Post-Petrarchism

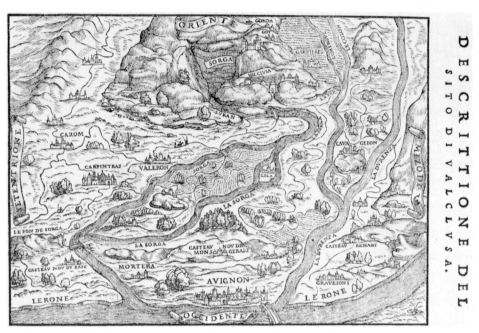

"Description of the Site of Vaucluse," from Alessandro Vellutello's edition of *Il Petrarcha* (Venice, 1547). (By permission of the Houghton Library, Harvard University.)

Post-Petrarchism

ORIGINS AND INNOVATIONS

OF THE WESTERN LYRIC SEQUENCE

Roland Greene

PRINCETON UNIVERSITY PRESS

PRINCETON, NEW JERSEY

Library of Congress Cataloging-in-Publication Data

Greene, Roland Arthur.
Post-Petrarchism : origins and innovations of the western
lyric sequence / Roland Greene.
p.   cm.
Includes bibliographical references and index.
1. Lyric poetry—History and criticism. 2. European poetry—
History and criticism. 3. American poetry—History and
criticism. I. Title.
PN1356.G74   1991   809.1'4—dc20   90-44496   CIP

ISBN 0-691-06840-2 (acid free paper)

CONTENTS

ACKNOWLEDGMENTS

FOR LOVE and support, my first debt is to my mother and sister. From the time I began this project, Earl Miner and Thomas P. Roche, Jr., were the best of advisers: generous with support of every kind, free with criticism, and deeply sympathetic to critical aims and practices that often conflicted with their own. A number of colleagues at Princeton, Harvard, and elsewhere read one or more chapters and offered useful criticism: my thanks to Barbara K. Lewalski, A. Walton Litz, William Arrowsmith, Emory Elliott, James E. Irby, Dorrit Cohn, Elizabeth Fowler, Joseph Lease, Suzanne Keen, Katherine Rowe, and Wojciech Kotas. Two distinguished scholars of comparative literature read the manuscript for Princeton University Press and remarked a number of things about the project I had not seen before; wherever I followed their advice, I improved the book. Other colleagues, friends, and correspondents gave advice and support that has gone into the project: thanks to Daniel J. Donno, Anthony P. Esposito, Marjorie Garber, Thomas M. Greene, Seamus Heaney, Efraín Kristal, Julio Ortega, Charles Perrone, Chip Phinney, Madeleine Picciotto, Stephanie Sieburth, Nancy Vickers, and Susanne Woods. Besides those who have materially helped with the book, I would like to acknowledge several scholars of Petrarchism whose work has deeply conditioned my own: this cohort includes not only Greene and Vickers, but Robert Durling, John Freccero, Ann Rosalind Jones, and Giuseppe Mazzotta. At the Press, Bob Brown waited patiently for the manuscript and, when it came, treated it scrupulously; I especially appreciate his tact and encouragement. Jane Lincoln Taylor improved my work in many places. Emery Snyder was an indispensable research assistant at the beginning of the project. Lita Orefice's contribution in that job went into every corner of this book; no formal acknowledgment can tell what I have gained from our friendship.

I would like to thank the libraries that have made my work possible. The most important have been Firestone Library, Widener and Houghton Libraries, and the other collections at Princeton and Harvard. I have also used the Huntington Library, the Folger Shakespeare Library, the W. B. Yeats Archive at the State University of New York at Stony Brook, the Speer Library of the Princeton Theological Seminary, and the Benson Latin American Collection at the University of Texas at Austin—and through interlibrary loans, a number of other collections. In each case I am grateful to the library staff for making a project of this scope feasible.

Grants from the Hyder E. Rollins Fund and the Clark Fund, both at Harvard, contributed toward the preparation of the book.

For quotations from copyrighted material, I acknowledge the following: Martín Adán's *La Mano Desasida* (1964) and Alberto Hidalgo's *Patria Completa* (1960) are reprinted by kind permission of Juan Mejía Baca; my translation of *La Mano Desasida* by permission of Cecilia Bustamante from "The Hand Let Go," trans. Roland Greene, *Extramares 1*, copyright © 1989; C. H. Sisson's translation of Du Bellay's *Regrets* by permission of Carcanet Press Limited from *The Regrets*, trans. C. H. Sisson, copyright © 1984; T. S. Eliot's "Burnt Norton" by permission of Harcourt Brace Jovanovich, Inc., from *Four Quartets*, copyright © 1943 by T. S. Eliot, renewed 1971 by Esme Valerie Eliot; Robert Lowell's "Home After Three Months Away" by permission of Farrar, Straus and Giroux, Inc., from *Life Studies*, copyright © 1956, 1959 by Robert Lowell, renewed 1987 by Harriet Lowell; Pablo Neruda's *Alturas de Macchu Picchu* and *Veinte poemas* by permission of the Agencia Literaria Carmen Balcells, S.A., respectively from *Canto General*, copyright © 1950 by Pablo Neruda and the Fundación Pablo Neruda, and *Veinte poemas de amor y una canción desesperada*, copyright © 1924 by Pablo Neruda and the Fundación Pablo Neruda; Nathaniel Tarn's translation of *Alturas de Macchu Picchu*, by permission of Farrar, Straus and Giroux, Inc., from *Heights of Macchu Picchu*, trans. Nathaniel Tarn, copyright © 1966; James Wright's translation of *Alturas de Macchu Picchu*, Canto 3, by permission of Robert Bly, from *Neruda and Vallejo: Selected Poems*, ed. Robert Bly, copyright © 1962, 1971; Clayton Eshleman's translation of Neruda's "Ritual de mis piernas" by permission of the translator from *Residence on Earth*, trans. Clayton Eshleman, copyright © 1962; W. S. Merwin's translation of Neruda's *Veinte poemas* by permission of the translator from *Twenty Love Poems and a Song of Despair*, trans. W. S. Merwin, copyright © 1969; Rolfe Humphries's translations of Ovid's *Amores* and *Metamorphoses* by permission of Indiana University Press from *The Loves* and *The Metamorphoses*, copyright © 1957 and 1955; Robert M. Durling's translation of Petrarch's *Canzoniere* by permission of Harvard University Press from *Petrarch's Lyric Poems*, ed. and trans. Robert M. Durling, copyright © 1976 by Robert M. Durling; Ezra Pound's *Cantos* by permission of New Directions Publishing Corporation from *The Cantos of Ezra Pound*, copyright © 1959 by Ezra Pound; Edward Taylor's *Preparatory Meditations* by permission of Donald E. Stanford from *The Poems of Edward Taylor*, ed. Donald E. Stanford, copyright © 1960, renewed 1988; Brooks Otis's translation of the *Aeneid* by permission of Oxford University Press from Otis's *Virgil: A Study in Civilized Poetry*, copyright © 1964; Walt Whitman's *Leaves of Grass* by permission of New York University Press from *Leaves of Grass*, ed. Sculley

Bradley et al., copyright © 1980; W. B. Yeats's *A Man Young and Old* by permission of Macmillan Publishing Company from *The Poems of W. B. Yeats: A New Edition*, ed. Richard J. Finneran, copyright © 1928 by Macmillan Publishing Company, renewed 1956 by Georgie Yeats; *A Woman Young and Old* and other texts by Yeats by permission of Macmillan Publishing Company from *The Poems: A New Edition*, ed. Finneran, copyright © 1933 by Macmillan Publishing Company, renewed 1961 by Bertha Georgie Yeats; and the illustrations from Alessandro Vellutello's *Il Petrarcha* and Thomas Watson's *Hekatompathia* by permission of the Houghton Library of Harvard University.

I think of *Post-Petrarchism* as having lived at certain addresses, especially 47 Park Place and 34 Kirkland Street. I see my friends of both places on the pages of the book, and always will. Kathryn Burns has been at those addresses and more: this book is also the record of our *innamoramento*, which has in turn enabled me to write it.

A NOTE ON TEXTS AND PROCEDURES

Most quotations from non-English texts, except for lyric poetry, are given only in translation, either mine or the most appropriate available version. Lyrics are quoted in both the original and a translation as often as it seems justifiable to do so: for instance, the extenstive quotations from *Alturas de Macchu Picchu* by Pablo Neruda, an accessible text, are given largely in English, while *La Mano Desasida* by Martín Adán is unfamiliar to most readers and should appear in Spanish as well as English. Quotations from Petrarch's *Canzoniere* are always given in the original and in Robert Durling's translation. In a few places I alter quoted translations to achieve a version better adapted to some argument of mine; in such cases the imposed reading appears in brackets. Once in a while I silently change the spacing of a translation—adding or subtracting a blank line, for instance—to bring it into conformity with the original.

In the chapters, all dates cited with titles are dates of publication except where I specify otherwise. In the notes, page numbers of lyrics in sequences are usually omitted in favor of poem- and line-numbers.

Post-Petrarchism

POST-PETRARCHISM: TOWARD A POETICS OF LYRIC AND THE LYRIC SEQUENCE

I CALL this book *Post-Petrarchism* because it is concerned with the vernacular lyric sequence, a poetic form invented by Francesco Petrarca, in the ages and cultures of its influence. Contrary to what many readers assume, Petrarchism is neither static nor one sort of thing; perhaps most startling, it is not dead. It emerges out of European humanist culture as a lyric discourse adapted to representing amatory and other experience through unities of process and person—in the largest sense, to making fictions. Abiding its exposure to events such as the Reformation and Puritanism, the settlement of the New World, and the various modernisms of Europe and the Americas, Petrarchism answers a certain need where lyric and fiction intersect: then and now, it is (in Frank Kermode's phrase) a way of "finding things out" that changes "as the needs of sense-making change."[1] This book is the story of those changes.

But if in one sense Petrarchism has existed continuously since Petrarch himself, in another sense it never was. Belatedness is more than the tone or theme of Petrarch's voluminous works in verse and prose—it is, in every sense, their testament. They witness it, and they bequeath it. Petrarch's posteriority to a classical past, his cultural isolation, has been much observed by historians and literary critics.[2] That condition finds its analogy, I think, in a certain post-Petrarchan belatedness in lyric discourse, where poets born at least two centuries after Petrarch look directly or refractively to his *Canzoniere* (written 1330–74) as the model of what I call lyric fiction. A highly adaptable complex, the Petrarchan sequence seems under a compulsion to change all the time but remains recognizably the same; it has a role everywhere that poets and readers have need of a fictional medium in a specifically lyric (rather than a narrative or other) order. In this sense, there never is a Petrarchan lyric sequence other than Petrarch's own, for all the texts that follow represent specific solutions to local cultural and aesthetic problems. As soon as a European poet of the 1500s lifts pen to write as a Petrarchan, he or she inevitably becomes a post-Petrarchan, reinventing the idea of a broadly scaled, self-oriented poetry for present circumstances; when an American poet of the nineteenth or twentieth century reinvents the genre again, post-Petrarchism lives again.

The book addresses a question of this sort: within a general theory of lyric's properties as discourse, how can we account for the prevalence over five centuries, in many literary cultures of the Old and New Worlds, of the lyric sequence? My argument maintains that the Western vernacular sequence is largely a type of fiction, and proposes ways of reading its specimens as such across their cultural and linguistic settings. The credibility of the argument depends on the representative force of its examples. These are, I think, chosen as fairly as they can be; their varied successes as lyric achievements, their mutual unlikeness, and their widely dispersed origins within the post-Petrarchan family are oblique but honest proofs of that. Each lyric sequence in the study is isolated and examined as far as it demonstrates something vital to the form's beginnings or development, and no further. Whatever else there may be to say about the *Canzoniere*, or Edward Taylor's *Preparatory Meditations*, or Whitman's *Leaves of Grass*—and there is always much more—cannot detain me here.

I have made one basic assumption that should be admitted from the start, though it will be evident everywhere in the book. My experience with texts such as the ones treated here convinces me that the Western lyric sequence from Petrarch to the present day is a single form with a more or less constant set of principles. To any reader with an eye for unities and a tolerance for the superficial changes in literary habit over time, this proposition will command clear support: the line of inheritance, and the evidence of a collective tinkering with these goods held in common, are plain enough. But this departs from a convention of treating works composed during the Renaissance—or even the Renaissance as it happened in a particular place—as though they are necessarily at one with each other but innocent of later developments, or of describing modern and postmodern varieties of the lyric sequence as though they were entirely new. Ever since a turn-of-the-century spate of important essays on aesthetic *variatio* in classical lyric collections, for example, it is striking how often critics of one series or another have rediscovered the same principle and called it their poet's own.[3] Just as often, where criticism has struggled to adapt a lexicon for the work of modern lyric sequences without the context of a post-Petrarchan poetics, it has tried to account for such sequences as "epics": the term seldom achieves much significance, but it stands there, nonetheless, as the signpost of the critics' collective helplessness. To me, the continuing elusiveness of the poetic object despite all this effort—and not only the form itself as a body of principles, but its transhistorical value to a range of very different poets—merely confirms the need for a theoretical argument pitched as widely as possible to include lyric sequences from the Renaissance to the present.

Aside from defining the form in its settings, I want to contribute fresh terms to the understanding of my principal examples and see them emerge better defined one against another. My readings of such texts will often leave critically travelled ground on their way to fresh conclusions: thus my treatment of the properties of fictional space in Pablo Neruda's *Alturas de Macchu Picchu* (1945) gives extended articulation to what is often seen as "the physical immensity, the natural massiveness, the awesome geographical monotony of that Chilean's poetry,"[4] but also says much more in the context of a post-Petrarchan fictional poetics. This is not only to honor the several very different and immensely stimulating dialogues that have informed this book; it is to adjust my argument to receive ideas of order that may go unseen or unelaborated by those commentators who establish their discussions of the generic sequence on a smaller foundation of poets, times, and cultures.

A brief definition of my principal terms is in order here. My ruling premise is that lyric discourse is defined by the dialectical play of ritual and fictional phenomena, or correlative modes of apprehension that are nearly always available in every lyric, though particular specimens, collections, and schools may try to protect one at the expense of the other. I know there are many equally valid categories and approaches through which one might get at the nature of lyric—it might be defined entirely in terms of its social functions, for instance, or as a certain way of handling tropes—but in this book I rely on a phenomenological understanding because it is best prepared to recover the lyric sequence within the genre at large.

By lyric's ritual element, I mean the poem's office as directions for a performance—a script, that is, compounded of sounds that serve referential or expressive purposes in nonpoetic contexts, other sounds (such as "hey-nonny-nonny" or "oba-la-la") that have no other contexts, and the patterns that organize these sounds in the reader-auditor's experience. Rhythm and other objective events are the most obvious of such patterns. The anthropologist Stanley Jeyaraja Tambiah writes of the "unpleasant restlessness" likely to be felt by auditors who resist the pull into measured utterances or acts that are germane to their cultures, and observes that when such an auditor turns collaborator, "the experience of constraint of a peculiar kind . . . induces in him, when he yields to it, the pleasure of self-surrender. The peculiarity of the force in question is that it acts upon the individual both from without (as a collective performance) and from within (since the impulse to yield comes from his own organism)."[5] In the full play of its ritual mode, which goes well beyond prosodic elements to include rhetorical, semantic, and symbolic features, lyric is utterance uniquely disposed to be re-uttered. In performance it may be not only compulsory but coercive discourse, for the nature of lyric's ritual dimension, simply stated, is to superpose the subjectivity of the scripted speaker on the reader, and that substitution can entail a kind of violence. Thus the drama of authoritarianism that appears in much theory of lyric, such as Roman Jakobson's notes on the "coercing, determining" role of the poetic function, or Barbara Johnson's remarks on the mutual implication of violence and figurative language. Thus, too, the continual possibility of lyric's becoming the most insidious of ideological discourses, a (perhaps) politically charged speech that we believe nonetheless to be our own or our culture's transparent expression.[6] Its ritual phenomenology is probably the first place that historically minded critics might inquire after a politics of the lyric. In fact, reading for ideology in lyric without attending to the genre's elementary modes of apprehension risks a fundamental incompleteness.

At the same time, its ritual dimension is where lyric generally appears to remain more contemporary to its audiences than other kinds of literary discourse; hence perhaps the common remarks by lyric's auditors and practitioners, such as Denise Levertov: "The poet—when he is writing—is a priest; the poem is a temple; epiphanies and communion take place within it. The communion is triple: between the maker and the needer within the poet; between the maker and the needers outside him—those who need but can't make their own poems (or who do make their own but need this one too); and between the human and the divine in both poet and reader," and C. S. Lewis: "A good sonnet (*mutatis mutandis* and *salve reverentia*) was like a good public prayer: the test is whether the congregation can 'join' and make it their own. . . . [In] this respect the Elizabethan sonnet is comparable to the Elizabethan song. It does not matter who is speaking to whom in 'Since there's no helpe' any more than in 'Oh mistress mine.' . . . The whole body of sonnet sequences is much more like an erotic liturgy than a series of erotic confidences."[7] In fact, lyric's sheer availability, its openness to performance as sound, rhythm, and form, marks the point of entry to its likeness to liturgies and other structures of devotion. Through the enactment of the poem as a collective score, the participant typically transcends the prosaic uses of its constitutive elements and attains an experiential identity with a subset of his or her culture. Entering the poem as a timeless, infinitely repeatable act, he or she discovers "the reality of an all-together in which everybody—composer, performer, listener—stands together and gazes, as it were, with the eyes of the work in the same direction."[8] With such a discovery, the participant might be said to shed his or her all-too-specific person, and to take on the speaking self of the poem. After meeting in the society of the text and submitting to its revalorizations—of what we bring to it, and of its own sounds and meanings—we take those everyday selves back, restructured or reanimated. Lyric's ritual process in general tends to celebrate the idea and experience of selfhood—this is, of course, a commonplace—but implied in the reader's acting-out of such a celebration is a self-abandonment or self-dismantling that can be stunningly mercurial. Gilbert Rouget discerns this plot, for instance, where he observes the relations between music and trance: "Trance always manifests itself in one way or another as a transcendence of one's normal self, as a liberation resulting from the intensification of a mental or physical disposition, in short, as an exaltation—sometimes a self-mutilating one—of the self."[9]

As the theorist of music Victor Zuckerkandl insists, the passage out of the prosaic self into another dimension "is not a passage to a 'beyond.' The 'new dimension' is not another world, is not something mysterious as opposed to the self-evident, is not something supernatural. . . . [It is] another reality of the world, not the reality of another world."[10] Zuckerkandl's is about as good and concise an explanation of lyric's ritual mode as any: the "other reality" is simply the experience of a radically collective, synchronous text situated in the everyday world, of a performative unity into which readers and auditors may enter at will. The final cause of the ritual mode is this collective act itself, which distributes a uniform event among actors who may be otherwise held apart by time, space, ideology, or other divisions. However lyric rituality differs from other secular rituals—perhaps in its latent synchrony, its abstract collectivity, its extreme availability—the issue of the mode, as far as it goes, remains the same: to "restructure and integrate the minds and emotions of the actors,"[11] to contribute to the joining of cultures, one poem and one reader at a time.

I am most interested in the structures that activate lyric's ritual mode, and the propositions they entail, such as revalorization, or as Levertov puts it, the idea that "poetry makes its structures, its indivisibilities of music and meaning, out of the same language used for utilitarian purposes, for idle chatter, or for uninspired lying";[12] or the precept that, as with any ritual, in doing this—reciting and reconstituting the poem—we are even now doing something else, something of larger moment. In small gauge, where words and phrases are involved, such processes of appropriation and transvaluation have been studied forever: they are the basis of paronomasia, catachresis, "ungrammaticality." Michael Riffaterre has described "the reader's praxis" of lyric semiosis as "akin to playing, to acting out the liturgy of a ritual—the experience of a circuitous sequence, a way of speaking that keeps revolving around a key word or matrix reduced to a marker."[13] There are, however, both smaller and larger gauges that ought to interest us, particularly (as I will soon show) in the context of the vernacular lyric sequence. On the one hand, glossolalia or pure sound—which we might call pre- or postreferential language, speech that indicates only that someone is speaking—implies revalorization of sound at the very point of utterance, and always exerts a strongly ritual pull on its auditors. They repeat it attentively and lovingly, fully aware that they participate in something of much greater import than noise. No matter how canonical or culturally appreciable the poetry, it always resorts to nonverbal discourses: "ducdame," riprap, *Trilce*. When we look directly at this type of lyric speech, we are perhaps looking, as closely as possible, at the ritual constitution of lyric itself—the imperative that keeps us listening with an ear to quoting, quoting with a mind to claiming and (where lyric speech turns referential) believing.[14]

On the other hand, especially in its sequences, lyric is heavy with large-scale ritual structures such as calendars, acrostics, and numerologies, where (again) to read the poem is to do something else as well, to bring an event out of latency and into actuality. Particularly in Renaissance literary studies, where many of them have been recovered, these structures have been neglected by criticism. They seem antiquarian, superstitiously pious, vaguely embarrassing. But they invariably open onto lyric's ritual mode, giving body and reach to a phenomenon that in fact appears in the formal aspect of every poem, from what is more concrete than the morpheme to what is more abstract than the plot. One of my incidental projects in this book is to show how the relatively overlooked elements of the ritual phenomenon, from glossolalias to numerologies, might be vindicated for interpretation, and their poems or sequences made whole again. Aside from the present effort, I think it is extremely important that those types of analysis (in the main, structuralist) that have done much for our understanding of lyric's small-gauge ritual phenomena be invited to account for the more distant and unfamiliar manifestations of the same impulse.[15]

Lyric is, then, doubly general property: it is made of borrowed and revalorized factors large and small, and it fuses these into speech that potentially belongs to any of us. Its character as common property sometimes makes the genre seem translucent, its interpretation obvious. In this ritual sense commentators often remark, as Hans Robert Jauss does, that lyric "seems by its very nature, the fact that it is an event purely of language, to be furthest removed from any kind of mimesis or 'referential illusion.' "[16] Formulations of this type—like Archibald MacLeish's sharper dictum, "A poem should not mean / But be"—have long been a convenient abbreviation of the ritual capacities of lyric. Particularly in European poetics, they have tended, perhaps by their appealing simplicity, to impede further investigation of how readers and writers engage the poem as immediate experience. As one recent critic has aptly remarked, once "we go beyond the relatively infrequent and obvious cases of sound patterns and rhythmic structures which seem to imitate what is being described we enter a shadowy realm where no one speaks with confidence. We recognize patterns and are certain that they contribute to the effect of poems but cannot say with assurance in what way they contribute."[17]

The theorist of genre Käte Hamburger extends the ritual premise, and reminds us how it complements what I will shortly call the fictional one. She states unequivocally that

> a poem presents no such formal and structural problems as fictional litera-
> ture does—narration, the creation of time, the mode of being of fiction itself,
> etc.—and is absolutely identical with its linguistic form. . . . [There are] two
> opposing logical possibilities over which thought expressed in language pre-
> sides: the potential to be either the statement of a subject about an object, or
> the function (in the hands of the narrator or the dramatist) which creates
> fictive subjects. . . . *That* creative language which produces the lyric poem
> belongs to the statement system of language. And this is the basic, structural
> foundation for the fact that the manner in which we experience a lyric poem
> as literature is quite different from the way we experience a fictional, i.e., a
> narrative or a dramatic work of literature. We experience it as the statement
> of a *statement-subject. The much disputed lyric I is a statement-subject.*[18]

Hamburger goes on: "What distinguishes the experience of lyric poetry from that of a novel or a drama is that we do *not* experience a poem's statements as semblance, as fiction or illusion. Our grasping the poem through acts of understanding and interpretation is to a large extent a process of 're-experiencing.' We must consult ourselves, if we will under-stand the poem."[19] And again: "The function of the word as such is dif-ferent for the fictional from what it is for the lyrical genre. Whereas in the lyric it has an immediate function, the same as in every statement outside of literature, its function in fiction, on the other hand, is one of mediation. . . . What we encounter in the lyric poem is the immediate lyric I."[20] Pre-sumably this "I" and its statements, which constitute "an open struc-ture," are entertained by the reader as elements in his or her own life, are tried on and "re-experienced" from the inside.[21] Certainly most of us know the sensation of enacting a lyric utterance as if it were our own speech: such an imaginative operation precedes any interpretation, in fact creates the conditions for interpretation, and presumably allows us to ex-pand the experiential dimensions of our selves by adding to a store of domesticated memories. As one reader puts it, "the sense we have [is] that the experience [of a ritual phenomenon] in these poems is cognate with our own experience of the natural world. . . . [The] experience in effect takes place *in* the real world, the world we and the poet are in."[22] Readers of fictions will recognize right away that this apprehension of lyric—which prompts lovers to quote each other poems not written by them-selves, adopting the poems as their own utterances in the real world—must clash with the notion of fictions as discrete, virtual worlds that readers may "step inside . . . and more or less lose touch with the nonfictional realm."[23] Has anyone ever quoted a complete utterance from *Pride and Prejudice* to a loved one as though it were his or her own speech?

By fiction I mean the poem's other identity for apprehension, not as potentially immediate but as represented speech. Barbara Herrnstein Smith designates speech of this mode as "fictive utterance": "[What] is central to the concept of the poem as a fictive utterance is not that the 'character' or 'persona' is distinct from the poet, or that the audience purportedly addressed, the emotions expressed, and the events alluded to are fictional, but that *the speaking, addressing, expressing, and alluding are themselves fictive verbal acts.*"[24] For Smith, poetry differs from the other arts and literary genres principally in what it takes as its object of representation: "paintings are fictive instances of what, in nature, are visually perceived objects. . . . [Novels,] a distinctively post-Gutenberg genre, have typically been representations of chronicles, journals, letters, memoirs, and biographies. . . . And poems are fictive utterances."[25] From a ritualist standpoint, a poem's spokenness points up its function as common property, as the text of a collective act. For a fictionalist like Smith, however, the same event suggests an implicit plot that unfolds within a hypothetical world. Even in treatments less extreme than Smith's, where the fictionalist standpoint does not always exclude recognition of lyric's presentness and materiality, nor argue so hegemonically for fiction—for Smith believes that even musical texts are "fictive instances of acoustically perceived events"[26]—it will still tend to insist on arguing from the same properties, the same textual evidence. And why not? The linguistic features called shifters or deictics, for instance, are the text of both phenomena: the "I" of lyric speech will often invite a person-representation, and the construction of a fictional situation, quite as easily as it refers to me, the reader who speaks a poem aloud on a certain occasion and entertains it as my own utterance.[27]

A lyric's fictional capacities are enlisted in various ways: where the reader is able to construe the poem as a "speaking, addressing, expressing, [or] alluding" within a hypothetical context that articulates and holds the boundaries between self and things, subject and object, and so on; where the history evoked by the work is not merely coextensive with its performance; where the poem's voice is posited not as the reader-auditor but as a character; where temporality has been addressed through some formal strategy equivalent to a plot; and where the fortunes of tone, rhetoric, and meter are susceptible to analysis within that plot. If lyric's ritual dimension often presents shards of experience that we welcome into our empirical world, fiction represents an alternate world into which we enter not as assimilators but as respectful observers: hence Hamburger's telling ritualist remark that "one cannot speak of a relation of literature to reality with respect to lyric poetry in the same sense that one can speak of such a relation with respect to narrative or dramatic literature."[28] We can impose the continuing plot of our own lives on the ritual layer of lyric, but a fiction, with its "empirical alternativeness to the actual world,"[29] requires that we submit to its temporal, causal, and moral laws as a means of gaining relief from, and fresh perspective on, our own here and now. And where the worldmaking of fiction posits a relation of "alternativeness" or embassy between the real and hypothetical worlds, ritual tends to imagine a reversible immanence, where each of these worlds dwells inside the other: the poem is a microcosm that, when brought into speech, takes its place as someone's utterance, a real-life element of the empirical world.

These modes of apprehension are theoretically available in every specimen of lyric, and give onto each other easily and often. They are the factors in a dialectical operation that produces many of the outcomes we recognize as belonging to lyric discourse, as well as most of the responses we call its criticism; each of the modes, hardly impervious to the other, recapitulates and contains that dialectical movement. For example, the oxymorons of feeling ("living deaths, deare wounds, faire stormes and freesing fires") that summarize the fiction of Petrarchan lyric may concurrently articulate the ritual constitution of poetry itself, since sensory reversals (where "cold may be experienced as warmth and heat experienced as cold") often occur in rhythmically driven trances.[30] On the other side, a deliberately severe manifestation of lyric's ritual mode, such as psalmody, concrete poetry, or the prose poem, may acknowledge its fictional imperatives by insisting that it maintains subgenres such as georgic, epithalamium, or utopia.[31] A poem that seems to embody one of these phenomena will nearly always see the alternate mode break forth, suddenly and incontestably, to interrogate it, and the critic who reads by passing over these interrogations will discover that certain of lyric's resources, and much of its appeal, must remain unaccountable.

Even so, poets have often chosen to propose or renew a contemporary version of one mode at the expense of the other: in various times and places, they have turned to the (largely fictional) amatory sonnet series when a plainspoken, inscriptive poetry was exhausted, to a (ritualized) "selection of the real language of men" when lyric's extant fashions of worldmaking grew stale, to (newly fictionalized) long poems when plot, character, and ideas had become foreign to poetry again.[32] In fact, a political or institutional history of lyric discourse and its interpretations might be elaborated from the relations of these modes over time, not only in schools of poetry and literary theory, but in such areas as pedagogical practice, translations from biblical poetry, and supposedly neutral criticism and reviews. To write or interpret lyric is to decide, at least unconsciously, on a fashion of ordering these phenomena, of putting them into a definite relation to one another; even to privilege one is usually a matter not of ignoring the other, but of subsuming it so that it helps rather than hinders the establishment of the other's primacy. In the continual struggle of these phenomena to define themselves against each other—or in the tireless efforts of poets and critics to justify and enable one against the other—neither alternative can prevail, though the dicta of movements will always try to give one or the other finality.

Before turning at last to the poetics of the lyric sequence, I might suggest that the names given to these modes here are perhaps only general, provisional covers for a variety of other terms, all topical of late, that have gone largely unreconciled with one another in recent theory. As phenomena, the fictional and ritual dimensions of lyric are here much more broadly conceived, and less particularly defined, than the several concepts that are properly included within them and that give an account of their active practice. Paul de Man's influential treatment of the unequal modern relations between symbol and allegory, for example, might be considered a chapter in the history of interactions between lyric's ritual and fictional dimensions. Several of the contradictions of Romantic thought among which de Man moves might be provisionally resolved by allowing the symbol its considerable debt to a (mostly implicit) ritual poetics: if Coleridge's theory maintains the values of both materiality and transcendence in the symbol, or if his poetry allows that "closer attention to surfaces engenders greater depth," we need not look hard for an explanatory model to enable these transfigurations and reversibilities, nor to justify in Romantic poems those final affirmations of self that seem to follow from very different, external beginnings.[33] On the other side, de Man offers a good deal of evidence to associate allegory with lyric fiction on the grounds of its carefully disposed temporality, its affinity with irony, and its alienation from "the point of view of the self engaged in the world." If we stand apart from and interpret his argument to conclude that irony— a "synchronic structure" that "comes closer to the pattern of factual experience"—is the outcome of an internal dialectic toward ritual within fiction, and is its concession to ritual, we can well appreciate de Man's knowing remark that "one is tempted to play [allegory and irony] off against each other . . . as if one were intrinsically superior to the other," and his deciding that "the dialectical play between the two modes . . . [makes] up what is called literary history."[34] Obviously my argument corresponds to his. Mine gains or suffers, however, from a stricter generic focus and a wider attention to ritual structures of poetic knowledge not always identified or acknowledged in canonical European lyrics.

But while de Man is perhaps the recent theorist who fills out these dimensions most generously, several others have recorded episodes of their own. I might indicate, without elaboration, the pertinence of Michael Riffaterre's ambitious and provocative encounter between local, emphatic "ungrammaticalities" and a mimesis that gives way to the more general praxis—the coercive "ritual" or "game"—of semiosis; Octavio Paz's occasional contrast between *habla* and *escritura*, which tends to endorse the former; and even Jacques Derrida's critique of phonocentrism, which has the incidental result of producing in some deconstructionists a willful blindness to the fact that lyric-as-ritual always condones *aporia* and deferrals of meaning, that the crises of indeterminacy disclosed in some deconstructive readings are the making of critics using a monistic, implicitly allegorical model of poetic discourse.[35]

The major canon of the European lyric sequence from Petrarch's *Canzoniere* to the early twentieth century represents the development of lyric's fictional mode; my first chapter, therefore, proposes to show how Petrarch's series emerged from an unstable generic situation in the late Middle Ages to establish the founding model of the fictional sequence.[36] Through various strategies of elaboration, the *Canzoniere* and its epigones define the possibilities of the mode: they advance plots, establish characters, arrange space—and above all, create worlds—as though to project the contingent fictional dimension of every lyric. Nearly always they give a compensatory expansion of lyric's ritual mode as well—sometimes in the calendars and numerologies mentioned above, sometimes in more acute outbreaks of nonverbal music or pure shape—but where the poets of the post-Petrarchan line communicate and extend one another's work, they are largely writers of (what I will often call) fiction. In fact, a generic perspective on the fate of the sequence ought to contribute a fresh sense of a post-Petrarchism that involves not simply the usual stylistic devices and attitudes, but the idea of poetry that contains them, the highly influential conviction that lyric poetry can attain the properties of any other type of fiction. For present purposes, then, "Petrarchan" means "fictional" as a standpoint in the theory of lyric I have been describing. Any number of lyric sequences that few readers would consider Petrarchan (post- or otherwise) in the usual, ossified sense of that term— works such as Hart Crane's "Voyages" (1926), H.D.'s *Trilogy* (1944– 46), or the Caribbean poet Shake Keane's calendrical series *One a Week with Water* (1979)—will be understood as such for the purposes of this study. The work of the Petrarchan program for the lyric sequence—the events that befall it under the pressures of new aesthetics and ideologies, mightier cultural forces, and its own process as a variety of fiction—is most of the story of this book.

As fiction, the lyric sequence undergoes a development that approximates the histories of several other such varieties. It begins with a humanist phase in which each work is largely concerned with representing the states and actions of a unitary human self—or a self struggling to seem unitary. I call such works nominative because they posit and name selves (Louise Labé, Astrophil, Babbling Will), and are, in turn, often themselves named after those person-representations. Their charter of lyric's serial possibilities often holds out for the linear, the characterological, the confessional; allegorically speaking, they point us insistently to a logic bounded by the potentialities of a hypothetical speaker. Further, the nominative sequence puts its speaker in relation to another character cast in the role of object—*Délie (Object de Plus Haulte Vertu), Willobie his Avisa, Pamphilia to Amphilanthus*—and largely invents its politics, society, and world from the exchanges of these two. Because these fictions play out the humanist conviction that selves ought to be unified and the equally humanist terror that they are not, the second person is often appropriated so as to cover the gaps and inconsistencies in the first, which is to say there is likely room for only one speaking voice in such texts. More implicit but probably most important, the reader enters a mutually determining and completing relation with the speaker, and the humanist engagement is achieved. Conceding de Man's argument that autobiography is not a genre in itself "but a figure of reading or understanding that occurs, to some degree, in all texts," I might propose that because of its internal disposition and cultural uses, the nominative lyric sequence is a dense, highly developed technology for activating "the autobiographical moment," where two subjects face each other—in a sense, constructing each other—across the fictional divide.[37] The nominative mode maintains itself, I think, by sending experimental impulses in certain directions. In my chapter on *Astrophil and Stella*, for example, I suggest that Sidney's sequence takes advantage of lyric's characterological possibilities in order to fictionalize the urge toward nominativity. As Astrophil becomes particularized, as we attend the fashioning of a fictional person, the property of transitivity, or lyric's ritual application to the reader's condition, is ironized and gradually discredited by the poet. Sidney may be not simply making a nominative sequence but giving that mode a polemical urgency—arguing, in effect, for a humanist convention of reading lyric as fiction.

Since the first decades of this century, however, the lyric sequence has tended toward a new formal and ideological disposition, which I choose to call artifactuality: several independently realized voices contributing to a composite fiction, and the series itself forcing nominativity, including the idea of unitary selfhood and the humanist engagement between poetic speakers and readers, into a trenchant reexamination. This new disposition often entails an acknowledgment that the work does not tell of experience lived or seen, but is a thing made. The artifactual mode takes in most of the major modernist sequences, such as T. S. Eliot's *Waste Land*

(1922), Mário de Andrade's *Paulicéa Desvairada* (1922), William Carlos Williams's *Spring and All* (1923), and the definitive work of that bent, Pound's lifelong *Cantos*; its most programmatic recent instance might be *Renga* (1971), the multilingual series of twenty-seven sonnets composed jointly by Paz, Charles Tomlinson, Edoardo Sanguineti, and Jacques Roubaud, where the project is the "irritation and humiliation of the I."[38] One fact of genre often lost in commonplace discussions of "the modernity of the fragment" in post-Romantic poetry is that the lyric sequence has always, and necessarily, announced its internal fragmentation. Recall the Latin title of Petrarch's *Canzoniere*, for instance: *Rerum vulgarium fragmenta* ("Fragments of Vernacular Things"). The only change of mind worth recording concerns the implicit wholes from which such fragments are broken, and the nature of the fashioning that arrays them into a purposeful order. For the modern artifactual sequence, the relevant whole is unlikely to be represented as an individual psyche, in the manner of Petrarchism, but instead is often seen to be something unmanageable or unknowable in its totality—a dynamic relationship between genders, or an entire culture, or perhaps the world itself.[39] And as the entirety and virtuality behind the sequence become untenable, the fictional phenomenon admits its own criticism, its own unraveling, from the alternate standpoint of the ritual mode. The act of definition that established the lyric sequence as a complex of fictional priorities, that installed fiction over ritual with the aim of getting certain things done, allows the proliferation of those resorts to decompose fiction and cast it out of power. The principal modernist and later sequences, then, tend to display vestiges of their origin in a post-Petrarchan fictional impulse, and these traces must be attended in a way that entails a concern for the internal history of the genre. But as the products of that impulse's turning back on itself, they also demand a reading that has much to do with ritual values in lyric, including the experience of materiality as sheer sound or shape, the property of transitivity, and the necessity of collective realization in lieu of solitary, interpretive reading. In arriving at ritual again as the furthest elaboration of its move toward fiction, the lyric sequence reenacts, on a diachronic scale, the motions that define the phenomenology of the single lyric.

Nominativity and artifactuality may be generally discriminated according to the properties of specific works, but like the more basic modes of ritual and fiction, they are implicated in an endless plot of interrogation and exchange. Thomas M. Greene has recently emphasized that the values of artifactuality—its polyvocal realization, its spatiality, its patchworking of heterogeneous fragments from other texts—are always latent in the classic humanist fictions, lyric and otherwise; he suggests that while humanist poetry often contains a struggle to appropriate subtexts and artifacts, it covers these, as in the *Canzoniere*, with a different struggle to "compose a self which [can] stand as a fixed and knowable substance."[40] As I see it, Petrarchan poetries put their artifactual tendency under the supervision of the nominative illusion, much as a fictional lyric will master ritual elements for its own ends; generations of readers have been fulfilled, of course, by naturalizing whatever they find back into the smoothness of an exaggerated nominativity. With work such as Greene's concerning the deep structures of Petrarchism behind me, and aware that the nominative and artifactual modes are heavily implicated in each other, I will concentrate on episodes of crisis within and between the two.

There exists as well a vigorous minor tradition that subdues lyric's fictional dimension in favor of a sustained ritual phenomenon. After my first two chapters, both exploratory essays on the fictional constitution of major European sequences, a third chapter takes up that minor tradition, first in the work of Edward Taylor, one of North America's first poets, and then in *Leaves of Grass* (1855). I describe Taylor's lyric achievement in the context of ostensibly similar but far less radical devotional sequences by John Donne and George Herbert, and propose fresh terms for understanding Taylor's reconception of the devotional sequence in America. Taylor makes a convenient expository gate onto the ritual sequence: he has several authentic predecessors in the tradition of the devotional series realized as lyric ritual (including some, like the psalmists of the sixteenth century, whose commitment to the performative element of their work has provoked a critical consensus to deny them to be poets altogether), and many worldly successors, especially in the United States. One of the successors, Walt Whitman, has much less to do with predecessors; his sequence, in contrast to Taylor's *Meditations*, can be said to create its own context by reimagining the possibilities of the form more thoroughly than any poet since Petrarch. I consider *Leaves of Grass* the founding text of a poetics that sets ritual over fiction, the *Canzoniere* of its mode. In fact, the modernist lyric sequence can be roughly described as the confluence of the major and the minor traditions I have sketched here, both asserting a program valuing lyric's ritual mode but each having come to that value in its own way—the one as the outcome of an oscillation or development, the other as a more or less constant principle.

My fourth chapter treats a representative moment in post-Petrarchism's arrival at modernism out of nominativity, and its turn into a new, artifactual order. I take *A Man Young and Old* (1928) and *A Woman Young and Old* (1929) by Yeats as inexact but instructive turning points in this reorientation of the sequence: answering the male speaker of the first series, Yeats's woman does not really reject a nominative poetics so much as she hints at the possibility of a fully integrated second voice and, with suggestive revisions of post-Petrarchan norms, invites a new understanding of lyric. The two works by Yeats are perhaps too schematic in their reconception, and still too faithful to Petrarchism, to strike anyone as genuine modernist sequences or "long poems" like those of Pound, H.D., or Basil Bunting. But enough has been written on these poets' contributions to the lyric sequence to forestall any need for one more such essay, and even so the event of generic change is unfamiliar enough to deserve an accounting through a neglected but highly appropriate text.

The final chapter recognizes one of the many alternate orders that become feasible in the modern series, especially that of the New World. I treat two Spanish American works, *Alturas de Macchu Picchu* by Neruda and *La Mano Desasida* (1964) by Martín Adán, as built on spatial and geographical conceits that reweigh the mutual inflections of ritual and fiction while maintaining a palpable debt to the original Petrarchan program, in which a geographical order was always latent. If this essay opens the way to further explorations of the New World sequence as an outcome of European lyric poetics, it is also meant to suggest that there are innumerable available orders for such works in the free-fire zone of modern and postmodern poetry, and that the recovery of such arrangements depends only on the critic's openness to the generic capacities of the sequence. Doubtless there is much more to say about recent writing in the form, but I have tried to stop where the present-day multiplicity of lyric conceits and critical strategies just becomes visible; my subsequent silence will indicate, I hope, that I see the present book as a foundation on which other readers may want to elaborate.

As a whole, this study relies on a few occasional terms that should be concisely introduced here. Throughout the chapters I tend to refer to the sequence, considered as a transhistorical generic production, as a "form"; it should be clear that on empirical evidence I share the formalist belief that, in Hugh Kenner's words, "forms remember."[41] For a demonstration of the idea that forms remember their histories, that they move their authors and readers to treat certain received issues, one need not look any further than Petrarch's and later poets' management of the motif of *spargimento*, the scattering of members or fragments. Out of its Western sources in the first Psalm and the Song of Songs, the matter of scattered fragments is crucial to the fiction of the *Canzoniere*. Certainly it has other significances for Petrarch, but from the standpoint of poetics, the main job of the motif is to articulate as a struggle within the fiction—in spiritual, psychological, stylistic terms—what the work accomplishes on the generic scene by proposing a fiction at all, namely the establishment of an *unus*, an *integer*, from *rime sparse*.[42] The act of founding the phenomenon of fiction on lyric fragments is the originary, traumatic event in the history of the form, and Petrarch's successors cannot forget it even where, like the New Yorker Louis Zukofsky in *"A"* (1928–74) or the Peruvian

Adán in *La Mano Desasida*, they might seem to have little direct acquaintance with the *Canzoniere* itself.

This form remembers, of course, because it is more than a form. Everywhere that I use the shorthand of "form" for the sequence, it should be understood that I mean to invoke it as a complex of formal and generic properties: in many texts of the Renaissance, for instance, as the intersection of the formal values of sonnets and *canzoni* with what I have described as a cultural bent toward lyric's fictional dimension. It stands therefore in parallel to other subgenres that come into being in the intersection of forms and attitudes—such as narrative romance, tragedy, the short story, and so forth—and has its own history quite as much as these do. This generic history, however, has been greatly overlooked in the case of the sequence, partly because the play of two modes or dimensions that defines lyric as aesthetic experience permits it to be marginalized—its assertions can always be read ritually as our own speech, its discoveries treated as obvious or inevitable—and partly because as a collocation of lyrics, the sequence is naturally susceptible to disintegration. The alternate identities with which most sequences have been implicitly tagged in criticism ("poetic sequence" or "assortment of short poems"), in fact, caricature and redouble the two modes of lyric proper, and so the form has been broken down insensibly by generations of readers and critics.

In treating these several possibilities for lyric's identity, I have chosen to put into use a working idea of the other literary kinds that a few readers may find too strict or conservative. Narrative is the principal object of contrast. I hold that narrative requires the presence of story and plot, and call the joining of these threads the genre's quintessential act: the result is a mutual order that often gives a distinct emphasis to the values of causality and followability, and to the proportional relation between the two lines. The impact of narrative largely depends on the exactitude of its temporal specifications through any particular plot, on the integrity of the causal and historical relations among its elements. Further, since much more time goes into their evoked history than into their realization as performance, most narratives theoretically—and some manifestly—gain on the present tense in which they are read or spoken. Narrative is translatory. In any narrative the fulfillment of these properties may be deferred for one effect or another, but it can seldom be utterly denied.[43]

In lyric, however, the lines of priority and causality are often considerably blurred. My chapter on the *Canzoniere* maintains that, in perhaps the most well-articulated case of fictional process in the lyric genre, the constituents of that process—the utterances that correspond to the events of a narrative or drama—could be literally rearranged into numberless alternate orders (though not every lyric piece could fit into every available setting). Most readers will agree that the temporal stipulations of such works as *A Man Young and Old* and *Alturas de Macchu Picchu*, while present and necessary, are far looser and more ambiguous than those of nearly any novel or play. One must consider, moreover, lyric's characteristic interplay between fictional and ritual temporalities: the former may be vacated episodically (as in bursts of sheer sound), or at length (again, some psalms and concrete poems come to mind), with the result of setting the two modes in fresh relation. By contrast, narrative's now-proverbial *erzählte Zeit* (story time) and *Erzählzeit* (narrating-time) hardly exchange priority as liberally. If narrative typically implies a gaining on the present of the utterance, as I indicate in the first chapter, we might say that its ritual mode does not relieve and restore fiction, but is held in suspense as its hypothetical completion, the projected moment in which the narrative arrives at us and our doings here and now. Disposed into a stable, periodic relation for narrative, the two modes interact dynamically in lyric, with a restorative effect on particular specimens and on the genre as a whole. When I say narrative, then, I mean these general principles of proportion between story and plot, causality, and advance on the reader or hearer, and nothing more specific or limiting.

One generic constituent that figures discreetly in the first chapters on Renaissance sequences, then more explicitly where I treat modern innovations, might be considered the counterpart of narrative distance: I call it lyric interval. It might be defined as a phenomenological structure, the sum of the several deictic settings on which a poem or a collocation of poems is founded—temporal, personal, spatial, social—and therefore a kind of measure of the lyric's implied distance between intelligence and object. A poem firmly cast in the present tense and consistently based in a *here*, which moves only from the first- to the second-person and back again (take Shakespeare's Sonnet 76), will probably constitute a very different report than another that shifts in the matter of temporality (Fulke Greville's *Caelica* 63); a sequence such as the *Canzoniere* that often replays a contrast between a *then* and a *now* tends to establish conditions that prefer a fictional phenomenon, while another such as *Leaves of Grass* in which "past and present and future are not disjoined but joined," in which the speaker "places himself where the future becomes present" and "scorns intervals," will practically compel a ritualist reading.[44] I introduce the term *lyric interval* not because it always implies prior or certain conclusions about how these texts ought to be read, but because I think one's understanding is advanced by absorbing a poem's deictic facts together, as an overall adjustment of controls. Seeing these features as a cohort enables readers to construe how a lyric's identity as fiction or performance is constituted, and perhaps how the deictics operate as the dynamic factors in a type of plot. Many lyrics, for instance, dramatize the plot of seeking to close their intervals altogether, to escape the straits of discourse in favor of the (imagined) freer conveyances of music, where subject and object collapse on each other, where concreteness is everything: Tennyson's *In Memoriam* 106 ("Ring out, wild bells") talks about this urge, while several portions of Zukofsky's *"A"* enact it. Many sequences that articulate a strong fiction also contain a palpable longing for ritual, part of the genre's incessant alternation of the two modes: this is vital to Spenser's *Shepheardes Calender* (1579) and to *The Waste Land*. It is impossible, of course, for a poem to close down its lyric interval; it is also impossible for a sequence to give one mode unqualified rule over the other. But in poetics, impulses and attitudes often matter as much as achievements. While criticism is laden with local, untheorized observations of particular deictic facts, it is time to suggest that these be measured in the wider contexts of lyric interval and the play of alternate modes.

   If this book is often about unities (as any study of fiction must be), it is also about junctures, or the white spaces that separate poem from poem, stanza from stanza, utterance from utterance in the body of Western lyric sequences. Any reading of lyric as fiction must accommodate discontinuity as well as continuity, allow for the spatial dimension of lyric temporality, and offer a means of getting into and over the white gaps between the poems without brutally closing them. In order to test my approach against the most demanding texts, I have preferred many junctures over few, so Renaissance and modern sequences with many internal episodes appear much more prominently than works such as Eliot's *Four Quartets* (1943), with its twenty-odd breaks. In this and other ways, the need for a body of sequences with urgent claims on lyric theory largely determines the canon of the book. No further statement about the literary value or cultural position of these works is implied; where such statements are intended, I explicitly make them.

   Finally, as a frankly generic reading of a vernacular form with an especially long history, this book has to rely heavily, and look glancingly, on more copious studies of what happened at certain times in art (outside the form) and culture. I see my argument as anything but an alternative explication of, say, modernism in poetry; instead I offer a version of the story that tries to corroborate both narrower- and wider-ranging accounts with its special, limited focus on the lyric sequence, which has a generic identity and a cultural history of its own. My errand of getting past the Renaissance and my interest in large-scale poetic structures ensure that I have little to say about certain things (such as the sonnet) that critics of Petrarch and the sixteenth century are usually occupied with; on the other hand, my critical etiology in Petrarchan poetics, and (again) the scale of my texts, mean that I give little attention to certain things (such as the image) that scholars of modern poetry write about all the time. To that extent, perhaps, my conversation with these camps is impeded. On the other hand, I hope a new book that slights some cultural and literary detail about familiar things for a range much longer and wider than usual will seem refreshing rather than stunted. My paramount idea for *Post-Petrarchism* is to articulate a single poetics, and with it to demarcate a common critical space, in which readers and scholars of many poetries— of the European Renaissance, the colonial United States, the high modernisms of Europe and the Americas, postwar Latin America—might exchange perspectives. Whatever the success of that idea, I hope to demonstrate why the Western lyric sequence seems to me to occupy a site where such an encounter can occur.

Chapter 1

FOUNDING FICTION: THE TEMPORALITY OF
PETRARCH'S *CANZONIERE*

THE WESTERN lyric sequence was born in the practice of Francesco Petrarca, whose fourteenth-century *Canzoniere* or *Rime Sparse* is the first and probably the most comprehensive specimen of the form. Petrarch's disparate models—including the collections of Roman lyricists such as Propertius and Ovid, the Provençal chansonniers, and the mingled prose and verse of Dante's *Vita Nuova*—were transformed by his infusion of several elements, and passed on, a new whole, to European and New World poets of five ensuing centuries. The most catalytic of these elements, I believe, is the conceit of temporal process, of a continuum that binds the entire sequence of "scattered rhymes" and activates what might be called the phenomenology of fiction. The patterns and devices that build process in the sequence are not the product of random, disinterested experimentation, but are in a sense historically determined (or at least historically explicable) events: they coincide with Petrarch's obsession with temporality as a cultural and epistemological problem, and represent perhaps an imaginative reworking of questions long familiar to him and his era of pause between the Middle Ages and the Renaissance. In another sense, some of the sequence's innovations are probably decided in the internal actions and reactions of the lyric genre, some of which I have just sketched. In this chapter, I will analyze the means and scope of Petrarch's temporal innovation, and in doing so, fit his *Canzoniere* more firmly into its accustomed (but often untheorized) place at the historical and generic wellspring of the vernacular lyric sequence. I take the view that nearly everything still to happen in the poetics of the sequence, down to the modernist and postmodernist innovations of our own time, depends on what is articulated as possible by Petrarch's master text. My discussion begins with linguistics, from which I appropriate some ideas and terms, and proceeds through a brief survey of varieties of temporal process in narrative and the single lyric, at last to an anatomy of the *Canzoniere* as founding fiction.

My exploration of Petrarch's achievement starts where time most radically enters language, with the words and phrases that make temporal reportage feasible. In his *Introduction to Theoretical Linguistics*, John Lyons writes:

Every language-utterance is made in a particular place and at a particular time: it occurs in a certain spatio-temporal situation. . . . The notion of *deixis* (which is merely the Greek word for "pointing" or "indicating"—it has become a technical term of grammatical theory) is introduced to handle the "orientational" features of language which are relative to the time and place of utterance. The so-called "personal pronouns" (*I, you, he,* etc.) constitute only one class of the elements in language whose meaning is to be stated with reference to the "deictic co-ordinates" of the typical situation of utterance. Other elements which include a component of deixis are such adverbials of place and time as *here* and *there* ("in the vicinity of the speaker" : "not in the vicinity of the speaker") and *now* and *then* ("at the time of speaking" : "not at the time of speaking"). These are just the most obvious instances of the way in which the grammatical structure of language may reflect the spatio-temporal co-ordinates of the typical situation of utterance.[1]

For the present chapter, naturally, I aim to concentrate on temporal rather than spatial, personal, or social deictics, though some of these other kinds are relevant to my argument now and then.[2] The former category extends well beyond the adverbs Lyons mentions, and includes a wide array of grammatical forms—such as adverbial and nominal phrases, and verb tenses—that give chronological shape to an utterance.[3]

A few examples will carry the point:

It is not *now* but *long and long ago*
I *have* you *served* as to my power and might
As faithfully as any man might do,
Claiming of you nothing of right, or right.

That you *were once* unkind *befriends* me *now*,
And for that sorrow which I *then did* feel
Needs must I under my transgression *bow*,
Unless my nerves *were* brass or hammered steel.

When lilacs *last* in the dooryard *bloom'd*
And the great star early *droop'd* in the western sky in the night,
I *mourn'd*, and *yet shall mourn* with ever-returning spring.

Long tiers of windows staring out toward *former*
Faces—loose panes *crown* the hill and *gleam*
At sunset with a silent, cobwebbed patience . . .
See them, like eyes that *still uphold* some dream
Through mapled vistas, cancelled reservations!

Time *past* and time *future*
What might *have been* and what *has been*
Point to one end, which *is always present*.[4]

What these underscored words and phrases share as deictics is that they set evoked experiences and events in time relative to the utterance itself. As Émile Benveniste puts it, "they have in common the features of being defined only with respect to the instances of discourse in which they occur."[5] Charles Fillmore adds the stipulation that "deictic expressions like *here* and *there*, *this* and *that*, are to be distinguished from non-deictic terms like *near* and *far*, *above* and *below*, *push* and *pull*, etc., where the positional relation is not with respect to the speaker at the time of speaking, but with respect to the objects named by the nouns these words are in construction with, and at the time indicated by the sentences in which they occur."[6] Another theorist, Rodney Huddleston, proposes a second order of deixis especially suited, I think, to literary analysis: "within-the-text deixis," which specifies a period of time by referring to some marker in the discourse. Among the examples he cites are the anaphoric *then, at that time, the next day*, and *some time later*.[7] Anaphoric or "within-the-text" deictics are crucial to any discussion of literary or fictional deixis exactly because any piece of literature coheres as a text, a fabric of utterances woven together by threads of external and mutual reference, and may have little to do with the discrete statements favored by linguists. Strict deixis on Fillmore's model is hardly extensible for the duration of the typical literary work: as a discourse enlarges and its author records events, states, and relations in ever-greater numbers, it is usually natural and economical to locate these in time against one another, not against the speaker's *now*. We say "two hours ago the first event happened, and an hour later the second," not "two hours ago the first, an hour ago the second." To use the latter construction programmatically would threaten to unravel the continuity of the discourse. Further, in fiction, "pure" deictic narration would radically divorce the reader's or auditor's experience from that of the characters: they would measure events, as we do in life, against other remembered or anticipated events and not in relation to a narrator's *now* they could never imagine. (Even in retrospective narratives that proceed toward a *now* known to the narrating protagonist, such as *Huckleberry Finn, The Good Soldier*, and *Invisible Man*, anaphoric deictics greatly overrun pure ones.) Because this essay and book are about literary discourse, I will use the term *deictic* from now on to mean either of the two varieties, and trust the reader to make any further distinctions.

The likeliest way of understanding the job of deictics in literary discourse, I think, is to see them as the contours of process. Linguists commonly use the term *process* to denote the range of experience encompassed by an utterance that has both a subject and a verb ("the action or the qualification expressed by the subject-predicate group").[8] One theorist defines the term specifically in view of its subjection to deictics, which are sometimes called "specifiers": "The term 'process' is understood in a very broad sense, to cover all the phenomena to which a specification of time may be attached—in English, anything that can be expressed by a verb: event, whether physical or not, state, or relation."[9] I use the term in a wider but related sense, to mean the temporality evoked in a longer utterance such as a poem and, I will argue, a lyric sequence; it is simply time articulated, which may respect any available phenomenological order—of ritual, of fiction, of history, of private intellection. As an utterance grows longer, so does the process it implies: so, too, it comes to involve more deictics of all sorts, and gives them occasions to shape the emerging process—and to contribute a version of the relevant phenomenon—in manifold ways. If each literary process is a temporal stream, deictics fashion the topography—the shortcuts, the obstructions, the reversals and clear channels—that determine the stream's pace, direction, and integrity, or the want thereof.

Where human beings create or experience a sense of process by design, deictics are usually among the instruments of that perception. For instance, Mircea Eliade has described "sacred time," a "primordial mythical time made present" by religious men and women on their highest occasions: "Every religious festival, any liturgical time, represents the reactualization of a sacred event that took place in a mythical past, 'in the beginning.' . . . [It] is the time that was created and sanctified by the gods at the period of their *gesta*, of which the festival is precisely a rehabilitation. In other words the participants in the festival meet in it *the first appearance of sacred time*, as it appeared *ab origine, in illo tempore*."[10] Here, naturally, is one of the most integral and exclusionary of human processes. Reminders of ordinary temporal duration (say, a factory whistle outside Mass) cannot interrupt the sacred process once it commences, but can only signal that other, simultaneous processes are underway. Eliade does not analyze the particular verbal formulas by which religious men and women recover their sacred time, but as the words of the quotation itself attest, these formulas—parts of the larger rites, including choreography, objects, and histrionics, that effect a passage from ordinary to mythical time—depend largely on deixis. Some pure deictic phrase, like the "in the beginning" of the book of Genesis, commences the ceremony or "reactualization" by carrying the community's imagination back to a single instant in sacred history, and there are presumably deictic structures of larger extent and regular recurrence that maintain the actors' participation in what amounts to an alternate temporality. In a festival, we are released into that revivified age to inhabit and domesticate it. In liturgy and scripture, we are guided through a compact rehearsal of divine history, and delivered at last into our own present. Both types of reenactment encourage the conception of the sacred past as bound up in process with the present: the festival by replaying that past over our own lives—having lived in both times, we remember them as temporally parallel and mutually accessible—and the liturgy by fashioning an explicit continuum between *then* and *now*. Following Eliade, it seems fair to say that the typical deictic patterns of sacred time (such as *in illo tempore* or "in the beginning") confirm the significance and holiness of the rite's present instant by showing its descent from indisputably sacred events of the past, and by allowing worshippers to live through that past, finally returning to their present, in the course of the ceremony.

Poems and other literary works may employ deictic formulas to enter heightened times, or simply to set about the basic technical matters of their kinds. Narrative probably comes first to mind. Writing of Proust, Gérard Genette maintains that every narrative is founded in some particular deictic utterance, and restates some traditional issues of the genre in terms of deictic categories:

> [Let] us accept the hypothesis that all narratives, regardless of their complexity or degree of elaboration . . . can always be considered to be the development of a verbal statement such as "I am walking," or "He will come," or "Marcel has become a writer." On the strength of this rudimentary analogy, the problems of narrative discourse can be classified under three main headings: the categories of time (temporal relationships between the narrative [story] and the "actual" events that are being told [history]); of mode (relationships determined by the distance and perspective of the narrative with respect to the history); and of voice (relationships between the narrative and the narrating agency itself: narrative situation, level of narration, status of the narrator and of the recipient, etc.).[11]

In most narratives, it seems, the relations that fall under Genette's temporal category remain fairly stable and predictable after the founding of some originary, governing orientation. The narrator elects an initial tense for the tale, usually the aorist or preterite.[12] Other temporal bearings may appear at the outset as well, such as adverbial deictics or the vaguer formulas descended from "once upon a time": "It was in the time that the earth begins to put on her new apparel against the approach of her lover," or "Here on this beach a hundred years ago. . . ."[13] From starting points such as these, narrative discourse literally advances: we understand that subsequent, unmodified verbs in the past tense represent a temporal movement toward the time of the utterance, which is often unmarked and implicit. This movement can be accelerated, slowed, or otherwise made explicit by the narrator's "within-the-text" deictics, such as the anaphoric *and* (as in many biblical narratives) or *then*: "But bad luck was still to come from Poseidon Earthshaker. He drove the winds against me, and barred my course, and stirred up the infinite sea, so that the waves would not let me get on; and there I sat despairing on my raft. Then the tempest broke it to pieces; and I went swimming across yonder gulf, until wind and water drove me to your coast. ... I was thrown up gasping for breath, and night came on. Then I got away from the swollen river, and sank down in the bushes, where I scraped up the leaves over me, quite worn out, and God let me fall into a deep sleep."[14] Narrative has, then, a regular deictic program, a drift that characterizes the genre: as the tale goes on, events grow nearer to the time of the speaker—and beyond him or her, and still more implicit, the reader. Time elapses during the telling, of course, but not often at a rate equal to (let alone greater than) the rate of time's passing in the story. Only in dialogue, and in some few passages that temporarily eschew narrative abstraction, does the evoked time pass at something like the rate of the utterance-time; it practically never lags behind. Accordingly, the relation between event and utterance, as it is established and regulated by narrative deixis, sees the former steadily and perceptibly gaining on the other, a fact that sometimes claims explicit recognition:

> My intention is to tell of bodies changed
> To different forms; the gods, who made the changes,
> Will help me—or I hope so—with a poem
> That runs from the world's beginning to our own days.[15]

This fact is not so recondite as to have no impact on the reader's or auditor's experience of a tale such as those in the *Metamorphoses*. Part of the nervous effect of a fictional climax, I think, comes from our sensation of being gained upon: the climax represents a sudden, stark revelation of how quickly circumstances change and plots get resolved, and pricks an inarticulate fear that we may be caught and swept up in a train of events we had thought safely stowed in the past. It is the moment where we are forced to observe the story's gathering forward impetus, where we have to suppress the thought that the momentum has knocked down all historical restraints and made the story ours.

This pattern of forward deictic movement holds true even in those narratives that begin in medias res, and those that enclose separate, digressive minor stories. In fact, it provides the momentum and binding that make these variations feasible. The narrative that starts "in middle things" puts its plot into segments, and rearranges these: each segment keeps its forward deictic movement, as it must if the ending of an intermediately situated but historically prior segment—such as the ubiquitous example, chapters 9 through 12 of the *Odyssey*, where Odysseus tells of his adventures immediately after leaving Troy—is to mesh with the start of a first-appearing but historically later segment, such as chapter 5, the tale of Calypso. The deictics advance each episode so that its terminus meets the opening of another, and the narrative comes together accordingly: "From that place I drifted for nine days, and on the tenth at night the gods brought me to the island of Ogygia. There dwells Calypso, that goddess so beautiful and so terrible, who can speak the language of man; and she loved me and cared for me. But why go on with my story? I have told it already, and no one cares for a twice-told tale."[16] In the pulse of *thens* and *laters* that hurries such expositions along, we hear the epic's march toward integrity, its struggle not to splinter in the face of its effort at nonlinear elegance. The episode gains a measure of interest and urgency just from its part in the technical drama of binding and unifying.

Digressions from the main plot that cast expository light on a new or subordinate character usually return at last to the *here* and *now*—which (again) is not the time of reading, but the path of its relentless forward movement. Recall the ending of the captive's tale in *Don Quixote* 1.41:

> The other released captives took their departure, each the way that seemed best to him, and Zoraida and I were left alone with nothing more than the crowns that the courtesy of the Frenchman had bestowed upon Zoraida, out of which I bought the beast on which she rides. For the present I am attending her as her father and squire, not as her husband. We are now going to find out if my father is living, or if any of my brothers had better fortune than mine has been, though as Heaven has made me the companion of Zoraida, I believe no other lot could be assigned to me, however happy, that I would rather have.[17]

That extraordinarily digressive novel also furnishes an example of a pure digression in the "Tale of Foolish Curiosity" (1.33–35). The curate reads a novella he has found in a trunk. Neither he nor his auditors has participated in the events of the novella, and as the digression is thus cut off from any discernible historical relation to the main story, it cannot fall in with the deictic march of the book at large. For its duration, too, the main story cannot advance: Cervantes admits this fact by interrupting the digression itself to churn up the main story again. But pure digressions are rare, and hard to get away with—Cervantes complains that his readers pass over them "hurriedly or in disgust, without noticing the elegance and artifice that go into them"[18]—and most narrative displacements fit my model of the genre's distinctive process in that they contribute to the extension of the main story.

Even while they collectively shape the general temporal relations between event and utterance, however, deictics can singly and locally defy the drift of those relations. Brooks Otis has observed that shifting verb tenses in Virgil's *Georgics* and *Aeneid* guide the reader's attention and response, as in the footrace from the latter poem's fifth book:

Primus abit longeque ante omnia corpora Nisus
emicat, et ventis et fulminis ocior alis;
proximus huic, longo sed proximus intervallo,
insequitur Salius; spatio post deinde relicto
tertius Euryalus;
Euryalumque Helymus sequitur: quo deinde sub ipso
ecce volat calcemque terit iam calce Diores
incumbens umero; spatia et si plura supersint,
transeat elapsus prior ambiguumque relinquat.
Iamque fere spatio extremo fessique sub ipsam
finem adventabant, levi cum sanguine Nisus
labitur infelix, caesis ut forte iuvencis
fusus humum viridisque super madefecerat herbas.
Hic iuvenis iam victor ovans vestigia presso
haud tenuit titubata solo, sed pronus in ipso
concidit immundoque fimo sacroque cruore,
non tamen Euryali, non ille oblitus amorum:
nam sese opposuit Salio per lubrica surgens,
ille autem spissa iacuit revolutus harena.
Emicat Euryalus et munere victor amici
prima tenet plausuque volat fremituque secundo;
post Helymus subit et nunc tertia palma Diores.

(First far beyond the other runners Nisus goes away.
He flashes faster than the winds or winged thunder bolt.
Next to him but next by a long interval
Follows Salius: finally then after another space
The third, Euryalus.
Helymus follows Euryalus: and then right on his track
Look! Diores flies and almost gets his heel
Straining upon him: and if there'd been more room
He would have gone ahead or left the race in doubt.
And now almost at the end and near exhaustion point
They were coming to the goal, when Nisus on slick ground
Slips, the unlucky, for a bullock's blood had there
Been shed and had made the grass slippery and wet.
Here the young man—so sure of victory—could not keep
His footing as he rocked and reeled, then headlong
Down he went in the foul mud and sacred gore.
Yet not Euryalus, yet not his love did he forget
For he threw himself on Salius, rising from where he slipped

And Salius now lay wallowing in the trodden sand.
Euryalus then flashes by, victor by his friend's gift,
And takes first place as he flies on to much applause and cheers.
Next Helymus comes in second; Diores is third.)

(5.318–39)

Otis points out how the differentiated tenses conform to the state of the
action: the present tenses (*abit, emicat, insequitur, volat, terit*) for the
moments when the race is a blur of immediacy and unpredictability as the
runners strain for the lead, the imperfect (*adventabant*) for the sensation
of incompleteness as the race draws to an end.[19] The most memorable
incident in the episode, Nisus's pratfall into the mud and his quick tackle
of Salius, is set apart and unified by the perfect tense. I notice other, related devices, including two close instances of anaphoric *deinde*
("then")—these "within-the-text" deictics speed up the pace of the narrative greatly—and the several occurrences of *iam* ("now") to narrow the
auditor's attention, particularly the double deictic *hic iuvenis iam* (literally, "now this young man") at line 331. These variations scarcely impede
the episode's careful development of a narrative process: the linguist
Martin Joos remarks that a narrator who resorts to the present (or "actual") tense for greater immediacy "will *always* use enough past-tense
forms, mixed in with his actual-tense forms, to reassure the listener that
he is 'keeping his feet on the ground.' "[20] They quicken or retard the pace
of that development, and assign agency to one or another character for
perspectival relief.

Likewise, local deictics tug against the historical tide in the *Poema de
Mío Cid* and the poems Lope de Vega called "an *Iliad* without a Homer,"
the Spanish *romances viejos*. In both cases the poets "used the historic
present . . . to bring details into the foreground, and the past tenses to
hold them at a remove."[21] The scholar of Spanish balladry Ramón Menéndez Pidal observed the indelible effects of the adverbs *he* ("here is")
and *ya* ("now" or "already") in actualizing and vivifying both the *Cid*
and the romances.[22] It is worth noting, too, the broad and irrevocable
impact on the *Cid* of the adjective *mío*, which modifies nearly every appearance of the hero's name. Though a personal rather than a temporal
specifier, the deictic pronoun serves to pull the hero out of a merely leg-
endary past, announcing continually and obsessively his proximity to
both the narrator and the listener. It may be the most purposive, unfet-
tered play of a single deictic in narrative.

Since these cases of shifting tenses and other varieties of linguistic play
are often said to mark the spots where these narratives most resemble
lyric, one vital generic difference ought immediately to come clear: lyric
discourse, unlike narrative, has no programmatic deictic movement, no

hierarchic association of event and utterance that we can map and predict. It has no ready formula for process that corresponds to the narrative's heaping-up of perfect verbs and anaphoric deictics, or its postponement of the speaking present. Instead of hurrying toward it but deferring it, lyric often sees that *here* and *now* burst into the discourse spontaneously, abruptly; the speaking present, when it claims enough textual ground, may come into identity with the temporal dimension that most narratives keep at two removes, namely the reader's own present. Therefore, the job of lyric deixis is to establish a context that both exploits and controls the immediacy of the present—that maintains its emotional charge, and lends that to past and future tenses, while preserving an appropriate relation between the ritual and fictional modes to which the present and other tenses, respectively, often contribute. In principle, such a relation is devised again for every poem; according to local or occasional purposes, the needs of a poem by itself or in a collocation, or the demands of an explicit poetics, lyric process is continually reconfigured.

The chief tense of lyric poetry is probably the simple present, which often proposes a narrower interval between event and utterance than that common in narratives.[23] Poets may widen or contract such an interval for particular aims—in my fourth chapter, I will treat two sequences by W. B. Yeats that demonstrate a deliberate expansion of interval as a way of gaining flexibility within a post-Petrarchan poetics—but for many lyrics, the temporal remove between the speaker's intelligence and the events, actions, or states he or she tells, tends to favor the (often ambiguous) specification of the present. Even when a lyric plumbs the past for much of its argument, or when a speaker fashions an especially diffuse pattern of temporalities, one is seldom led to question the relevance of a *then* to a *now*. Instead, as in Wordsworth's "She Was a Phantom of Delight," one's instinct for the poem's cardinal happening is drawn to the revelatory moment, lodged in the simple present, that (it is claimed) inspires the utterance:

> She was a Phantom of delight
> When first she gleamed upon my sight;
> A lovely Apparition, sent
> To be a moment's ornament;
> Her eyes as stars of Twilight fair;
> Like Twilight's, too, her dusky hair;
> But all things else about her drawn
> From May-time and the cheerful Dawn;
> A dancing Shape, an Image gay,
> To haunt, to startle, and way-lay.

I saw her upon nearer view,
A Spirit, yet a Woman too!

.   .   .   .

And now I see with eye serene
The very pulse of the machine.[24]

The poem might be considered a programmatic example of lyric temporality, in that it discloses much that is typical to operations of the genre
as though that were its only business. Everything we know from this lyric,
we know because of what happens *now*: the settling of a once "startled"
and "waylaid" lover into serenity, and his freshly complete idea of his
phantom-woman, provoke him to create the poem as we have it. The
present tense, amply figured with feeling, reaches back to draw the recollections into a contingent relevance, and keeps us at the end from noticing much lyric interval at all, except for a sensation of its narrowing. Even
so, the simple present is carefully held in check: drafted to close the production, it is let in according to a formal pattern already established for
reminiscences, and cannot—because it is not allowed to—take over the
utterance in the present it shares with its auditors. It has been conscripted
and hedged around in order to achieve a small fiction.

Like narrative, lyric must rely on deictics to maintain and adjust its
internal process, to found fictions. Some lyrics, it is true, may enact a
roughly narrative movement: such poems as "The Unfortunate Lover"
by Andrew Marvell and "The Fish" by Elizabeth Bishop build a fairly
regular, graded sequence of deictics—arranged in a continuous historical
line, and gaining slightly on the instant of utterance—to realize, finally,
something like a story. But more often, the lyric poem constructs fiction
not by deferring but by confronting and subduing the present. Often a
breathlessness over the times visited in a poem is part of its self-advertise-
ment and affect. In a certain class of poems, the lines seem to radiate the
speaker's own dazzlement at what the lyric genre allows him to do. Robert Herrick's "How Lillies Came White" is one of these:

White though ye be; yet, Lillies, know,
From the first ye were not so
     But Ile tell ye
     What befell ye;
Cupid and his Mother lay
In a Cloud; while both did play,
He with his pretty finger prest
The rubie niplet of her breast;
Out of the which, the creame of light,
     Like to a Dew,
     Fell downe on you,
     And made ye white.[25]

Of course, this is not narrative: in its quick, ungraduated retrieval of a distant moment, the poem calls on strictly lyric resources. Lines 3 and 4 communicate the speaker's eagerness to sift one particular episode out of the broad past: he does not care to tell a story, in the sense of the term that implies a structure of events and a deictic gain on the instant of utterance. He creates an occasion for lyric recovery of the past, first by barring the flowers from claiming congenital whiteness—"from the first ye were not so," he announces, and casts the process behind their present condition into obscurity—and then by restoring to them a history, a fresh temporal development. The juncture of the last two lines holds an immense leap forward in time, compressing the span between the onset of their whiteness and the instant of utterance into a smooth, eventless continuity, and returning to the present by repeating two of the poem's first three words as its last two (one of these, the deictic second-person pronoun *ye*). The speaker's efficacy at halting the initial present tense and then replacing it with one of his own making is a demonstration of power not only over the flowers, but over the present: with its symmetrical first and final verses, the poem is a kind of exertion that keeps the *here* and *now* away and in check, a stay against the simple present. In poems like this one where the speaker-poet shows such unsophisticated glee at the reach of his deictic tools, one sees something of how lyric temporality always involves a coming to terms with the time of the utterance itself, no matter how seamless and exhilarating the evoked process may appear to speaker or auditor. There are enough explicit poems of this sort in Herrick's sequence *Hesperides* (1648) and in other works and literatures—such as Wordsworth's "Poems on the Naming of Places," or the Irish subgenre called *dinnseanchas*—to suggest that their bold, abrupt reach, and the astonishment it inspires, have something to do with the appeal of lyric discourse in general.[26]

Of the various patterns that a single lyric's temporal process may take, one especially interests me now because it forms the basis of Petrarch's invention of the lyric sequence as a type of fiction. It is perhaps the simplest or most schematic, but also (if these things can be judged) one of the most expressive. I mean the plain contrast of past and present, *then* and *now*, in a short lyric. Such poems—in effect, concentrations of the structure already observed in Wordsworth's "Phantom"—epitomize the fictional mode at work within a brief extent: they exploit the immediacy of the simple present but control its spread against the poem's bottom edge, so that the local affect involves a potential slippage from the fictional into the ritual mode, no more, perhaps like the aforementioned sensation of narrative climax. Sketched by a few conspicuous deictics and their modifiers, this pattern has possibilities for inflecting the emotional quality of the past and present tenses, and for relating them to each other, that are remarkably varied. Depending on how feeling is distributed among its temporal dimensions, a poem's process may seem smooth or discontinuous, brief or protracted, charged or neutral. For instance, the speaker may name the present as only the latest point in an emotional continuum unqualified from the past. This construction, comparatively rare in poetry, tends to diminish the integrity and urgency of the present instant and so to throw away one of the genre's precious commodities. One notices how peculiar, how vaguely unlyric, such a poem seems:

> The years have gathered grayly
>   Since I danced upon this leaze
> With one who kindled gaily
>   Love's fitful ecstasies!
> But despite the term as teacher,
>   I remain what I was then
> In each essential feature
>   Of the fantasies of men.[27]

Or the poem can qualify the past's likeness to the present by striking a concurrent note of difference. An *again* construction often manages this result, compressing the deictic distinction of *then* and *now* into one term: although the adverb *again* explicitly insists on a similarity of past and present, it seems not to cancel the present tense's implicit, automatic affirmation of its own distinctiveness. The two notes resound at once to create an affecting sense of the anniversary when much has changed, as in the first lines of "Lycidas": "Yet once more, O ye laurels, and once more / Ye myrtles brown, with ivy never sere."[28] Sharon Cameron has astutely suggested that "poems which call attention to themselves as a repetition with a difference are often elegiac in nature, and the purpose of the 'again' is not to chart sameness but disparity, to distinguish the unique event recorded by the poem from its too easy resemblance."[29] Clearly there may be an almost palpable relation between the temporal phenomenon of a lyric utterance—the way its speaker organizes experience in time, fills out that elementary structure, and ascribes value to it— and such larger matters as genre, ideology, and participation in a culture outside the poem.

I choose this particular construction of process because it affords a way of closing in on the *Canzoniere* both aesthetically and historically, and of crossing from the basic structures of temporal apprehension to wider matters. For many of the poets who must be considered begetters of Petrarch's lyric sequence, the *then-now* pattern seems to have been a regular way of initiating their long poems and anthologies. The lyric poets of Augustan Rome, who gathered their elegies into loosely organized volumes, can probably be called Petrarch's earliest secular models.[30] Like other Italians of the late fourteenth century, for instance, Petrarch knew the works of Propertius well: he had them copied into a manuscript that became the foundation of a textual tradition. In the first lines of the proem to the *Monobiblos*, Propertius's first book of elegies, the speaker's emotional history cleaves into a distant age of proud innocence and a continuing time of bittersweet experience:

> Cynthia prima suis miserum me cepit ocellis,
> contactum nullis ante cupidinibus.
> tum mihi constantis deiecit lumina fastus
> et caput impositis pressit Amor pedibus,
> donec me docuit castas odisse puellas
> improbus, et nullo vivere consilio.
> et mihi iam toto furor hic non deficit anno,
> cum tamen adversos cogor habere deos.

(Cynthia first caught me, poor wretch, with her eyes; before then, I did not know desire's touch. At that moment Love cast down my steady, proud eyes, and pressed down my head with his planted feet, until perversely he taught me to hate chaste girls, and to live wildly. Now a year has gone by with my passion undiminished, though my case still suffers the hostility of the gods.)[31]

At the start of a long collective or sequential work, this deictic construction can accomplish several tasks. It locates the onset of the emotional turn that inspires the collection, making each subsequent utterance seem to belong, even vaguely, to a single current of thought and feeling. It allows for expansion between its tenses, as the poet lengthens and dramatizes the moment of change. And it evokes the distant past enough to show how sharply *now* differs from *then*, and so binds the next poems into a loose temporal association.[32]

Compare the first of Ovid's *Amores*, where the *then-now* construction is slightly concealed because the body of the lyric consists in the stretching of that interval between tenses, filled here by a dialogue between the once innocent poet and his antagonist Cupid:

> Arma gravi numero violentaque bella parabam
> edere, materia conveniente modis.
> par erat inferior versus—risisse Cupido
> dicitur atque unum surripuisse pedem.
> "Quis tibi, saeve puer, dedit hoc in carmina iuris?
> Pieridum vates, non tua turba sumus.
> quid, si praeripiat flavae Venus arma Minervae,
> ventilet accensas flava Minerva faces?
> quis probet in silvis Cererem regnare iugosis,
> lege pharetratae Virginis arva coli?
> crinibus insignem quis acuta cuspide Phoebum

instruat, Aoniam Marte movente lyram?
· · · · · · · · · · · ·
cum bene surrexit versu nova pagina primo,
   attenuat nervos proximus ille meos;
nec mihi materia est numeris levioribus apta,
   aut puer aut longas compta puella comas."
Questus eram, pharetra cum protinus ille soluta
   legit in exitium spicula facta meum,
lunavitque genu sinuosum fortiter arcum,
   "quod" que "canas, vates, accipe" dixit "opus."
Me miserum. certas habuit puer ille sagittas.
   uror, et in vacuo pectore regnat Amor.

(Arms and violent wars, with meter suited to matter,
   Arms and violent wars, all in hexameters,
I was preparing to sound, when I heard a snicker from Cupid;
   What had the rascal done, but taken one foot away?
"Why, you bad boy!" I said, "who gave you this jurisdiction?
   We are the Muses' own, not your contemptible throng.
What if Venus should snatch the arms of fair-haired Minerva,
   What if Minerva should fan torches of love into flame?
Who would approve it if Ceres ruled on the ridges of woodland,
   Tilling the fields that law gave to Diana for hers?
How would Apollo learn to brandish a sharp-pointed spear-shaft?
   Wouldn't Mars look like a fool strumming the Orphean lyre?
· · · · · · · · · · · · · · · · · ·
My first line rose well, noble and lofty in measure,
   But the one you brought next surely corrupted the text.
What can I do in light verse? I have no boy I can sing of,
   No nice long-haired girl making a theme for my lays."
So I complained, and he drew out a shaft from his quiver,
   Taking his time to choose just the right arrow to use,
Bent the bow, moon-shaped, at his knee, and "Poet," he told me,
   "Take what I send; this barb surely will sting you to song!"
Never was truer word spoken; that boy shot straight with his arrow,
   I am on fire, and my heart owns the dominion of love.)[33]

Here as well, the *then-now* construction sets the forthcoming lyrics together in a loose series, compared by the poet to the start of a new reign. I cannot help thinking that the imperfect *parabam* ("I was making ready") in line 1 softens the otherwise hard distinction between past and present, allowing us to see an incipient trace of *now* in *then*: it shows the speaker-poet working repeatedly at his martial composition, as if trying to keep down thoughts of other things. His limp protests to Cupid about a slackening style, like his obviously informed description of the girl he does not possess, hint at the same infiltration. Still, the elementary *then-now* structure already remarked in Propertius's proem is unquestionably here, and for the next poems in the *Amores* the same temporal and emotional binding follows.

But in Propertius, Ovid, and most of the Augustan lyricists, the temporal organization of the collections stops there: typically, poem meets poem in the body of the series without promoting a sensation of continuity among them or (however else they might be ordered) enacting what might be called fictional process. The lyrics are independent, seemingly random episodes of the lover's experience. Any idea of temporal coalition that attaches to them follows largely from the proem's single effort to set the rough boundaries of the collection, to sound the limits of its recoverable history. Eric Havelock seems to dismiss the phenomenon of process within Catullus's *libellus* when he argues that the arrangement of the 118 lyrics is "purely formal. . . . On the one hand it pays no regard to the poetic substance of the verses, nor on the other does it attempt, presumably, to reproduce their chronology."[34] When Archibald W. Allen considers the temporality of Propertius's elegies, he concludes sternly that

> There is no progression in time in the elegies. The opening elegy is an introduction to love, and the last elegy of the third book is a valediction to love. Between these two are elegies which treat all the aspects of love, fruition and loneliness, renunciation and renewal, hope and despair, jealousy and penitence. But there is no plot which unites them and determines the order in which they shall appear. Propertius is not concerned to tell a story, but rather to impart the quality of an experience. Explicit statements of time, place, person, and circumstance have meaning . . . as details which serve to enforce perception of the essential and typical aspects of experience in love.[35]

Gordon Williams observes that "Propertius, in collecting his poems together, was interested in the effects observed by sequences of poems which could display either similarity or variety," and remarks that in Propertius's second book, the poet "seems to have composed in a series of cycles, in each of which [he] progresses not through a historical sequence of events or episodes, but through a range of emotional crises ending in the death of love or a retreat into poetry."[36] James E. G. Zetzel adds that in the typical Roman collection, "the persona of the poet may vary, the overt subject may change, and only rarely (as, for instance, in the case of Propertius I 7 and I 9) does the author provide a clear and objective link between one poem and another, a link visible enough to allay the doubts of those scholars who feel that such structures are more often in the mind of the critic than in the intention of the poet."[37]

In fact, most readers who hold out for the logic and design of the so-called Augustan poetic books deny any version of temporal process in those texts. Despite the occasional rudiments of a temporal unity—the shifting historical orientations in single lyrics, and the continuities among subcollections within the books—the collections of Catullus, Propertius, Ovid, and the rest seem to fit Roland Barthes's prospectus for his own atemporal, amatory "fragments": "No logic links the [fragments], determines their contiguity: [they] are non-syntagmatic, non-narrative; they are Erinyes; they stir, collide, subside, return, vanish with no more order than the flight of mosquitoes . . . the lover speaks in bundles of sentences but does not integrate these sentences on a higher level, into a work; his is a horizontal discourse: no transcendence, no deliverance, no novel (though a great deal of the fictive)."[38] If this is true of the Augustans, it is even more so of Petrarch's other principal model for the lyric collocation, the twelfth- and thirteenth-century chansonniers or songbooks of the Provençal poets. Their influence along the small gauges of Petrarch's poetics is substantial: his Canzone 70, a tribute to Arnaut Daniel and other vernacular lyricists, attests as much. The songbooks' inclusion of the poets' *vidas* is surely important in the founding of the post-Petrarchan ideology of lyric I have called nominativity. But temporally and collectively speaking, the chansonniers can only have suggested to Petrarch the value of parataxis between and among poems, for they are scarcely unified, were generally not assembled by the poets themselves, and often even lack proems.[39]

As for another major complex of influence on Petrarch's *Canzoniere*, readers have often noticed the resemblance between the form called Menippean satire—a fictional discourse built of both prose and verse, and represented in Petrarch's age by the *Vita Nuova* of Dante—and the lyric sequence.[40] In this case, where a few strokes can assemble disparate materials and get the fiction underway, one often sees a similarly patterned exposition. These are the first lines of the opening poem in Boethius's *Consolation of Philosophy*:

> Carmina qui quondam studio florente peregi,
>   Flebilis heu maestos cogor inire modos.
> Ecce mihi lacerae dictant scribenda Camenae
>   Et ueris elegi fletibus ora rigant.
> Has saltem nullus potuit pervincere terror,
>   Ne nostrum comites prosequerentur iter.
> Gloria felicis olim uiridisque iuuentae
>   Solantur maesti nunc mea fata senis.
> Venit enim properata malis inopina senectus
>   Et dolor aetatem iussit inesse suam.

(I who once wrote songs with keen delight am now by sorrow driven to take up melancholy measures. Wounded Muses tell me what I must write, and elegiac verses bathe my face with real tears. Not even terror could drive from me these faithful companions of my long journey. Poetry, which was once the glory of my happy and flourishing youth, is still my comfort in this misery of my old age.)[41]

There are notable differences, however, in how Propertius and Boethius follow such a proem. Unlike the Augustan collections, Menippean satire has more than a thematic or vocal unity, is more than an anthology. It is a species of narrative. The prose segments add context and momentum to the metrical elements, while the poems contribute lyric reflection and the weight of feeling. Often the lyrics actually further the narrative, as in the poem by Publius that Trimalchio reads into the record of the *cena trimalchionis* in the *Satyricon*. Like other narratives, Menippean satire is bound up by the fact of continuous fictional process, by a sense of the integrity and advance of the historical present laid out in the proem.

Written circa 1300, the *Vita Nuova* shows in its first lines still another version of this contrastive construction, and suggests—by its relentless stipulation of a "before" and "after" in the speaker's life—how adeptly such an opening can prepare for an extended fictional process:

Nove fiate già appresso lo mio nascimento era tornato lo cielo de la luce quasi a uno medesimo punto, quanto a la sua propria girazione, quando a li miei occhi apparve prima la gloriosa donna de la mia mente, la quale fu chiamata da molti Beatrice li quali non sapeano che si chiamare. Ella era in questa vita già stata tanto, che ne lo suo tempo lo cielo stellato era mosso verso la parte d'oriente de le dodici parti l'una d'un grado, sì che quasi dal principio del suo anno nono apparve a me, ed io la vidi quasi da la fine del mio nono. Apparve vestita di nobilissimo colore, umile e onesto, sanguigno, cinta e ornata a la guisa che a la sua giovanissima etade si convenia. In quello punto dico veracemente che lo spirito de la vita, lo quale dimora ne la secretissima camera de lo cuore, cominciò a tremare sì fortemente, che apparia ne li menimi polsi orribilmente; e tremando disse queste parole: "Ecce deus fortior me, qui veniens dominabitur michi." In quello punto lo spirito animale, lo quale dimora ne l'alta camera ne la quale tutti li spiriti sensitivi portano le loro percezioni, si cominciò a maravigliare molto, e parlando spezialmente a li spiriti del viso, sì disse queste parole: "Apparuit iam beatitudo vestra." In quello punto lo spirito naturale, lo quale dimora in quella parte ove si ministra lo nutrimento nostro, cominciò a piangere, e piangendo disse queste parole: "Heu miser, quia frequenter impeditus ero deinceps!" D'allora innanzi dico che Amore segnoreggiò la mia anima, la quale fu sì tosto a lui disponsata, e cominciò a prendere sopra me tanta sicurtade e tanta signoria per la vertù che li dava la mia imaginazione, che me convenia fare tutti li suoi piaceri compiutamente.

(Nine times already since my birth the heaven of light had circled back to almost the same point, when there appeared before my eyes the now glorious lady of my mind, who was called Beatrice even by those who did not know what her name was. She had been in this life long enough for the heaven of the fixed stars to be able to move a twelfth of a degree to the East in her time; that is, she appeared to me at about the beginning of her ninth year, and I first saw her near the end of my ninth year. She appeared dressed in the most patrician of colors, a subdued and decorous crimson, her robe bound round and adorned in a style suitable to her years. At that very moment, and I speak the truth, the vital spirit, the one that dwells in the most secret chamber of the heart, began to tremble so violently that even the most minute veins of my body were strangely affected; and trembling, it spoke these words: "Here is a god stronger than I who comes to rule over me." At that point the animal spirit, the one abiding in the high chamber to which all the senses bring their perceptions, was stricken with amazement and, speaking directly to the spirits of sight, said these words: "Now your bliss has appeared." At that point the natural spirit, the one dwelling in that part where our food is digested, began to weep, and weeping said these words: "Oh, wretched me! for I shall be disturbed often from now on." Let me say that, from that time on, Love governed my soul, which became immediately devoted to him, and he reigned over me with such assurance and lordship, given him by the power of my imagination, that I could only dedicate myself to fulfilling his every pleasure.)[42]

Here the initial deixis has been raised to a kind of touchstone, to be rubbed repeatedly as it marks the start of love's governance over the speaker. The three human "spirits" who respond to the vision of Beatrice, though they express their amazement in different idioms according to their rank, throng around the first moment of her impact on Dante as the original boundary of his unitary *vita nuova*: "Behold! Here she is, and now it begins," they agree, and the reader's perception of the poem's background could not be more severely parted into seasons of *then* and *now*. The paratactic, incantatory phrase *in quello punto* ("at that very moment") encourages a fascinated attention to the texture of that instant of *innamoramento*, stalling the incipient narrative there; the trembling, weeping, and wonder Beatrice inspires add an emotional body to the moment; and the inevitably serial relation of three simultaneous utterances gives it a remembered length and resonance. The poem's temporal frame in place, the deictic *d'allora* ("since then") reaches out to claim the ensuing work as the body of the proem's *now*, and the process of the *Vita Nuova* is set unstoppably in motion. It will be reaffirmed at innumerable points along the course of the work by every anaphoric *and* and *then*, by the continual forward drift these deictics direct. Temporal indicators in the introduction and the rest of the *Vita Nuova* pull together to draw the limits and generate the impetus of a steady progress through narrative time, relieved by lyric interludes scattered along the way.

When we arrive at the first poem of Petrarch's *Canzoniere*, then, we ought to be able to read it, in one sense, as an installment in a familiar line of deictic openings:

> Voi ch'ascoltate in rime sparse il suono
> di quei sospiri ond'io nudriva 'l core
> in sul mio primo giovenile errore
> quand'era in parte altr'uom da quel ch'i' sono,
>
> del vario stile in ch'io piango et ragiono
> fra le vane speranze e 'l van dolore,
> ove sia chi per prova intenda amore,
> spero trovar pietà, non che perdono.
>
> Ma ben veggio or sì come al popol tutto
> favola fui gran tempo, onde sovente
> di me medesmo meco mi vergogno;
>
> et del mio vaneggiar vergogna è 'l frutto,
> e 'l pentersi, e 'l conoscer chiaramente
> che quanto piace al mondo è breve sogno.

(You who hear in scattered rhymes the sound of those sighs with which I nourished my heart during my first youthful error, when I was in part another man from what I am now:

for the varied style in which I weep and speak between vain hopes and vain sorrow, where there is anyone who understands love through experience, I hope to find pity, not only pardon.

But now I see well how for a long time I was the talk of the crowd, for which often I am ashamed of myself within;

and of my raving, shame is the fruit, and repentance, and the clear knowledge that whatever pleases in the world is a brief dream.)[43]

As an announcement of the collection's matter and style, this lyric stands as a proem much like the signature poems of the classical elegists.[44] Through the unobtrusive workings of deixis in the first quatrain's verb tenses and the first tercet's adverbs and adverbial phrases, it sets out temporal dimensions of *then* and *now* just as they do. But it has another, crucial enterprise. Here for the first time in a Western lyric collection, I believe, the proem does not stand alone at the head of a chain of temporally polymorphous fragments. Rather, this proem introduces a temporal program, an alternation of tenses in single lyrics that will remain in force throughout the *Canzoniere*. Keeping a *then* and a *now* accessible at closely intermittent points in the longer work, Petrarch creates a fictional process that holds the entirety of the *Canzoniere*. He makes, in effect, a large-scale lyric fiction by the systematic repetition of what had been merely a local strategy in lyric anthologies and narratives.

How does this establishment of fictional process work? In fact, it depends on several technics, which I will trace in turn. The first among these is the recurrent construction of *then-now*, the temporal frame of about one-fourth of the 366 poems in the *Canzoniere*.[45] In a single poem, this pattern is an economical, not very remarkable way of refining a speaker's psychic history into a cleanly differentiated statement. As I have indicated, the construction concedes certain advantages when it appears at the head of a collection of lyrics. But inevitably and maybe unexpectedly, it has another notable issue when it appears consistently in sequence: it counterfeits the phenomenon of passing time. At each point along a series of such poems, the speaker and the reader orient themselves against a past, and see the stirrings of the present there. To put it a little differently, each lyric charts its process with the same deictic arrangement, setting perfect and present tenses—with their respective, sustaining adverbs such as *d'allora* ("then") and *ora* or *omai* ("now")—against one another for analogical or contrastive ends. And just as in lived experience, each of these dimensions constantly extends its range, for the past seems to engulf each lyric as it slips out of the reading present, and our serial assimilation of the work ensures that the fund of present moments (or "axes of orientation," as the linguists have it) stretches inexhaustibly forward. Since each lyric quickly joins the accumulating past, the series never arrives at the flat, continuous present of a ritual poetics; what we have already seen as a common expedient for determining a short poem's situation among lyric modes, organizing its fictional errand while admitting and controlling the axis of the present, is here greatly elaborated toward the same phenomenological issue. Soon the later pieces in the sequence appear to look back at the anterior ones, and before we get very far we notice the sensation of our passing, not across 366 lyrics gathered into a book, each with a native, independent history, but through a single span of fictional time, a process.

An acutely condensed outline of that process, and a run through it, may be in order now.[46] Every reader of the entire *Canzoniere* notices that, while the poet constantly discriminates past and present, these periods seem to shift their boundaries forward in time as the work advances. In Sonnet 3, for instance, the past includes the lover's preromantic innocence as in Propertius 1.1, the present his extravagant sufferings:

Era il giorno ch'al sol si scoloraro
per la pietà del suo factore i rai,
quando i' fui preso, et non me ne guardai,
ché i be' vostr'occhi, donna, mi legaro.

Tempo non mi parea da far riparo
contra colpi d'Amor: però m'andai
secur, senza sospetto; onde i miei guai
nel commune dolor s'incominciaro.

Trovommi Amor del tutto disarmato
et aperta la via per gli occhi al core,
che di lagrime son fatti uscio et varco.

(It was the day when the sun's rays turned pale with grief for his Maker when
I was taken, and I did not defend myself against it, for your lovely eyes, Lady,
bound me.

It did not seem to me a time for being on guard against Love's blows; therefore I went confident and without fear, and so my misfortunes began in the
midst of the universal woe.

Love found me altogether disarmed, and the way open through my eyes to
my heart, my eyes which are now the portal and passageway of tears.)

(3.1–11)

A few poems further along, the past has gained in extent—including not
only the speaker's innocence (com'era or "before," line 8) but a thousand
subsequent imprecations—while the present is a moment of fresh uncertainty:

Mille fïate, o dolce mia guerrera,
per aver co' begli occhi vostri pace
v'aggio proferto il cor; mâ voi non piace
mirar sí basso colla mente altera.

Et se di lui fors'altra donna spera,
vive in speranza debile et fallace:
mio, perché sdegno ciò ch'a voi dispiace,
esser non può già mai cosí com'era.

Or s'io lo scaccio, et e' non trova in voi
ne l'exilio infelice alcun soccorso,
né sa star sol, né gire ov'altri il chiama,

poria smarrire il suo natural corso:
che grave colpa fia d'ambeduo noi,
et tanto piú de voi, quanto piú v'ama.

(A thousand times, O my sweet warrior, in order to have peace with your lovely eyes, I have offered you my heart; but it does not please you to gaze so low with your lofty mind;

and if some other lady has hopes of him, she lives in weak and fallacious hope; mine—since I disdain what does not please you—mine he can never be as before.

Now if I drive him away, and he does not find in you any help in his sad exile, nor can stay alone, nor go where some other calls him,

his natural course of life might fail, which would be a grave fault in both of us, and so much the more yours as he loves you the more.)

(21)

Sometimes the *then-now* construction portrays a temporal partition not in the speaker's personal history, but in someone else's:

> Amor piangeva, et io con lui talvolta,
> dal qual miei passi non fur mai lontani,
> mirando per gli effecti acerbi et strani
> l'anima vostra de' suoi nodi sciolta.
>
> Or ch'al dritto camin l'à Dio rivolta,
> col cor levando al cielo ambe le mani,
> ringratio lui che' giusti preghi humani
> benignamente, sua mercede, ascolta.

(Love, from whom my steps have never strayed, used to weep, and I with him at times, to see by the strange and bitter effects that your soul was freed from his knots:

now that God has turned it back to the right path, in my heart lifting both hands to Heaven I thank Him who in His mercy listens kindly to just human prayers.)

(25.1–8)

When this signature turns up even in topical poems like Sonnet 25, we ought to recognize that it came to serve as a compositional habit or topos with Petrarch, a way of generating structure and matter for poems by seeking out significant divisions in whatever history he was immediately concerned to celebrate. The construction is as fully "Petrarchan," I believe, as that of transposing deep feeling into a language of paradox, another sort of slashing formulation borrowed from classical and medieval models that has been known as his since the Renaissance. The principal virtue of this retrospective topos for occasional poetry is that it goes far toward answering the constant generic difficulty of aggrandizing the occasion. It tends to place a poem's present moment or occasion on the cusp of a gathering temporal movement, of an incipient *vita nuova*, as in Sonnet 25 or this poem of condolence:

> La bella donna che cotanto amavi
> subitamente s'è da noi partita,
> et per quel ch'io ne speri al ciel salita,
> sí furon gli atti suoi dolci soavi.
>
> Tempo è da ricovrare ambe le chiavi
> del tuo cor, ch'ella possedeva in vita,
> et seguir lei per via dritta expedita:
> peso terren non sia piú che t'aggravi.
>
> Poi che se' sgombro de la maggior salma,
> l'altre puoi giuso agevolmente porre,
> sallendo quasi un pellegrino scarco.
>
> Ben vedi omai sí come a morte corre
> ogni cosa creata, et quanto all'alma
> bisogna ir lieve al periglioso varco.

(The beautiful lady whom you so much loved has suddenly departed from us and, I hope, has risen to Heaven, so sweet and gentle were her deeds.

It is time to recover both the keys of your heart, which she possessed while she lived, and to follow her by a straight and unimpeded road: let there be no further earthly weight to hold you down.

Since you are lightened of your greatest burden, you will be able to put down the others easily, rising like a pilgrim who carries little;

you see now how every created thing runs to death, and how light the soul needs to be for the perilous crossing.)

(91)

Much has been written about the topical poems in Petrarch's sequence, mostly out of a perceived need to reconcile these elements to the dominant amatory and devotional strains in the fiction.[47] It is, I think, worth weighing the idea that the *Canzoniere* is an especially agreeable site for so many non-amatory poems, first because its programmatic deictic construction fits their needs so exactly—accustomed to sifting and organizing experience in this fashion, Petrarch may well have composed many more occasional poems than did poets whose responses to public and nonpersonal events were less rehearsed—and second, because poems organized like Sonnets 25 and 91 go to unfold the sequence's temporality as well as the love lyrics do: taking them in, the *Canzoniere* loses nothing of its fictional integrity and momentum. The sequence's capacity for absorbing topical poems may rest in part on just such reciprocity.

More important, the retrospective topos is congruent with the ideas about time that Petrarch is often said to have communicated to Western culture in his various lyrics, narratives, and letters: the obsession with time's flight and its irretrievability to humankind, the impulse to weigh the present hour against past achievements, the need to give history a segmented order as a means of making it comprehensible to the present.[48] Further, the topos coincides with the random or uncodified element in Petrarchan ideology that Thomas M. Greene has called humanist pathos. In Greene's words,

> Petrarch precipitated his own personal creative crisis because he made a series of simultaneous discoveries that had been made only fragmentarily before him. It was he who first understood how radically classical antiquity differed from the Christian era; he also saw more clearly than his predecessors how the individual traits of a given society at a given moment form a distinctive constellation; he understood more clearly the philological meaning of anachronism. In view of his humanist piety and his literary ambition, these perceptions created a problem that he would bequeath to the generations that followed him: the problem how to write with integrity under the shadow of a prestigious cultural alternative. To be a humanist after Petrarch was not simply to be an archaeologist but to feel an imitative/emulative pressure from a lost source.
>
> In Italy the word after Petrarch is cast out of the maternal circle of *Latinitas*; it begins to betray its exile, its finitude, its relativity. The sense of privation, which was certainly present in medieval culture, became better informed and less resigned, became an incitement. History betrayed a rupture.[49]

The retrospective construction materializes the Petrarchan idea of disjuncture between past and present; its frequent appearances in the *Canzoniere* represent the habit of a mind used to playing over this contrast obsessively, provocatively, reproachfully. It mimics the intuition of anachronism. Yet the accumulation of *then-now* lyrics creates a fiction of continuity from these unlikely factors, and in doing so answers the humanist dilemma of admitting anachronism or rupture while overcoming it, defending against it with itself. Of course in these lyrics Petrarch translates humanism's cultural crisis into personal life, substituting utterly ephemeral experience in love—always in freshly varied examples—for the classical past, and other moments, quite as ephemeral, for the medieval-turned-Renaissance here and now. Parodically, only the structure of the humanist crisis remains the same: Petrarch seems almost to be comparing great things with small. But like other humanist texts that address the problem in their ways, and more successfully than many, Petrarch's lyric sequence "mitigates the choice between awareness of otherness and its refusal"; it "permits a fiction of historical flow that reconciles and bridges."[50] In this sense, the seemingly mundane and overexplicit dimension of the *Canzoniere* simply means that the series is the lyric restatement of a cultural event with which Petrarch (and later, others) struggled on many fronts. It finds a solution on its own terms, exclusive to its genre, where a material construction much repeated can shade into something we have to call fiction.

As the poems accumulate, the recoverable past gets still larger: in Sonnet 164 the present is a particular night when Petrarch stays awake with thoughts of Laura, the past everything previous:

> Or che 'l ciel et la terra e 'l vento tace
> et le fere e gli augelli il sonno affrena,
> Notte il carro stellato in giro mena
> et nel suo letto il mar senz'onda giace,
>
> vegghio, penso, ardo, piango.

(Now that the heavens and the earth and the wind are silent, and sleep reins in the beasts and the birds, Night drives her starry car about, and in its bed the sea lies without a wave,

I am awake, I think, I burn, I weep.)

(164.1–5)

Four sonnets later, the present consists in a new burst of hopeful speculation, and the past, again, in all that came before (including, one assumes, the wakeful night of Sonnet 164):

> Amor mi manda quel dolce pensero
> che secretario anticho è fra noi due,
> et mi conforta, et dice che no fue
> mai come or presto a quel ch'io bramo et spero.

(Love sends me that sweet thought which is an old confidant between us and comforts me and says that I was never so close as I am now to what I yearn and hope for.)

(168.1–4)

And after Canzone 264 opens the work's second historical phase, *in morte di Madonna Laura*—her death is first explicitly announced in Sonnet 267, but 264 marks the renewal of the sequence after a deliberate pause—the remembrance of Laura *in vita* takes over most uses of the *then-now* construction, in poems such as Canzone 270:

> Passata è la stagion, perduto ài l'arme,
> di ch'io tremava: ormai che puoi tu [Amor] farme?

(The season is past, you [Love] have lost the arms at which I trembled: what can you do to me now?)

(270.74–75)

and Sonnet 282:

> là 've cantando andai di te molt'anni,
> or, come vedi, vo di te piangendo:
> di te piangendo no, ma de' miei danni.

(Where I went singing of you many years, now, as you see, I go weeping for you—no, not weeping for you but for my loss.)

(282.9–11)

Here the "singing" he mourns includes all 281 prior poems, and the range of emotional climates they show: remembered against Laura's death, everything that came before sounds like singing.

At the last, the lover's mind turns strongly to thoughts of his impending death and reunion with God, and chords of repentance for his lifelong, profane love of Laura fall closer to one another and more loudly. Sonnet 364, the antepenultimate poem in the *Canzoniere*, takes the longest retrospective scope of any poem so far:

> Tennemi Amor anni ventuno ardendo,
> lieto nel foco, et nel duol pien di speme;
> poi che madonna e 'l mio cor seco inseme
> saliro al ciel, dieci altri anni piangendo.
>
> Omai son stanco, et mia vita reprendo
> di tanto error che di vertute il seme
> à quasi spento, et le mie parti extreme,
> alto Dio, a te devotamente rendo:
>
> pentito et tristo de' miei sí spesi anni,
> che spender si deveano in miglior uso,
> in cercar pace et in fuggir affanni.

(Love held me twenty-one years gladly burning in the fire and full of hope amid sorrow; since my lady, and my heart with her, rose to Heaven, ten more years of weeping.

Now I am weary and I reproach my life for so much error, which has almost extinguished the seeds of virtue; and I devoutly render my last parts, high God, to You,

repentant and sorrowing for my years spent thus, which ought to have been
better used, in seeking peace and fleeing troubles.)

(364.1–11)

In a certain sense, however, the longest backward glance of all belongs to
Sonnet 1, the proem I have already quoted. It is uttered at a time hypo-
thetically nearer to the reader than any other poem in the sequence, and
identifies all the succeeding lyrics—including those written *in morte di
Laura*—as casualties of the speaker's spiritual renaissance, his "shame"
and "clear knowledge." Commenting on the rest of the *Canzoniere*, Sonnet 1 is actually outside the temporal span of the series, and asks us to
enter just as the process from Sonnet 2 through the 364 succeeding poems
is about to begin.

With this rough outline of the process of the *Canzoniere*, I mean only
to point out a few of the many spots where Petrarch weighs the accumulating past against the advancing present, and to suggest that the reiteration of the retrospective topos confers a sense of temporal movement on
the entire lyric sequence. I do not maintain, for one thing, that the *Can-
zonïere* is unrelieved of such seemingly two-dimensional lyrics: there are,
properly, many poems in the sequence that do not contribute to the illusion of process in any notable way, like the much-imitated Sonnet 132
("S'amor non è, che dunque è quel ch'io sento?"). Nor do I maintain that
the sequence has a narrative logic: in fact, it is critical to the intellectual
and generic assimilation of the *Canzoniere* that we understand exactly
how it does not. In its story—meaning the original chronology of events
implicated in an epic or novel, quite distinct from the order of its telling
in particular versions or plots—a narrative typically has a structure of
events that cannot be much altered without shattering the sense and progress of the work. Our sense of time's passing comes out of this structure,
realized in a chain of perfect verbs and anaphoric deictics: events cause
later events, characters grow and change in the heat of circumstances, and
long-stated goals are finally realized. For the sake of the narrative's life,
the abstract order of events must hold: Odysseus cannot come home before he meets Calypso, and Don Quixote cannot fight over a barber's
basin before he loses his wits and sets off as a knight.

In the implied process of the *Canzoniere*, however, most of the lyrics—
which approximate the "events" of a narrative—can be freely substituted
for one another with no loss to the fiction. The success of the Petrarchan
temporal enterprise depends not on any structure the lyrics build in con-
cert, not on a logic at all, but on the sheer additive force of the *then-now*
poems, each trailing an illusory thread of retrospection behind it. Certainly some lyrics in the sequence, as we have them, must fall roughly or
exactly where they do: these are the few poems that respond to unique

events such as Laura's death, the fifteen or so dated poems (which I will discuss shortly), and the poems that participate in clear-cut thematic developments. If we provisionally except the strains of theme and topic, however, and isolate the temporal construction of each lyric, it is hard not to concede that the lyrics on the *then-now* deictic pattern are astonishingly variable in the combinations they allow, impossible not to see that as we reshuffle them they seem to lose nothing of their fictional process. Compare E. H. Wilkins's textual explanation of the same phenomenon:

> [There] is no evidence that [Petrarch] was ever concerned to establish a precise chronological arrangement for his poems, or to give to his readers the impression that the poems stood in a precise chronological order. The several self-dated poems of the Pre-Chigi form ... stand in the order of the dates they bear; and while among the poems that are not self-dated there are several that stand out of the order which modern scholarship has shown to be the probable order of their composition, there is among the poems included in the Pre-Chigi form no instance of a dislocation that would be likely to impress the reader with the idea of a breach of chronology. That was enough for Petrarch; and it is enough for the reader. Petrarch was the poetic master of his chronology, not its slave.[51]

However the poems get arranged, each *then* will seem to look back at preceding pieces in the sequence and still earlier moments, each *now* to name the present as a traceable extension of that visible past.

"The primary illusion created by poesis is a history entirely experienced,"[52] proposes Susanne Langer in her arch-fictionalist poetics of lyric, and the much-repeated retrospective construction amounts to a formula for resolving the experience of passing time into the structure of a chain of lyrics; it is a conceit for that experience, a calculated and selective play of deictic terms that deepens the sensation of reading until we feel that we have given over years, not merely hours or days, to the unfolding of the *Canzoniere*. Again and again Petrarch gambles that the formula will hold, framing his own sense of duration in exclamations that would necessarily strike us as facile and empty if his sense were not ours, as well:

> Il tempo passa, et l'ore son sí pronte
> a fornire il vïaggio,
> ch'assai spacio non aggio
> pur a pensar com'io corro a la morte.

(Time passes and the hours are so swift to complete their journey that I have not enough time even to think how I run to death.)

(37.17–20)

Misera, che devrebbe esser accorta
per lunga experïentia omai che 'l tempo
non è chi 'ndietro volga, o chi l'affreni.

(Miserable soul, who should have been aware by now, through long experience, that there is no one who can turn back time or rein it in!)

(86.9–11)

O tempo, O ciel volubil, che fuggendo
inganni i ciechi et miseri mortali,
o dí veloci piú che vento et strali,
ora ab experto vostre frodi intendo.

(O Time, O revolving heavens that fleeing deceive us blind and wretched
mortals, O days more swift than wind or arrows! Now through experience I
understand your frauds.)

(355.1–4)

With the successful transmittal of that experiential "illusion," we can actually watch this lyric collection draw itself and its epigones into the phenomenological condition of fiction. It becomes a type of work through
which it means something to pass, a long poem that, in describing a virtual life, claims for itself a certain integral range of our lives as readers—
exchanges *vita* for *vita*. It is no string of trifles, but sustained lyric of a
new order: as demanding, and therefore as fertile of possibilities, as a
drama or novel. This is the opening of Petrarchan fiction, with all the uses
and adaptations poets during and after the Renaissance have given it.

There is another, fulfilling element in the fictional process of the *Canzoniere*, a continual erecting and elaborating of fixed limits around the
sequence's irresistible movement. This element consists in the regular
glances, forward and back, at the definite historical extremes of the sequence's temporal span: I mean the moment of Petrarch's *innamoramento* with Laura, recalled in Sonnets 2 and 3 and many following poems, such as 61:

Benedetto sia 'l giorno, e 'l mese, et l'anno,
et la stagione, e'l tempo, et l'ora, e 'l punto,
e'l bel paese, e 'l loco ov'io fui giunto
da' duo begli occhi che legato m'ànno.

(Blessed be the day and the month and the year and the season and the time
and the hour and the instant and the beautiful countryside and the place
where I was struck by the two lovely eyes that have bound me),

(61.1–4)

and the moment of his death, which he foretells recurrently from early on in the sequence:

> Quanto piú m'avicino al giorno extremo
> che l'umana miseria suol far breve,
> piú veggio il tempo andar veloce et leve,
> e 'l mio di lui sperar fallace et scemo.

(The more I approach that last day that makes all human misery brief, the more I see that Time runs swift and light and that my hope of him is fallacious and empty.)

(32.1–4)

> veggio a molto languir poca mercede,
> et già l'ultimo dí nel cor mi tuona:
> per tutto questo Amor non mi spregiona,
> che l'usato tributo agli occhi chiede.

(I see little reward for much yearning, and already the last day thunders in my heart. But for all that, Love does not set me free, for he demands the usual tribute from my eyes.)

(101.5–8)

Keeping these absolute limits in view, Petrarch counters the freely selective deixis of most of the retrospective lyrics, which can, in principle, choose any *then* for contrast with *now*. He iterates what his predecessors, the classical lyricists and Menippean satirists, did largely in their proems. He suggests again and again the dimensions of the temporal frame in which his *Canzoniere* oscillates and advances, and compels a renewable sense of bounding around the process of the fiction.

This combinative formula of fixity around temporal movement, continual alternations of *then* and *now* framed by a recalled *innamoramento* and an anticipated death, is to Petrarch's lyric sequence what the chain of perfect verbs and anaphoric deictics is to the typical narrative: a generic prescription for engendering a large-scale fiction out of a latent history. Petrarch's fictional accomplishment—never named before this but always an implicit basis of his poetic influence—is to fuse the fragmented lyricism of the traditional collections, Roman, Provençal, and Italian, with the fictional continuum of Menippean satire; he creates a chain of lyrics as integral as the latter, as interchangeable as the former. The sense of passing time inaugurated in the *Canzoniere* becomes, in a few generations, a natural and unquestioned resource of the post-Petrarchan lyric sequence. It is never reproduced, I think, with a formula as radical as Petrarch's, but then it does not need to be: his example had the force to make poets and readers irrevocably identify the form with the phenomenon, a memorability that precluded any second exercise of his thoroughgoing deictic program.

A third element remains to be reckoned in with Petrarch's temporal program. His critics have long remarked on the "self-dating" poems in the *Canzoniere*, the fifteen or so lyrics, like Sonnet 62, that announce their distance in absolute time from the day of the speaker's *innamoramento*:

> Or volge, signor mio, l'undecimo anno
> ch'i' fui sommesso al dispietato giogo
> che sopra i piú soggetti è piú feroce.

(Now turns, my Lord, the eleventh year that I have been subject to the pitiless yoke that is always most fierce to the most submissive.)

(62.9–11)

Many readers, in fact, confuse the dates for the primary element in the work's time-scheme, proceeding to explain from them the sensation of passing days and hours.[53] But these dates are nearly superfluous to the reader's impression of passing time. They are only the most explicit layer of a process that runs strongly and steadily throughout the sequence, only fifteen out of 366 poems. The phenomenal difference between a few baldly stated dates and a fiction built from the constant play of deictics is like the difference between looking at a calendar and living through a year. The aim of the dates is to confirm the sense of duration that hangs, independent of them, over the *Canzoniere*: they afford some widely spaced, incidental glimpses of the calendar. They show that the span from Sestina 30 to Canzone 50 is three years long; that a year separates 50 and 62; three more years, 62 and 79; and so on. Where they fall into a smooth numerical logic, they add only an agreeable concreteness to the accumulating process. And where they defy such a logic—Sonnets 145 and 266, for instance, both appear to be dated earlier than their respective forerunners in the self-dating series—they cannot harm the fiction, because it has accumulated a force, a laying-up of phenomenal experience, much greater than any calendrical irregularity. In fact, the disordered dates actually enable a properly nuanced understanding of the temporality of the *Canzoniere*. For many readers they are Petrarch's most visible sedition against our automatic assumption of a narrative logic, and they encourage us to look and look again at the interchangeability and deictic play of these 366 lyrics. Further, when epigones of the *Canzoniere* deliberately arranged their anniversary lyrics out of chronological order, they were honoring the conviction that somehow Petrarch brings the condition of fiction to what might have seemed (and often still does seem) a mere collocation of poems; they were trying, superstitiously as I see it, to summon the same effect into their sequences.[54]

At this point, a closer view of temporality in one or two particular poems may seem desirable. Sonnet 118 offers a conspicuous example.

> Rimansi a dietro il sestodecimo anno
> de' miei sospiri, et io trapasso inanzi
> verso l'extremo; et parmi che pur dianzi
> fosse 'l principio di cotanto affanno.
>
> L'amar m'è dolce, et util il mio danno,
> e 'l viver grave; et prego ch'egli avanzi
> l'empia Fortuna, et temo no chiuda anzi
> Morte i begli occhi che parlar mi fanno.
>
> Or qui son, lasso, et voglio esser altrove;
> et vorrei piú volere, et piú non voglio;
> et per piú non poter fo quant'io posso;
>
> et d'antichi desir' lagrime nove
> provan com'io son pur quel ch'i' mi soglio,
> né per mille rivolte anchor son mosso.

(Now remains behind the sixteenth year of my sighs, and I move forward toward the last; yet it seems to me that all this suffering began only recently.

The bitter is sweet to me, and my losses useful, and living heavy; and I pray that my life may outlast my cruel fortune; and I fear that before then Death may close the lovely eyes that make me speak.

Now here I am, alas, and wish I were elsewhere, and wish I wished more, but wish no more, and by being unable to do more, do all I can;

and new tears for old desires show me to be still what I used to be, nor for a thousand turnings about have I yet moved.)

The poem dates itself in the first line and, in the remainder of that quatrain, alludes to both the starting- and ending-points of the sequence's fictional process. For the speaker as for the reader, the fact of sixteen spent years means less, as experience and hence as poetic statement, than the subjective sense of his position. He expresses that sense paradoxically: though passing through time steadily (lines 2–3), he remains only a short span away from the remembered start of his *innamoramento* (lines 3–4). For us readers, the regular flashbacks in the sequence have kept the beginning fresh in mind, and our subjective experience of the series' process to this point agrees with the paradox. The second stanza continues the rhetoric of paradox—the best-known of Petrarchan metaphors, and the most widely imitated emotional analogy of the Renaissance—and looks ahead to the gathering conclusion. This poem is one of the first in the *Canzo-*

niere to invoke the telos of Laura's death overtly; in later poems, anticipation of death, both hers and the speaker's, pulls insistently on his every thought, and makes the closure of the sequence seem profoundly urgent and immediate.

In the third stanza, the speaker pauses among the past and future tenses whose ends he has measured, inhabiting the present moment with both a temporal (*or*) and a spatial (*qui*) deictic. In the poem's spirit of paradox, he wishes he were "elsewhere," anywhere: suspended midway between a fresh past and an impending future, he wants progress. He can measure his elapsed experience absolutely—sixteen years exactly—but he measures nothing of development or change. The final tercet states this problem convincingly, in the slightly hyperbolic language of subjective experience (*per mille rivolte*) rather than of objectivity or exactitude.

Process without progress, time's relentless passing without perceptible advancement in the fortunes or attitudes of the lover: this is the basic emotional fact of Sonnet 118. If the surrounding sequence does not enforce the impression of passing time, one loses experiential sympathy with the speaker, and with that everything. The affect of the piece depends on the deictic paradoxes and hyperboles, as well as on the continual deictic patterns of the 117 preceding poems, nearly a third of the whole work. In this poem, the self-dating adds an objective counter to the speaker's subjective view of time's march, setting up the initial paradox and moving everything else toward the poem's end. But if we had to rely on the date alone for a sense of this lyric's place in process, we would do without most of its practical force.

Here is Sonnet 205, another lament over process without progress:

> Dolci ire, dolci sdegni et dolci paci,
> dolce mal, dolce affanno et dolce peso,
> dolce parlare, et dolcemente inteso,
> or di dolce òra, or pien di dolci faci:
>
> alma, non ti lagnar, ma soffra et taci,
> et tempra il dolce amaro, che n'à offeso,
> col dolce honor che d'amar quella ài preso
> a cui io dissi: Tu sola mi piaci.
>
> Forse anchor fia chi sospirando dica,
> tinto di dolce invidia: Assai sostenne
> per bellissimo amor quest'al suo tempo.
>
> Altri: O Fortuna agli occhi miei nemica,
> perché non la vid'io? perché non venne
> ella piú tardi, over io piú per tempo?

(Sweet angers, sweet disdains and sweet returns to peace, sweet harm, sweet suffering and sweet weight of it, sweet speech and sweetly understood, now a soothing breeze, now full of sweet flame!

Soul, do not complain, but be patient and still, and temper the sweet bitterness that has harmed us with the sweet honor that you have in loving her to whom I said: "You alone please me."

Perhaps once someone will say, sighing, colored with sweet envy: "This man endured much in his time for a most noble love."

Another: "O Fortune the enemy of my eyes! Why did I not see her? Why did she not come later or else I earlier?")

The anaphoric phrases in the first stanza enact a verbless counterfeit of temporal movement: the fact becomes explicit in line 4, where Petrarch introduces the deictic pattern *or . . . or* ("now . . . now"), which here and everywhere carries the narrative force of the anaphoric *then . . . then*, only with a greater urgency and immediacy. With the second stanza, the lover hushes his own protests against his want of progress. Imprisoned in advancing time, his consolation is this: someone will say *anchor* ("yet," or "still," or "once") that this man suffered greatly for Laura *al suo tempo* ("in his time"), that perhaps his example of enslavement to process will be celebrated and envied by another lover whose point in time he likes to imagine as loose, indefinite, free. The contrast between the vagueness of *anchor* and his own fixity in process—dramatized in the deictic phrase *al suo tempo*—is a momentary stroke of the lover's fancy that holds off despair. The final tercet restates the consoling thought in fresh terms, imagining another future student of Petrarch who will explicitly wish to trade his spot in time for contemporaneity with Laura and the chance to be enslaved (the phrase for "early," *per tempo*, reverberates here) in Petrarch's way. This sort of reflection on his reputation among future, ostensibly free lovers necessarily primes the speaker to endure further the pains of process. It is, again, only if we share the speaker's sense of subjection to a boundless string of *now*s that we can absorb the force of the ironic consolation, can understand what is being overcome in his imaginative resolution to go on.

All that I have described so far pertains to the establishment of a fictional poetics for the Western vernacular sequence. No series and no lyric, however, is unrelievedly fictional in its generic orientation. In many poems of the *Canzoniere*, perhaps where sound dominates sense, in the intricately repetitious sestinas, or where verses by earlier poets are explicitly patched together to make a new utterance, the ritual dimension of lyric discourse finds its outlet. Here I would like to draw some attention to one of the most intriguing constituents of the series, the well-defined calendrical order that runs alongside the fictional process. The principal scholar of numerology in the *Canzoniere*, Thomas P. Roche, Jr., discerns "a calendrical framework that places the *Canzoniere* unequivocally in the context of fourteenth-century Christian morality. . . . The hypothesis is quite simple: if we number each poem with a day of the year, beginning with the sixth of April, we will find that when we reach 264 we have also reached the twenty-fifth of December, Christmas Day. In short, I am suggesting that the division of the *Canzoniere* is based on two of the three most important events in the Christian calendar. Part I, dealing with the inception and growth of his love, begins with the death of Christ; Part II, dealing with the death of his love, begins with the birth of Christ."[55] While there is nothing unequivocal about such a framework—in fact it is one standpoint among many—it is still highly important to the understanding of Petrarch's fiction. If the date of Petrarch's infatuation, April 6, was also associated with the crucifixion, and if the end of the sequence can be allied as well with a prominent event on the Christian calendar, the limits around the fictional process gain a cultural as well as a personal relevance, and seem to enclose another integral cycle of significance. In one sense, we might say that Petrarch arranges his sequence so that the beginning and end of his *innamoramento* coincide with the boundaries of sacred time. Religious men and women of all sects are practiced in the piling-on of important dates from earthly and cosmic history to reinforce one another and to support the integrity of humankind's arbitrarily defined periods: as Eliade observes, often "the New Year coincides with the first day of Creation."[56] Petrarch's appropriation of integrity from sacred time merely complements or fulfills the experience of process communicated by deictics, and underlines the professions of faith and repentance in the proem and later pieces. And the Christian calendar, when perceived here, gains back what every sacred history loses over time, its charge of immediacy and passion; its alignment with the lover's strenuous life indicates how much of the emotional experience of scripture we forget as it stales for us, how little we feel of its durational unity. From a generic perspective, something like this has to happen in response to the subordination of the ritual mode by Petrarch's fictional poetics. The ritual conditions that cling to ordinary short poems—including the idea that the lyric might be not only a completed record but the text of an event in our own lives, that in realizing the first-person poem we simultaneously do something collective and momentous—are here elaborated into a large-scale structure. Like other numerological structures from the English sonnet boom of the 1590s to Pound's *Cantos*, the calendar here emerges from the displacement of the ritual phenomenon in single poems, junctures, and clusters.[57] For the bracketed ritual mode, it amounts to a plot of its own.

Petrarch's immediate successors sometimes call on the retrospective construction to instill their collections with a sense of history, dynamism,

and change. As a more or less random example, here are Sonnets 30 and
72 from the sixteenth-century poet Luigi Tansillo's *canzoniere*:

> Se quelle voci, che m'uscîr del petto,
>   mentr'io di voi mi dolsi, e quelle carte
>   ch'io vergai d' ira, e son tra molti sparte,
>   riaver potessi indietro, or che soggetto
> cangiar convien (poi che ragione ha stretto
>   quel nodo in tutto, ch'ira sciolse in parte),
>   preda d'oblio ciò che disdegno ed arte
>   han scritto, io farei, donna, e ciò che han detto.
> Non perché macchia al vostro onor né danno
>   fess' io già mai con lingua o con inchiostro,
>   ma acciò che quei che dopo noi verranno
> (s'avvien che tanto viva il nome nostro),
>   sappian com'io v'amai piú d'anno in anno,
>   e nacqui, e vissi sempre, e morrò vostro.

(Those sounds that escaped from my breast while I ached for you, and those
letters I scribbled from anger that are now scattered among many: I would
have these back again. And now my subject must change, for reason has
closed the knot entirely, that anger loosened in part. Whatever disdain and
art have written, lady, and whatever they have told, I would make oblivion's
prey. Not that I ever contrived with tongue or ink to harm you, or to blot
your honor; but in order that those who will come after us—if it should
happen that our name lives so long—may know how I loved you more year
by year, and how living and dying I was yours.)

> S'Amor mi fu di libertade avaro,
>   ecco che Sdegno or m'è cortese e largo,
>   già spezzo di mia man, non pur allargo,
>   quei nodi che sí stretto mi legaro.
> Con gli occhi, ond'arsi et tanto umor versaro,
>   Or su' l mio foco acqua di Lete spargo.
>   Piú veggon questi due, che cento d'Argo,
>   poiché la benda del desio squarciaro.
> Il tiranno de l'alma, abbandonato
>   da' seguaci pensier, cede lo scettro,
>   e la Ragion rientra nel suo regno.
> Ond'io, lodando il mio felice stato,
>   con altra voce omai, con altro plettro
>   quanto dissi d'Amor, dirò di Sdegno.

(If love was greedy of my liberty, look how disdain is kind and liberal to me
now. Already I break in my hand, hardly widening them, the knots that

bound me in their pinch. With the eyes that poured out so much water, I spill the waters of Lethe on my fire. And these two eyes see more than the hundred of Argus, since desire's blindfold was torn off. The tyrant of my soul, abandoned by slave-thoughts, hands over the scepter, and reason reigns again. And with another voice, another poetry from now on, and praising my happy state, I will speak of disdain as much as I spoke of love.)[58]

As managements of deixis for fictional purposes, these sonnets move without comment in the path of Petrarch's innovation. What is notable, I think, is simply that the success of the retrospective topos has encouraged Tansillo here and elsewhere to set his poem on an edge between two states of mind, and to have the later ones emphatically renege on the earlier ones. One hardly doubts that a later poem will take back the harsh words of Sonnet 72, and contrast a fresh *innamoramento* of the present with the "disdain" of the past. These mechanical swings of mood do not create a fiction so much as they participate in, and allude to, a phenomenal condition already established for the lyric sequence in the *Canzoniere*; they reflect Tansillo's practical admission that a lyric version of fictional process has been created and passed on by Petrarch, and his very Petrarchan impulse to seize on liminal instants as occasions for song.

In the main, the writers of lyric sequences in the Renaissance and after are able to rely on the reader's intuition that a chain of poems gathers up a fictional process recording days, months, years. In many collections, the poet takes the shortcut of simply referring to an emotional fact—the sense of imprisonment in a charged and bounded temporality, a psychic fatigue—that the sequence at hand has not necessarily communicated in any fictional way, that is merely inherited through the form. Appeals to such a borrowed emotion rise out of early modern sequences all the time, as in Juan Boscán's canzoniere (1543):

> Yo voy siguiendo mis processos largos,
> y stoy incierto del estado mío.
>   Llévame'l desvarío
> del pensamiento a differentes partes,
> y, a mi pesar, tras todas ellas guío.
> Son por doquiera muchos los embargos.

(I go pursuing my long processes, uncertain of my state. The madness of thinking carries me to different parts, and to my sorrow, I drive among them all. Everywhere there are many impediments),[59]

Bernardino Rota's *Rime* (1572):

> Gran tempo hauer fera seguìto alpestra,
> Che de la stratio altrui si pregi, & goda;
> Hauerla poi con santa, & dolce froda

Hauuta in man per sorte amica & destra;
Piangerla al fin de la magion terrestra
Con mio dolor fuggita, & con sua loda;
Estato il viver mio.

(For a long time to have followed a wild mountain-woman, who in the harms of others praises and enjoys herself; then to have had her in hand with a holy and sweet fraud, by a friendly, clever fate; at last to weep her, fled from the earthly mansion with my pains and her praises: such has been my life),[60]

Shakespeare's Sonnet 115 (written 1590s, published 1609):

Those lines that I before have writ do lie,
Ev'n those that said I could not love you dearer.
Yet then my judgement knew no reason why
My most full flame should afterwards burn clearer.
But reck'ning time, whose millioned accidents
Creep in 'twixt vows, and change decrees of kings,
Tan sacred beauty, blunt the sharp'st intents,
Divert strong minds to th' course of alt'ring things—
Alas, why, fearing of time's tyranny,
Might I not then say, now I love you best,
When I was certain o'er incertainty,
Crowning the present, doubting of the rest?
   Love is a babe; then might I not say so,
   To give full growth to that which still doth grow,

and Mary Wroth's *Pamphilia to Amphilanthus* (1621):

How many nights have I with paine indur'd
   Which as soe many ages I esteem'd
   Since my misfortune? yett noe whitt redeem'd
   Butt rather faster tide, to griefe assur'd?

How many howrs have my sad thoughts indur'd
   Of killing paines? yett is itt nott esteem'd
   By cruell love, who might have thes redeem'd,
   And all thes yeers of howres to joy assur'd.

O doting Time, canst thou for shame lett slide
   Soe many minutes while ills doe beguile,
   Thy age, and worth, and faulshoods thus defile
   Thy ancient good, wher now butt crosses 'bide.[61]

As the next chapters will show, the received process of the post-Petrarchan sequence makes a stable base for poets who elect to innovate against the form. Nearly every instance of the fictional sequence mentioned or implicated after this, from Spenser to Yeats, assumes the currency of such a process and uses it to define that work's identity against the originary *rime sparse*. Even for a poet who was young in the 1920s, traces of Petrarch's phenomenology linger in a major love sequence:

> Te recuerdo como eras en el último otoño.
> Eras la boina gris y el corazón en calma.
> En tus ojos peleaban las llamas del crepúsculo.
> Y las hojas caían en el agua de tu alma.
>
> Apegada a mis brazos como una enredadera,
> las hojas recogían tu voz lenta y en calma.
> Hoguera de estupor en que mi sed ardía.
> Dulce jacinto azul torcido sobre mi alma.
>
> Siento viajar tus ojos y es distante el otoño.
>
> (I remember you as you were in the last autumn.
> You were the grey beret and the still heart.
> In your eyes the flames of the twilight fought on.
> And the leaves fell in the water of your soul.
>
> Clasping my arms like a climbing plant
> the leaves garnered your voice, that was slow and at peace.
> Bonfire of awe in which my thirst was burning.
> Sweet blue hyacinth twisted over my soul.
>
> I feel your eyes travelling, and the autumn is far off.)[62]

That sequence, Neruda's *Veinte poemas de amor y una canción desesperada* (1924), concludes with a "song of desperation" that assumes process through the preceding twenty poems, and mourns the mix of energy and brevity that sets this fiction apart in quality from the vast, eventless Petrarchan story:

> Mi deseo de ti fue el más terrible y corto,
> el más revuelto y ebrio, el más tirante y ávido.
>
> (How terrible and brief was my desire of you!
> How difficult and drunken, how tensed and avid.)
>
> ("La canción desesperada," 31–32)

Here, too, is a post-Petrarchism struggling both to honor and to get free of the origins of the fictional sequence, in a continuing revision of the complex—the "unstable furor" of private emotion, the pathos of cultural crisis, the interest in fictional innovation—that moved Petrarch himself.[63]

Though it must be rendered less acutely and exactly in later works, Petrarch's conceit of process, the founding phenomenon of the vernacular lyric series, will be supposed to exist, even by allusion or association, in nearly all of the fictional sequences treated in the following chapters. One of the constituting paradoxes of lyric discourse in general, as I see it, is that such an exemplary lyric fiction can be compounded of elements (such as deictic formulas and calendars) that by themselves seem to have everything to do with rituality. But in its role as the founding text of the discursive mode I call nominative, Petrarch's *Canzoniere* introduces a further, enveloping paradox, namely that despite its set of thoroughly constructivist conventions—its self-consciously and programmatically modern response to the competing claims of past, present, and future that the poet as artificer continually negotiates—this sequence could have come to be naturalized into an undifferentiated, idealized, unthreatened unity of style and attitude: into the parody of itself, perhaps, that the original humanist poets would hardly have recognized themselves, but that many readers have (tacitly and oversimply) believed the nominative mode to represent.[64] My brief allusions to Tansillo and some of the other early modern poets, if followed back to their sources, might be taken to imply that such a reduced understanding of nominativity is not merely a modern blind spot, that the naturalization of Petrarchism began early in the sixteenth and continued long into the twentieth century. But my treatment of the *Canzoniere* itself in this chapter, and my foregrounding of certain highly aware post-Petrarchans of the sixteenth and twentieth centuries such as Rota, Shakespeare, and Neruda, are meant to provoke the observation that the building of the nominative mode is, in close-up, an artifactual event, that the constructivism of (say) Shakespeare's sonnets might be seen to originate as much in a certain way of reading the *Canzoniere* as in anything else. For all its demonstrated influence, then, and for all readings, counter-readings, and (perhaps) misreadings, Petrarch's fiction is an exemplary event in lyric poetics: it is the original aesthetic and ideological fusion that makes a viable form; it is the premise with and against which succeeding poets of nearly all eras and inclinations—amatory and devotional, European and American, nominative and artifactual—develop other versions of lyric fiction for their times and places. In chapter 2, I treat a major English sequence not only temporally but characterologically determined in its search for a working order.

Chapter 2

CONSTRUCTING CHARACTER: SIDNEY'S
ASTROPHIL AND STELLA AS NOMINATIVE FICTION

IN THE WEST, every literary genre, subgenre, or form with a claim to importance and capacity tends to be a vessel for the construction we call character. As the plot element of a work offers its readers the appeal of teleology and order, the characterological element has the appeal of identity, and offers a store of figures, however schematic in constitution, that we are tempted to judge by personal, cultural, and ideological measures. Even when we consider characterization analytically, however, our terms are often excessively rigid or imprecise. In this chapter, I briefly treat the constitution of literary character, in a sketch that accommodates the several dimensions—personal and structural, synchronic and diachronic— that occasionally contravene the loose or intractable terms of critics. This theoretical sketch makes no claim of describing fictional characterization in general, of course, but goes far enough to explain the workings of nominative fictions within the generic history of the lyric sequence. Although a stripped-down, conservative characterological event, the nominative mode demands an exposition in terms cognate with other types of fiction. The lyric sequence ought to be an especially attractive site for assembling character and elucidating its poetics, I believe, largely because it has the capacity to give us something like "pure" character—in other words, because its utterances can be coextensive with the very units of character itself. Certainly it belongs to the nominative moment to make them seem so: in a thoroughgoing self-making sequence such as the *Canzoniere, Les Regrets* (1558) by Du Bellay, or Shakespeare's *Sonnets*, nearly everything in the poems goes into the characterological fiction and is conditioned there. Elements of a ritual poetics, when they break in, may stand for self-denial, or self-dissolution, or otherwise mark phases in the personal history at hand, but they are carefully disposed to do practically nothing more. As an ideology of genre that holds a strong position in its literary cultures from the earliest post-Petrarchans to at least the end of the Renaissance, the nominative mode, when it rules, rules tyrannically— though subtle readers can and do locate traces of the elisions, violations, and confusions that go into its program.[1]

When a theoretical base is fairly established, I will go on to explore Philip Sidney's *Astrophil and Stella*, the lyric sequence that readers have often singled out—or deplored—for its successes in characterization, and that in fact maintains Astrophil's person, contingent on a Petrarchan temporal process, as its most conspicuous principle of order. I think we have done poorly by the fiction of Sidney's sequence. Its fictionality is evident in interpretations all the time—not least, in the assumptions of recent historicist critics—but the terms that would investigate that phenomenon have gone more or less undeveloped.[2] Somewhere between the standard-issue personae of some late sixteenth-century sequences and the uniqueness of the *Sonnets* as a subjective record, Sidney's characterological achievement stands as the model of its moment. Alongside my reading of *Astrophil and Stella*, I will examine the tensions that beset lyric sequences when they undertake to represent character thoroughly and vividly, as well as the daring, sometimes impressive solutions that Sidney—also, of course, a writer of prose narrative and a major theorist of fiction—extemporizes for his compelling Astrophil and his definitive *Astrophil and Stella*.

Since characterization is a notoriously elusive matter for critics, I should suggest early on the set of terms that rules my thinking. There are, it seems to me, three more or less distinct elements in any realized character: function, attributes, and development. Function implies the part of the plot a character holds up, or in plotless works, the terms and proportion of his or her impact on the emotional or histrionic process of the whole.[3] The norms of function wear a mantle of timelessness, but they are deeply implicated in not only the literary, but the ethical, political, and economic life of a culture. Protagonist, villain, chorus, and clown are some fairly stable functions in Western literature, and there are many more available depending on where and when. A character's attributes are those qualities, often a seemingly original complex, that he or she carries toward the fulfillment of function. The play of function and attributes probably accounts for much of literary characters' lastingness and force, and explains their failure to come off now and then. For instance, it answers the persistent question why Shakespeare's John Falstaff, an artfully constructed clown in *Henry IV*, cannot achieve anything like his original impression when he lives again as the protagonist in *The Merry Wives of Windsor*. His delicate composition of attributes—say, to single out one of these, his extravagant lying in the manner of the miles gloriosus or braggart soldier of Roman comedy—exactly fits his function in the *Henry* plays, where he soars alone against the current of verifiable history. He is a clown framed for that particular setting. It is no wonder that the same complex of attributes falls short in the nonhistorical comedy of the *Wives*, where lying is not in the formula for comic friction, where Falstaff as hero cannot defy the play's drift but must himself steer it.

Function and attributes lay what we might call the synchronic base of a character. Although they are serially realized like everything else in literature—so that, in most works, there are seemingly random and uncoordinated instants when function and attributes are not fully clear for one character or another, and one has to grope through an exceptionally lifelike uncertainty—they remain fairly stable once set.[4] The construction must hold: we have to be able to recognize Pyrocles, Emma Bovary, or Bigger Thomas as the same character from one chapter to another. Development, as the complement to function and attributes, offers a field for diachronic play on their foundation, for a continually fresh sounding and emphasis occasioned by the plot's events. Of the three constituents of character, it is the nearest to plot: in works with one prominent character (as in "The Double" by Dostoevsky), or with a centripetal cast of dramatis personae (as in *Othello*), development of character may, in design and end, be the plot itself. In any case, the terminus of a character's development is a last balancing of attributes and function traceable to his or her accumulated experience in the fiction, a resolution at the level not only of plot, but of person as well.[5]

Advancing these terms for the dissection of character, I suggest that the synchronic elements of characterization—our perception of the characters' functions and attributes—do not greatly depend on the logic of the plot's unfolding. As rhetorical constructions, characters can be retrieved from a disordered plot, or from no plot at all. In *Romeo and Juliet* or *Henry IV*, for instance, if Shakespeare's arrangement of scenes were transposed by an especially crazy Nahum Tate or Colley Cibber, the spectator's understanding of the main figures would not suffer beyond what a few moments of reflection could repair: we would charge these poetasters with ruining the plot, not the characters. The most fundamental set of facts to be grasped about any character, function and attributes, would emerge relatively (maybe surprisingly) unscathed from such tinkering. We would perceive Romeo and Juliet in their function as protagonists, and Falstaff's rich array of attributes, in any sequence.

Anyone who has ever entered a movie theater just too late to catch the thread of a film's story knows something of character's independence from plot: at such times we are tantalized by a frustrating sense of incompletion, of grasping one line of advancement (character) but not what fulfills it (plot). Consider one of the most successful experimental films of the postwar years, Alain Resnais and Alain Robbe-Grillet's *Last Year at Marienbad*. Here the two authors strive to banish plot from the movie, at least in the ordinary sense: scenes float past one another in chronological disengagement, exposition is slighted, and the camera's objects of attention remain seemingly indiscriminate throughout. Notice that, in Robbe-Grillet's preface to the film's script, his explanation of the deliberate violation of the plot assumes that the attributes of characters come through inviolate:

> [The] movie audience seemed to us already well prepared for this kind of story by its acceptance of such devices as the flashback and the objectivized hypothesis. It will be said that the spectator risks getting lost if he is not occasionally given the "explanations" that permit him to locate each scene in its chronological place and at its level of objective reality. But we have decided to trust the spectator, to allow him, from start to finish, to come to terms with pure subjectivities. Two attitudes are then possible: either the spectator will try to reconstitute some "Cartesian" schema—the most linear, the most rational he can devise—and this spectator will certainly find the film difficult, if not incomprehensible; or else the spectator will let himself be carried along by the extraordinary images in front of him, by the actors' voices, by the sound track, by the music, by the rhythm of the cutting, *by the passion of the characters* . . . and to this spectator the film will seem the "easiest" he has ever seen: a film addressed exclusively to his sensibility, to his faculties of sight, hearing, feeling. The story told will seem the most realistic, the truest, the one that best corresponds to his daily emotional life, as soon as he agrees to abandon ready-made ideas, psychological analysis, more or less clumsy systems of interpretation which machine-made fiction or films grind out *ad nauseam*, and which are the worst kinds of abstractions.[6]

Compare this description from the shooting script, where Robbe-Grillet makes clear how much of his characters' functions survive in the "subjective" film: "The series of views of the hotel ends with a stationary shot possessing all the same characteristics, carried to their extreme. A slow scene. The image includes, at the far left, a blurred close-up of a man's head, cut by the edge of the image and not facing the camera. It is X, *the hero of the film*."[7] The daring experiment of *Marienbad*, then, challenges its audience's expectations at one stratum only, and leaves other objectivities—for what could be more objective, more conventional, than the notion that a narrative must have a "hero"?—quite unadjusted. Whatever else the experiment accomplishes, it does not prevent the summing-up of each character by the conclusion of the film.

For a literary demonstration of character's freedom from plot, one only has to reimagine the folktale as anatomized by Vladimir Propp. Analyzing a body of Russian folktales from a nineteenth-century collection, Propp discerns a single chain of thirty-one actions that contains the abstract narrative pattern of each tale. The chain's first links are actions that strike an early note of incompleteness or promised danger, as

> I. ONE OF THE MEMBERS OF A FAMILY ABSENTS HIMSELF FROM HOME. "The prince had to go on a distant journey, leaving his wife to the care of strangers" . . . "once, he (a merchant) went away to foreign lands."

II. AN INTERDICTION IS ADDRESSED TO THE HERO. "You dare not look into this closet" . . . "don't pick up the apples" . . . "don't pick up the golden feather" . . . "don't open the closet" . . . "don't kiss your sister."[8]

Later a villain appears, the hero meets a donor, a search ends in success or a battle in victory, and the hero marries and becomes a king:

VIII. THE VILLAIN CAUSES HARM OR INJURY TO A MEMBER OF A FAMILY. This function is exceptionally important, since by means of it the actual movement of the tale is created.

. . . .

XIV. THE HERO ACQUIRES THE USE OF A MAGICAL AGENT.

. . . .

XXX. THE VILLAIN IS PUNISHED. The villain is shot, banished, tied to the tail of a horse, commits suicide, and so forth.

XXXI. THE HERO IS MARRIED AND ASCENDS THE THRONE.

These actions occur in a sequence that cannot be disrupted. As Propp has it, "by no means do all tales give evidence of all functions. But this in no way changes the law of sequence. The absence of certain functions does not change the order of the rest."[9] Naming the links in this chain, Propp gives us not only a blueprint of the tales' construction but a recipe for disintegration, as well: if the actions were rearranged out of their numerical logic and into a less satisfactory one—if the donor appeared before his gift were needed, say, and if the hero left home at the end of the tale— then the plot would splinter, an unavoidable casualty of the new order. Propp suggests an analogy with judicature: "if witnesses distort the sequence of events, their narration is meaningless" on the ground of plot, of story.[10]

What of the characters? Propp sometimes calls the tale's constituent events the "functions of its dramatis personae," sometimes the functions "of the course of action." It is plain that the actions have little to do with function or attributes in characterization in the sense of these terms I use: they are really segments of the plot, "stable, constant elements in a tale, independent of how and by whom they are fulfilled."[11] Concerned only to enumerate pieces of the action that must be held up, Propp concedes that in his view "to speak of the fact that the villain may be a dragon, a witch, an old hag, robbers, merchants, or an evil princess, etc., or that the donor may be a witch, an old woman, a backyard-grandma . . . , a forest-spirit, or a bear, etc., is not worthwhile."[12] Each of the actions adduced by Propp supposes the job of characterization to have been done at another, subordinate level of discourse. Therefore the rearrangement of the actions ends in the moving-around of single segments of the plot, and that falls to pieces; but within each plot-segment are many segments or elements of characterization, which stay joined and intact as they are shifted together to a new place in the tale, and which work to assemble character there as anywhere. To disintegrate characters in Propp's tales would demand finer tools than he gives us, some rhetorical eggbeater that would attack a single action until it had scrambled the construction called "hero"—function, attributes, and all—beyond identification.

Our critical repertory lacks, then, a common language for describing the serial elements of a character's unfolding. The received terms for the sequential constituents of a literary work, when they are not merely linguistic or formal, are oriented toward plot—*episode, scene, chapter*, and the like—after the traditional primacy of plot in post-Aristotelian literary theory. And these terms do well enough for their usual aims. But when the argument turns to characterization, these plot-divisions are plainly ham-fisted, for what they gather up is too large, too unmanageable and inchoate, to get at the factors of characterization. While we hold to them, the devices by which writers populate their fictions invariably slip out of sight.

In view of these difficulties, it seems pragmatic to suggest, after M. M. Bakhtin, that the radical factor in characterization is the utterance.[13] By *utterance* I mean the fundamental integer of literary context available in any work according to the formal gauge of that kind of work: a discrete speech of one or a hundred lines in a novel or play, a paragraph in this essay, a sonnet in a series of sonnets. In some works, such as long stichic poems or formally undemarcated prose, the utterance's exact boundaries may be liable to several interpretations—or largely irrelevant. Generally, however, an utterance is probably complete where its constituent words, lines, or sentences have assembled a context, where sense has accumulated consecutively and is framed by some formal or logical marker. The utterance can therefore be compared (and often in poetry, equated) with the stanza, which carries in its etymology the sense of a "room" or "station" of meaning. The utterance is distinguished from other, less cardinal units of speech and meaning by its frequent infiltration of the larger movements of plot or argument, its appearance of completeness in thought and feeling, and its seeming capacity for transport to a new setting (or to no setting, since it carries its own context) as an epigraph, a dictum, an anthology piece.[14] In fact its completeness is realized only in the continuous process of the work where it appears, because it is a completeness of response, a temporary exhaustion of one pose or stance toward the extant issue. A fresh orientation toward topic and auditor, nothing less, will bring about another utterance, and so goes the work. On this supposal, all utterances are the constituents of a dialogue, even when—as in the Pindaric ode, the sonnet sequence, or the essay—the other voice is fully received into the single speaker's dramatic awareness, and has no independent, perspicuous life. The literary utterance is the product of a submerged dialogue in the mind of the author, of hidden reconnaissances of his or her purpose and positions, the terms of which can be mastered only from attention to the entire work. Adjusting our sights in this way, we perceive that the two features, plot and character, lay up their parts in a concurrent but syncopated relation to each other: events and characters arrive at their realizations in a staggered overlap—several of character's parts falling into place for each one of plot's—until the closure of the play or narrative, which presumably brings the two rhythms into synchronization for the first time and resolves them at once.

The primacy of the utterance in literary characterization is tacitly corroborated in a few passages of Aristotle's *Poetics*, as where he proposes to show the detachment of character from action or plot, and its basis in speech "showing what kinds of things a man chooses or avoids."[15] Aristotle does not explicitly confirm that the single utterance is to the abstraction called "character" as the single act is to the abstraction called "plot," but from every vantage the claim is well-grounded. No one will dispute for long that a figure in literature who does not speak—or who does not develop an alternate semiotics—remains unrealized, uncharacterized, in the elementary sense: not addressing proximate events and persons, he or she makes no decipherable choices. No amount of inarticulate action or of discourse about the figure will fully avail, because these are only incidental checks on the immediate reception of the figure's words and signs. They may set or undermine what speech reveals, but alone they cannot achieve a character.

The indispensability of the utterance in characterization is evident in those modal characters built on the repetition of a single tag in all circumstances: Mrs. Micawber, Bartleby, McGinty.[16] As they force their short, characteristic sentences to serve in every sort of dialogue, and seem to participate only in a single context of their own making, these characters effectively treat mere speeches as integral, all-purpose utterances. In every dimension, these figures are as sparsely realized as anyone in literature can be, but they must cling to their peculiar utterances as long as they wish to remain characters. Readers and writers alike instinctively know what Bakhtin affirms, that "the outwardly actualized utterance is an island rising from the boundless sea of inner speech,"[17] and we insist that inner substance, however thin or unvaried, show itself in language. Moreover, each of the factors of characterization I have laid out—function, development, attributes—depends on available speech for its construction. The former two factors come out in the character's attitudes at large toward events and other characters, while the latter, the attributes, are read minutely in the fabric of every utterance, in every choice and avoidance.

Perhaps to the surprise of some readers, lyric discourse is a rich site for looking at one factor of characterization, the ascertainment of attributes in utterances. It is just as fruitful in this way as narrative or drama. Lyric speakers commonly display no development, true, and they are nearly all protagonists in function. But where we are concerned to see the laws by which attributes are brought out and maintained, they can show us everything. Fernando Ferrara proposes a character-centered anatomy of literary fiction that sees the penetration of character into lyric:

> The field of fiction . . . embraces manifestations of every level (from the most courtly to the cheapest) and of every language (from pictures to gesture, to music, to words); it is evident that such distinguishing elements are considered variables, while the relevant constants must be seen implicitly or explicitly in the character. In fact one could also define fiction as "communication through characters." This must be understood in the widest sense; according to this conception, for example, both *Robinson Crusoe* and Petrarch's *Canzoniere*, both the frescoes of the Scrovegni Chapel and the last sequence of Pheiffer, are communications imparted through characters, and therefore they all belong to the field of fiction. Much of the so-called "lyric" is nothing but poetry through character which must be attributed to the author who proposes his own poetic persona . . . as the protagonist. One must imagine it as being recited not by the author but by that character whom the author proposes as interpreter; no one believes that the "I" in the *Rime* coincides with Francesco Petrarca. In the case of the lyric "I" would tend to have the so-called "inspiration" coincide with the assumption of all those recognizable elements (poses) which constitute the characterization of the "I" which is the protagonist and voice of the lyric.[18]

How are these "poses" or attributes recovered? What are the protocols of our experience with the qualities of characters, and what particular import does the bundle of attributes possess in its cooperation with the other factors of the characterological complex?

On the way to suggesting how characters gather attributes, perhaps I can demonstrate how they do not. Consider a speech that occurs late in *Macbeth*. It is spoken by Malcolm, the rightful king of Scotland, to Macduff:

> I think our country sinks beneath the yoke:
> It weeps, it bleeds, and each new day a gash
> Is added to her wounds. I think withal
> There would be hands uplifted in my right;
> And here from gracious England have I offer
> Of goodly thousands. But, for all this,
> When I shall tread upon the tyrant's head,
> Or wear it on my sword, yet my poor country

Shall have more vices than it had before,
More suffer, and more sundry ways than ever,
By him that shall succeed.

. . . .

It is myself I mean; in whom I know
All the particulars of vice so grafted
That, when they shall be open'd, black Macbeth
Will seem as pure as snow, and the poor state
Esteem him as a lamb, being compar'd
With my confineless harms.

. . . .

    I grant him bloody,
Luxurious, avaricious, false, deceitful,
Sudden, malicious, smacking of every sin
That has a name; but there's no bottom, none,
In my voluptuousness. Your wives, your daughters,
Your matrons and your maids could not fill up
The cestern of my lust, and my desire
All continent impediments would o'erbear
That did oppose my will. . . .

. . . .

    With this, there grows
In my most ill-compos'd affection such
A stanchless avarice that, were I king,
I should cut off the nobles for their lands,
Desire his jewels, and this other's house,
And my more-having would be as a sauce
To make me hunger more, that I should forge
Quarrels unjust against the good and loyal,
Destroying them for wealth.

. . . .

The king-becoming graces,
As justice, verity, temp'rance, stableness,
bounty, perseverance, mercy, lowliness,
Devotion, patience, courage, fortitude,
I have no relish of them, but abound
In the division of each several crime,
Acting it many ways. Nay, had I pow'r, I should
Pour the sweet milk of concord into hell,
Uproar the universal peace, confound
All unity on earth.

. . . .

If such a one be fit to govern, speak:
I am as I have spoken.[19]

Certainly no one who has ever read or heard this speech has believed Malcolm's self-characterization for more than an instant or two: the chief dramatic interest excited by the utterances, I imagine, is the question *why* he should extravagantly denounce himself. When Malcolm reveals that he has deliberately spoken falsely to test Macduff's "truth and honor," we feel no surprise at the fact, only at the motive. The reason we are not taken in, I think, is that in drama as in narrative and lyric, characters are not usually permitted to scrutinize their own functions and attributes, to define themselves finally and overtly. In a word, they do not recognize themselves as constructions, as characters. In most dramatic utterances, characterization happens when the speaker insists on his or her reality as a person, as Macbeth does earlier in the play:

> This supernatural soliciting
> Cannot be ill; cannot be good. If ill,
> Why hath it given me earnest of success,
> Commencing in a truth? I am Thane of Cawdor.
> If good, why do I yield to that suggestion
> Whose horrid image doth unfix my hair
> And make my seated heart knock at my ribs,
> Against the use of nature? Present fears
> Are less than horrible imaginings:
> My thought, whose murther yet is but fantastical,
> Shakes so my single state of man that function
> Is smother'd in surmise, and nothing is
> But what is not.

(1.3.130–42)

Here and in other speeches, the audience is enabled, even required, to complete the circuit that runs to the declarative statements: "Macbeth is superstitious," "Macbeth is irresolute." The speaker declines from direct self-commentary, leaving qualities and states of being implicit and ready for our assembling. I suggest that utterances add to characterization in proportion as they permit readers and auditors to bend them toward a flat statement of quality or value. With no opening that calls for our intervention and completion, a character will not be effectively constructed.

Declarations that "I think," "I feel," "I want," and so forth all hold out the possibility of assembly, the chance for an auditor to go beyond them in postulating a theory of the character's attributes. So does the "I do" or "I will do" sort of utterance, as in Hal's often-remarked soliloquy early in *1 Henry 4* (1.2.195–217). Part of that speech's fascination comes from the adeptness with which a highly self-knowing character avoids direct admission of his shrewdness and steely heart, the attributes that prompt his late "reformation." Hal's resort to a simile for his conduct before we know the grounds of comparison (lines 197–203) belongs to the same bent for softening and indirection, as everywhere he dances around the hard fact of his cunning. The only version of "I am" (line 210) appears needlessly, where "I will be" would serve as well to express the temporary state of fulfilling an unoffered promise; there briefly, at the climax of the soliloquy, Hal fakes a step toward an overt self-evaluation, only to retreat at last. Shakespeare keeps him clear of the stroke that must fulfill his characterization, because it cannot be done by him, because it is ours.[20]

There are exceptions to this seeming rule, certainly, but they carry consequences:

> Plots have I laid, inductions dangerous,
> By drunken prophecies, libels, and dreams,
> To set my brother Clarence and the King
> In deadly hate the one against the other;
> And if King Edward be as true and just
> As I am subtle, false, and treacherous,
> This day should Clarence closely be mew'd up
> About a prophecy, which says that G
> Of Edward's heirs the murtherer shall be.
>
> (1.1.32–40)

Here in Shakespeare's early historical tragedy *Richard III*, the protagonist's self-characterization sounds an initial note of melodrama: other elements will deepen the play's high-pitched sensationalism, but the vital touches of melodrama that sustain it—including the king's "jolly" murder of the "gentle babes" (4.3), and the succession of ghosts toward the conclusion (5.3)—have their start here, as Richard hands over his characterization, analyzed and accomplished, to the audience. As a style that shrinks from the indeterminate, and often collapses the fruitful patches between its abstract patterns and their realization, melodrama is the natural, and, I suppose, inevitable end of this kind of self-interpretation. Perhaps the reason we think it fair to respond vocally to a performance of melodrama—cheering the hero, hissing the villain, and the rest—is that we have been shut out of participation in realizing and completing these characters; we vent our impulse to comment in the only way left.

Here is Shakespeare's Sonnet 121:

> 'Tis better to be vile than vile esteemed,
> When not to be receives reproach of being,
> And the just pleasure lost, which is so deemed,
> Not by our feeling but by others' seeing.
> For why should others' false adulterate eyes
> Give salutation to my sportive blood?

> Or on my frailties why are frailer spies,
> Which in their wills count bad what I think good?
> No, I am that I am, and they that level
> At my abuses reckon up their own;
> I may be straight though they themselves be bevel.
> By their rank thoughts my deeds must not be shown,
>   Unless this general evil they maintain—
>   All men are bad and in their badness reign.

The speaker's impulse is not only lyric, of course, but rhetorical: to justify himself against the opinions of others. But it is hard not to notice how little he says about himself, how strenuously he resists any direct self-characterization. His closest approach, in fact, is the tautology "I am that I am," a virtual invitation for the reader or auditor to construct him from what he tells us indirectly. The phrase contains a glance at Exodus 3:14, where Yahweh charges Moses to lead Israel's children away from Egypt in his name. But that redundant self-announcement—in Hebrew, a writing-out of the materiality of the tetragrammaton—fits a God of sheer presence. It means something else, perhaps even a devastating self-disclosure, from a lyric speaker who exists only in a material chain of words, whose ostensible aims are to enable the assembly of those words into a person-representation and to lead us to a certain ethical conclusion.[21] The verbal energy spent vilifying the unnamed antagonists—he tells us with particular feeling that they are "false," "adulterate," "bevel," and "rank"—is countered and fulfilled only by the cipher of the self-revelation. Against the portraits of the others, who does the speaker's self-portrait weigh? How can we ever know enough about him to share his outrage? The characterological suspense of the sonnet comes, I believe, out of its mixed purposes and clashing imperatives, where the demands of persuasion meet the obliquity of fiction. Its polemical aim and substantial effort at invective call for a positive, ethical proof far stronger than either the compass of this short poem or the limits of self-characterization will allow. Stalling and blocking the poem's embarked purpose, the imperative of indirection hovers destructively over the speaker's effort to transmit the ground and force of his passion.

Compare Sonnet 129 as an alternate characterization of Shakespeare's speaker:

> Th' expense of spirit in a waste of shame
> Is lust in action, and till action lust
> Is perjured, murd'rous, bloody, full of blame,
> Savage, extreme, rude, cruel, not to trust,
> Enjoyed no sooner but despised straight,
> Past reason hunted, and no sooner had,

Past reason hated as a swallowed bait,
On purpose laid to make the taker mad;
[Mad] in pursuit, and in possession so,
Had, having, and in quest to have, extreme,
A bliss in proof, and proved, [a] very woe,
Before, a joy proposed, behind, a dream.
    All this the world well knows, yet none knows well
    To shun the heav'n that leads men to this hell.

Here the speaker makes no rhetorical contrast between "our feeling" and "others' seeing," so there is no chance of a destructive but unavoidable imbalance in the poem's characterizations. Instead, he tacitly includes himself among the members of lustful humanity, and synecdochically— "lust" in line 2 standing for its votaries—calls these by more bad names than Duncan's Malcolm ever gave himself. But maintaining the plurality and synecdoche at once, the speaker achieves a double feat of indirection that forestalls his representing himself as a distinct character: the complex of attributes he names is transferred to him by the reader or auditor, and it will seem to be our work, not his. The speaker confirms his sharing in "th' expense of spirit" when he describes lust's fruits not as static vices, but as the ends of a process that leads from extreme enjoyment to disproportionate scorn, from fervent search to temporary satisfaction and then hatred: we perceive that the speaker has enacted this sequence himself, standing between the "joy" and the rueful "dream." He knows its phases well enough. But when the implied self-references accumulate and the poem edges toward personal narrative, the speaker retreats behind the mask of plurality again ("all this the world well knows"), and pointedly exempts himself, the author of this diatribe, from the saving knowledge that would spell lust's end ("to shun the heav'n that leads men to this hell"). Still, the ferocity of the self-contempt is diluted by the patent clarity that goes into the speaking of the lyric. He could not, one imagines, discern the causes and stages of lust so starkly if he were not different in quality from the rest of the "world" and "men" he describes. The acuteness of his commentary, the sharpness of his unmistakable swerve away from personality in line 13, mark him as an individual who assumes a choral mask. And in that instant of our inference, characterization happens: we assemble a provisional persona who combines the admitted vices of the first twelve lines with a superintending vision and discretion.[22]

Joachim Du Bellay's *Regrets* is an emphatically social fiction. In fact, Du Bellay deliberately reverses much of what is often thought to be Petrarchan: as such poetry usually finds a virtual society among lovers and intimates, Du Bellay's speaker discovers his passions in his oblique angle on public events in Rome. The sequence's characterization is unobtrusive, but Sonnet 39, "J'ayme la liberté, et languis en service," is put in early, perhaps as a statement of program:

> I love liberty, but I am a servant,
>   I don't like servile manners, but must have them,
>   I do not like pretence, but I pretend,
>   I like straightforwardness, but I am learning:
> Property bores me but I work for avarice,
>   I do not care for honours, but must act as if I do,
>   I like to keep my word, my employer says no,
>   I look for decency, and find only vice:
> I look for peace, and find something else,
>   For pleasure, and I do not get it myself,
>   I don't like argument although on the right side:
> I am not fit, and yet I have to travel,
>   I am born for poetry, but my job is to manage,
>   Am I not, Morel, the unluckiest man alive?[23]

The sonnet's aim is not to discredit the social world that envelops the speaker, but actually to blur the boundaries between the two—to find what is psychic in what is social, and vice versa. Contradictions between his public role and his private urges have the status here that Petrarchan poetries usually give to wholly emotional or spiritual conflicts. He is characterized not by the lines' first clauses alone, as he seems to insist, but by the full assertion of each verse. And because person and society overlap, characterization and social criticism are indistinguishable. Instead of deciding that this speaker had better leave Rome or quit his job, most readers will want to see how the personal and the public are engaged and reengaged throughout *The Regrets*, how the setting—with this voice installed in it as an impulse—operates as a dilated character. In Shakespeare's Sonnet 129, we acknowledge the speaker's place in "the world" but finally subtract him from it in order to realize his character; here he and we do the opposite, also to achieve character.

From another nominative sequence, here is Robert Lowell's "Home After Three Months Away":

> Gone now the baby's nurse,
> a lioness who ruled the roost
> and made the Mother cry.
> She used to tie
> gobbets of porkrind in bowknots of gauze—
> three months they hung like soggy toast
> on our eight foot magnolia tree,
> and helped the English sparrows
> weather a Boston winter.

Three months, three months!
Is Richard now himself again?
Dimpled with exaltation,
my daughter holds her levee in the tub.
Our noses rub,
each of us pats a stringy lock of hair—
they tell me nothing's gone.
Though I am forty-one,
not forty now, the time I put away
was child's-play. After thirteen weeks
my child still dabs her cheeks
to start me shaving. When
we dress her in her sky-blue corduroy,
she changes to a boy,
and floats my shaving brush
and washcloth in the flush. . . .
Dearest, I cannot loiter here
in lather like a polar bear.

Recuperating, I neither spin nor toil.
Three stories down below,
a choreman tends our coffin's length of soil,
and seven horizontal tulips blow.
Just twelve months ago,
these flowers were pedigreed
imported Dutchmen; now no one need
distinguish them from weed.
Bushed by the late spring snow,
they cannot meet
another year's snowballing enervation.

I keep no rank nor station.
Cured, I am frizzled, stale and small.[24]

Almost by reflex, one assembles the speaker's character from everything
but what he tells us blatantly about himself: from the qualities in his per-
ceiving and composing his restored life at home, from the passion of his
final asseveration but not its substance. In fact, the last line's claim is
contradicted, point for point, by the preceding verses. "Frizzled": we can
call the "gobbets of porkrind" that, and the open amusement and muffled
scorn of the speaker's description effectively remove him from any likeness to them. "Stale": the wonder of his seeing ("after thirteen weeks /
my child still dabs her cheeks") affirms an abiding freshness that contra-
dicts that label. "Small": the vivid physical contrast between him and the
child, their mutual revel in an assumed analogical relation that makes him

a comparative "polar bear," denies that epithet, too. We cannot finally believe any of the speaker's allegations about himself—implicitly, the poet does not wish us to believe them—but we understand that he believes them, and respond with an unquenchable compassion to the sincerity of his conviction, the loneliness of its detachment from the clear facts of his life. The poem works as characterization, again, by leaving a little space between its direct assertions and what we can observe indirectly about the truth of the character.[25]

As the preceding sketch indicates, the construction of character is often a matter of ironies large and small, for irony is among the events that enable us to differentiate between fiction and other literary phenomena, and in lyric, between fiction and the alternative, ritual orientation that often exercises a claim on our terms of reading. Kenneth Burke sees the natural alliance of character and irony in terms that extend their implications well beyond the argument at hand:

> A human rôle (such as we get in drama) may be summed up in certain slogans, or formulae, or epigrams, or "ideas" that characterize the agent's situation or strategy. The rôle involves properties both intrinsic to the agent and developed with relation to the scene and to other agents. And the "summings-up" ("ideas") similarly possess properties derived both from the agent and from the various factors with which the agent is in relationship. Where the ideas are in action, we have drama; where the agents are in ideation, we have dialectic. . . .
>
> Irony arises when one tries, by the interaction of terms upon one another, to produce a *development* which uses all the terms. Hence, from the standpoint of this total form (this "perspective of perspectives"), none of the participating "sub-perspectives" can be treated as either precisely right or precisely wrong. They are all voices, or personalities, or positions, integrally affecting one another. . . .
>
> [Insofar] as terms are thus encouraged to participate in an orderly parliamentary development, the dialectic of this participation produces (in the observer who considers the whole from the standpoint of the participation of all the terms rather than from the standpoint of any one participant) a "resultant certainty" of a different quality, necessarily ironic, since it requires that all the sub-certainties be considered as neither true nor false, but *contributory* (as were we to think of the resultant certainty or "perspective of perspectives" as a noun, and to think of all the contributory voices as necessary modifiers of that noun).[26]

In the nominative sequence, of course, the "perspective of perspectives" is a proper noun, a person-representation. In constructing characters as part of building such fictional "wholes," writers and readers shun the relativism of the single perspective, of Malcolm's offered self-defamation.

Writers invent and readers await other "voices" to collate the accumulating composition of a character's attributes. But in many specimens of narrative, dramatic, and especially lyric characterization, the contributory voices may be expressed through the medium of the character's own utterances, so that he tells *about* himself and tells *on* himself at the same time—in lyric, that is, the noun modifies itself. Lowell's poem represents this kind of subversive invalidation, as the implicit and explicit layers of the several utterances disjoin and quietly fight.

Complication or contradiction can exist on one level among the attributes, as in the "potent and submissive" Good Bad Boy whom Leslie Fiedler finds in American fiction,[27] or on several levels at once. Slipslop in Fielding's *Joseph Andrews* realizes the second possibility. Her foremost distinguishing mark on the plane of style is her tiresome malapropisms, but these only figure the more deep-seated conflict between her pretensions to chastity and respectability and the evident quality of her mind and passions. Her malapropisms—unhappily italicized as though one might miss them—call out that here is a gathering of contradictions to be assimilated, a character. Style often dispatches this signal. Considered abstractly, two major characterological events of Renaissance fiction, Falstaff and Sancho Panza, are built from identical clashes of attributes: in both cases an abundant corporeal indolence is topped, to every reader's and spectator's astonishment, by a furious verbal energy.

FALSTAFF. 'Sblood, you starveling, you [eel-]skin, you dried neat's tongue, you bull's pizzle, you stock-fish! O for breath to utter what is like thee! you tailor's yard, you sheath, you bowcase, you vile standing tuck—

PRINCE. Well, breathe a while, and then to it again, and when thou hast tir'd thyself in base comparisons, hear me speak but this—

(*1 Henry 4*, 2.4.244–51)

"Let God look after [my use of maxims]," answered Sancho, "for I know more proverbs than a book, and so many of them come all together into my mouth when I speak that they fight one another to get out; and the tongue seizes hold of the first it meets with, even though it mayn't be just to the point. But from now on I'll take care to bring in only those that suit the gravity of my office [as governor]. For in a well-stocked house the supper is soon cooked; and a good bargain doesn't hold up the business; and the man who sounds the alarm is safe; and giving and taking need some sense."[28]

Just as commonly and effectually, a character may come into weight through a contradiction between the attributes taken together and his or her function, the other term in the synchronic makeup. This sort of conflict animates most of Shakespeare's extracategorical characters: the villains who seem more sympathetic than villainous, fools whom we cannot laugh away, savages whose claims to humanity sound strangely convincing. The first sentence of *David Copperfield* ("Whether I shall turn out to be the hero of my own life, or whether that station will be held by anybody else, these pages must show")[29] marks Dickens's strategy to suspend Copperfield's realization of the protagonist's function, and to infuse the identity, when it is finally seen, with a lingering sense of unlikelihood and paradox. Such a design carries the aesthetic risk that events will disentangle the seeming paradox, and the character will suffer a dissolving interest over time. But in its most deliberate realizations, such as the Shakespearean characters and Milton's Satan, the clash of function and attributes finishes by redefining the function to accommodate new reserves of thought and emotion, new patterns of fulfillment.

Having sketched these principles as a working model, I arrive now at what is probably the premier lyric sequence of the sixteenth century in English, Philip Sidney's *Astrophil and Stella*. The special vividness of Astrophil and his mistress has been often remarked, but no one, so far as I know, has thought to use the sequence as a testing-range for a theory of characterization, nor to make the point I am stalking here: that the lyric sequence, including Sidney's work in the form, allows a construction of character as fully realized as in narrative or drama—admits, that is, function, attributes, and development—without a plot external to the character and without attenuating the lyric properties of its single poems. Its internal divisions do not gather up the radical units of character in bunches, as in narrative or drama, but they are those units, those utterances. Then and now, the sequence holds out the possibility of a thoroughgoing invention of character away from the straits of story, linearity, and causal logic. The admission of this possibility by poets as a matter for practical exploration defines lyric fiction's nominative mode. Such a program circumstantiates the humanist idea that lyric discourse occasions a commerce between individual personalities, the reader and the constructed speaker; that lyric is about experiences elaborated from a few strong emotions, and thus its other feasible interests—for instance, examining politics and society on the one side, questioning its own poetics on the other—are properly subordinated to this personal impulse; and that the evoked experiences, hedged by ironies large and small, have to be critically interrogated (in present-day terms, explicated) by a reader in order to gain pertinence, let alone universality. *Astrophil and Stella* is probably the most thoroughly developed characterological sequence of its time, and as such it deserves close attention to the means and implications of its emphasis on lyric person. It will not tell us everything we might learn about nominativity—no single text in the line that runs from the originary *Canzoniere* to the reactionary *In Memoriam* (1850) would—but like the other specimens treated in this book, it invites us to fill its generic context by inference and conjecture.

Sidney's distinguished proem starts to lay the synchronic base of his Astrophil and his Stella.

> Loving in truth, and faine in verse my love to show,
> That the deare She might take some pleasure of my paine:
> Pleasure might cause her reade, reading might make her know,
> Knowledge might pitie winne, and pitie grace obtaine,
>   I sought fit words to paint the blackest face of woe,
> Studying inventions fine, her wits to entertaine:
> Oft turning others' leaves, to see if thence would flow
> Some fresh and fruitfull showers upon my sunne-burn'd braine.
>   But words came halting forth, wanting Invention's stay,
> Invention, Nature's child, fled step-dame Studie's blowes,
> And others' feete still seem'd but strangers in my way.
> Thus great with child to speake, and helplesse in my throwes,
>   Biting my trewand pen, beating my selfe for spite,
>   "Foole," said my Muse to me, "looke in thy heart and write."[30]

Every reader here provisionally assigns the protagonist's function to Astrophil. As with most protagonists, his desires and acts occasion the work—the first lines announce that fact starkly, though elegantly—and there are other dramatis personae against whom Astrophil defines himself (including the object of his love, "deare She," and the as yet undifferentiated lot of "strangers"). Further, there are the often-discussed hexameters, which Sidney borrows from narrative models and which by association may bring a measure of centricity, of protagonism, to their speaker as they add epic consequence to the collection. Astrophil's function of hero already enacts a mild conflict with his attributes in this first sonnet, in his avowals of helplessness and confusion and their sudden confirmation in the speech of the Muse. It is a little startling to see the hero we are assembling called a "Foole," with obvious justice, so summarily and soon. But the sonnet represents a war among the lover's attributes, too. That he claims to be both "great with child to speake" and tongue-tied intimates a struggle of impulses, an ambivalence in his love, that will be enlarged and anatomized in the rest of the sequence. And there is a war, which is ours to mediate, between his evaluation of himself as "halting" and "helplesse," and the smooth volubility of this proem. Like "Home After Three Months Away" and most lyric self-criticisms, it is belied by the generic fact that we tend to identify the intelligence that selects and fulfills the poem's materials with the speaker, and (in a successful poem) to attribute to him a clarity of sight that nearly cancels the force of his recriminations, or mixes with it to inspire a response drawn from regret and admiration together. All these features have been noted before in Sidney's proem and sequence. I propose to inspect them as elements in a sustained achievement of nominativity or pure character, Burke's "noun" situated at the center of the fictional text.[31]

Astrophil's function as protagonist, once constituted, needs only a few strokes—an occasional demonstration of his singularity, and some glances at his relations with the other characters who enter and depart his plotless chain of utterances—to keep it available. The apparent scarcity and modesty of the strokes that maintain function have more to do with the intractability of that feature than with any peculiarity of the lyric sequence or Sidney's version of it: of the two relatively synchronic elements in character, function is by far the more stable. It seems especially secure in the case of protagonists, who seldom step away from centricity to take up another function in the span of the same lyric, dramatic, or narrative fiction. In part, this stability has to do with the relentless human urge to personalize assertions about the world, and with the early alignment of some character with the protagonist's function in the conception of a work: what may have been conceived more or less abstractly as a piece on, say, the psychology and morality of sexual love becomes, upon the choice of Astrophil as hero, the more or less specific story of him and his experiences. Naming a figure as a protagonist is one of the original impulses to the writing of a book, and a cardinal principle of unity, and to shift that function onto another character in medias res is to reconceive the work in motion, tantamount to starting over. When protagonism moves its site, it is likely to move a great number of things with it.

Sidney's singling out of his hero from received attitudes is an insistent note in *Astrophil and Stella*, from the early, offhand glances at Petrarchans and other poets who work in schools,

> Not at first sight, nor with a dribbed shot
> > *Love* gave the wound, which while I breathe will bleed:
> > But knowne worth did in mine of time proceed,
> Till by degrees it had full conquest got.
>
> > > > > > > (2.1–4)

> Let daintie wits crie on the Sisters nine,
> That bravely maskt, their fancies may be told:
> Or *Pindare's* Apes, flaunt they in phrases fine,
> Enam'ling with pied flowers their thoughts of gold:
> > Or else let them in statelier glorie shine,
> Ennobling new found Tropes with problemes old:
> Or with strange similes enrich each line,

> Of herbes or beastes, which *Inde* or *Afrike* hold.
> For me in sooth, no Muse but one I know.
>
> (3.1–9)

> I never dranke of *Aganippe* well,
> Nor ever did in shade of *Tempe* sit:
> And Muses scorne with vulgar braines to dwell,
> Poore Layman I, for sacred rites unfit.
>   Some do I heare of Poets' furie tell,
> But (God wot) wot not what they meane by it:
> And this I sweare by blackest brooke of hell,
> I am no pick-purse of another's wit,
>
> (74.1–8)

to the more generalized dismissals of those "fooles" who cannot share Astrophil's perspective:

> Envious wits what hath bene mine offence,
>   That with such poysonous care my lookes you marke,
>   That to each word, nay sigh of mine you harke,
> As grudging me my sorrowe's eloquence?
> Ah, is it not enough, that I am thence,
>   Thence, so farre thence, that scarcely any sparke
>   Of comfort dare come to this dungeon darke,
> Where rigrows exile lockes up all my sense?
>   But if I by a happy window passe,
> If I but stars upon mine armour beare,
> Sicke, thirsty, glad (though but of empty glasse:)
> Your morall notes straight my hid meaning teare
>   From out my ribs, and puffing prove that I
>   Do *Stella* love. Fooles, who doth it deny?
>
> (104)

From the standpoint of character, it hardly matters if these claims do not always match Sidney's poetic program, as readers now and then aver they do not, nor should anyone rush to figure out the membership of the various parties that draw Astrophil's scorn. We count the energy of self-discrimination more than the precise terms of that effort. His struggles to disentangle himself leave us with the luminous but indistinct memory of a violent individuality.

The starkness of his willful singularity is only improved by the few poems that admit a "fellowship" and identity with like minds:

With how sad steps, ô Moone, thou climb'st the skies,
  How silently, and with how wanne a face,
  What, may it be that even in heav'nly place
That busie archer his sharpe arrowes tries?
Sure, if that long with *Love* acquainted eyes
  Can judge of *Love*, thou feel'st a Lover's case;
  I reade it in thy lookes, thy languisht grace,
To me that feele the like, thy state descries.
  Then ev'n of fellowship, ô Moone, tell me
Is constant *Love* deem'd there but want of wit?

(31.1–10)

Desire, though thou my old companion art,
  And oft so clings to my pure Love, that I
  One from the other scarcely can descrie,
While each doth blow the fier of my hart;
Now from thy fellowship I needs must part.

(72.1–5)

Yet sighs, deere sighs, indeede true friends you are,
  That do not leave your least friend at the wurst,
  But as you with my breast I oft have nurst,
So gratefull now you waite upon my care.

(95.1–4)

Like most of the fifty-odd apostrophes in the sequence, these sonnets draw the lineaments of a psychic world where the lover converses "streight" with the passions that rule his life, not with the human schools and individuals who process and resolve them into ideas; where he struggles with these elemental feelings as with "voices, or personalities, or positions," and makes himself appear both lonelier and more heroic than other lyric speakers because he is a defiant equal to other lovers' masters; and where the dramatis personae are mostly these personified abstractions, rarely other human beings (except, of course, Stella).[32]

Astrophil's reiteration of his function by setting himself apart from other poets, lovers, and "fooles" suggests, however, that another roster of dramatis personae stands behind this sequence and others in the Petrarchan vein, and its induction into *Astrophil and Stella* tells us something about the pressures on the lyric sequence when it attempts to show character. Bakhtin properly reminds us that the monologic utterance such as Sonnet 1, and the unitary chain of utterances such as *Astrophil and Stella*, are after all, already an abstraction, though, to be sure, an abstraction of a "natural" kind. Any monologic utterance, the written monument included, is an inseverable element of verbal communication. Any utterance—the finished, written utterance not excepted—makes response to something and is calculated to be responded to in turn. It is but one link in a continuous chain of speech performances. Each monument carries on the work of its predecessors, polemicizing with them, expecting active, responsive understanding, and anticipating such understanding in return.

. . . .

Dialogue, in the narrow sense of the word, is, of course, only one of the forms—a very important form, to be sure—of verbal interaction. But dialogue can also be understood in a broader sense, meaning not only direct, face-to-face, vocalized verbal communication between persons, but also verbal communication of any type whatsoever. A book, i.e., a *verbal performance in print*, is . . . discussable in actual, real-life dialogue, but aside from that, it is calculated for active perception, involving attentive reading and inner responsiveness, and for organized, *printed* reaction in the various forms devised by the particular sphere of verbal communication in question. . . . Moreover, a verbal performance of this kind also inevitably orients itself with respect to previous performances in the same sphere, both those by the same author and those by other authors. It inevitably takes its point of departure from some particular state of affairs involving a scientific problem or a literary style. Thus the printed verbal performance engages, as it were, in ideological colloquy of large scale: it responds to something, objects to something, affirms something, anticipates possible responses and objections, seeks support, and so on.[33]

Addressing antecedent poets and lovers directly, then, Sidney makes a rhetorical topos of something that obtains, tacitly but irrevocably, in any utterance. In every way imaginable, in fact, *Astrophil and Stella* seems determined to be the most concrete of personal fictions, naming every influence and impulse and letting nothing get away from its drama of selfhood. Its overt dialogism is merely part of Sidney's highly programmatic model of the nominative sequence.

What generates the urgency of Astrophil's apostrophes? It seems to me that when a poet works in a largely monologic, unpeopled lyric form such as the post-Petrarchan sequence, and when he is interested in creating and sustaining character, he faces a special difficulty. Like every character of that function, the protagonist needs dramatis personae, a cast of interlocutors and antagonists, against whom to affirm and define himself. The bare fact of his protagonism will stand out in any event—he must only introduce desire into the poem, and shape its progress after his own search for fulfillment, to become the hero—but for any more exact realization, he demands a challenge. Unthwarted by a contrary figure, the protagonist's extemporaneous means of pursuing an object will not come clear; untested by competing values, his ethical intelligence will likely remain inactive. A complete achievement of the three factors of characterization will wait on the peopling of the work, or on some improvised substitute for a population. Under this kind of pressure, the lyric sequence can bring down its monologic limits and call in a range of contemporaneous voices to converse with the main character. Many modern sequences, especially of the generation after the rise of the artifactual mode, have chosen this measure. Or in reaction to the same pressure, the sequence can be made to reach back diachronically and find interlocutors in its own fictional tradition. Speakers such as Astrophil wrestle with their predecessors to justify the love of the moment against all the foregoing others, to reframe the meaning of devotion until it accommodates only their own, to become the protagonist of the instant.

What does Sonnet 15 stand for, if not an explosion into diachrony against this imperative?

> You that do search for everie purling spring,
>> Which from the ribs of old *Parnassus* flowes,
>> And everie floure, not sweet perhaps, which growes
> Neare therabout, into your Poesie wring;
> You that do Dictionarie's methode bring
>> Into your rimes, running in ratling rowes:
>> You that poore *Petrarch's* long deceased woes,
> With new-borne sighes and denisend wit do sing;
>> You take wrong waies, those far-fet helpes be such,
>> As do bewray a want of inward tuch:
> And sure at length stolne goods do come to light.
>> But if (both for your love and skill) your name
>> You seeke to nurse at fullest breasts of Fame,
> *Stella* behold, and then begin to endite.

Here Astrophil speaks to his antecedents, near and far, through a generic continuum, and draws them from their dispersed historical sites into a temporary simultaneity. He pushes them into the role of failed protagonists who "take wrong waies," like the witless older brothers in a folktale. The lyric exists, it seems, entirely for its sharpening of his function and attributes against these assembled brother-poets. The turning point of the poem arrives when Astrophil switches into the imperative mood, and reverses the consecutiveness of his relations with the other poets: he proposes that they start their works again from infancy, and follow his influence. This time, we assume, they will not be Astrophil's failed rivals but his avatars, and their success will validate his version of protagonism. The sonnet's smooth, almost invisible shifts between temporal stances toward the conscripted dramatis personae—from diachronic to synchronic, and then back in reversed sequence—ought to disclose the shrewdness of the expedients by which this writer of fiction, especially in the early lyrics, populates his long poem. In the compensatory mechanics of this sequence, the diachronic, dialogic stratum of the sonnets rises to prominence as the construction of character demands.

As these emphatic discriminations take Astrophil out of every sort of crowd, and fortify his protagonism by setting him in a superior isolation, Sidney forces a few widely scattered skirmishes between our received, insensible expectations of Astrophil's function and the attributes that fulfill it. Like most clashes of function and attributes, these point to a redefinition of the protagonist's function according to the imperatives of the work at hand, and expand that function's available means of fulfillment. Sonnet 41 is the site of such a skirmish:

> Having this day my horse, my hand, my launce
>> Guided so well, that I obtain'd the prize,
>> Both by the judgement of the English eyes,
> And of some sent from that sweet enemie *Fraunce*;
> Horsemen my skill in horsmanship advaunce;
>> Towne-folkes my strength; a daintier judge applies
>> His praise to sleight, which from good use doth rise;
> Some luckie wits impute it but to chaunce;
>> Others, because of both sides I do take
> My bloud from them, who did excell in this,
> Thinke Nature me a man of armes did make.
> How farre they shoote awrie! the true cause is,
>> *Stella* lookt on, and from her heavenly face
> Sent forth the beames, which made so faire my race.

As a treatment of character, much of this poem's purpose is to place Astrophil in the martial saddle where sixteenth-century literary heroes often sit, to admit (or even boast) his faultless achievement of the hero's tasks, and finally to insist that these successes flow from love and answer only its demands. The implications of the argument touch softly on Astrophil's function, for he is first a lover—and hence susceptible to Stella's invigorating influence—and second, a heroic "man of armes." His "strength" and "skill" are merely the incidental attainments he sweeps up in love's pursuit. The poem amounts to a signal that Astrophil's heroic qualities do not make his protagonism but stand weakly, perhaps irrelevantly, beyond it. They are its consequence, not its cause.

If we miss the admonition, Sonnet 53 makes the point again in stronger terms:

> In Martiall sports I had my cunning tride,
>   And yet to breake more staves did me addresse:
>   While with the people's shouts I must confesse,
> Youth, lucke, and praise, even fild my veines with pride.
> When *Cupid*, having me his slave descride
>   In *Marse's* liverie, prauncing in the presse:
>   "What now sir foole," said he, "I would no lesse,
> Looke here, I say." I look'd, and *Stella* spide,
>   Who hard by made a window send forth light.
> My heart then quak'd, then dazled were mine eyes,
> One hand forgott to rule, th'other to fight.
>   Nor trumpets' sound I heard, nor friendly cries;
>   My Foe came on, and beat the aire for me,
>   Till that her blush taught me my shame to see.

What love gives, it easily takes away. Cupid yanks all the heroic attainments of Sonnet 41 from Astrophil's grasp, and stresses that to serve love and to serve Mars are not necessarily congruent affairs. Moreover, he calls Astrophil "foole," as the Muse does in the first poem when Astrophil wanders from his lonely lover's errand. The epithet in Sonnet 53, and the lyric's climax as Astrophil is paralyzed by confused ardor, drive us to the understanding that his protagonism accrues to the lover in him, not to the jousting hero: he may fulfill his function best when he is unmartial, "dazled," and ashamed. Sonnets 41 and 53 sort out this protagonist's particular charge from the irrelevant ideas projected onto the sequence by other heroes in other settings, to clear the way for what we must see sometimes as his foolishness and impiety. They invite a fresh vision of the lover-hero that admits the psychological and moral impulses behind this and earlier sequences, and warn us that love's results are not always emotionally consistent or morally laudable. If we seek to receive the experience of love in the several dimensions that Sidney renders, we had better adjust our expectations of the lover's role away from what does not matter here, toward the difficult, ambiguous patterns of fulfillment that do.[34]

In the characters of a nominative lyric sequence, the reader's discernment of attributes or qualities differs in means from the corresponding process in narrative or drama, conceding something to genre and structure. It does not, I think, differ in principle. In the other kinds of fiction, the things a character tells us about himself are joined, and perhaps altered or cancelled, by a variety of other reports: what we can infer about him from his choices of gesture and action, what the other dramatis personae and the narrator tell us about him, what we can see and hear objectively of his relations with these other figures. From these first-, second-, and third-person accounts, we construct a schematic program of attributes to ground the person from moment to moment, to set out the field of his development. We have, finally, what appears to be an abundance of helps from several sides to check and adjust that provisional attribution.

But the nominative sequence cannot offer these checks as a programmatic principle of structure and genre. Nearly everything in the sequence that goes toward characterization must issue, directly or not, from the speaker's first-person utterances, and not every lyric can comment on its own direct statements in the manner of Lowell's "Home After Three Months Away." So the sequence seems to hold to an improvised rule of objectivity by accumulating completeness, giving in quantity and variety of moods and attitudes what it cannot give in perspectives, and inviting the construction of character from a train of short, perhaps formally identical integers that exhaust the speaker's stances toward his or her matter. Lacking most recourses to the seemingly objective collation that runs through narrative and drama, the lyric sequence grounds its subjectivities, and makes character verifiable, by some conception, expression, or organization that emerges out of the sheer volume of the poems. The post-Petrarchan sequence, including nearly everything written in the form down to the end of the Renaissance, tends to find its ostensible objectivity in the contradictions that accumulate in the utterances: the records of different moods pile up, modifying one another with subtle or thorough disagreement:

> With what sharpe checkes I in my selfe am shent,
>   When into Reason's audite I do go:
>   And by just counts my selfe a banckrout know
> Of all those goods, which heav'n to me hath lent.

(18.1–4)

> No more, my deare, no more these counsels trie,
>   O give my passions leave to run their race:
>   Let Fortune lay on me her worst disgrace,
> Let folke orecharg'd with braine against me crie,
> Let clouds bedimme my face, breake in mine eye,
>   Let me no steps but of lost labour trace,
>   Let all the earth with scorne recount my case,
> But do not will me from my *Love* to flie,

(64.1–8)

and produce a sketch of person as representative, as mapped and inflected, as the genre will allow. Sonnet 6 glances at the result of this formula—a seemingly comprehensive, spatial survey of the character's mind—while looking away, ingenuously but understandably, from any admission of the method that takes us there:

> Some Lovers speake when they their Muses entertaine,
> Of hopes begot by feare, of wot not what desires:
> Of force of heav'nly beames, infusing hellish paine:
> Of living deaths, deare wounds, faire stormes and freesing fires:
>   Some one his song in *Jove*, and *Jove's* strange tales attires,
> Broadred with buls and swans, powdred with golden raine:
> Another humbler wit to shepheard's pipe retires,
> Yet hiding royal bloud full oft in rurall vaine.
>   To some a sweetest plaint, a sweetest stile affords,
>   While tears powre out his inke, and sighs breathe out his words:
> His paper, pale dispaire, and paine his pen doth move.
>   I can speake what I feele, and feele as much as they,
>   But thinke that all the Map of my state I display,
> When trembling voice brings forth that I do *Stella* love.

Sidney's effective plan for characterization, which shares more with the alternating "hopes" and "hellish paine" of Petrarch than Astrophil admits, is animated by the spirit of *variatio*, by the conviction that fullness of inquiry follows a dialogue of opposites. The lover's voice sounds its own answer, and we find our approach to completeness there.

Further, some writers of sequences, notably Petrarch and Sidney, spin a thread of collation in the temporal process of their works, which I have discussed in the preceding chapter. Each lyric has its moment in the continuum of the lover's life, and the consistency and extent of the process around it seem to confirm its representative accuracy in thought and mood. A sonnet such as Sidney's 72, set against the advance of time, witnesses for past utterances that have discovered the speaker in different moral resolutions:

> Desire, though thou my old companion art,
>   And oft so clings to my pure Love, that I
>   One from the other scarcely can descrie,
> While each doth blow the fier of my hart;
> Now from thy fellowship I needs must part,
>   *Venus* is taught with *Dian's* wings to flie:
>   I must no more in thy sweet passions lie;
> *Vertue's* gold now must head my *Cupid's* dart.
>   Service and Honor, wonder with delight,
> Feare to offend, will worthie to appeare,

Care shining in mine eyes, faith in my sprite,
These things are left me by my only Deare;
   But thou Desire, because thou wouldst have all,
Now banisht art, but yet alas how shall?

The competing resolves, both figured in the last couplet, are shown to be not errant, randomly chosen moral specimens, but parts of two steady, contemporaneous strains of mood. The background of running time creates contexts of mutual verification for the sonnets, a diachronic rounding to complement the synchronic completeness of the successive contradictions and moral shadings.

   Treating the fictional poet's want of corroborative testimony for his characterizations and his ad hoc adjustments to this lack, I have deliberately passed over the fact that, in Sidney's case at least, such corroboration is available in the songs. In general, the eleven songs set themselves at different intervals to the events than those of the sonnets. If most of the sonnets are talk—to Stella, himself, and others—directed to Astrophil's seductive purpose, most of the songs amount to something like action; in any case, they are closer to an unedited record, and farther from Astrophil's revisions, than anything else in the series. One thinks of the narrative Eighth Song, ostensibly spoken not by Astrophil but by an unnamed observer, and the dialogue between lover and lady in the Eleventh Song. For whatever other purpose Sidney introduces him or her, the Eighth Song's speaker collates the strong lines of Astrophil's character from a standpoint on the outskirts of the personae. He or she faithfully translates Astrophil's sense of himself as protagonist—and of Stella as object—into empirical, narrative action:

In a grove most rich of shade,
Where birds wanton musicke made,
May then yong his pide weedes showing,
New perfumed with flowers fresh growing,

Astrophil with *Stella* sweete,
Did for mutuall comfort meete,
Both within themselves oppressed,
But each in the other blessed.

Him greate harmes had taught much care,
Her faire necke a foule yoke bare,
But her sight his cares did banish,
In his sight her yoke did vanish.

Wept they had, alas the while,
But now teares themselves did smile,
While their eyes by love directed,
Enterchangeably reflected.

Sigh they did, but now betwixt
Sighs of woes were glad sighs mixt,
With armes crost, yet testifying
Restlesse rest, and living dying.

(Eighth Song, 1–20)

Besides the third-person perspective, the past tense adds another degree of hardening and recension to Astrophil's discovery of functions.[35] More important, the unnamed narrator testifies to the histrionic evidence of Astrophil's psychic conflicts, the alternating fits of ecstasy and despair, that come from his variously charged impulses toward virtue and passion, reason and idolatry. Astrophil's inner battle has been flattened and shaped to the stresses of the dramatic situation at hand; lacking a chart of the deeps in Astrophil's character such as the first-person lyrics offer, the narrator seeks no cause for Astrophil's oppression and mixed "sighs" but what he or she finds in this single meeting with Stella, and leaves us with the welcome ability to circumstantiate the oblique narrative, to verify it as it verifies our own perspective to this point.

I have said that a conflict of moods and qualities motivates the reader's cognitive struggle and, hence, fixes the character in mind. In this light, even the most unsophisticated version of Petrarchan love poetry—where the protagonist suffers a sweep of oxymoronic sensations, which may figure deeper battles among his attributes—can be fairly seen, in part, as a received formula for lyric characterization. A post-Petrarchan poet who chooses to explore character in his or her collection, such as Louise Labé, Thomas Watson, Sidney, or Barnabe Barnes, adjusts the attributes while keeping them in tension, and a certain substantiality of person follows. In *Astrophil and Stella*, one of the principal conflicts of attributes comes between Astrophil's moral intelligence and his passion for Stella. As Hallett Smith has it, "the most extended and pervasive conflict in *Astrophel and Stella* is the battle between Reason and Passion; aspects of this struggle provide the specific framework for about one-fifth of the sonnets, and these sonnets are disposed throughout the cycle in such a way that they influence most of the others."[36]

A poem such as Sonnet 10 is typical of the building of Astrophil, since it makes the psychic battle explicit and tentatively resolves it:

Reason, in faith thou art well serv'd, that still
Wouldst brabling be with sence and love in me:

> I rather wisht thee clime the Muses' hill,
> Or reach the fruite of Nature's choisest tree,
>   Or seeke heavn's course, or heavn's inside to see:
> Why shouldst thou toyle our thornie soile to till?
> Leave sense, and those which sense's objects be:
> Deale thou with powers of thoughts, leave love to will.
>   But thou wouldst needs fight both with love and sence,
> With sword of wit, giving wounds of dispraise,
> Till downe-right blowes did foyle thy cunning fence:
> For soone as they strake thee with *Stella's* rayes,
>   Reason thou kneel'dst, and offeredst straight to prove
>   By reason good, good reason her to love.

It matters most, as characterization, that the "fight" of impulses gives off a certain energy, that the struggle is vivified with the analogy of desperate and committed warfare: that energy comes to mind at every point in the collection where we assign utterances to their sources in Astrophil's radical person, and enforces an instantaneous sizing-up, a sifting of exquisitely balanced alternatives, that leaves behind its memory. If the force of the struggle is clear, then any attributes will do, and Sidney's election of reason and passion amounts to a minor inflection of Petrarch's tactic. "A Strife is growne between *Vertue* and *Love*," Astrophil will say in Sonnet 52, for the poet must keep the battle always alive to us. Sidney's mastery, here and elsewhere, comes from his keen structural sense of characterization. He seems to understand that the causes of a vivid character must be traced to the means of representation as much as to the matter, to the *how* of Astrophil and not only to the *who*. Again and again in his sequence, he recharges the mechanical features of Petrarch's program for lyric characterization while replacing the Petrarchan lover's particular composition, and achieves an independent protagonist who resembles his model more in plan than in person.

The resolution of Sonnet 10 is worth a look because it shows how Sidney continually calls truces among the attributes without calling off their wars, and so preserves the force of these clashes for the generation of character in later utterances. These truces are usually successful, not cancelling the founding dynamic of the characters, but now and then they falter. Here the glance of Stella's eyes gives the "downe-right blowes" that draw Reason's temporary surrender, but nothing is gained toward the permanent decision of the conflict: the final four lines effect a smooth dramatic and rhetorical conclusion without touching the emotional truth of the sonnet, and without imposing any conditions on the lyrics to come. The lines intrude only to shut down, for a few instants, the energetic and well-matched war of impulses, as a diversion might distract combatants.

The last couplet, and particularly the final, chiasmic line, peel away from the block of the sonnet like a thin, ornamental strip, and lessen the force of the utterance by opening that interstitial space, that chink in the unity of an emotional piece. The movement of the sonnet's characterization goes from more to less inquiry and exactitude. Of course, even a trifling piece like Sonnet 10 may contribute something to the cognitive impact of the character: Reason's fast, unanticipated surrender probably forces us to regroup our expectations, to look out for sudden victories by bents and attributes that seem to have the odds against them. It may fail to settle in the direction it commences, but the sonnet can still give an early memorial body to the figure of Astrophil.[37]

Sonnet 71 is much more successful as characterization, and answers the wants of Sonnet 10 in a noteworthy way.

> Who will in fairest booke of Nature know,
>   How Vertue may best lodg'd in beautie be,
>   Let him but learne of *Love* to reade in thee,
> *Stella*, those faire lines, which true goodnesse show.
> There shall he find all vices' overthrow,
>   Not by rude force, but sweetest soveraigntie
>   Of reason, from whose light those night-birds flie;
> That inward sunne in thine eyes shineth so.
>   And not content to be Perfection's heire
> Thy selfe, doest strive all minds that way to move,
> Who marke in thee what is in thee most faire.
> So while thy beautie drawes the heart to love,
>   As fast thy Vertue bends that love to good:
>   "But ah," Desire still cries, "give me some food."

The simplest way to explain the relative triumph of this poem as characterization is to observe that it suddenly shows us more about Astrophil instead of less, and transmits the experience of advent and progress. The first thirteen lines look through the eyes of a single disposition, Astrophil's continual impulse toward "vertue" and "reason." In fact, the disposition rules him so hard that he tries to gratify it by characterizing Stella—whose ways have drawn varying interpretations to this point, sometimes as "chastnesse" and good faith, sometimes as pride and "ungratefulnesse"—in quite one-dimensional terms. She is, he supposes, an unqualified reserve of virtue who inspires a similarly unrelieved "perfection" in others. No reader will give much weight to Astrophil's statements in the accumulating register of Stella's character; they are too reductive and interested for that. Instead, his hyperbolic praise throws light back on his own character, revealing how strong the sway of desired reason and virtue can be, and how extravagantly Astrophil can distort empirical reality under its rein. In the struggle of virtue and passion that energizes Astrophil's person, Sonnet 71 seems about to add to the force for virtue. The last line, of course, interrupts this one-way operation and renews the alternate bent with sudden vigor. Astrophil's character seems here to come into a special vividness, a sufficiency and closure, because of the revival of his ambivalent constitution. David Kalstone, one of Sidney's best critics, observes the result:

> For the first thirteen lines Sidney's poem appears to be a version of Petrarch's praise of Laura [in *Canzoniere* 248]; then in the last line the poem departs completely from its model and our attention is pivoted to Astrophel, forcing a re-evaluation of all the lines that have come before. Two different views of love are balanced against one another: one, noble and assured; the other, impetuous and unanswerable. It is a curious kind of balancing and testing, thirteen lines against one; but the point of the poem is to show the power of desire to bring a carefully created structure toppling to the ground.[38]

The late and sudden plunge toward Astrophil's center, where the attributes enact an endless, undecidable contest, makes Sonnet 71 one of the fiction's most notable adventures in characterization. The contest rages through Sonnet 72, which I have already quoted, and gets a fresh dramatization in the adjacent Second Song, where the lover's virtue turns practical but still inhibits the free play of passion.

As I have said, the nominative mode can be called such because, among other properties, it sets its speaker in relation to an object. The fixity of the two characters' orientation to each other is so much a part of the amatory lyric series that during the boom of the 1590s, many sequences were titled after their objects instead of their subjects because one naturally implied the other. To generalize briefly about the role of the object in *Astrophil and Stella* and other post-Petrarchan fictions, I would say that here more than anywhere, the imaginative dominion of the nominative sequence, as well as the limits around it, are exposed to view. How is Stella typical as an object? Her attributes are assembled only in the most general way; everything we assimilate about her is given context by Astrophil's representation. Though she is one of the more detailed female objects in the post-Petrarchan line, she achieves an elaboration that in any other type of fiction would be thought minimal (and in fact, she is like those one-tag speakers common in novels and short stories). Still, I think her subordination has as much to do with the generic and cultural limits on lyric fiction at this early modern moment as with the specific points of difference in her relations with Astrophil—gender, class, political status, or anything else. The nominative mode is a testing-ground for humanist convictions and anxieties, and its drama of self-examination and self-unification is often a zero-sum game where amatory and social relations are concerned. Someone has to be taken apart in order for the "noun" to be pulled even provisionally together. And because nominativity is an aesthetic and ideological program for lyric, it can take major inflections, but does not seem to suffer serious challenges, from the emerging class of new poetic voices in sixteenth-century Europe. In fact, one sees the same material disparity in a variety of contexts where the conditions of the fiction differ: say, where the speaker is female and the object male, or where the speaker is a worshipper and the object God. Though it may seem local, or reducible to a few rhetorical poses, or even invisible, the nominative program for lyric fiction is part of the substance of the texts we have, and is therefore implicated everywhere in their language, their semiotics, and their politics.[39] For instance, because such a program of generic purpose can be made to correspond to structures of belief in the relevant societies, there are surely political motives (among many others) for repeating this uneven bargain often in these professedly heartfelt, improvised chains of utterances. It goes without saying that ideologies are almost always insensibly fortified by appearing in the innocent-seeming medium of "sweete poesie."

Finally, what do we observe of Astrophil's development? I have said that a character's development entails a continual reweighing of his attributes after the impressions made by the plot, and a final balancing of qualities that resolves their conflict into a harmony just as the work's dramatic conclusion does for the action. In the post-Petrarchan fictional sequence, there is usually no plot in the narrative sense, but instead a few decisive events dispersed through the work. Between such events, the utterances are mostly paratactic and interchangeable. To chart Astrophil's development, then, one must identify these climactic junctures and examine the psychic redistributions that follow them.

I will now look into the last poems of the sequence, an experimental run of sonnets and songs, for signs of Astrophil's diachronic characterization.[40] Sonnet 69 opens onto the eventful center of the sequence, for here Stella apparently favors the lover's designs and, for the first time, alters his range of possibilities:

> O joy, too high for my low stile to show:
>   O blisse, fit for a nobler state then me:
>   Envie, put out thine eyes, least thou do see
> What Oceans of delight in me do flow.
> My friend, that oft saw through all maskes my wo,
>   Come, come, and let me powre my selfe on thee;
>   Gone is the winter of my miserie,
> My spring appeares, ô see what here doth grow.
>   For *Stella* hath with words where faith doth shine,

Of her high heart giv'n me the monarchie:
I, I, ô I may say, that she is mine.
And though she give but thus conditionly
   This realme of blisse, while vertuous course I take,
   No kings be crown'd but they some covenants make.

The metaphor of winter's turn to spring ("ô see what here doth grow") is particularly notable, as it announces the start of an appreciable movement in Astrophil's development. His compact with Stella, however, suggests trouble to the reader who has watched the laying of Astrophil's character: it demands what most of us cannot foresee, the raising of his "vertuous" and rational side over his elemental side. The explanation for the spectator's skepticism can be given in different terms by different spectators, but from the present point of view, the answer is unmistakable. If characters are framed for their functions and circumstances, and if Astrophil is built on the tension of his attributes, then his proposal amounts to nothing less than the dissolution of his substance and person—his death as a character. A changed emphasis among the attributes is not, of course, impractical; figures in narrative or drama often find their development in one of the qualities that fashion their synchronic base, and seem to grow along one division of their person over the course of a work. But such characters will replace their first, generating conflict with a fresh one: they keep their identity by shifting the site of their constituting battle, by keeping a conflict alive somewhere. At the same time, the fresh mix of attributes must maintain an engagement with the character's function. Again, none of these achievements is technically impossible, though completely successful instances are probably fewer than one expects.

But Astrophil's unusual, explicit program for self-transformation promises nothing so abstract and complicated as this feat. It holds out only a destructive challenge to the protagonist's person as we have learned to perceive it, and threatens to shut down the sequence as a nominative record. As a forecast of the speaker's development, it compares to Malcolm's self-characterization in *Macbeth*: it generates tension and expectation from its alarming frankness, and must, one imagines, form a piece in an ironic design. As it happens, the rest of the sequence tests and rejects Astrophil's resolution, and displays Sidney's efforts to save the character by ingenious, desperate solutions. Astrophil strives to change in accord with his promise to Stella, but he cannot; the sway of desire is too strong in him, as he discovers in sonnets like 71 and 72 (I have treated the former above), and in the Second Song, where he clearly fails Sidney's test of his supposed monistic attachment to virtue. If Astrophil cannot carry out the kind of willful development he wants, how will he "grow" instead?

The problem is trenchantly rendered in the most famous of the songs, the fourth. Here Astrophil meets Stella's determination that he may not retreat into a foreclosed path, but must conform to changed circumstances. With low, trochaic rhythms and a largely monosyllabic diction to whet the starkness of the scene, Sidney places his protagonist at a personal and fictional impasse:

> Onely joy, now here you are,
> Fit to heare and ease my care:
> Let my whispering voyce obtaine,
> Sweete reward for sharpest paine:
> Take me to thee, and thee to me.
> "No, no, no, no, my Deare, let be."
>
> Night hath closd all in her cloke,
> Twinckling starres Love-thoughts provoke:
> Danger hence good care doth keepe,
> Jealousie it selfe doth sleepe:
> Take me to thee, and thee to me.
> "No, no, no, no, my Deare, let be."
>
> Better place no wit can find,
> Cupid's yoke to loose or bind:
> These sweet flowers on fine bed too,
> Us in their best language woo:
> Take me to thee, and thee to me.
> "No, no, no, no, my Deare, let be."

(1–18)

Astrophil's bland proclamation that love's "yoke" may be loosened or straitened by the lovers' drawing together gives a rhetorical nod to possibilities that do not exist in fact, to a way of development he has lately admitted in speculation but cannot achieve. The song's structure represents a series of charismatic and argumentative attempts to recover the legitimacy of Astrophil's passion, and an answering series of rebuffs. It concludes with an affirmation of Stella's fondness for Astrophil and her wish to see him well,

> Wo to me, and do you sweare,
> Me to hate? But I forbeare,
> Cursed be my destines all,
> That brought me so high to fall:

Soone with my death I will please thee.
"No, no, no, no, my Deare, let be,"

(49–54)

but she surrenders none of her resolve.

Sonnet 86 and the Fifth Song show the results of Astrophil's inability to change. Stella reproves him with "lookes," he asks for lenience,

O ease your hand, treate not so hard your slave:
In justice paines come not till faults do call;
Or if I needs (sweet Judge) must torments have,
Use something else to chast'n me withall,
    Then those blest eyes, where all my hopes do dwell,
    No doome should make one's heav'n become his hell,

(86.9–14)

and when that "something else" fails to come, he lets go a flood of angers more acrid and voluminous than anything in the sequence until now:

Yet worse then worst, I say thou art a theefe, a theefe?
Now God forbid. A theefe, and of worst theeves the cheefe:
Theeves steal for need, and steale but goods, which paine recovers
But thou rich in all joyes, doest rob my joyes from me,
Which cannot be restor'd by time nor industrie:
Of foes the spoile is evill, far worse of constant lovers.

Yet gentle English theeves do rob, but will not slay;
Thou English murdring theefe, wilt have harts for thy pray:
The name of murdrer now on thy faire forehead sitteth.

(Fifth Song, 43–51)

As characterization, the Fifth Song is probably the most daring trial in *Astrophil and Stella*. It answers the emotional immobility of the protagonist at this point, where he struggles between a passion he cannot return to, and a growth he cannot realize; it blasts him out of the terrible stasis forced by the shifts of events around him and his own constructional limits. But because it differs so violently in tone and attitude from what has come before—because, in other words, it gruffly introduces an attribute of the speaker that we have scarcely seen yet—the song risks coming into the chain of utterances as an inconsecutive, unverifiable blunder. Sidney surely sees this danger, because he responds by stretching the poem out to considerable length and dividing it, like all the songs, into stanzas. A short lyric with this attitude in a monolithic stanza would have had almost no chance of inhabiting the sequence authentically, but its length shows the Fifth Song's shrewd effort to collate itself, to occupy enough

distinct utterances that the strong emotion will seem to have a context. It
gains entrance, subversively, as a kind of lyric sequence in miniature.

As the final stanza implicitly warns, the song has brought only a diversion from the protagonist's dilemma: he still loves Stella, and he still finds
no satisfactory answer in her. His insistence that she change her mind
covers transparently the facts that the imperative properly applies to
him—both as a moral agent and a literary construction—and that his position in both aspects is growing more desperate:

> You then ungratefull thiefe, you murdring Tyran you,
> You Rebell run away, to Lord and Lady untrue,
> You witch, you Divill, (alas) you still of me beloved,
> You see what I can say; mend yet your froward mind,
> And such skill in my Muse you reconcil'd shall find,
> That all these cruell words your praises shall be proved.

Some twenty poems after the avowed start of his growth, Astrophil as
character and his changed circumstances remain in an unproductive
standoff.

The terms of the standoff are vivified once again in the Eighth Song,
where Stella speaks her mind straight out. She iterates her challenge to
the construction of his character, urging him to live out only one of his
impulses and to throw away the worser part:

> There his hands in their speech, faine
> Would have made tongue's language plaine;
> But her hands his hands repelling,
> Gave repulse all grace excelling.
>
> Then she spake; her speech was such,
> As not eares but hart did tuch:
> While such wise she love denied,
> As yet love she signified.

> (65–72)

Here the series finally confronts the dilemma honestly, and meets its literary consequences. Astrophil as a man—and Sidney as the creator of a
person-representation—cannot dissolve at will everything that has led
him and us to this instant. A man in love, Sidney intimates, cannot change
passion into virtuous friendship by sheer volition, and keep his standing
with the woman, his proximity and intimacy, unchanged. For one thing,
the emotional resistance and consequent pain are too great. But more ad-
missible to the intellect than that, it is his particular combination of loves
that has brought him to seek a physical and emotional closeness, that has
drawn him into his present relation to the woman: to switch suddenly to
a lesser, passionless friendship is to render his circumstances untenable,

to force a distance and perhaps a separation. Mere friendship cannot justify Astrophil and Stella's prominence to each other. Analogously, Sidney
cannot subtract Astrophil's passion for Stella and think to keep his function, and the conditions of his readership's interest, available and intact.
To do so is to tamper with Astrophil's peculiar formula for appeal and to
replace the missing elements with nothing, and in a work as schematic as
the nominative sequence, there is simply nowhere for him to go, no one to
take his role as protagonist. The Eighth Song, then, like the sequence in
large, travels down to the only resolution it can manage under these conditions. It ends with an abrupt, downward spiral into silence and paralysis:

> "Therefore, Deere, this no more move,
> Least, though I leave not thy love,
> Which too deep in me is framed,
> I should blush when thou art named."
>
> Therewithall away she went,
> Leaving him so passion rent,
> With what she had done and spoken,
> That therewith my song is broken.

Astrophil's projected development has ended, and the sequence is effectively over.

   The rest of the sonnets show Sidney's experimental attempts to manip-
ulate events, settings, and conventions to keep Astrophil's radical person
vivid and alive. He makes Astrophil a complaining, self-indulgent shepherd, buying time for the protagonist by casting an unreality over his history with Stella. He absents Stella from the court, making Astrophil's passion and languor seem appropriate at a distance from their object, and
postponing again the press of circumstances against Astrophil's feeling.
He has Stella fall sick, exonerating Astrophil's ardor as fit for her condition. But these strategies of evasion cannot obscure the fact that the sequence goes nowhere after the Eighth Song, that Astrophil's paralysis admits no program for closure. So the last sonnet gathers its energies to
portray, as precisely and movingly as can be done, the sensation of paralysis that holds Astrophil fast:

> When sorrow (using mine owne fier's might)
>   Melts downe his lead into my boyling brest,
>   Through that darke fornace to my hart opprest,
>   There shines a joy from thee my only light;
> But soone as thought of thee breeds my delight,
>   And my yong soule flutters to thee his nest,
>   Most rude dispaire my daily unbidden guest,

Clips streight my wings, streight wraps me in his night,
    And makes me then bow downe my head, and say,
Ah what doth *Phoebus'* gold that wretch availe,
Whom iron doores do keepe from use of day?
So strangely (alas) thy works in me prevaile,
    That in my woes for thee thou art my joy,
    And in my joyes for thee my only annoy.

The resolution of person here involves not a final subordination of attributes and impulses, one to another, but a snapshot of the qualities in their perpetual struggle.[41]

In a sense, the moral and characterological dilemma of *Astrophil and Stella* is exactly that of lyric fiction's nominative mode, which creates a strong character within a certain emotional setting but shows difficulty in moving him or her about for a dynamic resolution. The notions of selfhood that keep such speakers at the epistemological and political centers of these works implicitly require that the fictions must draw whatever conclusions they have out of those framed, isolated selves. But few of the major sixteenth-century specimens are able to manage what one might call endopsychic endings; as it happens, one of the features of the nominative mode at the apex of its authority is that its fictions resist closure except in the most superficial terms.[42]

In England there are several amatory sequences, composed within ten years of *Astrophil and Stella*, that seem to find their way deliberately out of this nominative bind. To spring themselves, they shake up the defining structure of nominativity: they allow one or another instance of lyric's ritual mode to take charge of the matter of endings. The most famous of these works are Spenser's *Amoretti* and *Epithalamion* (1595), where the emotional history of the former text, an orthodox post-Petrarchan fiction, is gathered up and fulfilled in the rituality of the latter, which plots a wedding. The exquisitely patterned speech of the *Epithalamion*—with rhetorical, ceremonial, and numerological orders laid over one another—invites performance, and ritually oriented interpretations that treat the text as a potential script for "sweet consent."

Thomas Watson, in the one-hundred-poem *Hekatompathia* (1582), has his speaker consciously decide to throw off love's yoke, and to substitute for it a hatred of everything amorous that seems to war with "reason" just as his passion did: "[It] may appeare by the tenour of this Passion [that is, poem] that the Authour prepareth him selfe to fall from Loue and all his lawes as will well appeare by the sequell of his other Passions that followe, which are all made upon this Posie, *My Loue is past*."[43] The change of heart is literally signalled by one of the most intriguing appropriations of a ritual event for fictional purposes among the sixteenth-cen-

MY LOVE IS PAST.

ALL such as are but of indifferēt capacitie, and haue
some skill in Arithmetike, by viewing this Sonnet
following compiled by rule and number, into the
forme of a piller, may seeme iudge, howe much art &
studye the Author hath bestowed in the same. Where
in as there are placed many pretty obseruations, so these which I
will set downe, may be marked for the principall, if any man haue
such idle leasure to looke it ouer, as the Authour had, whē he framed
it. First therfore it is to be noted, that the whole piller (except
1 the basis or foote thereof) is by relation of either halfe to the other
Antitheticall or Antisillabicall. Secondly, note this posie (Amare
2 est insanire) runneth twyse through out y Columne, if ye gather but
the first letter of euery whole verse orderly (excepting the two last)
and then in like manner take but the last letter of euery ons of the
said verses, as they stand. Thirdly is to bee obserued, that euery
3 verse, but the two last, doth end with the same letter it beginneth,
and yet throegh out the whole a true rime is perfectly obserued, al-
4 though not after our accustomed manner. Fourthly, that the foote
or the piller is Orchematicall, y is to say, founded by transilition or
ouer skipping of number by rule and order, as from 1 to 3, 5, 7,
*Polygra- & 9: the secret vertue whereof may be learned in *Trithemius, as
Jhiæ tuæ lib. namely by tables of transilition to decypher any thing that is written by secret transposition of letters, bee it neuer so cunningly con-
ueighed. And lastly, this obseruation is not to be neglected, that
5 when all the foresaide particulars are performed, the whole piller is
but iust 18 verses, as will appeare in the page following it, Per
modum expansionis.

Passion 80 from Thomas Watson's *Hekatompathia* (London, 1582).
(By permission of the Houghton Library, Harvard University.)

LXXXI.

MY LOVE IS PAST.

A Pasquine Piller erected in the despite of Loue.

<pre>
            A   1   At
                 2 laſt, though
                 3 late, farewell
                 4 olde ſwell a da: A
         m   5 Mirth oz miſchance ſtrike
        a 6 vp a newe alarm, And m
             7 Cypria   la   nemica
       r 8   miA Retire to Cyprus Ile, a
      e 9 t ceaſe thy waRR, Els muſt thou pzoue how r
   E 10 Reaſon can by charmE Enfozce to flight thy e
  s 11 blindſolde bzaſte & thee. So frames it with mee now, E
  t 12 that I confeſS, The liſe I leaue in Loue deuoyde
 I 12 of reſt, It was a Hell, where none felte moze then I, I
 n 11 Joz anye with lyke miſeries ſozlozn. Since n
 s 10 therefoze now my woes are twered leſS, And s
  a 9 Reaſon bidds mee leaue olde ſwellad, a
  n 8   Jo longer ſhall the wozlde laughe mee
   i 7 to ſcozn; I'le chooſe a path that a
    r 6 ſhall not leade awzie. Reſt i
         5 then with mee from your
          4 blinde Cupids carR r
     c. 3. Each one of
            2 you, that
              1 ſerue,
             3 and would be
           5 ſre E. His dooble thzall e.
          7 that liu's as Loue thinks beſt, whoſe
          9 hande ſtill Tyrant like to hurte is preſſe.
</pre>

Huius Colu
næ Baſis, pro
ſillabarum
mero & lin
rum propo
one eſt Orc
matica.

L

MY LOVE IS PAST.

Expansio Columnæ præcedentis.

A At laſt, though late, farewell olde wellada;   A
m Mirth for miſchaunce ſtrike vp a newe alarm; m
a And Ciprya la nemica mia a
r Retyre to Cyprus Ile and ceaſe thy warr, r
e Els muſt thou proue how Reaſon can by charms e
E Enforce to flight thy blyndfolo bratte and thee. E
s So frames it with me now, that I confeſſ s
t The life I leade in Loue devoyd of reſt t
I It was a hell, where none felt more then I, I
n Nor any with like miſeries forlorn. n
s Since therefore now my woes are wexed leſſ, s
a And Reaſon bids me leaue olde wellada, a
n No longer ſhall the world laugh me to ſcorn: n
i I'le chooſe a path that ſhall not leade awry. i
r Reſt then with me from your blinde Cupids care r
e Each one of you, that ſerue and would be free. e
   * 'tis double thrall that liu's as *Loue* thinks beſt
   Whoſe hand ſtill Tyrant like to hurt is preſt.

τόν τοι Τύραν „
νον εὐσ'εβεῖν „
ὃ ῥάδιον.
Sophoc. in
Aia. flagell.

Passion 82 from Watson's *Hekatompathia*.
(By permission of the Houghton Library, Harvard Library.)

tury sequences. Passion 81 is a concrete chant, in the shape of a pillar, that bitterly lampoons love and banishes it from the series, an interruption in the fiction that actually enables the plot go on; 82 is an acrotelestic to the same purpose, taking up the imprecation of the former lyric—"amare est insanire," to love is to be insane—as its framing text. (Even in this satiric phase, however, the speaker's feelings are not unequivocal: *insanire* implies inspiration almost as easily as madness.) When the speaker is next heard in his fictional mode, in Passion 83, he has adopted the new attitude:

> Therefore all you, whom Loue did ere abuse,
> Come clappe your handes with me, to see him thrall,
> Whose former deedes no reason can excuse,
> For killing those which hurt him not at all:
>   My selfe by him was lately led awrye,
>   Though now at last I force my loue to dye.
>
>   (13–18)

Barnabe Barnes, the author of *Parthenophil and Parthenophe* (1593), is one of the most accomplished writers of fiction among the boom poets of the 1590s, but he also resolves his protagonist's situation with a resort to the ritual mode. Madrigall 17, where the speaker experiences orgasm through a kiss, carries out a breakthrough from one mode to another, like Watson's Passions 80 and 81. Its final verse, "this passion is no fiction,"[44] indicates Parthenophil's determination to get free of the programmatic rounds of suffering that enclose other fictional lovers, and to summon that climax again. After that utterance, *Parthenophil and Parthenophe* often shifts modes to accommodate incantation and charm, becoming something besides a fiction of seduction: the text of the magical spells directed against Parthenophe (as in the riveting Sestina 4), or the soundtrack of her rape (as in the appalling Sestina 5). Taking the countermeasure to Spenser's public-minded resolution, Barnes closes his sequence by relieving his speaker's frustration animally, where the luckless Parthenophe has been silenced and tied up.

Sidney's *Astrophil and Stella*, however, is more firmly committed to the aesthetic and ideological program of nominativity than nearly any contemporary work. With the vividness of its main character, it exaggerates the successes of the self-making disposition elaborated from Petrarch's original example; in its failures, too—its characterological overdetermination, perhaps, or what Joel Fineman calls its "stagey theatricalization of Petrarchan conceits"[45]—the series is a kind of nominative protocol. It could be argued that Stella actually represents the ritual voice in the sequence: her few speeches, whether heard directly or not, often stand out from Astrophil's discourse in their obvious materiality, their echoes and repetitions. "No, no, no, no, my dear, let be" and the paronomasias around "love" in Sonnet 62 and the Eighth Song interrupt the subjectivity of the fiction, at least for most readers; they would for Astrophil too if he were less capable of naturalizing them into his own worldview, as in 63. We hear her words through a crack in the self-making mimesis, as belonging to a dimension that opens onto the reading present; to that extent, we can see her side of things with remarkable sympathy considering the infrequency of her speech. But these episodes have no chance of taking over even a brief range of *Astrophil and Stella*, of contributing a ritual episode like those of Watson or Barnes. Sidney uses them to associate Stella's moral demands on Astrophil with a generic unraveling of the series itself, to conflate two kinds of danger to which Astrophil is liable. And while we are surely to look ironically on Astrophil's refusal to budge or change, there is no sign that the poet feels particularly curious or even-handed about the presentness, transitivity, or concreteness of a ritual poetics. In fact, this sequence and his highly fictionalized *Psalms* together suggest that Sidney as poet was uncomfortable with the ritual mode, and sought to write it out of power even more decisively than post-Petrarchan love poetry usually does—and of course the ritual mode could not then surface to set fresh terms for the ending of the sequence. Accordingly, Sidney's static conclusion, channelled entirely into character, goes somewhat as follows. He stalls Astrophil's contracted growth—and makes that stall evident to us again and again—to show that some wars among impulses, once started, can never stop, and to communicate the lover's predicament as the still eye of a whirling, oblivious world. The lyrics about Stella's absence, which imply that she has freed herself from participation in Astrophil's desire and that she roams through new fictions with fresh personae, sketch a dynamic, contrastive background to the fixity of Sonnet 108. She leaves Astrophil behind with a hero's function and no object to fulfill it, with a complex of attributes and no release from their imperatives.

While *Astrophil and Stella* distinctly plays down the temporal process passed on from the *Canzoniere* in favor of a still more person-oriented scope and order, other poets of Sidney's time are constantly refashioning the terms of their own self-making sequences. In Petrarch's and Sidney's texts one sees not what is typical of the others, but where and how the orders of time and person are most thoroughly developed in the form; and whether the disposition of these orders seems antiquarian or modern, idealized or constructivist, depends (I am convinced) on where one stands to observe, not on anything dependably fixed about the fictions themselves. It goes without saying that the self-consciously characterological dimension of *Astrophil and Stella*—the sense that one is watching the construction of character itself, and then its (potential) destruction—anticipates the play of (say) thematic and synthetic elements in modern fictions, although *Astrophil and Stella*, capacitated by the lyric genre, is necessarily less elaborate in its metafictional argument, and at the same time more at risk when it proposes its own dissolution through the erasure of Astrophil.[46] It would be interesting to trace the contemporary reaction to Sidney's utterly nominative fiction by means of a thorough reading of both the early critical literature and the many lyric sequences in English that present themselves as the children of Sidney's invention; it would be worthwhile, I think, to explore the question of whether that contemporary response understood *Astrophil and Stella* as reactionary or radical, and to know what those poets and readers thought lyric's nominative program meant in theory and practice. I suspect that Sidney's sequence, as a kind of nominative manifesto, immediately slips into its role as a set of stable conventions to be (loudly or quietly) innovated against, as a demonstration of what is possible that makes everyone's lyric work more definite and self-aware in the matter of fusing aesthetics and ideology. In any case, the two objects of these initial chapters, the *Canzoniere* and *Astrophil and Stella*, are the fictions that make modern innovations in the post-Petrarchan sequence possible—that lend context to such various person-representations as Whitman's speaker in *Leaves of Grass*, Pound's *Hugh Selwyn Mauberley* (1920), and the lover of John Berryman's *Sonnets* (written 1940s, published 1967). Unstable and provisional as they are, they have to seem the models of a certainty to be undermined and overcome. The next chapter concentrates on a fissure in post-Petrarchan lyric poetics that was already opening in Sidney's time, and that, much later, makes room for the modern sequence.

Chapter 3

TWO RITUAL SEQUENCES: TAYLOR'S
PREPARATORY MEDITATIONS AND WHITMAN'S
LEAVES OF GRASS

THE FICTIONAL program for the Western sequence holds its aesthetic and ideological legitimacy only by conceding a subordinate place for the countertrend in lyric, the ritual mode with which fiction converses in nearly every poem and volume. Traces of that other phenomenon cannot be obliterated, not while poems are composed of material signs to be performed and experienced; nor does fiction aspire to anything so drastic for its opposing principle, for the ritual mode is a valuable foil, and has much to offer by defining and corroborating the former. While the school of Petrarch rehearses its generic program, however, a countertradition of sequences built on ritual principles keeps producing its specimens on the quiet margin of European and American poetic cultures, and insists on adapting fictional strategies to its own uses, or criticizing them, or decomposing them. Because of several common liabilities, many of the works that belong to that tradition are hard to identify today. Some are almost too eccentric to be taken seriously: when the Italian poet Girolamo Malipiero (*Il Petrarca Spirituale*, 1536) and other Roman Catholic poets explicitly adapt Petrarchan and post-Petrarchan sequential forms—and "translate" particular poets' actual language—for wholly devotional aims, they carry out one mode's subordination to its counterpart more openly and forcibly than many readers will allow except in parody. Some are judged bad poetry by implicitly fictional standards: though it contains perhaps the most widely read English poetry of the sixteenth century, the psalter of Thomas Sternhold and John Hopkins has never prospered with critics and theorists, and accordingly has not been received as literature. And some works remain obscure for obscure reasons, while the fortunes of lyric fiction—and its particular development after the fourteenth century, the canon of nominative lyric sequences—are followed lovingly and exhaustively.

This chapter attends to the nearly clandestine history of the ritual sequence through two of its better-known examples: Edward Taylor's *Preparatory Meditations* (written 1682–1725) and Walt Whitman's *Leaves of Grass* (1855). I choose these works not because they are now more often read than other contemporaneous specimens, but because of their historical positions for the Western lyric series, the import of their Americanness, and their strategic revisions of available models. I take Taylor's *Preparatory Meditations* as coming at the end of a phase in the life of the form, where his ritual poetics represents the revision and dissolution of a common program for treating devotional experience in lyric. The *Meditations* effectually brings the original line of devotional sequences to its end. Whitman's *Leaves of Grass*, by contrast, articulates the potential of the ritual sequence in a climate where—as chapter 4 will show in more detail—the continuing dominance of a fictional poetics is under pressure from intellectual fashions and fatigue from its own longevity, its lack of a strong model after (the now very distant) Petrarch. Whitman comes to serve as such a model for a newly ritual poetics of the lyric sequence: especially in its original version of 1855, his series anticipates the situation of the next century's first decades, in which the fictional sequence finds the path of its development in formal and intellectual pluralities that call for readings more appropriate to ritual texts than to the closed, characterological fictions of the Renaissance. The anything but simple affinity between Whitman and the New World poets of the early twentieth century—the latter, poets who might be expected to embrace his premodern example eagerly—has much to do, I believe, with Whitman's place in a ritual rather than a fictional poetics, at the head of a line instead of its terminus. The shared fact of modernity simplifies, and perhaps ironizes, the relations between Whitman and such poets as Pound and Eliot, who know that they are neither the natural heirs of the ritual mode nor able to get across their highly advanced poetic fictions without relying on the means of reading that *Leaves of Grass* exacts and enables.[1] In the center of a book that finds its proper "origins" and its major "innovations" in the poetics of lyric fiction, then, this is an essay about the alternative at several instants of obscurity, crisis, and influence.

In order to recover the emergence of Edward Taylor's poetry from the compromises and exhaustion of a post-Petrarchan religious lyric, it is perhaps best to look briefly at how, in the Renaissance, the common interests of amatory and devotional sequences are identified; how a fictional poetics is transposed into the terms with which poets and theorists acknowledge their practice; and where the stresses might wait to undo that practice and give voice to its countermeasure, the ritual mode, in the service of devotional aims.

Throughout this book, I try to elucidate highly explicit terms with which to describe the post-Petrarchan lyric sequence, but naturally such terms would seem unlikely to, say, a poet or critic of the sixteenth or seventeenth century. Among the humanist and Christian commentators of his age, perhaps the most common way of remarking Petrarch's fictional achievement is to invoke the idea of variation. His technic, described as a deliberate program ("del vario stile in ch'io piango et ragiono") in the first sonnet of the *Canzoniere*, is ostensibly derived from the aesthetic doctrine, called *variatio*, by which Greek and Roman poets set unlike poems together and like poems apart.[2] As Georg Luck has observed, classical *variatio* may appear as "a contrast of mood or style, of content or metre."[3] Of course by extrinsic or editorial standards, the *Canzoniere* is a triumphantly varied collection of lyrics: it combines formal variety—317 sonnets, 29 canzoni, 7 *ballate*, 9 *sestine*, 4 *madrigali*—with innumerable shifts of tone, pace, and style. But Petrarch's innovative handling of *variatio* occurred chiefly in the conceptual phase of his composition, when he saw the limitless possibilities of serial variation for the dynamic representation of the mind in love. He makes it not merely a textural norm—"a negative approach to arrangement, the avoidance of certain obvious groupings and collocations"[4]—but a fictional strategy. Parcelling his lyric speech into discrete and often contrasting segments, Petrarch accumulates a portrait of conflicted love out of 366 poems. In large, this method provides a comprehensive, practically systematic view of love's parts, causes, and consequences; in little, it often creates startling junctures that seem to evoke love's dynamic psychology, as in the adjacent Sonnets 229 and 230:

> Cantai, or piango. . . .
>
> (I sang, now I weep. . . .)
>
> (229.1)

> I' piansi, or canto. . . .
>
> (I wept, now I sing. . . .)
>
> (230.1)

The physical properties of disjunction and formal equality on which *variatio* is predicated seem to lead unavoidably into fiction: one twentieth-century poet celebrates the vitality of "the pause, of the empty space, of the transition between one state and another. What distinguishes classic from primitive art," writes Octavio Paz, "is the intuition of time not as an instant but as succession, symbolized in the line that encloses a form without imprisoning it."[5] The facts of juncture and continuity invite poet and reader to counterfeit life's temporal and experiential flow between instants and not simply observe its bounding by instants alone. (Even the temporality itself enlists a *variatio* in realizing its effects: the process of the *Canzoniere* is compounded from a variation between the historical rhythm of the sonnets and the paces of the other forms, such as the highly concentrated sestine.) If the formal parity of the units were interrupted and the work's voice dispersed into several, the fictional mode might break down into ritual, the characterological might come apart to be re-cuperated only as choral; but within the professed limits of the idea, we can conclude that the more *variatio*, the less avoidable the values of suc-cession, character, dynamism—in short, of fiction.

Another outcome of *variatio*—what might be called its ethical or polit-ical result—deserves a word here as well. Petrarch's serial construction of his speaker out of resonant lyric moments necessarily splinters the por-traits of other figures, particularly the donna Laura. As Nancy Vickers has it, "Laura is always presented as a part or parts of a woman. When more than one part figures in a single poem, a sequential, inclusive order-ing is never stressed. Her textures are those of metals and stones; her image is that of a collection of exquisitely beautiful disassociated objects. Singled out among them are hair, hand, foot and eyes: golden hair trapped and bound the speaker; an ivory hand took his heart away; a marble foot imprinted the grass and flowers; starry eyes directed him in his wandering."[6] The atomizing of Laura follows in part from the dislo-cated quality of the poet's attention: a gaze that turns only on separate instants in the speaker's life will naturally catch even more estranged frag-ments of the other principal person, without finally pulling her together into a coherent character. The means of representation that achieve the speaker's immediacy and force also provide that Laura will be dissolved but not reassembled. As most readers of the *Canzoniere* at least implicitly understand this uneven fictional bargain, it suits Petrarch's interest to ex-aggerate Laura's fragmentation in particular lyrics and thus to strengthen the speaker's unity of mind: we fleetingly wonder at but really compre-hend the detached hand, the hovering eyes, the disembodied voice. For Petrarch's successors, notably Clément Marot and many poets who carry his influence down to Daniel and Donne, this disintegrative tendency finds its fulfillment in the *blason*, a lyric convention given to approaching a lady's essence through a serial catalogue of her attributes.[7] Though it gained a livelihood apart from its origin in Petrarch's sequence, the blason codifies the strategy of contrastive segmentation that nominally rules the *Canzoniere* and every other fictional series of the Renaissance; in hard-ened, scaled-down fashion, it reflects his fictional transvaluation of the editorial norm of *variatio*.

Because of its success as a fiction, Petrarch's practice—from editorial means to phenomenal issue—determined much about the poetics of Re-naissance lyric sequences. The *Canzoniere* came to exemplify the original, definitive relation between a topic and its fictional treatment. From here forward, the form carries the charge of dealing through voice or person with large, dynamic topics, of which love is thought to be the most natu-ral. There is always something paradoxical, perhaps sublime, in the disproportion between the scope of the work's concern and the smallness of each poetic unit. But many poets and critics grow to see that disproportion as natural, even desirable. Before the start of the English sonnet vogue in the 1590s, George Puttenham explicitly proclaims what might be called the poetics of the topic in lyric sequences of his day. Notice that, like Petrarch in *Canzoniere* 1, he treats *variatio* as a fictional strategy:

> The first founder of all good affections is honest loue, as the mother of all the vicious is hatred. It was not therefore without reason that so commendable, yea honourable, a thing as loue well meant, were it in Princely estate or priuate, might in all ciuil common wealths be vttered in good forme and order as other laudable things are. And because loue is of all other humane affections the most puissant and passionate, and most generall to all sortes and ages of men and women, so as whether it be of the yong or old, or wise or holy, or high estate or low, none euer could truly bragge of any exemption in that case: it requireth a forme of Poesie variable, inconstant, affected, curious, and most witty of any others, whereof the ioyes were to be vttered in one sorte, the sorrowes in an other, and, by the many formes of Poesie, the many moodes and pangs of lovers throughly to be discouered; the poor soules sometimes praying, beseeching, sometime honouring, auancing, praising, an other while railing, reuiling, and cursing, then sorrowing, weeping, lamenting, in the ende laughing, rejoysing, & solacing the beloued againe, with a thousand delicate deuices, odes, songs, elegies, ballads, sonets, and other ditties, moouing one way and another to great compassion.[8]

The lyric sequence, in effect, has an official topic, *variatio* a modernized application, and love a requisite means of treatment.

The boom in English love sonnets was largely over by 1600, though editions and revisions of sequences were still published for another generation or so. In the early years of the seventeenth century, a new strain of lyric sequences emerged, though its roots went back well into the past. I refer to the devotional lyrics of John Donne, George Herbert, Henry Vaughan, Thomas Traherne, John Milton, and, in New England, Edward Taylor. It is surprising how seldom these two historical developments have been analyzed for their aesthetic and intellectual similarities.[9] Renaissance readers and critics saw a similarity between love and worship in terms of their properties as topics for poetry, and many poets participated in both impulses. Thomas Wyatt, who introduced the imitation of Petrarchan models into English, wrote paraphrases of the Penitential Psalms (circa 1540) that together form one of the earliest English religious sequences; Philip Sidney and his sister, the countess of Pembroke, produced a complete psalter that flourished its *variatio* as fully as did *Astrophil and Stella*; Barnabe Barnes complemented *Parthenophil and Parthenophe* with a devotional series called the *Divine Centurie of Spiritual*

Sonnets (1595); and Donne himself had a foot planted firmly in each tradition, inspiring Thomas Carew to celebrate him as "two Flamens, and both those, the best, / Apollo's first, at last, the true Gods Priest."[10] Fulke Greville, Henry Constable, William Drummond of Hawthornden, Robert Herrick, and Henry Vaughan are among the English poets who wrote both sacred and profane sequences or sub-sequences. A comparable division of interests occurs in some Continental poets of the Renaissance, especially in France and Italy. Clément Marot had the makings of an amatory sequence in his strenuously varied chansons and elegies, but his most conspicuous work was his adapation of the Psalms (circa 1540); Jean-Antoine de Baïf, Philippe Desportes, and Jean de Sponde, as well, turned out both love sonnets and psalms. In Italy, Pietro Bembo (1530), Francesco Maria Molza (circa 1540), Bernardino Rota (1572), and Torquato Tasso (circa 1582), among many others, freely mingled amatory and religious lyrics in their *rime*. Even George Herbert, who has no such double oeuvre, saw that love of woman and love of God share some kind of affinity for the sequence. In trying to claim the form for pious purposes, he shows how naturally the two topics were perceived as pendants, or rivals, to one another. He insists in a letter to his mother that "I need not [the Muses'] help, to reprove the vanity of those many Love-poems, that are daily writ and consecrated to *Venus*; nor to bewail that so few are writ, that look towards *God* and *Heaven*," and asks his God,

> Why are not *Sonnets* made of thee? and layes
> Vpon thine Altar burnt? Cannot thy love
> Heighten a spirit to sound out thy praise
> As well as any she?[11]

I have maintained that Petrarch's poetic representation of love set a standard for the treatment of that (obviously) inexhaustible topic. To the devotional writers, of course, their topic—which Herbert tersely announces as "My God, My King"—is much vaster, much harder to contain in verse. Explicit remarks on the size of the matter are a commonplace in this tradition. Herbert addresses the Bible, "O Book! infinite sweetnesse!" and says of God's providence:

> Thou art in small things great, not small in any:
> Thy even praise can neither rise, nor fall.
> Thou art in all things one, in each thing many:
> For thou art infinite in one and all.[12]

Donne's divine poems include scattered references to Christ's "immensity," the endlessness of heaven and hell, the intricacy of man's making, and the "numberlesse infinities" of human souls under God's dominion.[13] Vaughan calls Christ's redemption of man "that vast, almighty measure," and contrasts his own smallness and God's magnitude ("I am but finite, He is Infinite"). His most famous poem opens with a hushed confidence, "I saw Eternity the other night / Like a great *Ring* of pure and endless light."[14] And Taylor frequently pauses over the difficulty and indescribability of his topic, as in Meditation 2.66:

> O! what a thing is Love? who can define
> Or liniament it out? Its strange to tell.[15]

Most of these poets answer the problem of their immense topic with Petrarch's fictional strategy, though they are likely to acknowledge the Psalms as their model.[16] With the same phenomenal imperative that moved Petrarch, they segment and vary their discourse, allowing a comprehensive picture of their religious subjects to accumulate processively out of multiple emotions.

The doctrinal roots of this aesthetic program are deep and reasoned in Christian thought. Perry Miller has described their workings in Puritan theology, but they have their origins much earlier, and in the Renaissance extend their sway more widely, than any strictly Puritan principle:

> Should human beings be required to contemplate forever an incomprehensible essence, their religious life might become an anarchic surrender to ineffable impulses. . . . Therefore Puritan textbooks hastened to assert that while we cannot define God we may piece together "an imperfect description which commeth neerest to unfold God's nature." This imperfect description was achieved by enumerating in logical sequence what were called God's "attributes." Strictly speaking the attributes have no existence outside the human intellect. God is one, indivisible, timeless act, but as such He is utterly meaningless to us: "we must needs have a diversified representation of it." . . . Diverse aspects of the divine essence cannot in fact be separated; yet from the human point of view they must be distinguished, and in thinking of them men are compelled to separate one from another "notionally." "They are not distinguished at all in God, but onely to us-ward, according to our manner of conceiving." . . .
>
> Puritans did not invent this reasoning. The discovery that man can conceive of God only by clustering the attributes . . . had been fully exploited by scholastics. In Puritan thought the doctrine received a renewed importance because they, in common with Augustinians of every complexion, medieval or Protestant, accused other theologians of abusing it.[17]

Christians had become used to thinking of their God in terms of contrastive segmentation or *variatio*, and at the same time were aware that these ways of representing him were necessary only because of humankind's limited imagination and immersion in time. In the Renaissance, Roman Catholic and Protestant writers of all sects struggle with the paradoxical relation of the timeless deity and its unavoidably serial representation. The Puritan divine John Preston reminds his listeners in the early seventeenth century that

> [God] is a being without succession: the creatures have not this; there is something to them, which was not before; and something shall be, which is not for the present: this is true of every creature; of men and Angels; but with God there is no succession . . . with the creature there is flux of time, the creatures enjoy one thing one minute, which they doe not another; but God enjoyes all at once . . . as, suppose all the pleasures that are in a long banquet, were drawne together into one moment; suppose all the acts of mans understanding, and will, from the beginning of his life to the end, could be found in him in one instant; such is eternity.[18]

The only way for human beings to comprehend God, then, is to distribute his qualities into the literary version of a "long banquet," a portrait whose main formal constituents are sequentiality and variation. God's real essence is something "incomprehensible . . . which we cannot expresse to you; yet this is an expression which we may helpe our selves by, and is used every where in Scripture. . . . fixe thy mind chiefly on his Attributes."[19]

From an Anglican perspective, Isaac Newton emphasizes serial variation in humankind's conception of God. He plays down its fallacy, though, and makes God seem like a Petrarchan lover: "by way of allegory, God is said to see, to speak, to laugh, to love, to hate, to desire, to give, to receive, to rejoice, to be angry, to fight, to frame, to work, to build. For all our notions of God are taken from the ways of mankind, by a certain similitude which, though not perfect, has some likeness however."[20]

Thomas Ken, bishop of Bath and Wells, devised a sequence of hymns called the *Hymnarium: or, Hymns on the Attributes of God* (probably written before 1704, published 1721) that affirms the serial idea of God with unusual clarity. Each of the thirty-one songs takes up a different attribute, and the collection as a whole is rich with formal *variatio* ("Variety, successive of Delight / [I] thought might greater Joy excite").[21] Doubtless the *Hymnarium* both reflects and promotes a sense of correspondence between God's "back-parts" and the formal order of a lyric series. The poet-worshipper knows his praise will have come as close to the mark as it can when he completes his multiform assault on the topic:

> I in that Grace have lib'ral Share,
>   And will in Hymn thy Love declare;
> Though Hymns can never reach the Height,
>   A Heart sincere is God's Delight;

> I'll, when each Hymn has done its best,
>   In Admiration vent the rest.[22]

Ken constantly warns his readers and himself not to confuse the solution of an intellectual and aesthetic bind with God's ontology:

> All the Duration I conceiv'd
>   Of divisible Parts was weav'd,
> Thou, O my God, art what thou art,
>   Eternity admits no Part,[23]

but all the while the assembling of the *Hymnarium* makes that solution seem attractive and inevitable.

As late as 1726, three years before Edward Taylor's death, the Massachusetts Puritan Samuel Willard is still turning over the theological and aesthetic problem: "If [God] should reveal himself fully to the Creature, it must be either in one word and moment, or in a speech and space of time: but not in a word and moment, because there can be no one word formed, which can draw forth and comprehend the whole sum of the perfection of the First Being; not in a speech, or many words & space of time; because if God should speak concerning himself throughout all Eternity, it would not explain to us all the perfection that is in him. . . . Let us therefore admire and adore this incomprehensible Being. Here we have a proper subject for our Admiration to work upon."[24]

Accordingly, the devotional sonneteers join the conception of lyric that began when Petrarch rejected mere textural *variatio*. The ideology of a natural incommunicability between God's essence and his representation sustains a parallelism with the fiction of a highly influential amatory poet, and the two topics come to be treated in the same way: Augustinian doctrine supports post-Petrarchan practice, which in turn validates the theory of divine representation such that these notions become indivisible for the Renaissance. The rise of a fictional poetics around religious topics in the sixteenth and seventeenth centuries belongs to the story of post-Petrarchism's hegemony over lyric. In England, for instance, it extends the experimental climate of the sonnet boom at least another fifty years. One easily sees how the fictional lyric sequence became a prime vessel for representing that "proper subject." Of all the age's received forms, it is the "long banquet" that best reconciles an inseparable, timeless deity with the human world of hours and divisions. It admits "a diversified representation," according to humankind's preference for variation. And it inherits from Petrarch a characterological or confessional dimension that allows, say, a sequence on the topic of love to build a strongly individual voice—another "proper subject"—who examines in turn himself, the loved one, the situation, and ancillary topics to assemble a compre-

hensive picture of amatory experience. Herbert probably drew a prece-
dent for the subjectivity of his *Temple* (1633) from the Pauline epistle
which, he notes with interest, combines *variatio* and strong passion without losing its piety: "What an admirable Epistle is the second to the Corinthians? how full of affections? he joyes, and he is sorry, he grieves, and
he gloryes, never was there such care of a flock expressed, save in the great
shepherd of the fold, who first shed teares over Jerusalem, and afterwards
blood."[25] Introspection and "affections" are the natural results of a poetic form that structurally and phenomenally resembles a diary; they
make the devotional sonneteers' practical topic something like the workings of God in the cosmos, the world, and the heart of the individual
Christian.

The agreement in the Renaissance over how these two matters ought
to be treated, and the general perception of their mutual resemblance as
poetic topics, figure notably in the Roman Catholic poet Henry Constable's amatory sequence *Diana* (1592). That work begins with a run of
twenty-one sonnets on the "variable affections of loue." After the first
seven poems in this group, which reflect in Petrarch's manner on the
speaker's *innamoramento* and his alternating bouts of hope and despair,
the sequence moves into a subsection called "the second 7 of his Ladies
prayse." Here is the initial sonnet of the subsection, a blason titled "An
exhortation to the reader to come and see his Mistrisse beautie":

> Eyes curiouse to behold what nature can create
> Come see come see and write what wonder yow doe see
> Causing by true reporte oure next posteritye
> Curse fortune for that they were borne to late
>
> Come then and come ye all, come soone least that
> The tyme should be to shorte and men to few should be
> For all be few to write her least parts historie
> Though they should euer write and neuer write but that.
>
> Millions looke on her eyes millions thinke on her witte
> Millions speake of her [lip] millions write of her hand
> The whole eye or the lip I doe not vnderstand
> Millions to few to prayse but some one parte of it
>   As eyther of her ey or lip or hand to write
>   The light or blacke the tast or red the soft or white.[26]

The woman's "least parts," like what the divines call the "back-parts" of
God, are too praiseworthy for the best of man's poems; we could praise
her forever, and never capture her graces (recall Willard: "if God should
speak concerning himself throughout all Eternity"); her elements, a lip or
an eye, are incomprehensible to the speaker. The remainder of the subsec-

tion includes sonnets on "the excellencye of his Ladies voyce," "her excellencye both in singing and instruments," "the prowesse of his Ladie," and "the envie others beare to his Ladie for the former perfections." Of course, Constable's blason parodies the Christian construction of God, deliberately crossing the line between the sacred and profane uses of this type of *variatio*. But the critical point to notice is how easily this section called "his Ladies prayse" joins the conventional post-Petrarchan sequence. The two topics share an internal dynamic: each encloses two constituents, the lover-devotee with his (or her) variable emotions, and the lady-deity with her (or his) numberless laudable parts; each implicitly entails a disparity of powers across the lines of subjectivity, the subject's representational hold on the other, and the object's empirical or spiritual advantage over the voice. Apart from the rhetorical collusions that critics often remark, then, the likeness of the two topics as poetic concerns, and the ideologies that develop around them, insist on their similar treatment as fictions. These two topics have too much in common as poetic material to be effectively kept apart by the moral, non-aesthetic distinction of sacredness and profanity. If they could not often cohabit, they had to watch and learn from each other.

By any measure, Edward Taylor (1642?–1729) is probably the last poet in the continuous English devotional line begun in the 1500s and developed by Donne and Herbert. The full title of Taylor's work indicates the nature of the topic: "Preparatory Meditations before my Approach to the Lords Supper. Chiefly upon the Doctrin preached upon the Day of administration." The poet, minister to a congregation in Westfield, Massachusetts, composed each installment of the *Preparatory Meditations* as a lyric meditation on the day's sermon; the sermons, not the poems, were the primary objects of Taylor's skill and interest.[27] Nonetheless, I would like to suggest that the *Preparatory Meditations* is an important text in the history of the Western sequence. It enacts the dissolution of the post-Petrarchan fictional poetics on which so much seventeenth-century religious poetry is founded; and in its reinvention of a devotional poetry, the *Meditations* turns to a ritual mode in which temporal process, character, and even *variatio* are manifestly absent. Taylor composed the *Meditations* with the example of the European devotional poets very much in mind, and so his series observes superficial Petrarchisms everywhere. But he wrote at so many removes from the tradition—historical, cultural, and geographical—that for him the phenomenal and intellectual complex that served Herbert and Ken had lost its inevitability, and the immediate nature of his religious experience exerted more force, even on literature, than any received textual idea of that experience. Therefore Taylor's *Preparatory Meditations* reweighs entirely the conventional adjustment of a ritual mode to the (heretofore dominant) fictional dimension: it is a phenomenal overthrow of the latter, a new kind of lyric document.

One question that puts us in search of Taylor's poetics concerns *variatio*: how is it manifested in the *Preparatory Meditations*? What are its implications for the sequence's identity as ritual or fictional lyric? A first approach to an answer might be directed through the internal arrangements of the *Meditations*. Certainly Taylor aims to establish some clearly demarcated subsequences within the larger sequence. The most obvious of these are the "First Series," including more than forty-nine poems, and the "Second," which contains about 165 lyrics. Other clusters, loosely linked by topics and themes, appear within the two books. Louis Martz has pointed out some of these: "A sequence of seven Meditations (1.31–37) written on consecutive aspects of . . . [a] passage from I Corinthians 3:21–23"; "the thirty Meditations on 'Types' that begin Taylor's second series; the subsequent series on the nature, love, and power of Christ (2.31–56)"; "the series (2.102–11) in which Taylor deals with the doctrine of the Lord's Supper; and lastly, the long series on sequential texts from Canticles (2.115–53), running from September 1713 to February 1719."[28] A list of scriptural tags indicates how one of these subsequences ostensibly proceeds. I quote selectively from the titles of 1.8–17: "I am the Living Bread," "My Blood is Drinke indeed," "A Feast of Fat things," "Glorious in his Apparell," "All the Treasures of Wisdom," "A Great High Priest," "A Greate Prophet is risen up," and finally, "King of Kings." From elemental to material and then to spiritual symbols of God's love, the lyrics in the series advance toward a direct consideration of the deity himself, who presents such a stupefying object that the speaker-poet at first can only exclaim, "A King, a King, a King, indeed, a King / Writh up in Glory!" (17.1–2). This and other structures seem to indicate that Taylor means for his meditations to deal in process, to counterfeit a speaker's experience of advent, to collaborate in assembling a serial, recessed representation of devotion.

But while the topics of the poems seem to announce a developing series, the particular lyrics strain to free themselves: Taylor's poetic sensibility constantly shuns the ironies, deferrals, and equivocalities that go into poetic fictions. In its broad outlines, the dramatic situation of the poems never varies. Each meditation records a direct address of the Lord by the abject, anxious speaker. More than one hundred of the poems actually begin with a stark apostrophe, such as "My Deare Deare Lord," or "Oh Good, Good, Good, my Lord." And however they begin, most lyrics conclude like "The Experience," an early, undated poem that appears near the beginning of the *Poetical Works* manuscript:

Oh! that my Heart, thy Golden Harp might bee
   Well tun'd by Glorious Grace, that e'ry string
Screw'd to the highest pitch, might unto thee
   All Praises wrapt in sweetest Musick bring.
   I praise thee, Lord, and better praise thee would
   If what I had, my heart might ever hold.

Typically, Taylor proposes an implicit or open bargain to his God: save the speaker's soul, and gain greater praise. The final couplet acknowledges the inadequacy of his poem and ascribes the fault to the object's elusiveness. With his lament that he cannot "hold" the experience, the poem slips away.

Like several other Puritan writers of sequences, Taylor seems to think of each installment in the *Preparatory Meditations* as an independent and final statement to God about his emotional life and spiritual ends. Karl Keller argues that Taylor's poems are merely the vestiges of a process of spiritual toning that preceded each sermon, and that "it was a perfect preparation he was after, not a perfect poem. . . . Taylor's private poems are themselves for the most part accounts of the process that Taylor went through in preparing himself to be disposed for saving grace. They are not poems *about* the process, but poems showing Taylor *in the process* of preparation. They are miniature dramas in which Taylor is re-enacting over and over again that which was to him the most meaningful process of man's life."[29] The Puritan divine Richard Baxter, a generation older than Taylor, expresses the attitude in the practical advice of his handbook on meditation, *The Saints Everlasting Rest* (1650): "Make it thy business in every duty, to winde up thy affections neerer Heaven. . . . When thou kneelest down in secret or publick prayer, let it be in hope to get thy heart nearer God before thou risest off thy knees."[30] Taylor's notion of each poem as literally a meditation, a script for the speaker's immediate relations with Christ, produces a text that we recognize as pertaining to ritual rather than fictional lyric. Instead of compiling a varied, subordinated record of religious life, or fashioning a lyric allegory of time or person, he wants to enact the whole Christian experience at every turn, to achieve grace in every poem.

Obviously Taylor's is a "poetry of meditation" in something of the way that such a tendency has been identified in sixteenth- and seventeenth-century poetry. But it must be emphasized that the appropriation of meditative technics in poetry, as Louis Martz attests, promises no skew toward a ritual or a fictional mode of lyric discourse. "I believe," writes Martz, that such technics "are essential to the dominant qualities of Donne's poetry; but that is far from saying that they are responsible for all of Donne's poetry. Donne wrote in many genres besides the meditative: satire, Ovidian elegy, funeral elegy, epistle, song, epigram, epitaph, epithalamion—and the sermon. In all these genres he displays the style that we call metaphysical. And in some of them we may discern the impingement and even the amalgamation of meditative elements, along with the other qualities of the poem."[31] Applied to lyric, the discipline of meditation moves impartially between the genre's characteristic modes, just as it is ideologically neutral between "Jesuit and Puritan," and aesthetically moderate between "the baroque extragance of Crashaw and the delicate restraint of Herbert."[32] Meditative exercise is so thoroughly quotidian, so much a part of "the lower levels of the spiritual life,"[33] that it assumes much of the character of particular lives—and of individual poetic practices. While the exercises assembled by Saint Ignatius Loyola are themselves a performative text—in the everyday sense, a ritual, with their three phases of composition, analysis, and colloquy—they yet contain directions that could generate fictions in the minds of their actors: "composition of place" and the making of "similitudes" or parables are two such exercises. The perspectivism of the former is indicated by Loyola and other contemporary commentators cited by Martz:

> It is clear from the various practices mentioned by these writers that there were three different ways of performing this imaginary "composition." The first is to imagine oneself present in the very spot where the event occurred: "to see the arrangements in the holy sepulchre, and the place or house of our Lady, beholding all the parts of it in particular, and likewise her chamber and oratory." The second is to imagine the events as occurring before your eyes "in the very same place where thou art." And the third is performed when persons "imagin that everie one of these thinges whereupon they meditate passeth within their own harte"—a method strongly recommended by Fray Luis [de Granada], although St. François de Sales warns that this method is "to subtil and hard for young beginners." . . . The effect is an intense, deliberate focusing of the "mind and thought . . . within the bounds, and limits of the subiect . . . either by imaginarie representation, if the matter may be subiect to the sences; or by a simple proposing or conceit of it, if it be a matter above sence," or, for those following St. Ignatius, some concrete similitude dramatizing even spiritual matters.[34]

It is very much Taylor's circumstances—his Puritan ideology, his readings of Herbert and others, his own understandings of lyric and of meditation—that make the *Preparatory Meditations* so strenuously ritualized in their generic orientation. The reader or auditor justly has the impression that Taylor offers up the same poem 217 times; that each lyric, hardly subordinated to any larger purpose of the sequence, aspires to do the work of the entire series; and that the professed act of each lyric, the speaker's self-examination and bargaining for grace, is nowhere completed. In Taylor's example we find the furthest elaboration to date, even the exaggeration, of elements that often figure in lyric's ritual dimension and in large-scale ritual sequences.

Meditation 1.32 addresses the encounter between received strategies for devotional poetry and the poet's Puritan thought.

> Thy Grace, Dear Lord's my golden Wrack, I finde
>   Screwing my Phancy into ragged Rhimes,
> Tuning thy Praises in my feeble minde
>   Untill I come to strike them on my chimes.
>   Were I an Angell bright, and borrow could
>   King Davids Harp, I would them play on gold.
>
> But plung'd I am, my minde is puzzled,
>   When I would spin my Phancy thus unspun,
> In finest Twine of Praise I'm muzzled.
>   My tazzled Thoughts twirld into Snick-Snarls run.
>   Thy Grace, my Lord, is such a glorious thing,
>   It doth Confound me when I would it sing.
>
> Eternall Love an Object mean did smite
>   Which by the Prince of Darkness was beguilde,
> That from this Love it ran and sweld with spite
>   And in the way with filth was all defilde
>   Yet must be reconcild, cleansd, and begrac'te
>   Or from the fruits of Gods first Love displac'te.
>
> Then Grace, my Lord, wrought in thy Heart a vent,
>   Thy Soft Soft hand to this hard worke did goe,
> And to the Milke White Throne of Justice went
>   And entred bond that Grace might overflow.
>   Hence did thy Person to my Nature ty
>   And bleed through humane Veans to satisfy.
>
> Oh! Grace, Grace, Grace! this Wealthy Grace doth lay
>   Her Golden Channells from thy Fathers throne,
> Into our Earthen pitchers to Convay
>   Heavens Aqua Vitae to us for our own.
>   O! let thy Golden Gutters run into
>   My Cup this Liquour till it overflow.
>
> Thine Ordinances, Graces Wine-fats where
>   Thy Spirits Walkes, and Graces runs doe ly
> And Angells waiting stand with holy Cheere
>   From Graces Conduite Head, with all Supply.

These Vessells full of Grace are, and the Bowls
In which their Taps do run, are pretious Souls.

Thou to the Cups dost say (that Catch this Wine,)
This Liquour, Golden Pipes, and Wine-fats plain,
Whether Paul, Apollos, Cephas, all are thine.
Oh Golden Word! Lord speake it ore again.
Lord speake it home to me, say these are mine.
My Bells shall then thy Praises bravely chime.

In part, this confession addresses the same expressive problem that sonneteers, especially devotional ones, always have to face. No "ragged
Rhimes" represent the wealth of the topic ("thy Praises") fairly. But the
poet-speaker here also admits the looming supervision of "Grace"—that
is, his thoughts of his soul's already ordained, immediate condition—over
his lyrics, and allows that poetic plans go awry when a poet thinks of
personal salvation as consequent to writing.

At the start of the Meditation, as in many others, Taylor assesses his
views of grace, the "golden Wrack," with distance and ambivalence:
grace as topic, he concedes, acts directly on his efforts to encompass it in
a poem, and brings an unpleasant havoc to the creative act. It is not his
object in any sense of tameness or domitability, nor does it settle for the
bright but passive immediacy of other "back-parts," like "Love" for Herbert or "Eternity" for Vaughan. Instead, it meddles in its own representation ("screwing my Phancy" and "tuning thy Praises"); it is both active
and immediate, and thus puzzles, muzzles, and tazzles the speaker. The
couplet of stanza 2 puts the problem simply, even apologetically, in a
grammatical antithesis. He wants to sing grace—to stand in relation to it
as subject stands to object—but it insists on confounding him, playing the
subject and making him its object. The apology here marks a vital step in
what Keller would see as the poem's preparation, for one can actually
watch Taylor move away from the mixed feelings of the first lines, toward
a desperate, uncritical coveting of grace for his own heart. The third
stanza links to its forerunner by meditating on the grammatical relation:
man, Taylor sees, must be the "Object" of God's love if he will be "rec-
oncild" and "begrac'te." Salvation demands his surrender. The climax,
then, occurs with the half-ecstatic, half-terrorstruck pleas of the fifth
stanza, where the original expressive conflict that generated the poem has
disappeared. It reappears only when the speaker remembers that he is a
poet as well as a Christian, and tries to reassert his wish to sing grace
again. He does so in the poem's last verses. In most of Taylor's lyrics, this
formulaic ending shows the poet-speaker shelving his emotional and intellectual concerns in return for God's implied assent to the contract he
proposes. It is almost always annoyingly superficial, but never more so

than in Meditation 1.32, where he seems to have quite forgotten the poem's origins. How, one must ask, does he think he has resolved the issue of grace as a lyric concern? He may have bought time by an impulsive, momentary reconciliation with God, but will the same problems not return again and again?

The answer, of course, is that they will. Taylor's lyrics are a string of such attempts to buy time for his soul. The closure of Meditation 1.32, resolving nothing, hints strongly that the *Preparatory Meditations* is designed as a cycle more than a sequence—that its temporality projects a structure of repetition and return—and that we will see a version of this poem again. While there are many lyric sequences that draw cyclical elements into the more comprehensive unity of a temporal continuum, including the *Canzoniere*, there are few that convey a sense of continual return as fully as the *Meditations*. As Albert Gelpi puts it, "all the elements of the First Series of *Meditations* are given in the first poem or poems; then the poet associates, elaborates, builds, connects, spatializing the implications of the initial vision. There is little or no temporal development from one point to another, as there is in much of Donne's and some of Herbert's verse; the movement is not linear and progressive but circular and self-defining."[35] The vigorous imperative mood at the close of each poem is an effort to halt the cycle then and there, and to gain a final salvation. But the very regularity of the imprecations betrays their stopgap character, their rootlessness in the particular poems—and their rootedness in a conception that precedes any single poem. They will not work as fictional endings.

Even on the rare occasions that Taylor seems to attempt a sustained fiction, he insists that the poem travel the full distance from its particular starting-point to the threshold of grace. A remarkable example of this recoil from fiction occurs in Meditation 2.77, an improvisation on the passage in Zechariah that alludes to "the Pit wherein is no water":

> A State, a State, Oh! Dungeon State indeed.
> In which mee headlong, long agoe Sin pitcht:
> As dark as Pitch, where Nastiness doth breed:
> And Filth defiles: and I am with it ditcht.
> A Sinfull State: This Pit no Water's in't.
> A Bugbare State: as black as any inke.
>
> I once sat singing on the Summit high
> 'Mong the Celestial Coire in Musick Sweet
> On highest bough of Paradisall joy,
> Glory and Innocence did in mee meet.
> I, as a Gold-Finch Nighting Gale, tun'd ore
> Melodious Songs 'fore Glorie's Palace Doore.

But on this bough I tuning Pearcht not long:
    Th'Infernall Foe shot out a Shaft from Hell,
A Fiery Dart pilde with Sins poison strong:
    That struck my heart, and down I headlong fell.
    And from the Highest Pinicle of Light
    Into this Lowest pit more darke than night.

A Pit indeed of Sin: No water's here:
    Whose bottom's furthest off from Heaven bright,
And is next doore to Hell Gate, to it neer:
    And here I dwell in sad and solemn night,
    My Gold-Fincht Angell Feathers dapled in
    Hells Scarlet Dy fat, blood red grown with sin.

I in this Pit all Destitute of Light
    Cram'd full of Horrid Darkness, here do Crawle
Up over head, and Eares, in Nauseous plight:
    And Swinelike Wallow in this mire, and Gall:
    No Heavenly Dews nor Holy Waters drill:
    Nor Sweet Aire Brieze, nor Comfort here distill.

Here for Companions, are Feares, Heart-Achs, Grief
    Frogs, Toads, Newts, Bats, Horrid Hob-Goblins, Ghosts:
Ill Spirits haunt this Pit: and no reliefe:
    Nor Coard can fetch me hence in Creatures Coasts.
    I who once lodgd at Heavens Palace Gate
    With full Fledgd Angells, now possess this fate.

But yet, my Lord, thy golden Chain of Grace
    Thou canst let down, and draw mee up into
Thy Holy Aire, and Glory's Happy Place.
    Out from these Hellish damps and pit so low.
    And if thy Grace shall do't, My Harp I'le raise,
    Whose Strings toucht by this Grace, Will twang thy praise.

As an extended portrait of despair with a fully realized setting and a seem-ingly hypothetical speaker, the poem is almost unique in the *Meditations*. It gains considerable emotional depth from the contrast of past joys and present torments—otherwise there is seldom a recognizable past in a Tay-lor lyric—and from the alarming sense of despair's inescapability put across by a version of the retrospective topos: "and here I dwell in sad and solemn night"; "I who once lodgd at Heavens Palace Gate / With full Fledgd Angells, now possess this fate." A devotional poet who thought of his or her sequence as a fictional structure, a type of lyric plot designed to envelop different perspectives on the Christian life within an unques-

tioned intellectual unity, might remain content with the body of this poem
as an effective counter to poems of undiluted joy. It would then in some
ways resemble Donne's Holy Sonnet "Oh, to vex me, contraryes meet in
one," where the poet sketches an Astrophil-like character who inhabits a
past, present, and future. Such a fictional poet might add a conclusion
that looks hopefully but discreetly toward redemption, as the ending of
Donne's penitential sonnet "Oh my blacke Soule!":

> Yet grace, if thou repent, thou canst not lacke;
> But who shall give thee that grace to beginne?
> Oh make thy selfe with holy mourning blacke,
> And red with blushing, as thou art with sinne.

Or he might round off the established parable on its own terms, letting
irony—the agent of fictional lyric, and a principle often antithetical to the
ritual mode—complete the job of bringing doctrine to life. Such is Herbert's program in "Redemption":

> Having been tenant long to a rich Lord,
> Not thriving, I resolved to be bold,
> And make a suit unto him, to afford
> A new small-rented lease, and cancell th' old.
> In heaven at his manour I him sought:
>> They told me there, that he was lately gone
>> About some land, which he had dearly bought
> Long since on earth, to take possession.
> I straight return'd, and knowing his great birth,
>> Sought him accordingly in great resorts;
>> In cities, theatres, gardens, parks, and courts:
> At length I heard a ragged noise and mirth
>> Of theeves and murderers: there I him espied,
>> Who straight, *Your suit is granted*, said, & died.

But lyrics like these do not have to epitomize their sequences as nearly all
of Taylor's do, nor are they meant to serve in the direct commerce between deity and devotee. Whatever their performative aspects, whatever
their transitivities, these poems, like most of the *Temple*, the *Holy Sonnets* (1633), and Vaughan's *Silex Scintillans* (1650 and 1655), clearly set
much of their ritual dimensions below their greater import as fictions.

Taylor will not subordinate his meditation to any larger movement in
the sequence. Each lyric must conclude by representing grace as imminent, and any fiction he nurtures during the course of a poem will be
shattered by the ritual closure. So it is with Meditation 2.77. The final
stanza grafts on the usual pious affirmation and pleadings as though there
were no difference between the emotional climate here and in the rest of

the sequence, as though this explicitly, intrinsically sinful speaker can have no mixed feelings about God and sin. What might seem the original terms of the fiction invite us to expect some acknowledgment of salvation's difficulty for him, something like the "blushing" or "contraryes" that indicate ambivalence and self-awareness in Donne's poems. In fact, the last stanza calls the logic of the whole preceding fiction into question: if it does not help us to arrive at a new and revealing perspective on the emotional and spiritual consequences of sin and despair, why is it there at all?

One way of answering such a fundamental question might be to observe that even at the beginning of Meditation 2.77, the fictional dimension of the poem claims no primacy. The poem's parable unfolds with the second stanza; before that, the first six lines introduce the meditation and underscore its rituality as though placing a phenomenal frame around what follows. In fact, the lyric "plot" of that first stanza involves a counterpoint of metaplasms that insinuates itself against the fictional sense of the passage. Two words from lines 1 and 2, "state" and "pitcht," are moved around, tested for latent meanings, and (in the latter case) internally transposed; and while "state" has no internal contradictions, but remains intact throughout the stanza—a discovery that should say something about the fortunes of character in this anticharacterological series— the other term, "pitcht," undergoes a subtractive transformation. As it falls away from "pitcht" to "pitch" to "pit," the materiality of the poem is disclosed: as Michael Riffaterre describes the same event in a text by the seventeenth-century Jesuit Athanasius Kircher, the arresting "linguistic anomaly is thus the means of transforming the semantic unity of the statement into a formal unity, of transforming a string of words into a network of related and unified shapes, into a 'monument' of verbal art."[36] When the word has reached its smallest morphemic shape in line 5, Taylor brings it down still another level, and ties the implicit conclusion to his penitential argument. "Inke," the material basis of the diminishing word, becomes its final, figurative metaplasm in the stanza, as though to suggest that any discursive fiction in the succeeding poem is really no more or less than shapes in ink. "State"—not character, but the wretched, remediless condition of the speaker—is the only element here that may be neither diminished nor cancelled. It thwarts catachresis. These events along the ritual dimension of poetic language are played out before the fiction proper gets underway; to most readers, they probably hold more interest as semantic music anyway, though their implications may be only glancingly recognized. Meditation 2.77 represents the orientation of the *Meditations* at large, enclosing and defeating the fictions of Christian experience that matter so much for Sidney, Donne, and Herbert, and making the open, invariable plea for grace that has no place in those poets' works.

I have suggested that Taylor's poetics of the sequence emerges out of the disintegration of a compact: its tenets are the Christian idea of deity as compromised by human capacities, and a Petrarchan fictional poetics adapted to such capacities. I should perhaps insist, as well, that much of his lyric program seems determined by the ideology of Puritanism as it is translated into poetic practice. Especially when seen against other specimens of Puritan writing in this form and other well-articulated fictional genres of the Renaissance, Taylor's *Meditations* appears deeply and characteristically ambivalent to the value of serial structures.[37] In a certain practical sense, Calvinists—especially the embattled Puritans of sixteenth- and seventeenth-century England, and the settlers in New England—lived out an unconcern for teleologies, and a blindness to the deferral of one element in time in favor of another: rejecting the Covenant of Works as a means toward salvation, and affirming that their fates were decided and potentially discoverable at every turn, they could not think of their lives as other sects did, as edifices to be built methodically toward the sky. For them to think or act thus was to risk a fatal irrelevance to the Covenant of Grace. The Puritan life in Christ was synchronic more than diachronic, to put it plainly, and it was the latter only in ways that tended to blur or conflate the scales of history.[38] The transfer of this practical theology into the literary representation of experience, from Ann Lok's *Meditation of a Penitent Sinner* (1560) to *The Pilgrim's Progress* and beyond, makes a fertile topic of study, though it overshoots my range here. Nevertheless, the Puritan lack of interest in living subordinated structures has major consequences for the lyric sequence in the age of Petrarch, Ronsard, and Sidney, and one of the decisive features of Puritan long poems is their failure to put something away for the textual future, anticipating their telos everywhere. Instead of a varied record of the Christian mind, we get from such poets as Ann Lok, her son Henry Lok, and Taylor the continual return of a single lyric, a loop that reenacts the closed, self-confirming circle of Christian history perhaps even more than the poets could have wanted or imagined. The impact of their lyric cycles resembles what Mircea Eliade describes as the issue of other religious acts of repetition: "[The] abolition of time [occurs] through the imitation of archetypes and the repetition of paradigmatic gestures. A sacrifice, for example, not only exactly reproduces the initial sacrifice revealed by a god *ab origine*, at the beginning of time, it also takes place at that same primordial mythical moment; in other words, every sacrifice repeats the initial sacrifice and coincides with it. . . . [Through] the paradox of rite, profane time and duration are suspended. And the same holds true for all repetitions, i.e., all imitations of archetypes; through such imitation, man is

projected into the mythical epoch in which the archetypes were first revealed. . . . This eternal return reveals an ontology uncontaminated by
time and becoming."[39] The largely paratactic program of the *Meditations*
makes something dynamic and immediate of the essential facts of typology and covenant theology, forcing them into our serial experience much
as the *Canzoniere* coerces us into respecting its ontology—one very much
"contaminated" by, and celebratory of, time and becoming.

As Eliade remarks, ritual structures of return tend to bring into question the possibility of human individuality: an "object or an act becomes
real only insofar as it imitates or repeats an archetype. Thus, reality is
acquired solely through repetition or participation; everything which
lacks an exemplary model is 'meaningless,' i.e., it lacks reality. Men
would thus have a tendency to become archetypal and paradigmatic."[40]
From Taylor's standpoint, the cyclical plan of the series is well adapted
to his Puritan vision of the relation of humankind and divinity because it
prevents the inevitable heaping of personal attributes from producing any
distinctive character of the speaker. Taylor's forcing us over the same
patch of lyric ground does not merely suspend the delineation of the
speaking voice, it indicates that the speaker of the *Meditations* is a two-
dimensional appliance disinclined to suspend "state" and break into the
contradictory entanglements of psychic and social vicissitude, and the illusion of personal development, that pass for character in Renaissance
lyric fiction. He is, quite simply, a speaker designed by and for lyric's
ritual mode. But while they diminish him, the poems gather up our in-
trigue for the God that remains so distant and unapproachable to the
worshipper. The reversal of the usual Renaissance idea of character, as
Sacvan Bercovitch has observed, is direct and uncompromised:

> We have been told that the Puritans' personal literature is a major "manifes-
> tation of a growing self-consciousness," that every one of them "had to speak
> honestly of his own experience." Their writings yield a different conclusion:
> there, self-examination serves not to liberate but to constrict; selfhood ap-
> pears as a state to be overcome, obliterated; and identity is asserted through
> an act of submission to a transcendent absolute. . . .
>
> It has become fashionable to link the production of mirrors during the
> Renaissance with the growth of modern individualism. This may hold true
> for the humanist Renaissance. For Baxter, [William] Dell, and Richard
> Mather, the mirror radiated the divine image. They never sought their own
> reflection in it, as did Montaigne and his literary descendants through Rous-
> seau. They sought Christ, "the mirror of election," and "Prospective-Glass
> for Saints"—or rather mirror, prospective glass, and image all in one: com-
> munion meant "*a putting on of Christ*," transforming oneself completely into
> his image. Manetti, Ficino, and Pico held up the christic mirror to show man

his own splendor. The Puritans felt that the less one saw of oneself in that mirror, the better; and best of all was to cast no reflection at all, to disappear.[41]

This is perhaps to suggest more than that in certain cases such as Taylor's, humanist nominativity becomes Puritan logocentrism, that scripture is these poets' "infallible correlative for the self."[42] These things are true, of course: one hears the explicit Puritan reaction to humanist ideas of the self, and to post-Petrarchan lyric fictions, in Arthur Golding's commonplace exhortation, in his Elizabethan translation of the Psalter, to "[frame] yourself according to the rule of Gods most holy word."[43] For Puritan lyric, however, the value of person is not entirely obliterated by such dicta, but is transferred out of the poems proper, to God. In a compensatory action that implies again the mutual interrogation of ritual and fictional modes, the effacement of Taylor's speaker, and the continual turning of his gaze in the direction of "thy person,"

> Thy Godhead Cabbin'd in a Myrtle bowre,
>   A Palm branch tent, an Olive Tabernacle,
> A Pine bough Booth, An Osier House or tower
>   A mortall bitt of Manhood, where the Staple
>   Doth fixt, uniting of thy natures, hold,
>   And hold out marvels more than can be told,
>
> (2.24.13–18)

makes God the sort of character that an Astrophil is for lyric of a different mode and ideology. Cleansing their transitive poetic speakers of complications that might cause attention to linger over the human counterfeit, Taylor and the other Puritan poets create an interest in God as the conflicted self of the sequence. Such an interest is already countermanded by doctrine: Perry Miller quotes Preston and Willard insisting that "All the Attributes of God are equall among themselves" and "*not contrary one to another.*"[44] But these protests actually verify that men and women will construct character through contradiction wherever they can, and that with the Puritan notion of selfhood in place, God becomes the object of a certain displaced naturalization. As Miller affirms, "the mind will never fathom how these qualities exist side by side in one consistent being. . . . We must regard the balance of the attributes as both a fact and a logical necessity, but we must not expect to know how the balance is maintained."[45] Fictionally God is cognate with both the lovers of the post-Petrarchan sequences and their objects, the Lauras and Stellas: the former because he is the dominant character of the lyrics (though only by default), the latter because he is still the speaker's object (though an object to whom that speaker emphatically wishes to cede his subjectivity). But he cannot be the object to a self-erasing subject, or the fictional object in a ritual text. Finally, then, he is neither subject nor object, but the irruption of a fictional principle past the margins of the poems. His involvement in the sequence's ideas of selfhood indicates that the ritual sequence, like what I have called the post-Petrarchan, must create its mode out of the suppression and reorientation of its opposite dimension: here fiction, in the form of characterological interest, will appear anyway, and must be channeled according to a fashion that maintains for the *Meditations* the primacy of its ritual mode.

But Taylor's series represents more than the thoroughly Puritan adaptation of a post-Petrarchan form, however much ideology intervenes in its generic vision. The sonnet sequences by Ann Lok and Henry Lok might be described that way, but the *Preparatory Meditations* is more seriously implicated in the mode it seeks to disempower, in the post-Petrarchan aesthetic it does so much to criticize and overthrow. Any number of conceits might describe how Taylor's series, like other early American texts, answers its received European protocols. Leo Bersani has recently written of *Moby-Dick* as "[inviting] America *to dissipate its capital, . . .* [proposing] no object of loyalty or of desire except the continuously repeated gesture of not receiving the wealth it appropriates." Starting over, *Moby-Dick* "takes the same risks as the country it finally honors."[46] In Taylor's case, where something like what Bersani describes takes place, the most exact critical conceit might be one the poet plausibly had in mind, if not while disposing his lyric capital, then while instructing his congregation how to dispose their lives. Perhaps the *Preparatory Meditations* might fairly be said to abrogate the post-Petrarchan devotional fictions of his English and Continental predecessors, as for Calvinism the Covenant of Grace succeeds and abolishes the Covenant of Law. In this sense, Taylor's sequence repeats for lyric discourse what Puritan ideology and practice accomplish in the area of doctrine. As Karen Rowe has recently written, the expiration of one covenant in the Old Testament and its replacement by another in the New had consequences that reached well beyond the hermeneutics of typology. This original abrogation forms the supposed basis for social and congregational covenants that determined much about how early New Englanders lived and worshipped.[47] Likewise, Taylor's deliberate abrogation of one poetics by another—his elaboration of a fully developed ritual series out of other poets' anticipations and the hints embedded in texts of the dominant fictional mode—supports much ancillary innovation at the levels of figuration, tone, and so forth. It is not, of course, that the extant models of devotional poetry had some intrinsic association with the Old Testament covenant between man and god or its typal elements. But Taylor, as man and poet, is situated at a temporal and geopolitical site where several Old World compacts have run out of efficacy, where abrogation is a spiritual and political imperative for the committed Puritan, where—especially in poetry—the gulf between his own experience and the available templates is intolerably wide. As a succession that includes the foregoing principle but explodes its dimensions to find a new program, abrogation describes the generic event of this sequence perhaps better than any other likely terms. It prepares us to recognize the *Meditations* as an uncompromising reaction within a doctrinal and aesthetic dispute, and to see these areas of experience as really continuous: when ideology changes, poetry necessarily changes too—and vice versa, in an indivisible effect. For devotional poetry, the *Meditations* represents an eschatology of the sequence, a deliberate getting-ready for the end by revising and cancelling old ways.

In 1855 there appeared the second major instance of a ritually oriented lyric sequence in the United States. The peculiar circumstances around the first edition of Walt Whitman's *Leaves of Grass* are well known from the chronicles of Malcolm Cowley, Paul Zweig, and others: very much an object of material interest, "designed to trouble, more than to please,"[48] it was a book unlike perhaps any other of its time. To this day it has remained, for the most part, unconvincingly treated by the procedures of criticism but passionately accepted by readers and poets. A single theme is threaded across much of the critical literature, however, and largely accounts for the incomprehensions of some readers, the pleasures of many others, and the exertions of still others who would claim Whitman as an honorary first modernist. If the *Preparatory Meditations* is the antitype of a prior devotional series founded on post-Petrarchism and the imperatives of lyric fiction, *Leaves of Grass* of 1855 dispels the eschatology of genre with which Taylor's work is heavily invested, and achieves the rebirth of that ritual poetics. In its own mode, Whitman's sequence approximates the *Canzoniere*, a beginning, a master-text of lyric's possibilities that authorizes certain of these while deferring or subduing others; and its reception bears out the analogy, for *Leaves of Grass* is commonly taken by its latter-day expositors as a vital codification of generic potential, imitable but unanswerable.[49] Naturally Whitman's sequence is indispensable to those poets, like Allen Ginsberg and Galway Kinnell, who consciously identify with an experimental tradition begun in *Leaves of Grass*. But its position is quite as important, though far more ambiguous, for those works that belong to the other phenomenological inheritance. From the standpoint of the lyric sequence, the story of modernism tells of a ritual mode coming to new life in the Americas while the fictional sequence breaks apart its nominative cast to admit fresh realizations. With the emergence of what I have called artifactuality, lyric fiction swerves to anticipate or accommodate a ritual poetics; and the work of an authentic innovator such as Whitman, the Petrarch of his mode, poses some definitive questions of genre and ideology for modern and postmodern contemporaries. Reading *Leaves of Grass* for its generic dispensation, one can perhaps see something of the divided inheritances of recent poetry, an unusually broad-scaled and immediate reflection of the divisions in lyric itself.

Whitman shares Ann Lok's and Edward Taylor's notion of the lyric series as procedure rather than world, as "a passage way to something rather than a thing in itself concluded."[50] As Charles Feidelson has it in a classic account, a typical poem of Whitman's,

> instead of referring to a completed act of perception, constitutes the act itself, both in the author and in the reader; instead of describing reality, a poem is a realization. When Whitman writes, "See, steamers steaming through my poems," he is admonishing both himself and his audience that no distinction can be made between themselves, the steamers, and the words. Indeed, no distinction can be made between the poet and the reader: "It is you talking just as much as myself, I act as the tongue of you." His new method was predicated not only on the sense of creative vision—itself a process which renders a world in process—but also, as part and parcel of that consciousness, in the sense of creative speech. The "I" of Whitman's poems speaks the world that he sees, and sees the world that he speaks, and does this by *becoming* the reality of his vision and of his words, in which the reader also participates. Most of Whitman's poems, more or less explicitly, are "voyages" in this metaphysical sense.[51]

In this lyric program, of course, the temporal remove between the speaker and his auditors is dissolved: they inhabit a common present tense, and share a participation in the act of the utterance. The series offers an open history without pasts and futures to impede the movement of speaker or reader. The tension around the issue of temporality in such a poem is not the Petrarchan dread of instants that slip past one's grasp, of a disappearing history, but an electric sense of time's openness and availability. Contemporaneous and concomitant with the speaker, we can go anywhere and see anything with him: where next?

Whitman's production is distinct from that of Taylor and other forerunners owing to the thoroughness of his reconception. Unlike Taylor's annulment in general of a mode honored by many of his lyrics in particular, *Leaves of Grass* works remorselessly. Perhaps for the first time since Petrarch, the form's founding poetics is suspended and replaced with an entirely reimagined phenomenology. The events and states of the poems are not, and cannot be, transposed between our reading and our recollection in the way that the accumulation of elements in the *Canzoniere* amounts to years of suffering; we cannot measure the speaker of *Leaves* by the ironic means of characterization that Sidney, Du Bellay, and other fictional poets exercise. In fact, it should imply the radical conception of the 1855 book when one notices that there is not an ironic word or event in the whole of the series, for the form itself was originated in and compounded by ironies large and small, and has always depended on the reader's powers of observation and combination, even in the constitution of whole works out of discrete and perhaps fragmentary parts. What lack of *variatio* is in Taylor's *Meditations*, lack of irony is in *Leaves*: an index of fictional values refused. Instead of a distillation, an equation, a way of putting things, *Leaves of Grass* is literally our own experience.

It seems to be a nominative sequence. As Whitman's friend Richard Maurice Bucke declared, the diachronic *Leaves of Grass* from 1855 to the Deathbed Edition "is a gigantic massive autobiography, the first of its kind," and through several editions its major poem was titled simply "Walt Whitman."[52] But nearly every example of nominativity I have surveyed so far occurs in the fictional mode, and *Leaves of Grass* is emphatically a ritual series. Still, how else to read lines such as these that open the book,

> I celebrate myself,
> And what I assume you shall assume,
> For every atom belonging to me as good belongs to you,
>
> (1855 ["Song of Myself"], 1–3)[53]

or these scattered (*sparse*) through the first poem, telling of viewpoint and values:

> What is commonest and cheapest and nearest and easiest is Me,
> Me going in for my chances, spending for vast returns,
> Adorning myself to bestow myself on the first that will take me,
> Not asking the sky to come down to my goodwill,
> Scattering it freely forever.
>
> (252–56)

> What is a man anyhow? What am I? and what are you?
> All I mark as my own you shall offset it with your own,
> Else it were time lost listening to me.
>
> (390–92)

> Mine is no callous shell,
> I have instant conductors all over me whether I pass or stop,
> They seize every object and lead it harmlessly through me.
>
> (613–15)

> I know perfectly well my own egotism,
> And know my omnivorous words, and cannot say any less,
> And would fetch you whoever you are flush with myself.
>
>   (1079–81)

It might be said that *Leaves of Grass* mimics the nominative series—almost parodies it—by speaking outright of what happens in the temporal and characterological processes of fictions. It lays open the cognitive events that are elsewhere screened by ironies, that are the substance of plots, that are rarely named or described. In a late note on the sequence, Whitman reminds his readership unnecessarily that "the main part about pronounc'd events and shows, (poems and persons also,) is the point of view from which they are view'd and estimated."[54] He seldom stints this sense of control from the first lyrics in the original volume, where the speaker's disposition of his surroundings is made literal:

> The little one sleeps in its cradle,
> I lift the gauze and look a long time, and silently brush away
>   flies with my hand.
>
> The youngster and the redfaced girl turn aside up the bushy hill,
> I peeringly view them from the top.
>
> The suicide sprawls on the bloody floor of the bedroom,
> It is so. . . . I witnessed the corpse. . . . there the pistol had fallen.
> · ·
> The big doors of the country-barn stand open and ready,
> The dried grass of the harvest-time loads the slow-drawn wagon,
> The clear light plays on the brown gray and green intertinged,
> The armfuls are packed to the sagging mow:
> I am there. . . . I help. . . . I came stretched atop of the load,
> I felt its soft jolts. . . . one leg reclined on the other,
> I jump from the crossbeams, and seize the clover and timothy,
> And roll head over heels, and tangle my hair full of wisps.
>
>   (1855 ["Song of Myself"], 140–45, 160–67)

The first lines of the opening poem, titled "Leaves of Grass" in 1855 but later called "Song of Myself," explicitly state the humanist assumption that the relations of text and reader ought to be understood as a commerce between individual subjects. Other passages admit the idea that the assembling of a "self" is the poem's sole project, and that the elements of lyric are organized toward it ("[I] accrue what I hear into myself . . . . and let sounds contribute toward me," 584–85). A famous burst near the end of the poem identifies a cardinal principle of fictional self-making,

Do I contradict myself?
Very well then . . . . I contradict myself;
I am large . . . . I contain multitudes,

(1314–16)

which is both more germane, and far less directly acknowledged, in the lyric fictions of character from the *Canzoniere* to the contemporaneous *In Memoriam*. Extravagantly, Whitman flattens or even caricatures the means and purposes of the nominative sequence: whatever happens elsewhere gradually or implicitly or as the end of a process, he renders as though it occurs to everyone, between everyone, all at once. Whatever passes in fiction between a lover and a beloved, he makes happen between himself and himself. Where temporality is charged with difficulty or mystery, he moves in decisively to defuse it, insisting that everything in the poem happens now—and that "I am the clock myself" (852). Whatever is hoarded and organized in post-Petrarchism, he scatters "freely forever."

In another classic treatment of "Song of Myself," Roy Harvey Pearce has written that

> the Whitman of *Song of Myself* surveys his whole world, his milieu and ambiance—but not according to any necessary order or chronology. He looks when he wills and interprets as he wills. There is a movement here, but not a form. It is essential to the meaning of the poem that the movement be unique; for the movement derives from the motion of the protagonist's sensibility. What is relatively stable and fixed, because it has no end and no beginning, is the world of which that sensibility becomes conscious, the world in and through which that sensibility discovers itself. The world is too large, too much, to have an imitable order or pattern. It is just there. The hero's hope in *Song of Myself*, his "altogether . . . moral and political" object, is to know that the world is there, and in the knowing, to know that *he* is there. In effect, through such a transaction he would create himself, only then to "find" himself: to discover, as though for the first time, that he exists and is free—at once, in the words of the opening inscriptive poem of *Leaves of Grass*, "a simple separate person" and "En-Masse."[55]

Thus Whitman literally revises the poetics of the fictional mode ("what I assume you shall assume") into that of lyric ritual ("I act as the tongue of you"), and his sequence announces its own new beginning out of remnants of the old order. Like Queen Victoria revising *In Memoriam* to suit her own grief, he cuts, shapes, and adapts the received text of nominativity to create a new poem—and in his case, a new poetics as well.[56] For much of its substance—its Emersonian Platonism and Indian mysticism as well as its accounts of what poems like itself do—*Leaves of Grass* transliterates some very old dicta into a single modern idiom, and holds everything together not by any consistency of the materials themselves, but by the evenness of Whitman's effort at constructing a large-scale revelation in lyric discourse.

Inevitably, there are traces of Petrarch's practice in *Leaves of Grass*, and Whitman dutifully listed the poet of the *Canzoniere* among his readings.[57] First, *Leaves* is a calendrical work, though the exact terms of that structure are often disputed by its readers. Its main lyric contains fifty-two "chants," which are first made explicit in the 1867 edition; soon after he began revising the volume, Whitman envisioned a *Leaves of Grass* ordered into 365 chapters, "one to be read on each day of the year."[58] Lightly (some say arbitrarily) asserted, this calendrical pattern has nothing to play against in the experience of the poem: where the calendar of the *Canzoniere* writes large the ritual dimension of that series, Whitman's implicit weeks are cognate with the ruling conception of his sequence. Still, they suggest that Whitman's reinvention of the sequence has the scope of Petrarch's. It is feasible to think, however, that other ostensibly Petrarchan elements in *Leaves of Grass* have more to do with certain variable strategies and preoccupations of the generic sequence—something, that is, that Whitman might have inherited through the form itself—than with any direct influence from the *Canzoniere*:

> Alone far in the wilds and mountains I hunt,
> Wandering amazed at my own lightness and glee,
> In the late afternoon choosing a safe spot to pass the night,
> Kindling a fire and broiling the freshkilled game,
> Soundly falling asleep on the gathered leaves, with my dog and
>   gun by my side.
>
> (1855 ["Song of Myself"], 168–72)

It is difficult not to imagine that the speaker is amazed because his high spirits are unfamiliar to the hunt motif, because he and the entire sequence are awakening astonished in America from a long generic nightmare begun in lyrics such as *Canzoniere* 23 and 36 or Shakespeare's Sonnet 129. The hunt convention has always been important to the nominative series because, among other reasons, it frames and isolates the speaker's state of mind in an artificially depopulated landscape; we are able to interpret his or her responses to a virtually Gothic exposure to power and danger in extremes. Here the danger of the Petrarchan hunt—that the female object will turn his latent power back on him, as in the Actaeon myth retold by Petrarch—is entirely vitiated, for the speaker is his own object, his hunt already over as he sets out with his dog. Further, Whitman makes much of the bivouac in *Leaves of Grass* because it is to his poetry what the term *stanza* is to the poetry of another time, namely an architectural metaphor for the values associated with the regnant lyric forms. He will not "build in sonnets pretty rooms" and live in them, like Donne, but will carry his quarters on his back wherever impulse leads him. The blason survives here too—as in the entangled bodies of "The Sleepers," or the bodily parts catalogued in the original "I Sing the Body Electric" and much amplified in 1892—though it has surrendered to the chaos of enumeration, a new sensation that the entire world could be swept in and counted by the poem's seemingly unlimited scrutiny.[59] Whitman's occasional Petrarchisms, far from compromising his original conception, serve mostly to affirm the continuity of the form and to affiliate the two poets as major innovators of it.

As Pearce indicates, it is much more common for *Leaves of Grass* to depart from evidently Petrarchan designs to find fresh ways of self-definition. Whitman explicitly scatters the tensions of the Petrarchan retrospective topos, for example, to create a work that does not continually define its present moment against a differently colored past and future:

> There was never any more inception than there is now,
> Nor any more youth or age than there is now;
> And will never be any more perfection than there is now,
> Nor any more heaven or hell than there is now.
> (1855 ["Song of Myself"], 32–35)

> The past and present wilt . . . . I have filled them and emptied them,
> And proceed to fill my next fold of the future.
> (1309–10)

Here "there was never any more" means not that the present instant is fuller of the qualities and states mentioned, but that the past and present belong to an additive continuum in which all history dwells in the present instant and all instants are one and the same. Throughout *Leaves of Grass*, Whitman insistently spatializes time—urging us to see, as in "Kosmos" (1860), "the past, the future, dwelling there, like space, inseparable together"—and heightens the work's orientation toward the speaker's self, his will, and his imaginings.[60] A speaker who participates in every phase of time, to whom no date is closed, gains a significant measure of power for making the work in his self-image. He inhabits all moments, and all culminate in him; his first lyric of his series is not a proem but perhaps a protopoem, not introducing the rest of the series, but sharing its substance; he gathers in not the post-Petrarchan speaker's capacity for arranging and interpreting the past, but a new, literal warrant ("my going up and down amidst these years") for reliving it as well.

Where lyric's ritual dimension is under the domination of fiction in the

Canzoniere, the sensation of the present moment's identity with the past is principally available to the reader through such unspoken patterns as the calendrical structure and a number of ironic scriptural echoes, beginning with the title *Rerum vulgarium fragmenta* and its allusion to John 6:12, Christ's injunction to "gather up the fragments that remain, that nothing be lost." It cannot be dramatically evident to the speaker that his years of profane love enclose a calendar of all the history between the birth and passion of Christ; nor can he understand how much his unconscious scriptural allusions mock his immediate condition. Instead he lives and suffers with only an occasional attention to his entrance into eternity.

> Io penso: se là suso,
> onde 'l motor eterno de le stelle
> degnò mostrar del suo lavoro in terra,
> son l'altr'opre sí belle,
> aprasi la pregione, ov'io son chiuso,
> et che 'l camino a tal vita mi serra.
> Poi mi rivolgo a la mia usata guerra.

(I think: if up there, whence the eternal Mover of the stars deigned to show forth this work on earth, the other works are as beautiful, let the prison open in which I am closed and which locks me from the way to such a life. Then I turn myself again to my usual war.)

(72.16–22)

Often the Petrarchan speaker's utterances proceed ironically through the fixed structures and allusions that enclose them:

> Sí come eterna vita è veder Dio,
> né piú si brama, né bramar piú lice,
> cosí me, donna, il voi veder, felice
> fa in questo breve et fraile viver mio.

(As it is eternal life to see God, nor can one desire more, nor is it right to desire more, so, Lady, seeing you makes me happy in this short and frail life of mine.)

(191.1–4)

As time passes he becomes more concerned about the state of his soul, and toward the end of the *Canzoniere* he reaches toward eternity blindly and eagerly:

> Tennemi Amor anni ventuno ardendo,
> lieto nel foco, et nel duol pien di speme;
> poi che madonna e 'l mio cor seco inseme
> saliro al ciel, dieci altri anni piangendo.

Omai son stanco, et mia vita reprendo
di tanto error che di vertute il seme
à quasi spento, et le mie parti extreme,
alto Dio, a te devotamente rendo:

pentito et tristo de' miei sí spesi anni,
che spender si deveano in miglior uso,
in cercar pace et in fuggir affanni.

Signor che 'n questo carcer m'ài rinchiuso,
tràmene, salvo da li eterni danni,
ch'i' conosco 'l mio fallo, et non lo scuso.

(Love held me twenty-one years gladly burning in the fire and full of hope amid sorrow; since my lady, and my heart with her, rose to Heaven, ten more years of weeping.

Now I am weary and I reproach my life for so much error, which has almost extinguished the seed of virtue; and I devoutly render my last parts, high God, to You,

repentant and sorrowing for my years spent thus, which ought to have been better used, in seeking peace and fleeing troubles.

Lord who have enclosed me in this prison: draw me from it safe from eternal harm, for I recognize my fault and I do not excuse it.)

(364)

The temporal irony exists in the fact that the speaker cannot understand how near eternity has been all along. His salvation, the contingency that God will gather up these fragments lest they perish, has been dramatized implicitly through 366 lyrics; eternity is visible, if not quite obtainable, in the structure that suspends every one of these. In fact, much of the emotional force of the *Canzoniere* and its fictional epigones is predicated on the inaccessibility of temporal dimensions, whether everlasting or merely aorist, to a speaker who earnestly wishes to escape the present: Fulke Greville describes the ironic blindness of the Petrarchan existence as a riddle that,

till the vayles be rent, the flesh newborne,
Reveales no wonders of that inward blisse,
Which but where faith is, every where findes scorne;
Who therfore censures God with fleshly sprite,
As well in time may wrap up infinite.[61]

Whitman's signal innovation in the matter of temporality is to disengage this element of his sequence from the post-Petrarchan aesthetic of tensions, limitations, and continuities. His speaker knows as much at any instant of the poem as at any other; his self-awareness is revealed in spontaneous bursts without much apparent relation to the poetic forms involved (neither their order nor their internal or external patterns), without moral or psychological change, and with little need for reversals or climaxes. Though he makes explicit use of the present tense throughout his lyrics, the speaker is usually careful to show that it is scarcely different in any way from every other time of his history; what may seem to be climactic events often fall away under these stipulations.

> Space and Time! now I see it is true, what I guess'd at,
> What I guess'd when I loaf'd on the grass,
> What I guess'd while I lay alone in my bed,
> And again as I walk'd the beach under the paling stars of the morning.
>
> (1892 "Song of Myself," 710–13)

This speaker's liberation in time introduces certain dangers unknown to the Petrarchan fiction, dangers involved in the deliberate, innovative distance between the speaker's and the reader's experience. As solitary readers of fiction, we can inhabit only one poetic moment at a time, and the post-Petrarchan series struggles to exploit this condition: such is the fundamental purpose of the retrospective topos, for instance, and of every other lyric strategy that promotes an identity between the speaker's stranding in time and our own. We live as readers much as these speakers do as lovers, advancing through a process in which retrospection and anticipation are distinct activities and in which the present instant has a set of movable but distinct boundaries—this minute, this hour, this day—and a fullness of its own. Further, our reading lives comprehend an even more concretely shaped and limited present than our empirical lives, since in the former we mark the exchange of one instant for another in the accumulation of words, verses, and lyrics, while in life we have nothing so precise and unvarying to fill each moment except the heartbeats of which we are mostly unaware. Literature in general is well adapted— and the post-Petrarchan lyric sequence, in particular, exquisitely adapted—to embodying this one practically inescapable way of thinking about time, to showing the serial quality of our lives in its quintessential structure.

Literary works have, however, few ways of recreating eternity in our reading experience. In lyric, only the ritual dimension—with its properties of synchrony and collectivity, its suspension of the poem until performance—seems to promise an escape from quotidian patterns of reading and living, a free passage into, through, and from the poem. A poet such as Whitman who aims to summon a version of eternity through lyric's ritual means will reach for an approximation of Eliade's "sacred time," a

continuous present that is "indefinitely recoverable" and "indefinitely repeatable," a history identical to its telling: "always equal to itself, it neither changes nor is exhausted."[62] Such a poet must manage the appropriation of lyric's ritual dimension not allusively or ironically as Petrarch
does, but fully and directly. He will also traffic in incomprehension or
disappointment, as the usual naturalizations fail to cohere and his audience must adjust its readings—and even stretch its notions of what lyric
may do and be.

   That adjustment, when or if it comes (and for some Petrarchist readers,
insistent on a naturalized fiction, it never does), is neither an anticipation
from prior generic experience nor a habituated response to the beginnings
of a rite. It simply happens over the time of each reader's reading, as the
series unconcernedly fails to give us the experience of fiction but always
asserts its own phenomenal integrity; Whitman allows that crossing,
from (presumed) mode to (actual) mode, to happen at the reader's own
rate, within the inviolable mutual reaction of reader, text, and empirical
world. *Leaves of Grass* beats one's expectations down. As the technology
of criticism loses its object (for no series resists close reading as bravely as
this one does), as we hear an unfamiliar tone, as we, at first insensibly,
perceive ritual instead of representational process in "Song of Myself,"
we come to understand that the poetics of the lyric sequence has been
thoroughly reconceived, and to read accordingly. We even hear the
speaker, near the outset of the capital lyric, telling us what is at stake in
our understanding of this highly original text:

> Have you reckoned a thousand acres much? Have you reckoned the earth
>   much?
> Have you practiced so long to learn to read?
> Have you felt so proud to get at the meaning of poems?
>
> Stop this day and night with me and you shall possess the origin of all poems,
> You shall possess the good of the earth and sun . . . . there are millions of suns
>   left,
> You shall no longer take things at second or third hand . . . . nor look through
>   the eyes of the dead . . . . nor feed on the spectres in books,
> You shall not look through my eyes either, nor take things from me,
> You shall listen to all sides and filter them from yourself.
>
>   (1855 ["Song of Myself"], 22–29)

It is appropriate for the speaker to address his audience so directly because Whitman is testing his readership's capacities just as directly, inviting us to assimilate this sort of lyric production as we can and will. Because his introduction of the work's nature is gradual, the Petrarchist
response sketched above—the frustrated sense that the speaker's eternity

is irrelevant and unavailable to our experience—belongs to everyone at some stage of acquaintance with the sequence; because the work continues so long, and sustains its aesthetic unevenly, we probably fall back into that state of judgment again at various points. What matters mainly is that our expectation of a post-Petrarchan fiction come loose somehow and somewhere in *Leaves of Grass*, that we accept (even if we do not always maintain) the principle that animates the series, the lyric alternative that Whitman creates and celebrates.

> I laugh at what you call dissolution,
> And I know the amplitude of time.
>
> (420–21)

As one defines the generic achievement of *Leaves of Grass*, however, it becomes necessary to concede the differences between the many versions of the work, and to distribute one's judgment among them. The first edition enacts this program of ritual self-making consistently and impressively. As most students of Whitman know, the version of the series published in 1855 lacks many of the features that often identify a completed body of poems, and instead carries the signs of immediate, limitless process, in effect of sacred time. The name of the poet is not affixed to the title page but occurs more or less randomly in the main lyric ("Walt Whitman, an American, one of the roughs, a kosmos" (1855 ["Song of Myself"], 499). Further, the lyrics are undifferentiated from each other by titles or other marks of finishing. Six times the start of a new and autonomous lyric is accompanied by the reappearance of the title of the entire work—*Leaves of Grass*, again and again—as though to affirm that the sequence begins here once more, that the whole work is reconceived as often as the speaker starts out on a new utterance. Then as though tired of making that point, Whitman eventually leaves off titles altogether: the lyrics that were later to be called "Who Learns My Lesson Complete?" and "Europe, the 72d and 73d Years of These States" appear for the first time as abrupt, untitled utterances at the end of the 1855 edition. (The volume's only experiment with what might be considered a lyric tilted toward the fictional mode is the hair-raisingly awful "Boston Ballad.") Not only in its explicitly ritual discourse but in almost every element of its design, the original version of *Leaves of Grass* is one of the clearest and most daring approximations of a temporally unsealed act of poetry, probably the most striking and ambitious example in the language before the twentieth century.

The further editions from 1855, however, which Whitman came to see as steps to the fulfillment of *Leaves*, regularly undermine this achievement of openness in self-making.[63] In the second edition of 1856, each of the poems has acquired a title that, at least potentially, sets allegorical cues around it: the poem that was to become "Song of Myself" is here numbered and called "1—Poem of Walt Whitman, an American," and the future "Crossing Brooklyn Ferry" is introduced as "11—Sun-Down Poem." With its revisions, which eventually produce a considerable number of discrete utterances and junctures, *Leaves of Grass* is no longer consubstantial with each piece at once, but is the sum of subordinated parts, of carefully described and delimited "poems." In 1860 the work is segmented into titled sections—some of the now-familiar names are "Calamus" and "Enfans D'Adam," as well as "Crossing Brooklyn Ferry"—and numbered subsections after biblical fashion. And like a divine ritual turned to scripture and further hardened with continual redactions, Whitman's evolving series moves decidedly toward becoming "a completed act of perception."

As an example of the revisions toward fiction that appear after 1855— or as Paul Zweig acutely sees it, "the conservative impulse that would coax [Whitman] back toward 'literature' as the years passed"[64]—consider the deliberate intrusions of second voices into the speaker's discourse. It belongs to everything in Whitman's ideology—to his vision of politics, of science, of poetry—that a single poet-speaker should stand entirely for his time and place: one of the original sites of this idea is the 1855 "Song of the Answerer," in which what begins as a dramatic situation ("A young man came to me with a message from his brother") is overwhelmed by the stacking of "signs" that affirm the poet's identity as ritual speaker of, for, and through others.[65] The idea can only be treated ritually: fictionally, where it would have to be explained in view of the speaker's dramatized relations with others over time, it makes no sense. (Conversely, the suffering lover of European post-Petrarchan poetry could never be realized in a thoroughgoing ritual series like *Leaves of Grass*: we are witnessing the near-exclusive bonds between certain lyric stances and the phenomenal conditions under which they are created.) Nonetheless, the successive versions of *Leaves* tend to struggle toward allegorizing versions of Whitman's self-centering. Proposing situations and introducing characters, they counterpose voices against that of the speaker in order to demonstrate (rather than simply declare) the centrality of his perspective.

Certainly the most successful instance of this revisionary strategy is "Out of the Cradle Endlessly Rocking" (1860), where the intercalation of the birds' voices contributes to that speaker's self-making, to "the destiny of me" (1860.157). Whitman's notes for the perfunctory "Song of the Redwood-Tree" (1876) look back to the earlier poem and stipulate what must be done again: "The spinal idea of the poem I (the tree) have fill'd my time and fill'd it grandly All is prepared for you—my termination comes prophecy a great race—great as the mountains and the trees Intersperse with *italic* (first person speaking) the same as in 'Out of the Cradle endlessly rocking.' "[66] Actually, "Out of the Cradle" recapitulates the changes over the editions of *Leaves of Grass*. The speaker, a "chanter" and "uniter of here and hereafter," learns at second hand of death and the past tense. But if the ritual mode promises anything, it is not second-hand, but firsthand knowledge translated and reexperienced by its auditors. At the close, the speaker anticipates a fusion of songs: one is the birds' original mode, "singing all time, minding no time," while the other might utter "the cries of unsatisfied love" or tell of "death, death, death, death, death"—a lyric, in other words, with the sense of an ending. With its hypothetical fusion of ritual and fictional modes and its interplay of voices, "Out of the Cradle" comes to serve Whitman as both pattern and prophecy of his revisionary poetics. Each of the six major editions of *Leaves of Grass* probably has a lyric or two that summarize its ambitions, apart from the lyrics that simply carry them out. What "Song of the Answerer" is to the poetics of 1855—a statement of program, perhaps an irrefutable demonstration of a particular mode's power—"Out of the Cradle" becomes to 1860 and the era of Whitman's fictional revisions.

However, its success is anomalous. A more typical example of Whitman's handling of plural voices is the graceless turn in "The Centenarian's Story" (1865) where the original speaker takes over from the voice of the Revolutionary War veteran:

> Enough—the Centenarian's story ends;
> The two, the past and present, have interchanged;
> I myself, as connecter, as chansonnier of a great future, am now speaking.
>
> (1865.94–96)

In a sense, the surprising word *chansonnier* tells everything here, as the word *romanza* does when it is permanently added to the first line of the "Answerer" in 1867. The poet's notion of the series has turned Petrarchan according to the broad understanding of that term; around an original core of ritual lyrics he disposes the poems of a lifetime, recording the phases of psychic history and building a person-representation, Walt Whitman, much as earlier poets had developed their fictions of named speakers. Finally, what is left of the sequence's native orientation toward a ritual poetics is that transversal between modes that allows an empirical and public person, Whitman, to stride out of the poems: with the same short circuit of 1855 that condensed a humanist poetics and fashioned perhaps the most explicit nominative text of all time, Whitman sets himself at the center of *Leaves of Grass* and, even through countless revisions, never leaves that place. Like a city erected over the ruins of another, or over many, the so-called Deathbed version of *Leaves* adopted in many modern editions invites its readers to an archaeological dig where the lyric phenomena so often found in alternation with each other are now literally stratified, in textual matter, part against counterpart.

As we step across the walls that divide one mode from another, we are obliged to notice the incident that tells most about the creeping, reformatory post-Petrarchism of *Leaves of Grass*: its antiproem, the closing lyric called "So Long!" (1860). In later life Whitman experimented with proems that might introduce the sequence from a retrospective standpoint like that of the post-Petrarchans: such otherwise negligible lyrics as "Small the Theme of My Chant" (1867) and "One's-Self I Sing" (1871) were devised, obviously, to satisfy this impulse. But Whitman's closural motions are even more strenuous, and together their aim seems to be twofold. He wants to reiterate the original conception of *Leaves* as open process, as a sheer script for an identifying reader who goes "realizing my poems" ("Full of Life Now" [1860], 6), but above that he appears eager to ensure that all readers understand the speaker's life within a set of definite, closed terms—to see that a lifetime of self-making does not go wasted by a ritual poetics that, at the last, Whitman does not greatly trust. (In "As the Time Draws Nigh" he exclaims: "O book, O chants! must all then amount to but this?" [1881.6].) As much as the 1855 text exploited ritual means but borrowed and inflected a fictional account of itself, the later versions are found to mouth their ritual convictions while insisting that we leave having assembled a coherent person and a certain sensemaking of the lyrics. This is the preoccupation that makes so many of the later poems seem to go over the ground of the original texts, but less convincingly; this makes the innumerable situations and details that fill the last volumes a largely unnecessary rehash of the basic idea, though in a new mode. Thus in "So Long!":

I have press'd through in my own right,
I have sung the body and the soul, war and peace have I sung, and the songs of
 life and death,
And the songs of birth, and shown that there are many births.

. . . .

Hasten throat and sound your last,
Salute me—salute the days once more. Peal the old cry once more.

. . . .

What is there more, that I lag and pause and crouch extended with unshut
 mouth?
Is there a single final farewell?

My songs cease, I abandon them,
From behind the screen where I hid I advance personally solely to you.

Camerado, this is no book,
Who touches this touches a man,
(Is it night? are we here together alone?)
It is I you hold and who holds you,
I spring from the pages into your arms—decease calls me forth.

                                        (1881.9–11, 34–35, 49–57)

The thought that animates Whitman's almost desperate efforts to make *Leaves of Grass* "a completed act of perception"—though one that openly professes to be otherwise—is the same that forced change on his speaker in "Out of the Cradle": death, death, death, death, death. The more he anticipates his end, the more (like Petrarch) he announces that his long years are drawing to a close, the more the sequence enters the province of fiction, "an organization that humanizes time by giving it a form."[67] "So Long!" appears as an antiproem, claiming to "announce what comes after me," but it is actually Whitman's pronounced effort at registering a shape and intention for *Leaves of Grass*—a proem in reverse that conspicuously shows, by its late arrival and its position in the text, the fictional mode struggling to get in the last interpretive word over the relics of an earlier conception. Idiomatically, every American recognizes "so long" as meaning "goodbye," but here the phrase reverberates with a hard-won conviction of temporal extension, and of the speaker's tardiness in that process, that might have been Petrarch's. Whether or not the poet will admit it, he has come far from a time when he could say

> There was never any more inception than there is now,
> Nor any more youth or age than there is now.

If Whitman is the Petrarch of a newly ritual poetics, it is especially instructive to consider who his successors were—and are. Modernist poets of the Americas have innumerable discoverable antecedents, of course, and their critics rightly tend to emphasize the nearer of these—the symbolists, or the "antisymbolists," or the other contemporaneous European modernisms.[68] I choose to take the longer view and argue that, from a certain perspective, the American poets of the modern lyric sequence confront the divided identity and heritage of the form itself. A poet such as Ezra Pound, the exemplary maker of a twentieth-century long poem, descends from the *Canzoniere* in the sense that his namesake *Cantos* figures in the long story of the form's mutations and deformations as a species of fiction, and is perhaps generically determined—as what I call an artifactual sequence—by that history. Because the artifactual sequence convulses the aesthetic and ideological facts of its post-Petrarchan origins and opens such categories as time and voice to the reader's unmediated self-applications, it seems to anticipate and enable the type of interpretation common to ritual texts. In fact, we have several oblique and direct characterizations of *The Cantos* by Pound that seem to insist on this antinominative impulse ("this is not a work of fiction / nor yet of one man"),[69] and many theoretical and practical statements by him about poetry that argue for an irreducibly "ritual" element in the founding forms and modes of early modern poetics. The artifactual impulse represents, as I have said, a turning from fiction back toward ritual—the finding of a chink in the former, where the latter regains a foothold—that replicates the incessant alternations of single poems or collocations.

In the best recent book on *The Cantos*, Christine Froula describes the many senses in which Pound's project carries out literally ritual processes such as repetition, transport, and healing, and ends with a striking proposition: that the most important of these processes is error, in which Pound's actual mistakes in *The Cantos*, accidental or deliberate, open onto a condition of textual or semantic indeterminacy that sees poet, editors, and readers meet in collaboration, and in which the poem itself registers "such incursions of history into History, of actual experience into ideas about the world."[70] Froula concludes that "the authorial errors in the text of *The Cantos*, then, may be viewed as the 'foot-prints' of the unfinished and unfinishable wandering which Pound's epic discovers—against its author's initial hopes as well as its readers'—to be modern history, modern experience."[71] Radically incomplete, driven by error, and often literally open to its readers' exercises of participation and power, *The Cantos* is the exemplary artifactual text, perhaps even more so because its polemical bent involves appropriations and distortions of materials that once went into the making of humanist fictions. Like Whitman, Pound parodies and exposes these fictions in several ways: by making their conventions seem two-dimensional constructs, by installing an open reading process that shows by contrast how scripted and coercive the humanist engagement between selves can be, by making his sequence literally rather than figuratively coextensive with his *vita* ("Cantos won't be finished until my demise," Pound wrote in 1958, "shd always reserve possibility of death-bed swan").[72]

The encounter among Petrarch, Whitman, and the modernists, then, should be full of interest. Before I go on in the next chapter to show how the transition from nominativity to artifactuality is enacted in two particular fictions by Yeats, I would like to pause over a document of that encounter: Pound's early essay "What I Feel About Walt Whitman" (1909). As one might expect from my preceding sketch of poetic filiations, the essay is heavy with the language of "forebears" and "birthrights." Pound's attitude is that of a rightful heir who cannot quite fit this crude

but powerful presence, this "exceedingly nauseating pill," into the family
tree he has taught himself.[73] In the short course of the essay, however, he
offers one or two admissions that deserve some attention here, in a brief
Poundian digression that will close this chapter. First one hears the young
poet's frustration with the workings of a post-Petrarchan nominative poetics, a complex of lyric aesthetics and ideology that he traces to its distant cultural sources, and from which he, like Whitman, will struggle to
differentiate himself: "Entirely free from the renaissance humanist ideal
of the complete man or from the Greek idealism, [Whitman] is content to
be what he is, and he is his time and his people. He is a genius because he
has vision of what he is and of his function. He knows that he is a beginning and not a classically finished work." Pound then imagines the different relations he has to Whitman—historical, national, artistic—and
comes to admit each of these as inescapable.

And then appears the climactic passage of the essay, in which Pound
suddenly speaks through the factitious voice of his so far unmentioned
antecedent, a cry of anachronism:

> I am immortal even as [Whitman] is, yet with a lesser vitality as I am the
> more in love with beauty (If I really do love it more than he did). Like Dante
> he wrote in the "vulgar tongue," in a new metric. The first great man to write
> in the language of his people.
>
> *Et ego Petrarca in lingua vetera scribo*, and in a tongue my people under-
> stood not.
>
> It seems to me I should like to drive Whitman into the old world. I sledge,
> he drill—and to scourge America with all the old beauty.

However fleeting, this is an instructive admission. Superficially it echoes
Pound's early poem "Histrion" (1908), in which the speaker identifies
with poets Pound liked to claim, then and later, as models ("Thus am I
Dante for a space and am / One François Villon").[74] But the self-characterization veiled in mock-medieval Latin suggests a correspondence often
overlooked by Poundian critics who draw the poet's influences straight
from his own polemical testimony, or who ignore the literary politics of
his choices. Further, Pound's readers commonly confuse the poet's models with his affinities, a no less troublesome simplification of the matter
of influence. Pound's relations with Petrarch are striking in light of the
present argument, but perhaps need some small elucidation to bring them
out.[75]

As Stuart Y. McDougal has recently observed, "Pound attempts to pro-
mote a renaissance of English letters by defining a new tradition of lyric
poetry through his versions of the anonymous seafarer poet, the Provençal poet Arnaut Daniel, and Dante's contemporary, Guido Cavalcanti."
And like the vernacular revolution produced by these poets among oth-

ers, "a modern renaissance has to begin, Pound asserted, with the creation of a new tongue. . . . For each of these poets Pound strives to make a
new and different language. . . . He had trained himself with a rare self-
discipline to relive this medieval renaissance."[76] But situating himself by
analogy at a historical moment of vernacularity and generic dynamism,
and determining to build on the gains of poets such as Propertius, the
Provençals, and Dante, Pound sets himself all too deliberately—but still,
almost always implicitly—in the role of a Petrarch.[77] Moreover, his early
decision to write a long poem (perhaps as early as 1904, though he actually began writing in 1915) naturally put several poetic problems into
active consideration, and not the least Petrarchan of these was to learn to
use a historically sanctioned medium ("it took two centuries of Provence
and one of Tuscany to develop the media of Dante's masterwork") in a
way that transcends its moment—to achieve, as Kenner has it, "a lively
sense of forms asserting their immortality in successive material oppor-
tunities."[78] Hence the early years of Pound's career saw a number of self-
consciously anachronistic experiments with form, in collections such as
Personae (1909), *Provença* (1910) (which includes the section "Canzoniere, Studies in Form"), *Canzoni* (1911) (a "chronological table of emotions" which grew out of that section), *Hugh Selwyn Mauberley* (1920),
and of course *A Draft of XVI. Cantos* "for the Beginning of a Poem of
some Length now first made into a Book" (1925).[79] As much as he owed
intellectually to Dante and his other often-remarked sources, Pound was
obliged to find a cultural and generic prefiguration in Petrarch, a forerunner with strikingly modern problems; he reacted to the fact with a long
campaign of reduction and dismissal against his antitype, most often
treating "fat faced Frankie Petrarch" with extravagant disdain as a
merely and overly rhetorical poet ("Minor triumph, in 1932: I drove an
Italian critic, author of a seven volume history of Italian literature, to his
last ditch, whence he finally defended Petrarch on the sole ground that
'one occasionally likes a chocolate cream' ").[80] There is no reason to suppose that Pound did not really dislike his distant predecessor's style. But
his studied blindness in the critical writings to Petrarch's anticipation of
his own situation—including his generic discoveries, his classicism, his
adaptation of the Provençal *vidas* into more diffuse but substantial lyric
autobiography ("a cryselephantine poem of immeasurable length which
will occupy me for the next four decades unless it becomes a bore"), his
willfulness about starting a renaissance, and his particular dash of humanist pathos—suggests an intuition of correspondence deliberately
overwritten.[81] Therefore the *et ego Petrarca* of the Whitman essay is important as a concatenated admission: while confessing his uncomfortable
descent from one model, Whitman, he might as well do the same for his
notably coincidental situation with the other, Petrarch. In many ways

Pound stands between them, and his major sequence, *The Cantos*, will show their influences on his lyric project constantly and severely.

Thus the matter of his driving Whitman into the old world: in the generic sense, where ritual returns upon fiction in a continual process of renewal, this is exactly what Pound and his contemporaries will do.

NOMINATIVE TO ARTIFACTUAL: INTERVAL AND INNOVATION IN TWO SEQUENCES BY YEATS

THE JOB of describing modern innovations in the lyric sequence is a frustrating one because poets of the twentieth century have found innumerable ways to depart from the practice and assumptions of Petrarch and his successors past Tennyson—they have discovered so many ways to be modern, and then postmodern. In this chapter, I propose to examine the turn to a fresh program by an inveterate twentieth-century poet of sequences, William Butler Yeats. His twin series of the late 1920s, *A Man Young and Old* and *A Woman Young and Old*, live out both a profound debt to the essential facts of the post-Petrarchan sequence I have described, and an intense reaction to some of its now ossified means and conventions. In *A Man* and *A Woman Young and Old* taken as countertexts, Yeats confronts the problems that every recent writer working in this complex of genre and form must face: the problems, not his contingent solutions, will be most relevant to other works and careers. The most urgent such problem, as I see it, is to dismantle the conceits under which poems have been gathered, and their collective fictional mode constructed, from the fourteenth century through the modernisms. Each modern poet finds an attitude toward the received model of the Petrarchan breviary and, if like most contemporaries he or she largely rejects that model, reconceives such fictional values as temporality and character toward a fresh orientation, a new result. Yeats's tendency in *A Man Young and Old* is to shatter the calendrical conception of the lyric series by drastically rethinking the relations of particular poems to the times, states, and emotions they speak about: I call this net of relations the lyric interval, an implied distance between the poem's intelligence and the experience it gathers in.

A Woman Young and Old has been undervalued. In it, Yeats builds on the counter-Petrarchan example of the *Man* sequence while improving on its losses. The *Woman* series restores the proem that the pressures of the former work push out, varies its interval between intelligence and objects, and redefines the possibilities of sequential biography as a resource of lyric fiction. More important, the two works together repeat a general development that was then unfolding in European and American poetic culture during the 1920s—a movement away from the lyric sequence's

origins in an undivided speaking self, toward exogenous experience and
multivocal ways of divulging that experience. The turn away from lyric
nominativity, toward artifactuality, is a condition of primary import to
such modernist sequences as *The Waste Land*, César Vallejo's *Trilce*
(1922), William Carlos Williams's *Spring and All*, and Pound's *Cantos*;
it is a premise vital to remarking what such works choose, adapt, and
refuse of the Petrarchan inheritance.[1] The present value of Yeats's two
brief sequences of the 1920s is that they enact both nominativity and the
turn itself, indicating how the newer tendency depends on the model it
displaces. As specimens of modernist lyric fiction, then, they make a con-
spectus of the contemporary generic situation. In *A Man* and *A Woman
Young and Old*, Yeats plays the role of "the verifier" given by Apollinaire
to Braque: "[He] has verified all the innovations of modern art, and will
verify still others."[2] This essay reads the two series' common fiction, the
touches that qualify it, and the implications of Yeats's experiment for the
modern lyric sequence.

For readers steeped in the fictional values of Petrarch and his epigones
through the nineteenth century, *A Man Young and Old* figures some subtle but vital differences of aesthetic and attitude, starting in its first poem,
"First Love." Elementally, this lyric implies the obsolescence of proems—
not a pedantic, but a crucial revision:

> Though nurtured like the sailing moon
> In beauty's murderous brood,
> She walked awhile and blushed awhile
> And on my pathway stood
> Until I thought her body bore
> A heart of flesh and blood.
>
> But since I laid a hand thereon
> And found a heart of stone
> I have attempted many things
> And not a thing is done,
> For every hand is lunatic
> That travels on the moon.
>
> She smiled and that transfigured me
> And left me but a lout,
> Maundering here, and maundering there,
> Emptier of thought
> Than the heavenly circuit of its stars
> When the moon sails out.[3]

What are fictional proems for? A post-Petrarchan proem may enact a
moral distance from the succeeding poems' passion, segmenting the fic-

tion emotionally and spiritually: this is what the proem of the *Canzoniere* does. Some proems are not ripe commentaries on old passions as much as public explanations of their sequences' origins and natures: proems by Sidney (*Astrophil and Stella*) and Ronsard (*Second Livre des Amours* [1560]) are of this sort, the latter having been promoted from the epilogue of another series. But in every such case, the post-Petrarchan proem gives something to the fictional sequence that its constituent lyrics lack. It sets going a historical momentum that will sweep along the following poems, preventing the work's cold start and overcoming the inertia of its junctures. It throws a collective immediacy over the sequence, while the particular lyrics isolate and explore moments or episodes, inviolate or synthetic, from the lover's history. Even while it assures their unity and equality, however, the proem often breaks loose from the other poems, and seems—like Petrarch's proem, or Ronsard's "A son Livre"—more the first installment in a potential sequence than any part of the present one. The post-Petrarchan proem's work of framing, commenting, and equalizing is so fruitful that it should be no surprise to find poets who try to carry some version of it to distant settings: George Herbert's "Church-porch" makes an architectonic proem to his devotional *Temple*, and Louise Labé puts the first of her sonnets (1555) into Italian for little discernible reason other than to make it seem both more Petrarchan and more independent of the next twenty-three poems. We have already seen Whitman trying to introduce a fictional poetics retroactively into *Leaves of Grass* through a type of postproem.

But I am interested in observing what happens to the fictional sequence when a speaker such as Yeats's sets his intelligence at a further retreat from his experience than a Petrarch or a Labé does; when the fiction, specifically the implied relation between the told history and the present occasion of the utterance, is calibrated in a fresh way. What happens when the proem's potential distance and commentary are shared in some measure by every lyric, and nothing remains to be urgently framed or explained? As a general outcome, I think, it follows that the dimensions of a series such as *A Man Young and Old* contract sharply in length and scope, a comparative reticence displaces the post-Petrarchan exactitude of emotion—and in particular, the proem is forced out as superfluous. To inquire after the disappearance of the proem in *A Man Young and Old* is to ask a fundamental question about Yeats's reconstruction of the post-Petrarchan sequence, and to start to elucidate a theoretical feature of every poem and sequence, the lyric interval. It is as though Yeats's play with interval and its contractive result in *A Man Young and Old* represent a taming of the received amatory series—a radical, openly destructive admission to the form—that allows for the more settled improvisation of *A Woman Young and Old*. It is as though the post-Petrarchan standard must be shattered and cast out before the amatory, biographical sequence can be reconceived on a new model.

As I have shown, lyrics in the post-Petrarchan line are very often meticulous in their temporal specifications. Even when nothing like the deictic program of the *Canzoniere* is in place, such poets as Daniel, Spenser, and Tennyson commonly designate a lyric's component times with a deliberate, passionate clarity, and indicate the correspondence—which may break out, ritually, into the simultaneity—of a particular moment or episode and the utterance that records it.

> No Aprill can reuiue thy withred flowers,
> Whose blooming grace adornes thy glorie now:
> Swift speedy Time, feathred with flying howers,
> Dissolues the beautie of the fairest brow.
>   O let not then such riches waste in vaine;
>   But loue whilst that thou maist be lou'd againe.

> But love whilst that thou maist be lou'd againe,
> Now whilst thy May hath fill'd thy lappe with flowers;
> Now whilst thy beautie beares without a staine;
> Now vse thy Summer smiles ere winter lowres.

> This holy season fit to fast and pray,
>   Men to deuotion ought to be inclynd:
>   therefore, I lykewise on so holy day
>   for my sweet Saynt some seruice fit will find.

> To-night the winds begin to rise
>   And roar from yonder dropping day:
>   The last red leaf is whirl'd away,
> The rooks are blown about the skies.[4]

The accumulation of such poems often yields something like a lyric breviary: one, two, or three hundred poems that distribute the experience of the sequence as days apportion the history of a year. Each poem is a "moment's monument," for the sense of a clear *now* expressed or implied by deictics, and the small number of distinct events committed to each lyric, ensure that no single poem can represent much of the speaker's history. His or her emotions, each articulated by one subjective voice and tied to a clearly demarcated tense, have a certain immediacy but claim no representative force in single utterances: as I have argued in chapter 2, these feelings and the attributes they reveal must be made representative or collated, either by the testimony of what in the fiction's terms counts as an objective voice, or by the sheer accumulation of the poems. If an insensitive reader or anthologist were to ask whether *Astrophil and Stella* could not be condensed to ten or so of its best lyrics, there are several ways—for the sequence's several unities—to frame the inevitable "no." But the simplest of these answers, once we recognize it, is to say something like this: that the distance between a lyric speaker's intelligence and the times, emotions, and events he or she records—the lyric interval, as I call it—is set to different measures for different lyric fictions, and that the ruling interval in *Astrophil and Stella* needs about a hundred poems to gather, retell, and verify Astrophil's experience.

Lyric interval is reckoned in the accumulation of deictic elements scattered through a poem or sequence—temporal and personal inflections in nouns and verbs, spatial discriminations in adverbs and demonstratives, and so forth—and other indexes of recension, such as singular or plural objects that may particularize or conglomerate the speaker's vision, and rhythms that may imply immediacy or removal. Interval is seldom a fixed distance drawn between a lyric utterance and its objects; it often varies throughout the utterance. Local oscillations will tell much about how a poem works fictionally, and will entertain purposes shared with other types of nonlyric fiction, while shifts toward immediacy may figure an irruption of the ritual mode into fictional discourse. In a larger sense, interval represents the space in which lyric vacillates between its often-remarked affinity with music and its necessary pact with referentiality: as soon as the latter enters the poem, interval gains an opening and thereafter grows or contracts along a pattern that indicates where the poem stakes its place in the struggles of the genre to define itself. The reckoning of a poem's interval, even if carried out implicitly or instinctively, is vital to the relative assessment of ritual and fictional modes carried out in every act of interpretation.

Lyric interval somewhat resembles the idea of narrative distance that many readers, especially of nineteenth-century novels, have commonly recognized.[5] But interval in the lyric sequence can and does have a greater impact on the gross facts of a work than does distance in the novel. J. Hillis Miller, "taking 'form' as a term for the inner structuring principles of a work rather than for its external shape," demonstrates that the omniscient narrator in Victorian fiction is "a generative presupposition determining form and meaning";[6] but certainly narrative distance has a much less clear relation to a novel's identity within its genre than interval does to that of lyric. The fortunes of lyric interval over the course of a poem—modulations, for instance, of tense or person—are a dynamic part of that poem's fiction, and may entail a kind of plot of their own. On the other hand, narrative distance occupies a figurative "space" much more recessed than that of lyric interval: there are hardly any lyric speakers who invite us to "the other side of the looking glass,"[7] as Miller has it, where they admit their own artistry and talk about the passions and events of the work with a seemingly total detachment. Though lyric interval is a phenomenon more or less unexamined as such by poets and critics alike, its configurations can seize or banish immediacy, strengthen or deter affect, stabilize or deform the work at hand.

Though as an amatory sequence *A Man Young and Old* respects the outward facts of its fictional inheritance, "First Love," as I have mentioned, already shows some local marks of a counter-Petrarchan orientation to events. Its treatment of temporal relations appears vague and synthetic ("She walked awhile and blushed awhile"), as though purposely to obscure the lineaments of its history; and the speaker's conflation and concealment of times ("I have attempted many things") introduces a bent against confession that will determine much of this sequence's peculiar nature. We see these tendencies again in the lyric's last stanza, where Yeats combines and then abandons events that, to many post-Petrarchan poets, would seem crucial chapters in the lover's emotional history and geography.

> She smiled and that transfigured me
> And left me but a lout,
> Maundering here, and maundering there,
> Emptier of thought
> Than the heavenly circuit of the stars
> When the moon sails out.

In effect, Yeats accedes to the received conditions for lyric character, then veers deliberately away in details, declining to particularize his speaker.

Even the meter of "First Love," which represents that of the work at large, seems intended to glaze and planish the speaker's testimony in some deliberate way, to forestall immediacy. Consider for a moment the form Yeats does not use. With its changeable rhymes and easy maneuver of argument, the sonnet has always invited the post-Petrarchan stratification of tenses. Its formal concessions to imbalance—whether the octave and sestet of its Petrarchan version, or the Shakespearean sonnet's three quatrains and a couplet—is strophic, not stichic, and produces an asymmetry in the argument's shape without distorting the tone or rhythm of its component statements. As W. H. Auden remarks,

> considered in the abstract, as if they were Platonic Ideas, the Petrarchan sonnet seems to be a more esthetically satisfying form than the Shakespearean. Having only two different rhymes in the octave and two in the sestet, each is bound by rhyme into a closed unity, and the asymmetrical relation of 8 to 6 is pleasing. The Shakespearean form, on the other hand, with its seven dif-

ferent rhymes, almost inevitably becomes a lyric of three symmetrical quatrains, finished off with an epigrammatic couplet. As a rule Shakespeare
shapes his rhetorical argument in conformity with this, that is to say, there is
usually a major pause after the fourth, the eighth and the twelfth line.[8]

As a vessel for thought and history, the sonnet is amenable and achro-
matic. But the alternating tetrameter and trimeter of Yeats's sequence
largely prohibit temporal and psychic variation. They cast *A Man Young
and Old* as a chain of fairly monochromatic lyrics. Further, the associa-
tions of ballads and nursery rhymes that cling to the broken fourteener
make the emotional history in the sequence seem a sealed and hardened
thing, closed to confession and modulation. It may well be that the sonnet's symmetrical stichic structure and certain closure allow it to remain
impartial to tones and stands, to wed easily to any lyric attitude and make
that attitude seem more integral and convinced; and that the stichically
uneven and extensible forms like Yeats's fourteeners are the structural
analogue for such attitudes of imbalance as irony, hyperbole, and so on.
In any case, the meter of "First Love," in concurrence with the speaker's
inexpressiveness, imposes a rather wide interval on the poem and the sequence. Compare, for instance, Miller's corresponding observation of
narrative distance in *Oliver Twist*, where a "disproportion" between the
language that controls the fiction and the events to which that language
refers "maintains firmly the narrator's detachment from the events and
experiences he describes."[9] What may be a local effect for Dickens—ir-
respective of the speaker's exact identity or role in the novel, even less of
the novel's place in its genre—becomes something much more charged in
a lyric setting. Here it is, or is about to be, the means of a modern poet's
independence from an old and somewhat constraining program for lyric
fiction.

That impulse (for now, I will untechnically call it reticence)[10] is developed further in the second and third lyrics, "Human Dignity" and "The
Mermaid."

HUMAN DIGNITY
Like the moon her kindness is,
If kindness I may call
What has no comprehension in't,
But is the same for all
As though my sorrow were a scene
Upon a painted wall.

So like a bit of stone I lie
Under a broken tree.
I could recover if I shrieked

My heart's agony
To passing bird, but I am dumb
From human dignity.

THE MERMAID
A mermaid found a swimming lad,
Picked him for her own,
Pressed her body to his body,
Laughed; and plunging down
Forgot in cruel happiness
That even lovers drown.

"Human Dignity," in fact, names and justifies the sequence's confessional restraint. The lover protests the woman's aloofness, her self-absorbed ignorance of his real merits and purposes; deploring his own decomposed integrity, he says that expression might save him but he cannot manage it for pride. In protesting his removal from the woman's thoughts, of course, he merely repeats a familiar complaint of post-Petrarchan love poetry. But in his removal from the ears of "passing birds" and readers, he identifies, and only lamely explains, the peculiarity that will mark the *Man* sequence throughout, that shrinks its efficacy as much as its number of pieces. To the woman's broad personal removal from him, the speaker will answer with a wide lyric interval from the hard truths of his own condition, and so deliberately cut off the lyrics from an animating exactitude of tense and feeling. It is a requital he will "recover" from, one supposes, enough to stir our imagination and rescue the sequence. This lyric inertia and lassitude cannot last; we feel sure that he will come to hinder, not help, the woman's idea of him as blank and undifferentiated from others, that some version of the post-Petrarchan divide between the beloved's and the reader's opinions of the lover will start to open.[11]

Then, in the most ironic and revealing juncture of the series, we pass over to "The Mermaid," a lyric that presses the lover's emotional history into a still life—where the indefinite article *a* and the third-person narrative bleach out particularity and immediacy—or a scene "upon a painted wall." A calculated shock, the poem seems to reply instantly and contrarily to our expectations of his Petrarchan reform, and to validate (if not fully to adopt) the woman's diagrammatic notion of his condition. Here again is a recension that makes proems needless, and confirms that Yeats seeks a new program for the lyric sequence, a fresh aesthetic.

One wonders: does the poem treat the speaker's experience at all? Is there a speaker available to claim this utterance? When we read "The Mermaid" retrospectively in the context of the *Man* and *Woman* sequences, we might observe that besides the recalculated lyric interval,

Yeats's improvisations aim at securing a place for a special kind of analogy among lyric tropes: driving reticence to its natural limit, he tries now and then to turn the poems' intelligence entirely away from his protagonist, to render his history ambiguous and perhaps opaque by shielding it with that of another. There is no tenor to the analogy that is "The Mermaid," no discernible anchor in the lover's empirical history that the analogy will color or enliven. Nearly anything a reader can do with the poem is easier than bringing it into that history. One can treat it as interlude, or as chant, or carry it to other settings. Directing the work's main track through the analogy's vehicle, Yeats creates a structural blind much as if, say, Milton had given an entire book of *Paradise Lost* to a single epic simile and left the trope untied to the plot of the epic.[12]

"The Death of the Hare," the fourth lyric and a reconceived Petrarchan episode, marks the end of the speaker's juvenile phase.

> I have pointed out the yelling pack,
> The hare leap to the wood,
> And when I pass a compliment
> Rejoice as lover should
> At the drooping of an eye,
> At the mantling of the blood.
>
> Then suddenly my heart is wrung
> By her distracted air
> And I remember wildness lost
> And after, swept from there,
> Am set down standing in the wood
> At the death of the hare.

It is a sign of the sequence's advancing obscurity that even the flow of desire is indistinct in the first lines: is the speaker a hunter of the woman-hare, or is he her sentry against the hunt of others? And if the latter, has he abandoned his desire for her? The first quatrain throws off first a neutral and then a positive amatory charge, and lines 5 and 6 linger over his quiet joy so as to suggest that the speaker has ceased only to be an active hunter, not to be a lover. As in the preceding lyric, Yeats only partly dismantles a literary convention, and this an unequivocally Petrarchan one, to free his speaker from a role that would mean the poem's broaching of the man's feelings: the detached tenor of "The Mermaid" and the lover-spectator of this lyric are two specimens of the now-familiar impulse toward concealment. The tense structure of these first lines, such as the vague specification of the perfect ("I have pointed out the yelling pack") and the archaic and ambiguous shift toward a present ("the hare leap to

the wood"), produce more such instances. This is a distant, and now evidently a decided, lyric interval.

The expediency of the present perfect tense for introducing a wide lyric
interval is evident, I believe, in the linguist Geoffrey Leech's analysis of
that tense's "indefinite" reference: "by 'indefiniteness' here are meant two
things: first, the number of events is unspecified—it may be one or more
than one; secondly, the time is also left unspecified. Therefore to put it
more carefully, the meaning of the Present Perfect here is . . . 'at-least-
once-in-a-period-leading-up-to-the-present.' "[13] Instead of plunging into
a narrative of feeling as with the past (say, "I *pointed* out the yelling
pack") and deepening the engagement with a chain of further preterites,
the present perfect distracts its audience into an ineluctable search for the
time and number of the pertinent events. With the uncertainty it admits,
the present perfect inevitably loses some of the piquancy of feeling associated with the simple present and the past, settling instead for a softer
focus. It seems to be rarely used in lyric poetry, especially in English.[14]

The dismantling of the hunt conceit in "The Death of the Hare" exacts
some implications from which we can discern the courses of this poem
and of the amatory history that envelops and succeeds it. As I mentioned
in chapter 3, the Petrarchan lover's hunt offers a means of representing
precisely and dramatically a certain pattern in human affairs, with room
for ordering and coloring as individual circumstances may require. In
each of its historical phases, the lyric sequence has put a high practical
value on such patterns, their rapid demonstrations, their easy alterations
and reversals: in *Canzoniere* 6, for instance, the lover hunts his beloved
while in 209 he is hunted by Love, and the constant pattern over changed
roles obviously serves as a principle of both unity and complexity, a symbol of fate's die that molds lovers as it finds them, now and then, in
changed positions. Because its value lives in the pattern, the conceit cannot be imported only in part unless the poet aims to scatter and let slip
the energies it musters. If the woman is the hunted "hare" but the speaker
declines to play the hunter, then his love for her must be manifestly rede-
fined or lost to the poem. He cannot simply drop out of the conceit without changing his relation to the poem's terms of desire. And so he does
change in the lyrics after "The Death of the Hare," for the speaker will
love again only in memory, and his remembrances will harden into an
opinion of love colored by bitterness and cynical detachment. The lover's
disengagement here from the patterns of post-Petrarchan amatory experience is the bridgehead into the second part of *A Man Young and Old*,
where much that belongs to the Western amatory sequence is resisted and
finally transformed.

The second stanza of "The Death of the Hare" takes the work's furthest step away from Petrarchan means and attitudes, toward a radical

concealment. While many post-Petrarchan sequences are meticulously processive, the impulse of this sequence will tend sometimes to conflate events as in "First Love," sometimes to atomize them as here: the "suddenly" and "after" of this stanza are ironic indexes of a temporal discrimination that has been otherwise shut off, signs that point nowhere. The events they frame will not flow into one another, but are only the fragments of an inferential continuity that must proceed from the wringing of the lover's heart through the death of the hare. In its abstract implications, the atomizing here stands for the same condition in the speaker as does the abandonment of the hunt conceit in the foregoing stanza. They both suggest the speaker's growing habit of failing to connect means to ends, of falling away from the process that would see his objects realized. He cannot carry through the hunt but forfeits his role there to others, and is unable to retell the process that puts him finally "in the wood." The childish bent of incompleteness he remarked tremulously in the first lyric ("I have attempted many things / And not a thing is done"), and that stifled him so strangely in "Human Dignity" ("I could recover if I shrieked / . . . but I am dumb"), has become the pattern of his adventures in love, and its frank portrayal makes up the business of this pivotal fourth lyric. The lines between youth and age will be drawn here, where the speaker responds to his helplessness and missed connections by fairly dropping his ends: if he does not seek anything, he cannot fail to overtake and arrest it. And if the few ends he still fosters are incorporeal and already arrested, he need not enter any process of reclamation but will only meditate on them obsessively and inconclusively. He can look back on the failed chases in his past with detachment and disdain, and stand coolly entrenched until death.

A recollection of one of Petrarch's corresponding sonnets will suggest the shift in attitude achieved by Yeats, the interval widened:

Sí travïato è 'l folle mi'desio
a seguitar costei che 'n fuga è volta,
et de' lacci d'Amor leggiera et sciolta
vola dinanzi al lento correr mio,

che quanto richiamando piú l'envio
per la secura strada, men m'ascolta:
né mi vale spronarlo, o dargli volta,
ch'Amor per sua natura il fa restio.

Et poi che 'l fren per forza a sé raccoglie,
i' mi rimango in signoria di lui,
che mal mio grado a morte mi trasporta:

> sol per venir al lauro onde si coglie
> acerbo frutto, che le piaghe altrui
> gustando afflige piú che non conforta.

(So far astray is my mad desire, in pursuing her who has turned in flight and, light and free of the snares of Love, flies ahead of my slow running,

that when, calling him back, I most send him by the safe path, then he least obeys me, nor does it help to spur him or turn him, for Love makes him restive by nature;

and [then as] he takes the bit forcefully to himself, I remain in his power, as against my will he carries me off to death;

only to come to the laurel, whence one gathers bitter fruit that, being tasted, afflicts one's wounds more than it comforts them.)

(Canzoniere, 6)

One reads the unmistakable flow of desire from the sonnet's first lines, and the clear differentiation of phases in the lover's headlong and misguided pursuit. This speaker is at peace with the job of hunting—he will not retreat from the chase to watch. Like "The Death of the Hare," the sonnet tells of the lover's helplessness, his incapacity for arresting his object. But in the *Canzoniere*, these breakdowns often follow from the ungovernable force of his love for the woman, and are not related to any disengagement from the fact of loving. It is never a point of contemplation for the Petrarchan speaker whether he loves the woman, or whether he ought to confess his love in the lyrics. Further, with the last lines of "The Death of the Hare" the lover admits a finality—the hunt has been successfully completed by others without his participation—that forces him to a turning point, while the lover of the *Canzoniere* can keep loving and hunting through the extent of a fictional process that will continue even for a hundred poems after Laura's death. Both poems arrive at unforeseen conclusions, but the sonnet uses the sudden detour from anticipated "death" to the "laurel" to enroll the lover afresh in the work's chain of sufferings and confessions, the "bitter fruits" that only renew his pain. Yeats's poem announces in its conclusion the end of one of life's phases and of a particular cycle of frustrations, and—if the "wildness lost" can be in part the lover's as well as the beloved's—promises a new phase with an ulterior emotional detachment: a permanent, satisfied lovelessness. "The Death of the Hare" is a determined rewriting of this and many other post-Petrarchan poems into both a terminal statement and an account of the catalysis toward a *vita nuova*. As far as it portrays inaction, bewilderment, and withdrawal on the lover's part, it fulfills its purpose for the sequence.[15]

The fifth poem, "The Empty Cup," fills the intersection between the man's juvenile and mature phases with the remembrance of a love affair long past, an episode—like that in "The Mermaid"—with an ambiguous application to the more immediate history told in *A Man Young and Old*. It resembles the prior lyric in the means and attitude of its entrance into the series, though it is more explicitly and reliably connected to the continuing record of the other poems than "The Mermaid," joining the fiction by more than mere posteriority:

> A crazy man that found a cup,
> When all but dead of thirst,
> Hardly dared to wet his mouth
> Imagining, moon-accursed,
> That another mouthful
> And his beating heart would burst.
> October last I found it too
> But found it dry as bone,
> And for that reason am I crazed
> And my sleep is gone.

The speaker first tells an unnamed man's experience and then compares his own, admitting the personal tie he left out of the earlier poem. In neither poem does the speaker disclose that the "lad" or the "crazy man" and he are identical—nearly every reader will make that inference anyway—but in "The Empty Cup," he manages to imply as much with a significant indirection: the "man" and the speaker-lover are made affinitive to each other because they share an object, the alternately brimming and barren cup of sexual pleasure. As though to confirm that the crucial fact of character in this part of the sequence has much to do with the speaker's objects or ends, Yeats delivers our attention here to such an object while he splits his lover into past and present selves—revising and literalizing the retrospective topos of Renaissance love poetry—in order to forestall the stronger emotional charge that would come from one man's starkly contrastive experience of past and present.

Consider, too, the indirection in Yeats's handling of time. In chapter 1, I described the exercise of the Petrarchan retrospective topos, the structural ghost that plays around "The Empty Cup." Resolved to blur the emotional mordancy that often accompanies the convention, Yeats here extends and dilutes the present instant by defining its original boundary at a distant, preterite "October last." To put it a little differently, he disrupts the usually poignant Petrarchan balance between times with a broadening motion that pushes the poem's present back toward the past of the first sestet, that tacitly threatens to blend and reconcile these tenses. The historical balance betrayed, its tensions are dispersed and unavailable to the sequence. Especially in view of an extant draft of "The Empty Cup" that respects the typical balance of the Petrarchan topos much more exactly, the poem as we have it lacks the qualities Yeats has programmatically abandoned throughout *A Man Young and Old*: immediacy, retrospective clarity, confessional impact.[16]

The next five lyrics, "His Memories" through "His Wildness," make an obvious bloc. They represent little historical range or development, and are a continuous statement from the unvaried perspective of the man, now old. With "His Memories," the former lover bitterly recalls his involvement in the game of infatuation and the hunt of love objects. From his present stand of detachment, he thinks especially of the Iliadic Hector, the peripheral victim of a disastrous love whose burial concludes the most distended battle for a love object in Western cultural memory:

> We should be hidden from their eyes,
> Being but holy shows
> And bodies broken like a thorn
> Whereon the bleak north blows,
> To think of buried Hector
> And that none living knows.
>
> The women take so little stock
> In what I do or say
> They'd sooner leave their cosseting
> To hear a jackass bray;
> My arms are like the twisted thorn
> And yet there beauty lay;
>
> The first of all the tribe lay there
> And did such pleasure take—
> She who had brought great Hector down
> And put all Troy to wreck—
> That she cried into this ear,
> "Strike me if I shriek."

The woman's revolt at shrieking suggests her wish to remain unimplicated in love except as a distant, lunar object. The impersonality of her encounter with the man is admitted in the first lines of the second stanza, and in the coolly utilitarian adjective "*this* ear."

The former lover then turns his gaze on his friends of long standing, particularly on the objects they pursue in later life. In "The Friends of His Youth," one of the eeriest moments in *A Man Young and Old*, their wishes for offspring and power draw only his scornful laughter:

> Laughter not time destroyed my voice
> And put that crack in it,
> And when the moon's pot-bellied

I get a laughing fit,
For that old Madge comes down the lane,
A stone upon her breast,
And a cloak wrapped about the stone,
And she can get no rest
With singing hush and hush-a-bye;
She that has been wild
And barren as a breaking wave
Thinks that the stone's a child.

And Peter that had great affairs
And was a pushing man
Shrieks, "I am King of the Peacocks,"
And perches on a stone;
And then I laugh till tears run down
And the heart thumps at my side,
Remembering that her shriek was love
And that he shrieks from pride.

Much of our necessary disquiet follows from the speaker's convulsion here—his emotional states have been screened or guarded, after all, at nearly every prior point in the series—and its jagged disproportion among his recorded reactions. It is as though the sequence has held short of full disclosure of feeling until this instant of cynical laughter, this derision of the lover's former values as they now appear in others. Accordingly, many readers will perceive a lie in the work's portraiture of feeling. We may sense that the depiction of love in the earlier lyrics has been sold out to the expectation of this bitter turn, that it has been muted to allow for the old man's abjuration. These latter poems have the matter-of-factness and inertia of a point triumphantly proven at the expense of their forerunners.

The adjacent lyrics "Summer and Spring" and "The Secrets of the Old" give a demographic sketch of the old man's mature friendships, and especially of his objectless revision of his life. Now he holds fast to crowds that obliterate most traces of the love-hunt and of Petrarchan relations in general:

Though Margery is stricken dumb
If thrown in Madge's way,
We three make up a solitude;
For none alive to-day
Can know the stories that we know
Or say the things we say.
("The Secrets of the Old," 7–12)

While some of these friends remain entangled in desire (such as the proud Peter, who interrupts the sympotic ease of "Summer and Spring"), the speaker is serenely conscious that he and the other men were always out of congruity with their female objects, and meets Peter's interjection with a sarcastic reply:

> We sat under an old thorn-tree
> And talked away the night,
> Told all that had been said or done
> Since first we saw the light,
> And when we talked of growing up
> Knew that we'd halved a soul
> And fell the one in t'other's arms
> That we might make it whole;
> Then Peter had a murdering look,
> For it seemed that he and she
> Had spoken of their childish days
> Under that very tree.
> O what a bursting out there was,
> And what a blossoming,
> When we had all the summer-time
> And she had all the spring!

The last modulation of the sequence is a flare of the speaker's longing, not to love, but to follow his crowd of friends into death. With his final utterance, he gathers his lack of passion and reciprocity into this snapshot of an old man with his chosen object, which he clearly does not mistake for any living thing:

> HIS WILDNESS
> O bid me mount and sail up there
> Amid the cloudy wrack,
> For Peg and Meg and Paris' love
> That had so straight a back,
> Are gone away, and some that stay
> Have changed their silk for sack.
>
> Were I but there and none to hear
> I'd have a peacock cry,
> For that is natural to a man
> That lives in memory,
> Being all alone I'd nurse a stone
> And sing it lullaby.

His embrace of the stone reconciles him to the woman's hard heart that once made him suffer, and completes his reconstruction in her likeness. Yeats's formerly Petrarchan lover cancels his pain by endorsing the attitudes of his torturer. With the collapse of his persona into that of the woman who does not and cannot love, the preceding lyrics are retrospectively weakened or even discredited as the dead-end chronicles of a misprision. Seen against the post-Petrarchan love sequences, which conclude variously but always maintain distinct values and identities for lover and beloved, *A Man Young and Old* insists on an astonishing, original ending to its program.

A Man Young and Old concludes with a *stasimon* from one of Yeats's contemporary projects, a translation of *Oedipus at Colonus*. His adaptation of the ode joins some elements of the Sophoclean strophe and antistrophe in four stanzas of long lines.

> Endure what life God gives and ask no longer span;
> Cease to remember the delights of youth, travel-wearied aged man;
> Delight becomes death-longing if all longing else be vain.
>
> Even from that delight memory treasures so,
> Death, despair, division of families, all entanglements of mankind grow,
> As that old wandering beggar and these God-hated children know.
>
> In the long echoing street the laughing dancers throng,
> The bride is carried to the bridegroom's chamber through torchlight and
>   tumultuous song;
> I celebrate the silent kiss that ends short life or long.
>
> Never to have lived is best, ancient writers say;
> Never to have drawn the breath of life, never to have looked into the eye of
>   day;
> The second best's a gay goodnight and quickly turn away.[17]

The admission of a stasimon or "stationary song" as the last vessel for the man's late turn of mind allows for a striking harmony of form and attitude. Among the several changes that habituate the ode to the sequence, two seem to be especially purposeful. The chorus of old men that speaks the ode in the Greek play wants to rule out a future for the beggar, to reconcile him to the imminent end of his life. It gives voice to an impatience with human process and its entanglements, and seems to anticipate an impulse for holding oneself out of time and future events: the ode concludes with a simile that shows Oedipus's stillness under a rushing stream of times and troubles, an analogy for time's merciless assault and his desperation. The vivid transfiguration of temporal events into physical "waves," and the determined association of those waves with diurnal hours—by which the chorus unravels its own transfiguration, maintaining the waves' reference to time—suggest both the chorus's struggle to retain temporal exactitude (and with it, the full force of the complaint) and an emotional need to flatten and reduce time into space, to beat the ravages of process by rendering them into another dimension. Oscillating between temporal and spatial premises, the last lines betray an especially charged response to life's chain of reverses. This polemic against process is surely the fact that attracted Yeats's notice, recommending the ode to him as a terminal speech for his lyric series. But he matches the ode's obliteration of the future by cancelling the past, too, as it is a likely conductor of "longing": his chorus—which is not much discriminated from the old man himself, and might be a multiplication of his voice—demands that the speaker of "His Wildness" cease even to live "in memory," that he eliminate desire for the past as he has for the future, that he kill this last object of his existence in a thoroughgoing way. The second tercet holds explicitly that "memory" is a kind of longing that shares some of the values and consequences of love itself, and that it must just as urgently be discarded. Yeats's revision of the Sophoclean chorus here answers the terms of his sequence to this moment, cutting off an oblique path to love and "entanglements" that had remained open even in the mature lyrics.

A complementary stroke is the third tercet, which figures very differently in the Greek ode, and which introduces a special concreteness and luminosity to the old man's withdrawal from process and pursuit. In *Oedipus at Colonus*, the music, dance, and celebration are the losses of old age and death, not something for salvage. Yeats's old man prizes, at the last, a store of static, disconnected instants and sensations left over from his years as a lover. Are these the sort of reductions of amatory experience he railed against in the first poems, where he protested his being treated "as though my sorrow were a scene / Upon a painted wall"? He has shaken out passion from his life, pulled out of the hunt, and finally distorted his own history and substance with as little ruthfulness as any Petrarchan donna would show him and his kind. The final tercet, which for its air of unconcern might be spoken by such a woman, takes aim at the sense of process that I have already identified as the quintessential post-Petrarchan achievement in lyric fiction, and effectively carries the man's impulse of withdrawal over the last imaginable parallel. This biographical sequence ends by disaffirming the life's process that makes biography feasible, catching the old man in a terminal pose of "gay" and impossible detachment as he turns "away" to . . . what? where? when?

In *A Man Young and Old* Yeats seems to discover, as he goes, a compound of ways to dissent strategically from the post-Petrarchan program to which the series largely belongs; its chief claim to interest among Western sequences appears, I think, in its transmittal of new means for recovering the shape and rhythm of a lover's life. The sequence ends by repudiating the obsession with temporal process that is probably Petrarch's most lasting and distinctive mark on lyric fiction, but the denial is mostly rhetorical. It cannot imply a feasible practice for this sequence, which is still processive in the abstract, but can only designate Yeats's resistance to the usual idea of amatory fiction. Instead of abandoning a post-Petrarchan fictional process, in fact, Yeats innovates within it. Adjusting the lyric interval as he finds it in the received sequence down to the twentieth century, he opens his practice to the new models that his contemporaries were exploring: A Man Young and Old begins to enact the movement away from canonical post-Petrarchan models, toward more versatile experiments in lyric fiction.

A Man Young and Old is completed in every sense by A Woman Young and Old, which was written in 1926 and 1927 and first published in the American edition of The Winding Stair (1929).[18] In fact, A Woman Young and Old has two claims to singularity in the expansion of its iconoclastic countertext. First, it is the only lyric sequence, so far as I know, that uses the voice of the usually silent object, the beloved, to interrogate the fictional and intellectual unity of an original series by the same poet. It is not the first series spoken by a woman: the sequences of Vittoria Colonna (1538), Pernette du Guillet (1545), Stefano Colonna (1552), Louise Labé (1555), Veronica Franco (1575), and Mary Wroth (1621) represent female speakers, some in pursuit of male objects, and generally maintain the post-Petrarchan embargo against the speech of those mysterious others.[19] But A Woman Young and Old is one of the few sequences created out of the recognition that a single perspective on love is incomplete—to insist that a lyric fiction must be emotionally and intellectually differentiated by voice—and perhaps the first to be matched voice to voice against another sequence within a single conception. How much of this recognition is built into the compression of A Man Young and Old itself? With its wide interval and its general recoil from the post-Petrarchan program, that series is already vitiated as a fiction, inviting one's retrospective sense of its incompleteness before A Woman Young and Old. Refusing to sound the lover's feelings obsessively, it does not force the woman's view out into a text of its own—as works by Petrarch, Scève, or Sidney seem to do—but calls for the other series as a necessary, perhaps a saving complement. In the generic history of the lyric sequence, the diagrammatically mutual reliance of these voices in fulfilling Yeats's fiction is an original attainment, never quite repeated even in the disorderly run of twentieth-century poetry. Together, A Man and A Woman represent the turn of the moment more closely and comprehensibly than almost any contemporary lyric text.

The second claim follows from the first: that the common text of *A Man* and *A Woman Young and Old* enacts a shift from a nominative battery of conventions to what I call an artifactual conception of lyric fiction. As I have already indicated, a nominative fiction is one that maintains the primacy of one voice or subject, that franchises a more or less linear account of the subject's life over historical reversal and play, that rates confession and immediacy above less personal literary means. For lyric poetics, nominativity originally manifests an alliance with Renaissance humanism—for which Petrarch, and later Sidney, hold important citizenships in both camps—and later adapts to Protestantism, Romanticism, and other strong ideologies concerned with the mutual verifications of epistemology, selfhood, and personal experience. It is founded on the idea that even as its sequences represent unitary selves to whom the various formal and experiential elements accrue, its readers build and define themselves against the ordered sensibility of the fiction. An artifactual work, by contrast, accepts the value of fashioning the lyric sequence out of histories to which no single self, no character, may necessarily lay claim. It might include several fully realized voices, a synthetic treatment of time, and other instances of literary exogeny. Because its works are frankly artifacts—collocations of things obviously made, not always of experiences putatively lived—this type of lyric series admits a crucial, sometimes catalytic role for rituality in its fictions. Poems may affirm their materiality, whether aural or visual, with an explicitness that seldom figures in the Petrarchan amatory sequences. They may require readings (like that of "The Mermaid") that suspend characterological unities in favor of a more provisional and performative approach. They may be openly choral. Nominativity is not exactly discarded after the artifactual turn of twentieth-century poetry, for a principle with its history and potency can never be wholly abandoned. But its ideological urgency and contemporaneity quickly scatter and its means come to seem obsolete, so that even when a second modernist generation takes up a kind of nominativity in reaction to its immediate forerunners—for example, one thinks of the American confessional poets of the 1950s and 1960s—it has to quote the characterological mode more than profess it wholeheartedly, and it produces sequences, like Robert Lowell's late volumes or John Berryman's *Dream Songs* (1964–69), where nominative premises are highly compromised by artifactual devices.[20]

Though these terms belong only to the poetics of lyric, they undoubtedly correspond to tendencies in the internal histories of other varieties of fiction. A similar, revolutionary shift of purpose happens in the multiplication of actors on the earliest Greek stage, for example, which Aristotle describes in terms of a morphogenesis of tragedy and comedy away from their founding state of something like dramatic nominativity.[21] And versions of these competing impulses have been remarked in the history of fictional film: treating the evolution of the cinema from daguerreotypy, Siegfried Kracauer argues for the original competition of two tendencies, the "realistic" and the "formative," and for their reconciliation later in various measures. The realistic tendency, a positivistic enthusiasm for "the camera's unique ability to record as well as reveal visible, or potentially visible, physical reality," was first demonstrated by the reels of the Lumière brothers, while the formative tendency, which "involved the artist's creativity in shaping the given material," was evidenced in the work of Georges Méliès.[22] The "realistic" conception is only such, of course, because it posits the continuous presence of an observing self whose report of more or less objective phenomena is the film. One might argue that cinematic realism is composed and held together as a set of conventions by a plausibly human, empirical vision. And the "formative" tendency has much to do with the dissolution of that hypothetical self: it is the elaboration of the camera's possible perspectives to include such artifactual devices as the close-up, the dissolve, the jump cut, and the other spatial and temporal effects of movement and editing.

Whatever their available counterparts in other types of fiction, these two impulses should be most important here for their recapitulation and transvaluation of lyric's elemental modes. As I have indicated, nominativity is the original conception through which the fictional mode is elaborated into the lyric sequence. But according to the generic plot that sees ritual and fiction endlessly conversing with one another even in short poems, the development of the sequence as fiction finally takes its characteristically lyric turn, and entails its own dissolution into the ritual mode in its readers' eyes and voices. As innumerable readers and critics declare, the artifactual sequence often makes the procedures of fictional interpretation futile, and compels a different sort of satisfaction—perhaps in reweighing the poem's interaction with the empirical world, perhaps in treating the series, like *The Cantos*, as not only "reading matter" but "singing matter, shouting matter"—or in a recent critic's terms, "a true musical score waiting for performing voices."[23] I see the passage of *A Man Young and Old*, from a first-person confession (however undermined) in the first poem to a choral ode at the end, as imitative of the generic history of its age. When *A Woman Young and Old* reiterates that imitation in turn and carries its verification of contemporary poetics even further, the task of these peculiar tribunes is complete.

The first poem in Yeats's female series, "Father and Child," shows the work's opening to multiple voices: the father, who will not appear again, utters the exposition and allows the child, the young *Woman*, to speak only the clipped, romantic judgment of the last lines.

> She hears me strike the board and say
> That she is under ban
> Of all good men and women
> Being mentioned with a man
> That has the worst of all bad names;
> And thereupon replies
> That his hair is beautiful,
> Cold as the March wind his eyes.

Demeaning this poem for its "lack of wisdom" and overblown romanticism, Delmore Schwartz objected that "whatever the worst of all bad names may be, traitor, murderer, or pimp, it is hard to accept beautiful hair and cold eyes as being a counterweight from any rational point of view."[24] That is exactly the point, of course, for as a serial fiction, *A Woman Young and Old* has an interest in making us curious enough about the child's impractical aestheticism to want to keep reading. Her fleeting appearance, through the two veils of her father's disapproval and her own terseness, charges her with a measure of mystery, perhaps of sympathetic appeal.

As the proem to its series, however, "Father and Child" also tells against *A Man Young and Old* and the fictional mode that is under continuing examination here; building on the prior sequence's quarrel with nominativity, the poem introduces stricter qualifications of that program. If representativeness in view of the rest of the series is one of the qualities that makes a poem a proem, how should we read the father's screening of the child in this first lyric? Her identity refracted through a paternal sensibility, the female child seems to carry the agency of her sequence less firmly than male speakers usually do, and so to indicate something of women's unsteady grip on their circumstances in a male world. Her utterances, as here, will often be replies—very different from the self-started, interrogatory speech of even the most ardent post-Petrarchan lovers and of Yeats's man—and yet with the force of their conviction, these utterances can overturn men's (including Schwartz's) premises at once. In fact, this speaker's gender turns out to be crucial to Yeats's continuing quarrel with his models.[25] *A Woman* struggles against the notion that it is possible to recover the shape or body of a person's life through a collation of his or her utterances; argues implicitly that the contexts of such utterances—personal, social, political—are vital to and inseparable from the assembled life; and proposes to join *A Man* in an unbreakable counterpoint, a new nominativity that opens onto another sort of fiction, an idea of the lover's life as an assembly of social and cultural artifacts. "Father and Child" is hardly made for single evaluation but, like many other proems, rehearses the sequence's major concerns. The Petrarchan proem, forced out of the previous series, returns here to claim its place in *A Woman* because it works toward Yeats's dissent from the available models of lyric fiction; in fact, such a shift from omission to strategic inclusion, from reticent distance to the purposeful uses of interval, largely defines the crossing from *A Man* to *A Woman Young and Old* as successive installments in a modern proof of the form.

The easy juncture that leads from "Father and Child" to the second poem in the series, "Before the World Was Made," relies on the linked images of "eyes" as aesthetic objects:

> If I make the lashes dark
> And the eyes more bright
> And the lips more scarlet,
> Or ask if all be right
> From mirror after mirror,
> No vanity's displayed:
> I'm looking for the face I had
> Before the world was made.
>
> What if I look upon a man
> As though on my beloved,
> And my blood be cold the while
> And my heart unmoved?
> Why should he think me cruel
> Or that he is betrayed?
> I'd have him love the thing that was
> Before the world was made.

Now a little older, the daughter still answers male censors of her conduct, and she goes on in her aesthetic vein, though turning her gaze on herself. But her dreamy aestheticism is no longer unschooled. She has taken lessons in Platonism, and hit on a defense for herself. Here are the marks of a conflict that assembles character, a clash between the ostensible disinterestedness and exploratory range of Platonic inquiry on the one hand, and the woman's local, cosmetic lies on the other. She is inquisitive and dishonest, alert and thoughtless, abstract and vain. Further, the woman's dishonesty is a complex of attributes in itself. Because of the formal and verbal similarities of the two stanzas in "Before the World Was Made"— and the example of a morally blank aestheticism in "Father and Child"— one tends to associate the woman's dishonesty with her love of forms and images, as though the moral flaw inevitably belongs with the aesthetic turn. Yeats binds these several impulses into a complex that stands for youth, a formula that will be unraveled, and its elements recombined, when her intellect and conscience ripen.[26]

The battle between the woman's dissimulation and her concern for permanent truths is, then, the constituting ground of her character during these first installments:

> I admit the briar
> Entangled in my hair
> Did not injure me;
> My blenching and trembling
> Nothing but dissembling,
> Nothing but coquetry.
>
> I long for truth, and yet
> I cannot stay from that
> My better self disowns,
> For a man's attention
> Brings such satisfaction
> To the craving in my bones.
>
> Brightness that I pull back
> From the Zodiac,
> Why those questioning eyes
> That are fixed upon me?
> What can they do but shun me
> If empty night replies?

This third lyric, "A First Confession," seems to sort naturally with its antecedents: answering a male interrogator again, the young woman frames her reply in the familiar anatomy of "hair" and "eyes." But the composition of her character, one must observe, is changing. The title and the penitent tone suggest that a surge of conscience has overtaken her old purposes, and when she articulates her ruling conflict in the second stanza, she sounds its demise. The lyric portrays her first challenge to the childish complex of values that has composed her to this moment: when she regrets "dissembling" over the tangling of her hair, she apologizes for the worship of pure beauty—which "hair" and "eyes" have come to stand for in this series—as much as for the actual lies she told. And when she wonders at the man's "questioning eyes," she is aware of seeing those eyes for the first time as reflections of the mind.

As a post-Petrarchan fiction of process, her development represents a version of a flux we commonly see in life, namely the tendency of children to become less reflexly aesthetic, and more interested in objective truth, as they get older. Rudolf Arnheim describes the normative change with respect to the drawings of children and adults, observing that the adults' pictures often do not fulfill their task as completely as do the children's drawings. . . . The children are amateurs like the adults. But with their unspoiled sense of form they can still put all aspects of shape and color totally to the service of the intended meaning. In this sense, their work is like that of the accomplished artist. In the average adult of our civilization, however, the sense of form fades, rather than keeping up with the increasing complexity of the mind. His art work may contain elements of authentic expression—a woman hugging a child, a monster glaring into the darkness—but otherwise he mainly tells a story as best he can, without conveying its intrinsic meaning through the arrangement of the shapes and colors themselves.[27]

"A First Confession" finds the woman caught between the "unspoiled sense of form" and spoiled moral sense she shows in the first two lyrics, and a newly emerging "complexity of the mind" and spirit. As she grows, her aestheticism will move its place among her attributes, settling successively into combinations with those qualities that take ascendancy in her character at each particular utterance.

The poem's title is worth noticing, for the prior sequence admits nothing like a "confession" of longing: it will become evident that with *A Woman*, Yeats achieves a short, tractable sequence that largely keeps its distance from particular moments in order to shatter the exactitude and accumulation of the Petrarchan breviary—but now includes an adjustment of interval, a movement into immediacy, unrealized in *A Man Young and Old*. Here Yeats manages to separate the value of historical amalgamation from the risk of emotional sterility, and to demonstrate for the first time a closely constructed biographical series that is also an effectual critique of post-Petrarchism. The speech of "A First Confession" cuts to the center of the woman's emotional constitution as no lyric of the first series ever does for the man, and technically speaking, the interval between her intelligence and the states and objects she observes is quite short (as determined partly by the resort to the simple present: "I admit," "I long"). But placed against that confessional immediacy is another sort of interval that perhaps cannot be so handily closed: a political removal, say, that keeps the woman's shows of mind within the implicit frame of men's assumptions about her. The last word of the poem, "replies," describes the nature of all of these utterances. They are all fearful or defiant responses to things asked of her, and however close we may come to the naked display of her subjectivity, we can understand little or nothing of the woman as lyric character unless we have those questions.

The woman's despair vanishes with the unfolding of "Her Triumph," the fourth lyric in the series.

> I did the dragon's will until you came
> Because I had fancied love a casual

Improvisation, or a settled game
That followed if I let the kerchief fall:
Those deeds were best that gave the minute wings
And heavenly music if they gave it wit;
And then you stood among the dragon-rings.
I mocked, being crazy, but you mastered it
And broke the chain and set my ankles free,
Saint George or else a pagan Perseus;
And now we stare astonished at the sea,
And a miraculous strange bird shrieks at us.[28]

Each of the reasons that the lyric stands out from the series has something
to do, I think, with its interval. First, Yeats temporarily suspends the insistent meter of long and short lines brought over from *A Man Young and
Old*, and suspends with it the sensation of coolness and hardening that
holds to those earlier poems. The loosely rhymed pentameters of "Her
Triumph" admit a confessional ease unseen to this point, and a sense of
serious but improvisatory reflection. Further, the lyric is fashioned on the
clean opposition of tenses that often distinguishes poems in the calendrical sequences of the Renaissance. Much like a Petrarchan lyric, "Her Triumph" gathers up three distinct moments: the woman's age of immatu-
rity, when her shallowness and trifling were a moral "dragon" (or as she
calls it in an early draft from the series, "my monstrous coquetry") that
had to be mastered; the man's advent and mastery, introduced with an
anaphoric *then* in the seventh line; and the present tense of the utterance,
when her moral redemption through sexual initiation ("[you] broke the
chain and set my ankles free") is fully accomplished.[29] The lyric has all
the emotional piquancy of the retrospective topos, made perhaps more
striking by its occurrence in a chain of utterances that has not included
much retrospection. The lyric's entrance into the series opens the way for
two more pentameter monologues, and the three poems together make a
symmetrical pattern of windows in the formal and confessional program
of *A Woman Young and Old*.

   As an utterance that discloses character, "Her Triumph" is a remarkable transvaluation of the Apollodorian-Ovidian myths of Perseus and
Andromeda, where the virgin's inexperience is not the danger, but the
priceless treasure to be saved. In this redaction, it belongs to the same
ironic impulse that produced the convenient Platonism of "Before the
World Was Made." The hint of contradiction that animates her character
comes, once again, in her molding of mythological and philosophical authority to the shape of her own experience and purposes, in the coinci-
dence of knowing and innocence implied here. Her selection of the myth
is not a neutral act, but implies some participation in its conventional

values, while her parodic rewriting of it to map her own subjective circumstances tugs the utterance into another, conflicting path.

The lyric concludes with the lovers' presence by the symbol that serves as their familiar in these sequences, the "miraculous strange bird," and with the "shriek" of authentic pleasure we know from "His Memories." Having thrown off the ideas about love that clung to the first two lyrics and troubled her in the third, she knows from newly gathered experience that at its best love is not "casual," but a deliberate conditioning of the mind and heart; that it is not an "improvisation," but the reward of design; that it is no "game," but a serious and vital passion for both participants. Yeats called his poem "Her Triumph," I imagine, after a lyric by Ben Jonson. The fourth poem in the sequence *A Celebration of Charis* (1640), Jonson's "Her Triumph" proclaims the lady Charis's mastery of "the Chariot of Love" and control over her own romantic destiny.

Yeats's "Her Triumph" completes what might be called the first movement of the series. The fifth lyric, "Consolation," recharges the contradiction between her apparent grasp of "wisdom" and authority on the one hand, and her need to find a mightier authority in her own impulses:

> O but there is wisdom
> In what the sages said;
> But stretch that body for a while
> And lay down that head
> Till I have told the sages
> Where man is comforted.
>
> How could passion run so deep
> Had I never thought
> That the crime of being born
> Blackens all our lot?
> But where the crime's committed
> The crime can be forgot.

The lyric is plainly meant as a piece of backsliding, a song "not so innocent" to counter the strong current of innocence and sincerity in the preceding utterance.[30] The sequence's return here to a wide interval is accomplished partly by the meter, but also by the play of deictics: the orientational *that* in lines 3 and 4, used in an utterance of the present tense and evidently in the presence of the woman's apostrophized lover, actually implies a spatial distance between the partners that figures the emotional interval, the coolness and lack of involvement, that stretches between them. The remembrance of a similar turn of deixis in "His Memories" might suggest an order of declining immediacy in utterances that refer to the self of the speaker or others: *my* and, at a wider distance, *this* for describing oneself, and *this*, and farther, *that* for locating others. Yeats's consistent play at the far end of this order ("My arms are like the twisted thorn, / And yet *there* beauty lay") is pertinent to the dominant, wide interval of the two revisionary biographies.

I turn now to "Chosen" and "Parting," the two lyrics that have attracted more analysis and conjecture than any other parts of *A Woman Young and Old*.[31]

CHOSEN

The lot of love is chosen. I learnt that much
Struggling for an image on the track
Of the whirling Zodiac.
Scarce did he my body touch,
Scarce sank he from the west
Or found a subterranean rest
On the maternal midnight of my breast
Before I had marked him on his northern way,
And seemed to stand although in bed I lay.

I struggled with the horror of daybreak,
I chose it for my lot! If questioned on
My utmost pleasure with a man
By some new-married bride, I take
That stillness for a theme
Where his heart my heart did seem
And both adrift on the miraculous stream
Where—wrote a learned astrologer—
The Zodiac is changed into a sphere.

PARTING

He. Dear, I must be gone
    While night shuts the eyes
    Of the household spies;
    That song announces dawn.

She. No, night's bird and love's
    Bids all true lovers rest,
    While his loud song reproves
    The murderous stealth of day.

He. Daylight already flies
    From mountain crest to crest.

She. That light is from the moon.

He. That bird . . .

She.   Let him sing on,
    I offer to love's play
    My dark declivities.

The declarative first sentences of "Chosen" are the woman's reproving answer to the ecstasy of "Her Triumph," just as that poem responds to prior parts of the sequence. She calls up the incessancy and range of her romantic experience since then with the perpetually "whirling Zodiac," and the arduousness of her battle against time and age with the figure of the sun's constant motion. Recognizing the astrological imagery from "A First Confession," we ought to notice that her struggle "to keep the sun from rising"—to keep her lover from departing, that is, and to hold time back in its tracks—has grown more difficult since that poem's effortless address to the lover as "Brightness that I pull back / From the Zodiac." We observe that the coquetry of her early youth has now been fully replaced by what she bitterly calls a "maternal" quality.

"Chosen" is another poem of the kind that finds no place in *A Man Young and Old*, a direct confession by someone whose self-criticism permits no unexamined corners. Her suffering in love has been less than the man's at the corresponding point in his history, although her rage at the imperatives of process certainly equals his feelings there. For her, time's advance means the dissolution of the kind of moment that sparks her existence, such as the lovers' unity after intercourse. But we are obliged to notice how differently she handles her feeling: in this series there is no disappearing speaker, no interruption or blind in the historical record of the work, no retreat from experience into stasis and sterility. Instead, she assesses her circumstances with a disarming precision and responsibility, a frank reconciliation to the facts of her existence.

Further, "Chosen" supports other indications of the woman's maturity as it reweighs the attributes revealed in the first poems. Her original, childlike aestheticism has shifted into another channel. It has ceased to live for her in the appearances of admired people as in her earliest utterances, or to find its fulfillment in mere coquetry as in "A First Confession." She has learned to apprehend things as what they mean ("those questioning eyes," "the horror of daybreak") more than as what they look like, and given up her idle craving for men's attention. Now for her as for many adults, the old "sense of form" lives only in the rare moments when harmony and perfection are realized through sex. As experience has replaced mere teasing and pretense, the sense of perfect form has come out of increasingly deeper and more serious acts, from observation to expectancy and participation. Its aesthetic weight tends to give dominion in turn to each of the attributes we read in those acts: first her keen imaginative vision is her prime characterological pose, then her coquetry, and at last her capacity for a reciprocal loving. As it travels, her aestheticism lays bare the path of her development.

Immediately after the bittersweet confession, Yeats introduces the delicate aubade called "Parting." The two poems, as we know from Jon Stallworthy's study of their manuscripts, were once parts of a single lyric titled "The Two Voices." But if we did not know as much, what would we say about their juncture? The imagery of one is somber and eccentric, the other idealized and highly conventional; clearly the poems are stylistic alternatives. But the most important fact about the juncture—though perhaps not the most striking—is the implication it holds for the modernist turn in the post-Petrarchan sequence, for verifying the generic mobilization toward what I have called artifactuality. Manifestly, the two contiguous lyrics introduce a temporal discontinuity into the *Woman* series, which has so far kept a strictly historical order, and the disruption is all but impossible to naturalize: the situation of the dramatic lyric, that is, seems to precede that of the monologue, disrupting the historical logic that leads from seduction ("Consolation") to repose ("Parting") and bitter reflection ("Chosen"). According to Stallworthy, Yeats planned to respect that logic until the last stages of composition, when "for no apparent reason," he "reversed the beginning and the end" of "The Two Voices."[32]

In the vast, calendrical sequences, there are occasional (perhaps editorial) lapses in which a lyric that relates an event or a state enters the series before another poem that relates an earlier event. But as I have argued in the first chapter, these irregularities seem not to subvert the temporal program of these sequences; in the case of the *Canzoniere*, the sedition of the dates is conspicuous enough only to indicate the authenticity of the difference between Petrarch's fictional achievement and that of narrative, to provoke our conjectural inquiry into the nature of the work's process while we remain bound into the experience of the continuum. In any case, the force of the Petrarchan generic program was strong enough that his readers and imitators would always naturalize any disruptions—as I have just done—back into an assumed continuum, back into nominativity. And in *A Man Young and Old*, the possibility of temporal subversion is shaded by that sequence's chronic reluctance of expression, so that we might or might not call poems such as "The Mermaid" and "The Empty Cup" interruptions in the characterological fiction. That sequence's experimental impulse, though obviously necessary to the success of *A Woman*, seems subordinated to a primary mood of concealment and distance.

But "Parting" demonstrates Yeats's determination to alter the received means of the fictional series, to plant a historical reversal in a lyric chain—already greatly shortened and concentrated from the post-Petrarchan model—where its disruptive impact will be far greater than the discontinuities of the *Canzoniere* or its European imitators. In a single gesture, the fictional sequence represented or verified here gains an openly artifactual capacity, *A Woman* defines itself as the completion of its countertext, and "Parting" becomes a heightened moment, a shard of experience isolated from the pattern of consequence and history. To the naturalizing eye, the lyric seems something like a dream imbedded in an empirical sequence of waking moments. According to such an interpretation, the woman reenacts the morning's events in her imagination, and recasts the details in a romantic light. Most significant, she leaves the ending of this replayed scene ambiguous: does the man stay or not? Fictionally speaking, "Parting" may be a psychological balm for the actual "horror of daybreak," a romantic daydream that admits the possibility of a happy ending; or it may be the woman's imaginative demonstration of power over the man. It may even be an ironic interlude, as the woman mocks her old, naive expectations by showing, in the conventional language of Shakespeare's and Donne's aubades, how little the lovers really have to say to one another.

A good analogy for Yeats's disposition of "Parting" can be found in the cinema, where, as Francis Sparshott observes,

> the dream-relationships of film space and the narrative nature of film time combine to encourage an ambiguity that may be fruitful or merely irritating. One often does not know whether one is seeing what in the film's terms is real, or only what is passing through the mind of one of the film's characters. This ambiguity becomes acute whenever there is a temporal jump, for time (as Kant observed) is the form of subjectivity. A flash-back may represent a character's memory, or may simply be a narrative device; a flash-forward may stand for a character's premonition, or simply an anticipation by the filmmaker, and, where the temporally displaced scene is recalled or foreseen, it may stand either for the event as it was or would be, or for the way it is (perhaps falsely) conjured up.[33]

Of course there can be no single answer to the poem's place in the series. But just as the flashback and the flash-forward are the results of film's morphogenesis away from the requisite means of realism, nominativity, and other types of implied empirical record, Yeats's transport of his completed lyric to a new site, out of the sequence's line of history, must have the "apparent reason" of increasing the compliance of his fictional medium—and of fashioning a two-stage anecdote that implies the purposes and relations of his *Man* and *Woman* series together. As though to redouble the recognition of artifactuality dramatized over the two sequences, the aubade's dialogic mode ("two voices") plays out again, locally, the perspectival orientation of *A Man* and *A Woman Young and Old*.

The motif of the dream continues in the eighth poem, "Her Vision in the Wood," the last of the three confessions in the series.

> Dry timber under that rich foliage,
> At wine-dark midnight in the sacred wood,
> Too old for a man's love I stood in rage
> Imagining men. Imagining that I could
> A greater with a lesser pang assuage
> Or but to find if withered vein ran blood,
> I tore my body that its wine might cover
> Whatever could recall the lip of lover.
>
> And after that I held my fingers up,
> Stared at the wine-dark nail, or dark that ran
> Down every withered finger from the top;
> But the dark changed to red, and torches shone,
> And deafening music shook the leaves; a troop
> Shouldered a litter with a wounded man,
> Or smote upon the string and to the sound
> Sang of the beast that gave the fatal wound.
>
> All stately women moving to a song
> With loosened hair or foreheads grief-distraught,
> It seemed a Quattrocento painter's throng,
> A thoughtless image of Mantegna's thought—
> Why should they think that are for ever young?
> Till suddenly in grief's contagion caught,
> I stared upon his blood-bedabbled breast
> And sang my malediction with the rest.
>
> That thing all blood and mire, that beast-torn wreck,
> Half turned and fixed a glazing eye on mine,
> And, though love's bitter-sweet had all come back,
> Those bodies from a picture or a coin
> Nor saw my body fall nor heard it shriek,
> Nor knew, drunken with singing as with wine,
> That they had brought no fabulous symbol there
> But my heart's victim and its torturer.

The first stanza suggests a number of clear-cut continuities and developments with respect to prior lyrics. The woman's self-characterization as "too old for a man's love" is a romantic exposition, ratifying the implicit horror of aging in "Chosen." Her bitter admission of lines 3 through 8 only resonates when read in sequence, for one has to understand the continual importance of imagination to this speaker. Unlike the man, she is a fully realized lyric character, to whom imagination is an integral element. Until now her imagination has not stirred independently of her experience, but has depended on men, events, and longings to move it. To the woman's dismay, "Her Vision" finds her having to separate imagination from amatory experience for the first time, as she has no such experience in old age. Moreover, as an element in a continuing logic of character, her aestheticism requires an outlet to indicate for us the prevailing attribute in her development. Rather than submit to the "greater" pain of a detached and abstract imagination, she chooses the "lesser pang" of self-mutilation, as though to undo the dressing and painting of her youth, to find her aesthetic fulfillment in destruction and concealment. Her disfigurement here is a violent analogue to the man's impulse to withdraw from experience, an act of physical rather than psychic transformation because almost everything in her biography has been put in physical terms. Her framing and her imperatives are far more definite than the man's, so her disengagement from present and future loves will occasion a more arresting, tortuous poem than anything in *A Man Young and Old*.

In the latter three stanzas, the only sustained narrative in the sequence, the woman recounts the "vision" that appears to her spontaneously after both the exhaustion of her immediate experience and the offertory spilling of her blood. First, she is insensibly drawn into the "troop" of women in love who carry the wounded Adonis to a rite of healing. This ritual vision, like the Perseus myth in "Her Triumph," is a trope born in the woman's own mind and prompted by a physical trauma: it is the expression of her own grief at the loss of love. But while she maintained a steady, conscious control over the disposition of the conceit in "Her Triumph," she abandons herself to the vision, and is "suddenly in grief's contagion caught." Her confused notion, that she is no longer the source of the emotion but only a participant in its rites, is crucial to the sequence's ideas about old age. The loss of a sense of freshness, urgency, and authority in what human beings feel, the poem suggests, is a critical event in the process of aging. When that sense goes, activity becomes passivity, the heart settles not in a pair but in a "throng"—remember the man's retreat into a trio in the last poems of his series—and one's lyric history fuses with the collective experience of all. Most striking, the woman demonstrates her impotence by showing her amatory fiction transmuted into ritual: where once she had the conviction of a seemingly unique personal history, here she "[sings her] malediction with the rest." Even so, the throng affords her no safety, for the Adonis meets her eye and—all at once, with a "shriek" that sifts her from the group—calls back all the entanglements and double-edged emotion of her old amatory experience.

Yeats deepens his dissent from post-Petrarchan poetics to insist here that human experience eventually wears down the contours that make a first-person amatory history feasible, that no one should be such a character, and have his or her history meticulously told, over an entire life. This is to expose one of the necessary illusions of the nominative sequence, which, in its most traditional phase, diverted attention from the physical and emotional aging of its lover-speakers by remarking the periods *in vita* and *in morte* of its objects. Lyric's ritual mode, which post-Petrarchism subdues as part of its self-invention, will find its way back, Yeats suggests, simply because human subjects move among experiences appropriate to the two modes: passionate authority gives way to collectivity, consecutiveness turns to synchrony, and some songs are best sung in a throng. A rite that would once have seemed inexpressive and confining to the young woman is now necessary to her older self. She cannot bear love's strong feeling alone, for her capacity is too "withered" and the prospect of rejection too painful. "Her Vision in the Wood" is like those poems, situated in fictional sequences, that celebrate and perhaps fetishize lyric's ritual dimension: since at least *Canzoniere* 70, the canzone that accumulates its argument out of the poems of Petrarch's predecessors, this has been a common outbreak within lyric fiction—a large-scale consequence, again, of the continual alternation of modes. But not simply the ritual outlet in a thoroughgoing nominative series, "Her Vision" holds and strengthens the common evidence of the *Man* and *Woman* sequences: that nominative fiction will necessarily come apart under cultural pressure—that it has already come apart—and that it must rewrite itself chorally, as a document of the culture more than of the person. Difficult to any reading, "Her Vision" actually forces the woman, its protagonist, to the periphery while such a generic change is enacted front and center.

The lyric advances, then, through three psychic phases: a rage at the humiliating dislocation of imagination from experience; a surrender of emotional authority to the troop of women; and a sudden recovery, through ritual means, of love's subjective poignancy, an intuition that by contrast makes her present loneliness seem safe and habitable. Where does this final recognition come from? Not from memory itself, but from the "eye" of the Adonis, the organ that drew the charge of the woman's feeling through most of the preceding lyrics. In ritual fashion, as Taylor or Whitman would recognize, it is not the remembrance of experience that returns, but experience itself. The wounded man's gaze summons a last irruption of the authentic pain of loving, and forces the woman's conclusive withdrawal from amatory experience and its serious contemplation.

Her crisis and withdrawal here vindicate the wide lyric interval of the remaining poems, and give parabolic shape to the interval of the *Woman* series at large. Unlike *A Man Young and Old*, this sequence reasons its lyric interval dramatically, as development of character. The woman's first utterances assume a distance from their own history and feeling that approximates the man's constant interval, but then in youth she is meant to seem cold and unseeing; the interval matches her character in these poems. When experience and maturity arrive, the interval finds a new measure in such poems as "Her Triumph," "Chosen," and "Her Vision," where the woman looks at her circumstances much more clearly than before, and wins our involvement in her emotional life as the man never does. The shock of her renewed suffering at the close of "Her Vision" offers the psychic conditions for her retreat back to the wide interval and relative indifference of the sequence's last poems.

The ninth and tenth lyrics, "A Last Confession" and "Meeting," make a bloc much like the concluding poems in *A Man Young and Old*. Now the wide interval, though fictionally justified, is perhaps close to that in "His Memories" and "The Secrets of the Old," its traces of passion also arrested and transformed. The two poems' complementary designs are emphasized by their corresponding forms, for they are the only consecutive installments in this sequence to use the same stanza since "Father and Child" and "Before the World Was Made."

A Last Confession

What lively lad most pleasured me
Of all that with me lay?
I answer that I gave my soul
And loved in misery,
But had great pleasure with a lad
That I loved bodily.

Flinging from his arms I laughed
To think his passion such
He fancied that I gave a soul
Did but our bodies touch,
And laughed upon his breast to think
Beast gave beast as much.

I gave what other women gave
That stepped out of their clothes,
But when this soul, its body off,
Naked to naked goes,

He it has found shall find therein
What none other knows,

And give his own and take his own
And rule in his own right;
And though it loved in misery
Close and cling so tight,
There's not a bird of day that dare
Extinguish that delight.

MEETING

Hidden by old age awhile
In masker's cloak and hood,
Each hating what the other loved,
Face to face we stood:
"That I have met with such," said he,
"Bodes me little good."

"Let others boast their fill," said I,
"But never dare to boast
That such as I had such a man
For lover in the past;
Say that of living men I hate
Such a man the most."

"A loony'd boast of such a love,"
He in his rage declared:
But such as he for such as me—
Could we both discard
This beggarly habiliment—
Had found a sweeter word.

The woman's wariness of strong emotions and insuperable processes is undoubtedly vital to the closure of this sequence, as the corresponding feeling was to the other work. But as though he were freed by the nascent artifactual impulse of *A Woman* or startled by the sterility of *A Man*, Yeats allows the woman here to retain the intelligible features of human passion, to keep the molds of her past acts available for new uses. Where the male lyrics show an insistent and disquieting absence of goals or ends—portray an emotion, that is, that implies no desire for a fulfilling action or state—these female lyrics still give off the flicker of a commitment to such ends in their anticipations of the soul's transcendence after death, and in the imagined possibility of rejuvenation. Further, both imaginings preserve the vestiges of her past engagement with physical love, casting the soul's rapture in its terms and invoking its remembered sweetness and "delight." Consider, in contrast, how the man introduces the matter of the soul's ascent in "His Wildness." His urge to "sail up there" is passed off as the reader's or auditor's ("O bid me"), as though the man can evade its origination. And the envisioned scene "there" in the second stanza, appearing as though unsummoned by a wish of the speaker ("were I but there"), parodies the strivings of other characters and his former self in order to show his utter detachment. At its end, then, the *Woman* series denies its foreparts much less radically than its countertext does. She will not parody her old longings, but conserves their shape for different ends.

As an installment in a construction of character, the last poems in the *Woman* series encourage a bleak assessment of her final state. Yeats had a stark idea of the emotions that ruled him in old age, a notion that might have come out of an Aristotelian rhetoric for its flinty categorization of human behavior: he called these emotions "lust" and "rage," as in his lyric "The Spur," from the *Last Poems* of 1940 ("They were not such a plague when I was young; / What else have I to spur me into song?").[34] The two penultimate lyrics of *A Woman Young and Old* make a two-leaf portrait, almost too schematic, of these attributes in utterance. Lust is not new to the sequence, of course, but has regularly figured in the lyrics of wider intervals: the distance between the perceptible emotion in "Father and Child" or "Consolation" and the emotion's object in each case adds urgency to the moral questions we have for the speaker anyway, and makes her stand toward her lovers seem coldly playful. These lyrics are consistently redressed by the intercalated poems of the pentameter bloc, which profess a more serious feeling and introspection, and sharply close those intervals.

But after "Her Vision in the Wood," "A Last Confession" must be seen as a more decisive episode for the woman's development than those earlier swerves from responsibility and authority. This bloc is, one supposes, the inevitable product of her experience in love. In fact, the links to other elements of the sequence are numerous and telling. Awaiting the soul's disrobing as foreseen in "A Last Confession," the woman implicitly concedes the very different quality of her old age in the "cloak and hood" that mask her in "Meeting." That vision of the soul's freedom makes all her coverings and decorations, even the makeup in "Before the World Was Made," seem vain and cumbersome attentions to a dying animal, and suggest that the tyranny of the body is not the old woman's burden alone but a lifelong fact.

"Meeting" is the record of an empirical encounter that casts into sad relief all the earlier meetings between lovers in the sequence, from "Her Triumph" to "Chosen" to "A Last Confession." The former victims and torturers stare "face to face," as though trying to recollect the pure sensual appeal that shone through the first utterances in the series. With comic and pathetic overstatement, however, they profess only "hate" and "rage" for one another, and the wistful last lines indicate that this extravagant loathing, too, is founded only on appearances. At the end of a life's round of loves and lovers, these former friends have come no closer to apprehending each other's essence or "soul" than they were in the giddiest days of youth. The greatest reward love can offer in a lifetime—the climactic stillness of "Chosen"—proves to be entirely illusory. For if the lovers once attained a measure of peace and a seeing into perfection, these were personal, incommunicable returns; in "Meeting," as in "Parting," the lovers lack a language for recalling their finest moments together. The insights achieved on the plane of bodily communication cannot be captured on the plane of words, and the experience of love is therefore solitary in spite of intercourse. "His heart my heart did seem," and only seem.

   A Woman Young and Old, like *A Man*, concludes with a Sophoclean choral ode, the tribute to love and lament for the heroine from the *Antigone*.

> Overcome—O bitter sweetness,
> Inhabitant of the soft cheek of a girl—
> The rich man and his affairs,
> The fat flocks and the fields' fatness,
> Mariners, rough harvesters;
> Overcome gods upon Parnassus;
>
> Overcome the Empyrean; hurl
> Heaven and Earth out of their places,
> That in the same calamity
> Brother and brother, friend and friend,
> Family and family,
> City and city may contend,
> By that great glory driven wild.
>
> Pray I will and sing I must,
> And yet I weep—Oedipus' child
> Descends into the loveless dust.[35]

Here, too, Yeats engages a final analogy and dissolves his female speaker into the identity of a canonical figure of classical culture without any explicit link between the analogy's two parts. In both instances it is an appropriate motion for closure, indicating that the man and woman have lived out patterns of mind and feeling as old as Western experience. This is another argument, then, against nominativity: it has been implied that human lives are too entangled to corroborate the Petrarchan life-history, that as lover's lives change they resist a birth-to-death fiction, that lovers themselves cannot come to know each other's essences; now we confront the idea that none of us leads an original life anyway, so the recovery of a man's or woman's experience might as well reach for congruent fragments of transpersonal histories, old and new. In this conclusion to a pair of series that deliberately carry out the transition between fictional models, we find ourselves, appropriately enough, not hearing another confession but staring at a strangely contemporary artifact.

Compared with its original stasimon, a paean to love in the *Antigone*, Yeats's translation is not very clear about its topic. Most modern translators begin the paean with an explicit apostrophe to "Love," but Yeats banishes the word entirely from the poem, preferring to let the reader name the object from his or her experience of the ode. As the ode from *Colonus* searches out a justification and a strangely "gay" idiom for the old man's withdrawal from "entanglements," this paean rejoins that the woman has never sought nor achieved a release from love's governance. All her acts and wishes are stamped with its contours. All the figures of her discourse—the rampant mythological and zodiacal imagery, and the personal language of "bitter sweetness," of faces and eyes and hair—are in the field where love plays and rules. The ode draws a conclusion very different from the sterile ending of *A Man Young and Old*, for it allows that love wins impossible triumphs, though by their sheer force these acts may disrupt established orders. It holds out the hope that she will realize a permanent victory over birds of day and loveless dust, that her long service to love in its various base and ideal aspects will power a transcendence like that imagined in the concluding stanzas of "A Last Confession." The first words of each stanza in the translation ("overcome . . . overcome . . . pray I will") direct the tone here, as does the fact Yeats makes unavoidable in the last tercet: that the woman's consciousness has gone elsewhere, that the present speaker is some unfamiliar and unidentified observer. It is a significant index of the sequence's shattered nominativity, I think, that while the stasimon in *A Man* might have been spoken by the man himself, this poem admits an external, choral intelligence into the sequence with a clamor of personal pronouns, extending the principle of openness to other voices begun in "Father and Child" and carried out in "Parting." (Since Pound had a major hand in the revision of this poem, it is worth comparing Yeats's closing ode with Pound's Canto 95, the last of the *Rock-Drill* subsequence, which was probably composed with both the substance and the location of the former in mind. Canto 95 is the semiotic and emotional obverse of the Yeats's ode, establishing "LOVE" as center and guide, but widening the orbit of reference to show the weakening of its gravity.[36] Yeats's poem circles inward until one can feel the pull.) Like us, the speaker who uses the pronoun "I" barely suppresses his hope that the woman, an escapee of the bonds of men from

"Father and Child" to "Oedipus' child," will achieve her liberation at last; and that all the rest of us, loving ourselves as well as others, will too.

The turn into artifactuality across *A Man* and *A Woman Young and Old* not only verifies a contemporary change in the resources of the lyric sequence—on reading the "Antigone" ode, for example, one has to think of Tiresias in *The Waste Land* and a multitude of other choral figures in contemporary sequences—but enacts a shift in Yeats's poetics as well. These countertexts are the outlet that opens toward such late multivocal pieces as *Words for Music Perhaps* (1932), the twelve *Supernatural Songs* (1935), and *The Three Bushes* (1938). *Words for Music Perhaps*—"all emotion and all impersonal," as Yeats saw it—begins with a lyric that invites one striking, mysterious element into its otherwise nominative program: a refrain that may be the imagined words of the speaker Crazy Jane, or some redaction of her antagonist the Bishop, or (perhaps most likely) the comment of a sparsely realized chorus that speaks the poet's views.[37]

> Bring me to the blasted oak
> That I, midnight upon the stroke,
> (*All find safety in the tomb.*)
> May call down curses on his head
> Because of my dear Jack that's dead.
> Coxcomb was the least he said:
> *The solid man and the coxcomb.*
>
> Nor was he Bishop when his ban
> Banished Jack the Journeyman,
> (*All find safety in the tomb.*)
> Nor so much as parish priest,
> Yet he, an old book in his fist,
> Cried that we lived like beast and beast:
> *The solid man and the coxcomb.*
>
> ("Crazy Jane and the Bishop," 1–14)

A similarly impersonal voice occurs in the third lyric, "Crazy Jane on the Day of Judgment," to frame Jane's utterances and to relate the answers of a male interrogator. The remaining twenty-two poems of *Words for Music Perhaps* include the wonderstruck averments of two young people—a woman and man who may well be Jane and Jack, respectively, telescoped into their innocent pasts—and a set of lyrics that express male and female intelligences on an uncircumstantiated, synchronic model. These latter speakers utter a "wisdom" belonging more to their sexes than to any discernible "selves" of theirs, and speak things that would be out of character if they were particular constructions in the fashion of the woman young and old or Crazy Jane:

HER DREAM

I dreamed as in my bed I lay,
All night's fathomless wisdom come,
That I had shorn my locks away
And laid them on Love's lettered tomb:
But something bore them out of sight
In a great tumult of the air,
And after nailed upon the night
Berenice's burning hair.

HIS BARGAIN

Who talks of Plato's spindle;
What set it whirling round?
Eternity may dwindle,
Time is unwound,
Dan and Jerry Lout
Change their loves about.

However they may take it,
Before the thread began
I made, and may not break it
When the last thread has run,
A bargain with that hair
And all the windings there.

The location of the lyrics in the series implies that the personalities of Jane and Jack have been drawn back in time to their liminal days between innocence and experience—to their first mutual cognizance of each gendered essence away from its outer show—and then coarsened, their limits collapsed, into these very essences. This pattern of subtraction concludes with the fifteenth poem, "Three Things," in which a "bone upon the shore" remembers its nearest approaches to life in an intercourse of the soul, its moments of highest fulfillment. The original speaker of the series having dissolved, then, a fresh voice enters in "Lullaby" and "After Long Silence" who fairly resembles the amatory speakers in Yeats's earlier volumes. It is as though a version of the poet's amatory characters steps out of Crazy Jane's erasure, showing the final and irreducible self behind her purposes and particularities. The remainder of the sequence represents that speaker's transfiguration into the more particular character Tom the Lunatic, a counterpart to Crazy Jane.[38] The roughly symmetrical arrangement of distinct voices in *Words for Music Perhaps*—where a relatively differentiated female self goes back into the mixing bowl of identity, and a man emerges as her pendant—suggests something of the range of perspectives available to the artifactual sequence, and indicates Yeats's vocal play in the fictions of his later career.[39]

At this point, this book potentially comes into confederacy with the many recent studies of modern sequences that might be said to fill out a description of the tendency I call artifactuality. If those accounts have not seemed to resemble each other much until now, the reason is perhaps that by its own principles, its inbuilt resistance to norms, and its many alliances with cognate events in other arts and media, artifactuality is always hard to define except in specific practice—and even there, its innovations may seem to belong more to a particular artist or a local movement than to a widely situated, transhistorical trend in lyric poetics. Even a successful effort at fashioning these innovations into a single context, such as Victor Knoll's inventive reading of Mário de Andrade's entire body of poetry or Marjorie Perloff's indispensable essays on the Pound tradition, may implicitly (and rightly) put off the matter of still wider contexts.[40] But my work here is intensely concerned with such contexts; I will remain on my long-range trajectory to show an outcome of post-Petrarchism in Spanish American poetry of the last several decades. The next chapter, then, takes up two New World lyric fictions in view of the inflections—inseparably phenomenal, cultural, and political—they bring to the premises of the form.

MEASURING SPACE, BECOMING SPACE: THE SPATIALITY OF NERUDA'S *ALTURAS DE MACCHU PICCHU* AND ADÁN'S *LA MANO DESASIDA*

ONE WAY to consider whether a work of literature realizes the phenomenon of fiction is to see how readers have become involved with the world it evokes. Fictions, lyric or otherwise, tend to give the illusion of occurring in a knowable place, while ritually oriented poems are supposed to happen anywhere the reader or auditor might be.[1] As a founding text of lyric fiction, Petrarch's *Canzoniere* has always led its readers to explore its represented world. In 1525 Alessandro Vellutello, one of the great Petrarchist commentators of that century, published the results of his research into the sites of the *Canzoniere*, a serious effort to recover geographical unity from the fiction. I quote from the chapter called "Origin of the Lady Laura, with the Description of the Place in Vaucluse Where the Poet First Fell in Love with Her":

> Some have said, speaking as a matter of opinion, that the lady Laura . . . was from Gravesons, a village two leagues from Avignon, and that on Good Friday, she having come to the city for absolution, the poet was enamored of her in the church of Saint Clara. I take this to be a false, worn-out opinion of too many, especially those from Avignon. . . . Others have said that the lady Laura was not from Gravesons, but from a tiny place by the name of Borgetto . . . because of that line "And now from a small village (*picciol borgo*) He has given us a sun," which occurs in [*Canzoniere* 4.12]. What infinite providence and art that would be, for in that country there is no Borgetto or Borghetto to be found no matter how hard you look. But the place provokes a great deal of faith that she was not from Avignon, because if she were, the poet would have had no reason to say that God had given her from out of a small village—Avignon having always been a magnificent city, especially in the days of the Roman court.[2]

Vellutello's map, shown as the frontispiece to the present book, was reprinted in about a fifth of the editions of the sequence published over the next hundred years.[3] In 1564 a new edition presented a discussion, chiefly between the commentators Alfonso Cambi Importuni and Luc'Antonio Ridolfi, concerning "the exact day and hour of Petrarch's *innamora-*

mento."[4] Today these exercises matter not because of any information they turn up, but because they indicate the generic identity and phenomenological reception of Petrarch's lyric sequence. They invite us to think about the protocols that attend other major texts of lyric fiction. As Vellutello understood of the *Canzoniere*, many sequences organized by the *vita* of the speaker contain at least the rudiments of a geography—but to what purpose? The places evoked in such fictions might be construed to fashion a process of their own sort, a spatial conceit, across the lyrics; even where one finds only contingent or vitiated geography, there may still be at least the two axes, temporal and spatial, operating together to give the sense of a world.

For a number of reasons—including, I believe, the urge to stand apart from the emphases of European humanist culture, and to revise openly and directly the terms of its fictions—Latin American poets have given much more attention to lyric versions of space and geography than their European and North American counterparts. In this chapter, I propose to examine two modern reconceptions of the sequence as spatial fiction: Pablo Neruda's *Alturas de Macchu Picchu* (1945), the second part and spine of his ambitious volume of historical reinterpretation called *Canto General* (1950); and *La Mano Desasida* (1964 and 1980) by Martín Adán, an oblique reply to post-Petrarchan and Nerudean poets as well as an original, hermetic disposition of the form. Neruda's work adapts the properties of the sequence to express physical composition and movement, much as Petrarch and his successors evoke time; Adán's series breaks open the form to realize a far more radical evocation, in effect to challenge its forerunners on the energy and fidelity of their adaptation to space. Because my concern here is strictly for evoked space, as earlier for evoked time, I can say nothing about the Latin American texts that variously explore the space of the printed page, such as the concrete experiments of the Chilean Vicente Huidobro or the Mexican Marco Antonio Montes de Oca, or the distinguished achievements since the 1950s of the Noigandres circle in Brazil. This essay is an extension of the post-Petrarchan line I have already measured, not a departure from it; I aim only to communicate here something of the distinctly New World ideology of lyric understood by poets who aim to extend lyric fiction into a spatial dimension.

Neruda's *Alturas de Macchu Picchu* participates in the serial conceits of earlier European and American sequences, containing both a rendition of fictional process and a personal design in the figure of the traveling speaker.[5] It is, in fact, a nominative sequence according to the terms set down earlier in this book.[6] From the first, however, Neruda works to establish the primacy of a spatial unity based in geographical discriminations and the fictional conceit of progress through space; the original stroke in this conceit is a moral and emotional valuation of the speaker's movements through lyric space. With the speaker's upright body tacitly drafted as marker—and such an election is only one, particularly physical sign of this work's nominative centering on the adventures of the speaking self—the first poem establishes that horizontal, geodesic movement means incrimination in the commercialism and spiritual depletion of modern urban life, while vertical movement, subterranean or ascendant, evokes the possibility of physical and spiritual escape from worldly matters. The former kind of travel suggests the path of the salesman and the shopper, while the latter marks the line of climbers and diggers, the founders and recoverers of cultures. In plain fact, the traveling speaker adopts a Euclidean geometry as his moral correlative—showing at right angles the collision of two ideas of life—and claims to have measured both legs of the angle from his own experience. I quote the proem, which discloses the Euclidean grid and its moral implications:

> Del aire al aire, como una red vacía,
> iba yo entre las calles y la atmósfera, llegando y despidiendo,
> en el advenimiento del otoño la moneda extendida
> de las hojas, y entre la primavera y las espigas,
> lo que el más grande amor, como dentro de un guante
> que cae, nos entrega como una larga luna.
>
> (Días de fulgor vivo en la intemperie
> de los cuerpos: aceros convertidos
> al silencio del ácido:
> noches deshilachadas hasta la última harina:
> estambres agredidos de la patria nupcial.)
>
> Alguien que me esperó entre los violines
> encontró un mundo como una torre enterrada
> hundiendo su espiral más abajo de todas
> las hojas de color de ronco azufre:
> más abajo, en el oro de la geología,
> como una espada envuelta en meteoros,
> hundí la mano turbulenta y dulce
> en lo más genital de lo terrestre.
>
> Puse la frente entre las olas profundas,
> descendí como gota entre la paz sulfúrica,
> y, como un ciego, regresé al jazmín
> de la gastada primavera humana.
>
> (From air to air, like a net dragged empty,
>   I wandered between the streets and the atmosphere, coming and going,

in the advent of autumn the money extended
by the leaves, and between spring and wheat ears,
what the richest love, as deep in a dropped glove,
gives us like a benevolent moon.

[Days of radiance living in the intemperateness
of bodies: steels converted to acidic silence:
nights raveled to the last flour:
the stamens of the nuptial land assailed.]

Someone who awaited me among the violins
met a world like a tower interred
sinking its spiral beneath all the leaves
the color of harsh sulfur:
and deeper yet, in the gold of geology,
like a sword ensheathed in meteors,
I sank my turbulent and loving hand
into the most genital places of the earth.

I bowed my face between the deep waves,
descended like a drop among sulfurous calm,
and like a blind man, retreated to the jasmine
of our spent human spring.)[7]

This is confessional history, as in the proem of the *Canzoniere*, but it is a history told through itinerary, through movement.[8] The first two lines establish a terrestrial plane—as the second lyric will have it, the "corridors [of] air, land, or sea"—along which the speaker moves in his worldly doings. In the first paragraph, his superficial tour seems an affront to the earth: the principal emotion excited by the stanza, in the recollecting speaker and the reader alike, is a mixed regret and astonishment that the speaker swaddled in "streets" has so paltry an intercourse with the soil that loves him and offers him the harvest. The second paragraph, hypotactic to the first, further represents the unnaturalness of those wandering days, and closes on the image of flattened and "assailed" stamens, the yield both of humankind's invasive administration of the earth and of the speaker's walking. The original Greek sense of "stand" waits significantly behind *estambre* ("stamen") here, assuring the perpendicular clash of the movement set going in the first stanza and the object sown in the second. As far as the speaker's net of attainments comes out "empty," it is because his days are spent patrolling sterile corridors and trampling his proper fruits underfoot, chasing perhaps one variety of *moneda* and letting go the monies offered by the earth.

With the third stanza, the speaker tells of his withdrawal from temporal and civilized society. The companion who "awaited me among the

violins"—one sees, I think, the redundantly horizontal motions of the
bowing—encountered a speaker half in this world and half sinking below,
and the proem's last lines report the climax, the plunge of mind and hand
that releases him from his tour. Groping for vitals, he calls the earth on
its promise of love. The last lines introduce the rest of the sequence as the
dream of his release and an investigation of our common exhaustion, its
causes and prospects.

The personal or anthropomorphic dimension noted, it is worth remarking how little of the canto's stock of energies is directed toward the
elaboration of anything like a character, and how much toward the tuning of a Euclidean tension: the opposed purposes of man and earth meet
always at right angles, like flowers in the road. It hardly matters why the
speaker pursues his empty terrestrial course, or why he changes his orientation to "sink" in the proem's latter half. Instead it weighs that the
space of this world is fully charged as the scene of the speaker's oscillation, and that every likely equivalence of movement and morality is
framed and tightened. Further, the moral force of the three-dimensional
Euclidean grid is not only maintained but preferred through the rest of
the series. At places it gives a distinct shape to the speaker's recollections
of his worldly life and his former emotional solitude:

> How many times in wintry city streets, or in
> a bus, a boat at dusk, or in the denser solitude
> of festive nights, drenched in the sound
> of bells and shadows, in the very lair of human pleasure,
> have I wanted to pause and look for the eternal, unfathomable
> truth's filament I'd fingered once in stone, or in the flash a kiss released.
> (Tarn, 2.22–27)

> I could not love within each man a tree
> with its remaindered autumns on its back (leaves falling in their thousands),
> all these false deaths and all these resurrections,
> sans earth, sans depths:
> I wished to swim in the most ample lives,
> the widest estuaries,
> and when, little by little, man came denying me
> closing his paths and doors so that I could not touch
> his wounded inexistence with my divining fingers,
> I came by other ways, through streets, river by river,
> city by city, one bed after another,
> forcing my brackish semblance through a wilderness
> till in the last of hovels, lacking all light and fire,

bread, stone and silence, I paced at last alone,
dying of my own death.

(Tarn, 4.17–31)

And at places in the early cantos of the series, the geometry gives the sense
of a hidden unity beyond and above humankind's terrestrial venue, a Platonic zone from which only imperfect visions of man's higher purposes
are "thrown":

I could only grasp a cluster of faces or masks
thrown down like rings of hollow gold,
like scarecrow clothes, daughters of rabid autumn
shaking the stunted tree of the frightened races.

(Tarn, 2.34–37)

In short, this Euclidean grid is the initial controlling principle of *Alturas
de Macchu Picchu*, the pattern to which action and history must be fitted
to be made comprehensible.[9]

Owing to both historical and imaginative reasons, the Euclidean geometry of straight lines and right angles makes a natural and efficient
correlative for Neruda's moral discriminations. Geometry has been associated with ethical and spiritual improvement since Plato made it the second vital feature of his ruling caste's curriculum, and paeans to geometry's rational essence ("[geometry] would tend to draw the soul to
truth")[10] are intimately contemporaneous with the rise of endowing ideas
about the dignity of man. For many centuries, Euclidean geometry was
viewed as a corpus of "right" principles rather than the tentative conclusions of an experimental science: Kant's appointment of geometry as a
synthetic, a priori system of knowledge is notorious, and John Stuart Mill
holds up geometrical postulates as belonging to one of the few human
preoccupations "where there is nothing at all to be said on the wrong side
of the question."[11] Even after Carl Friedrich Gauss, Bernhard Riemann,
and other mathematicians of the nineteenth century began to chart the
discoveries that would unsettle and finally refute the necessity of Euclidean geometry, the dissolution of ideas of space based in the *Elements* occurred much more slowly than the changes of mind occasioned by coeval
discoveries in geology and anthropology.[12]

In the Western cultural imagination, then, the forms and axioms of Euclidean geometry have been and largely remain a body of "pure universal
statements"[13] more or less untainted by the possibility of untruth, a refuge of clean discriminations that seems to corroborate an idealist view of
humankind's powers. One hardly has to accept all of Wilhelm Worrin-

ger's bold theory of aesthetic abstraction—itself an important influence on the early modernism of Pound and the Vorticists—to agree with him that "[the] simple line and its development in purely geometrical regularity was bound to offer the greatest possibility of happiness to the man disquieted by the obscurity and entanglement of phenomena. For here the last trace of connection with, and dependence on, life has been effaced, here the highest absolute form, the purest abstraction has been achieved; here is law, here is necessity, while everywhere else the caprice of the organic prevails."[14] If the pictorial artist's quarrel with "phenomena" concerns man's or God's place in the universe, geometry affords ways of delivering centrality and distinctness to his icons of humanity or divinity. If the sculptor designs to assert the value of a particular act, geometry gives her the means of imparting vitality and stability to her thinker, her dancer, her lovers. And if the serio-temporal artist's obsession is a dynamic question—the soul's destination after death, or the proper path of life in this world—the spatial relations codified in the *Elements* allow him or her to figure such convictions with vivid, intuitive force, treating what is actually ideological and constructivist as though it were somehow inevitable and exemplary. As Jacques Derrida has it, "geometrical exemplariness undoubtedly results from the fact that, as an 'abstract' material science, this exemplariness treats the spatiality of bodies (which is only one of the body's eidetic components), i.e., treats what confers sense on the notion of horizon and object. Despite all the antagonistic motifs which animate phenomenology, space's privilege therein is in certain respects remarkable."[15] Consider the most ready-to-hand instance in English of such exemplariness in poetic use, the closing stanzas of Donne's "A Valediction: Forbidding Mourning":

> Our two soules therefore, which are one,
>   Though I must goe, endure not yet
> A breach, but an expansion,
>   Like gold to ayery thinnesse beate.
>
> If they be two, they are two so
>   As stiffe twin compasses are two,
> Thy soule the fixt foot, makes no show
>   To move, but doth, if the'other doe.
>
> And though it in the center sit,
>   Yet when the other far doth rome,
> It leanes, and hearkens after it,
>   And growes erect, as that comes home.

Such wilt thou be to mee, who must
Like th'other foot, obliquely runne;
Thy firmnes makes my circle just,
And makes me end, where I begunne.

Here the geometrical conceit is a local expression of the speaker's sense
of amatory completeness: offered under a conditional clause and sub-
sumed in a train of assurances, it serves the poem's principal, original
emotion. All horizons—of speaker, addressee, and reader—are coextensive with the literal shape of this hypothetical circle, and the closure of
the fiction is graphic and absolute.

Neruda's geometry, however, is even more than a local conceit, and
yields no priority to other orders. The poet calculates that the rational
inviolability of geometrical shapes and relations will support his moral
discriminations, will absolve them of their arbitrariness and tinge them
with rightness. He describes two ways of life in vague terms of unfulfill-
ment and approval, respectively, and allows the tension and differential
force of the implied right angle to make his intuition seem sound—or even
imperative. Here geometry is neither local nor subordinate as an element
of the lyric's argument, but is the argument itself.

These first cantos enact another, parallel program of filling imagined
space with emotion, here in Neruda's advance of the preposition *entre*
("between" or "among") from a merely literal to a virtually tropological
meaning. In the proem's second line, the first instance of the preposition
in the sequence seems strictly literal—locating the speaker on his ribbon
of travel—until the second *entre* arrives two lines further, to claim a metaphorical (because both spatial and temporal) sense of betweenness:

From air to air, like a net dragged empty,
I wandered between the streets and the atmosphere, coming and going,
in the advent of autumn the money extended
by the leaves, and between spring and wheat ears,
what the richest love, as deep in a dropped glove,
gives us like a benevolent moon.

(1.1–6)

The temporal element in the fourth line's prepositional phrase, which
might be translated "between spring and harvest," is qualified slightly by
the second noun's concreteness (*espigas* or "wheat ears"). This mitigation
or reversal of purpose—a turning of space into time and partly back into
body again, like the treatment of the waves in the choral ode of *A Woman
Young and Old*—has a clear result for the sequence: it loosens the import
and suggestibility of *entre*, liberating its reference from merely spatial or
temporal dimensions to exact both of these in some measure. The fall of

the divide between the preposition's two usual senses marks the origin of a trope of interposition, the instrument of the poet's conviction that location can imply season and history and much more, that place matters greatly as both origin and expression of the psychic lives of human beings. Always a gesture toward the succeeding noun phrase, the preposition *entre* will announce the divisibility of the states or objects named there, and will ask us to ponder the sense of such divisions. It works in opposite fashion to the Latin copulative particle *que*, which, when joined to the second of two words, invites us to contemplate in retrospect the union of things just named. Unlike the Latin conjunction, Neruda's *entre* runs over its merely grammatical function, and comes to indicate something neither temporal nor spatial alone, something finally emotional.

Already at the third paragraph, the preposition appears to represent something more than a spatial or temporal plotting of its object's orientation: "Someone who awaited me among the violins / met a world like a tower interred" (1.12–13). Here the *alguien* ("someone") sheds his humanity and assumes the air of an anonymous, bankrupt civility from his enclosure by violins. The refined, artificial nature of the instruments—an impression only heightened by our glimpsing them here in unspecified quantity—introduces an implied field of connotation bounded by the object of the preposition, an intimated space within which any object or action will take on the quality of what surrounds it. Wherever position indicates character, the trope of interposition is at work, opening figurative spaces that will contribute to a definition of the speaker and his world in emotional terms. Seen in the developing context of the poem's binary morality, the *violines* enter as the most attractive vessels of the mercenary culture the speaker roams and queries. They ensure that the juncture of lines 12 and 13 will carry us from a nightclub to a ruin as though to condense the larger tendency of the lyric, where the moral and psychic contrariety of the two "worlds" is stark.

Local prepositional fields on this model are common in the first cantos of the sequence, where the definition and emotional galvanism of space agree with the poet's larger purpose. The final paragraph of the first lyric shows two cases, both of which catch the states of the encircled *frente* ("face") and *gota* ("drop") as the speaker's thoughts turn toward peace and profundity:

> I bowed my face *between* the deep waves,
> descended like a drop *among* sulfurous calm,
> and like a blind man, retreated to the jasmine
> of our spent human spring.
>
> (1.20–23, emphasis added)

Still more examples occur in the second poem, where Neruda manages the trope of interposition to achieve not the mutual likeness and ingress of adjacent elements, but the disappearance of one into the other:

> Flower to flower delivers up its seed
> and rock maintains its blossom broadcast
> in a bruised garment of diamond and sand
> yet man crumples the petal of the light he skims
> from the predetermined sources of the sea
> and drills the pulsing metal in his hands.
> Soon, caught *between* clothes and smoke, on the sunken floor,
> the soul's reduced to a shuffled pack,
> quartz and insomnia, tears in the sea,
> like pools of cold—yet this is not enough:
> he kills, confesses it on paper with contempt,
> muffles it in the rug of habit, shreds it
> [*between* or *within*] a hostile apparel of wire.
>
> No: for in corridors—air, sea or land—
> who guards his veins unarmed
> like scarlet poppies? Now rage has bled
> the dreary wares of the trader in creatures,
> while, in the plum tree's coronet, the dew
> has left a coat of visitations for a thousand years
> pinned to the waiting twig, oh heart, oh face
> ground small *among* the cavities of autumn.
>
> (Tarn, 2.1–21, emphasis added)

Here the serial degradations suffered by the soul are framed by two images of betweenness and loss, first as the civilized man's spirit is raveled in the interpenetration of cloth and smoke after a carousal—that part of the lyric hums with the hidden logic of the nightclub and the violins—and finally as it is shredded deliberately through another man-made *vestidura*, some modern hair shirt that mutilates the soul but leaves the body intact. The fragility and elusiveness of the *alma* ("soul") in our world could not come over more strikingly than in the first stanza's final lines, where the modern everyman fidgets with it variously and obsessively like the comic hero of a Keaton two-reeler.

The speaker then considers the possibility of purifying, compensatory angers that restore the soul's dignity now and then: to a humanity pulverized by the less efficient remains of a slave trade, he utters his consolation, that human life is sold less freely now than once. The turn of the spatial trope toward the apostrophized audience ("oh heart, oh face / . . . among the cavities of autumn") gives a fresh urgency to his complaint, extending that desperate interposition to all of us who are decomposed and lost "between" or "among" the fixtures of a tawdry civilization. The rest of the second lyric struggles to make a personal statement of this modern problem, and to issue a vital question at last:

> I had no place in which my hand could rest—
> no place running like harnessed water,
> firm as a nugget of anthracite or crystal—
> responding, hot or cold, to my open hand.
>
> What was man? In what layer of his humdrum conversation,
> among his shops and sirens—in which of his metallic movements
> lived on imperishably the quality of life?
>
> (Tarn, 2.38–44)

Much of the force of these poems' concerns, then, has been decisively translated into a spatial register: the lyrics evoke a moral geometry and depend on a locative trope to carry their sense that space offers a vivid set of references with which to demonstrate what we have realized as a species, how well or badly we have departed from our nature and origins, how much further we might go. In these cantos the lexicon and imaginative universe of space are charged with a significance comparable to that of time in the first poems of Petrarch's *Canzoniere*. In fact, the basis of this spatial program must be found in ideology, the ground of Neruda's poetry. As Jaime Concha, Alain Sicard, and other critics have shown, Neruda's mature poetry is steeped in a devout materialism.[16] The poet writes from the conviction that matter speaks its own language, and that in principle he can apprehend its discourse by a determined attention to what might be called the moral order of things: the relations among matter, disclosed in its sensory properties, that seem to lay bare a telluric but preterhuman pattern of existence and feeling, and to show the impurity of humankind where men and women have touched things:

> It is worth one's while, at certain hours of the day or night, to scrutinize useful objects in repose: wheels that have rolled across long, dusty distances with their enormous load of crops or ore, charcoal sacks, barrels, baskets, the hafts and handles of carpenters' tools. The contact these objects have had with man and earth may serve as a valuable lesson to a tortured lyric poet. Worn surfaces, the wear inflicted by human hands, the sometimes tragic, always pathetic, emanations from these objects give reality a magnetism that should not be scorned.
>
> Man's nebulous impurity can be perceived in them: the affinity for groups, the use and obsolescence of materials, the mark of a hand or a foot, the constancy of the human presence that permeates every surface.
>
> This is the poetry we are seeking.[17]

A materialist lyric tends to treat space as a more conventional lyric treats time, selecting its geography as well as its history, combining objects and axes of movement into seemingly adventitious but revealing compositions, and inscribing the emotional quality of the speaker's place as well as his instant in time. Moreover, Neruda's materialism often implies a strong temporal element. Amado Alonso has written that Neruda's vision continually goes out to the inexorable disintegration of matter in time:

> The poet's eyes, ceaselessly open as if they never closed ("Like eyelids held forcefully and horrifyingly open"), see the slow decomposition of all existence in a sweeping and instantaneous gesture, like a motion picture camera which shows us in a few short seconds the slow development of plants. They see the never-ending task of death's scythe in a static flash of lightning, the suicidal tendency of all things to lose their identity, the tumbling of the erect, the decomposition of forms, the fire's ashes. The anarchy that is life and death, with its secret and terrible control. The thawing of the world. The anguish of observing all life incessantly dying: man and his works, the stars, the waves, the plants in the midst of their organic movements, the clouds through their whirling, love, machines, the wear and tear of furniture, and chemical corrosion; in short the crumbling of the physical world, all that moves and gives expression to life is dying. . . .
>
> There is not a single page of *Residence on Earth* where this terrible vision of decay is missing. It is what is invincibly and intuitively felt by the poet, both seen and contemplated. This is not known or comprehended through reason; it is felt, it is lived, and it is suffered in the very bloodstream.[18]

The poet's response to these sights, perhaps strangely, is to become still more convinced that the essence of being is to be found in matter, and to regard time as a winnowing agent that leaves a permanent essence—or as Concha names it, "the Fundamental"[19]—intact and available even while it destroys the corporeal husks of people and things. Neruda's metaphysics contains a truly spatial imperative, for the immanence of essence in matter means that his speakers must search and sift their surroundings relentlessly for traces of meaning left over time. The temporal dimension of most lyric sequences—the original measure of experience they refer to, and are built on—is seen contrarily by Neruda to serve the valuation of matter and space, with which the lyric genre and the form at hand have always had much less to do. As Concha puts it, "The Nerudean metaphysics is, then, a geography. Nothing more and nothing less. A profound geography, a tautology. Neruda gives to the land what is the land's, and he is extremely conscious of this quality of his poetry. . . . Neruda's metaphysics is 'immensely physical' not only because of his peremptory intolerance for every kind of transcendence, not only because of his unbreakable adherence to the truth of Nature. It is also *physical* as much as the planes of existence that it discovers, the plane of temporality and the plane of the Fundamental, present a concrete spatial situation which it is necessary to accept in all literalness."[20] And a spatial metaphysics inspires a spatial poetics. In the context of Neruda's thought, his appropriation of geometry as an instrument for moral distinctions is neither capricious nor reductive, but is his faithful recognition that a spatial register will best direct and convey humankind's most radical questions about its world; the trope of interposition, as well, returns psychic and moral concerns to the geographical lexicon where they ultimately belong. These principles, which first come to prominence in the volumes of *Residencia en la tierra* (1925–47), generally continue to appear in his most ambitious book of lyrics, the *Canto General* of 1950. Neruda's ambition "from the beginning," maintains Sicard, was "to write a canto that, instead of reducing or abolishing space and time, as one entire tradition of poetry had done, could embrace them in their totality."[21]

The materialist poet who claims the lyric sequence as I have described it in the preceding chapters will necessarily introduce into the received form some changes that follow from his or her peculiar vision. Replacing time with space as a first principle of fictional phenomenology, he or she will likely adapt the properties of sequentiality and juncture for original ends, making them respectively show physical or geographical composition and adjacence, the inner dynamic of a place and the map of its exploration. Its topoi will take up the invitation of their name and adopt a spatial register: Petrarch's retrospective topos gives way to Neruda's trope of interposition. And the Petrarchan fiction of temporal process will often diminish or fall to a sensation of movement in space, and that conceit will achieve the same efficacy in its setting that time does in the *Canzoniere*.

Something of the spirit of this transposition is already native to the post-Petrarchan line of works, of course, in the blason: in the purest instances of such a lyric the poet transposes the serio-temporal progress from line to line to represent not an advance in time but a survey of the topographical and material reality of the beloved's body. In the post-Petrarchan sequence, the blason generally allows a respite from the program of temporal exploration and allows instead a short-lived, hypothetical exercise of power over the body of the donna. That is, the speaker's means of control—historical and physical—find their relative precedence temporarily switched around, as though to allay some of the tension mounting over his empirical impotence. Even where Neruda manifests his liberation from many post-Petrarchan values and imperatives, as in the *Residencia* volumes, he manages to retain some of the means of the earlier phase and to redirect these practices with his specific ideological vision. The aim of the mock-blason "Ritual de mis piernas" ("Ritual of My Legs") is evidently to isolate and exaggerate the civilized, self-cherishing attitude Neruda will reject in *Alturas de Macchu Picchu*:

> So. My knees, like knots
> particular, functional, evident
> drily separate the halves of my legs—
> actually, two different worlds, two different sexes
> aren't as different as these halves.
>
> .   .   .   .
>
> In my ticklish feet
> hard as the sun, open as flowers
> [and perpetual, magnificent soldiers
> in the gray war of space,]
> everything ends, life ends in my feet,
> the alien and hostile begin there:
> names of the world, the limited and remote,
> the substantive, the adjective I've no heart for
> originate there with unrelenting density and coldness.
>
> Always
> manufactured products, hose, shoes or
> simply infinite air
> between my feet and the earth
> intensifying what's isolated, solitary in my being
> something taken for granted between my life and earth
> something hostile, unconquerable.[22]

Since it anticipates his development of the spatial sequence, there is no surprise in Neruda's early experimentation with the blason here and in the amatory sequence *Veinte poemas de amor y una canción desesperada*. In part, one might say that the lyric sequence seems always to direct its practitioners—Sidney, Whitman, Williams, Neruda—into propensities that must be used in one idiom or another; in another part, Neruda seemingly noticed that the post-Petrarchan blason had always sheltered his incipient serial values within the fictional sequence. The program of *Alturas de Macchu Picchu* extends the principle of the blason by animation, inviting its readership not to survey a stationary object but to enter a fresh level of awareness through movement in space.

But just as the most engaging uses of the sequence's properties for temporal play have not been simple, there is no reason to suppose that a mere correspondence between one poem and one place, between consecutive junctures and transits, will realize the possibilities of the spatial series. Wordsworth's example is instructive. In his preface to the *Poems* of 1815, he inspects the "moulds" and "forms" into which poetry may be gathered. He lists there, after the narrative, dramatic, and lyric kinds, "4thly, The Idyllium,—descriptive chiefly either of the processes and appearances of external nature, as the Seasons of Thomson; or of characters, manners, and sentiments, as are Shenstone's School-mistress, The Cotter's Saturday Night of Burns, The Twa Dogs of the same Author; or of these in conjunction with the appearances of Nature, as most of the pieces of Theocritus, the Allegro and Penseroso of Milton, Beattie's Minstrel, Goldsmith's Deserted Village. The Epitaph, the Inscription, the Sonnet, most of the epistles of poets writing in their own persons, and all loco-descriptive poetry, belong to this class."[23] In the present context, the most notable thing about these remarks is the lack of any intrinsic quality, structure, or aim in this sort of poetry: Wordsworth assumes that "external nature" ought to be represented for its own sake, of course, and that the poet will find his order in the world outside the work. He went on to demonstrate his conviction. Among several other productions that belong in the category of the lyric series, he wrote, and published in 1820, thirty-four sonnets entitled *The River Duddon* "which together may be considered as a Poem."[24] The sequence's structural tenet is a progress from the source of the river near Wrynose, on the borders of Westmoreland, Cumberland, and Lancashire, to its resolution twenty miles southwest into the estuary of Duddon Sands and the Irish Sea. The relation between the fictional mode and the geographical imperative is light, almost nonexistent: there is no strong sense here that, in pursuing the river, the speaker is discovering and charting himself in the post-Petrarchan or Nerudean vein. His interest in the Duddon is merely levelheaded and affectionate:

> I seek the birthplace of a native Stream.—
> All hail, ye mountains! hail, thou morning light!
> Better to breathe at large on this clear height
> Than toil in needless sleep from dream to dream:
> Pure flow the verse, pure, vigorous, free, and bright,
> For Duddon, long-loved Duddon, is my theme!
>
> (1.9–14)

The conceit of movement, from Wrynose Pass to Ulpha and Broughton in Furness and beyond, is heavily laid onto the junctures without the involvement of the lyrics as fictions of space. The poems are largely snapshots of such sites as "The Faery Chasm," the view from Pen Crag, and Seathwaite Chapel, and nothing in the series moves between the interstrophic spaces, where invariably one is roused to continue the forced march along a southwesterly route. The lyric tendency to offer temporal change in heaps and layers, to paraphrase Sharon Cameron's memorable elucidation, finds no spatial complement here, and the speaker appears to have little to say about the human implications of space.[25] In fact he is more concerned with time than with space as a phenomenon in the life of humankind, as in his banal "After-Thought":

> I thought of Thee, my partner and my guide,
> As being past away.—Vain sympathies!
> For, backward, Duddon! as I cast my eyes,
> I see what was, and is, and will abide;
> Still glides the Stream, and shall for ever glide;
> The Form remains, the Function never dies;
> While we, the brave, the mighty, and the wise,
> We Men, who in our morn of youth defied
> The elements, must vanish;—be it so!
> Enough, if something from our hands have power
> To live, and act, and serve the future hour;
> And if, as toward the silent tomb we go,
> Through love, through hope, and faith's transcendent dower,
> We feel that we are greater than we know.

(34)

So *The River Duddon* turns out to be a shell of a lyric sequence: a series of sonnets, certainly, but hardly a fiction of any efficacy.

Its structure and orientation to space have much in common with a recent work, *The Shires* (1974) by Donald Davie. Alert to the energies for binding and innovation in modern sequences, however, Davie deliberately withdraws from the fictional mode by putting his lyrics into alphabetical order from "Bedfordshire" to "Yorkshire"; this is, of course, to return emphatically to the extrinsic, editorial strategies of organization that ruled lyric collections before the *Canzoniere*. Davie, like Wordsworth the author of several adept sequences in the conventional post-Petrarchism of his day, knows to reach for something looser and more modest in *The Shires*. He realizes, perhaps, that he has no conceit fit for the chore of reconceiving the modern sequence in spatial terms. The attenuations of these two "loco-descriptive" works indicate how comparatively seldom the lyric sequence has achieved the fictional rigor of the *Canzoniere* or *Alturas de Macchu Picchu*—or Saint-John Perse's *Anabase* (1924), or Raul Bopp's *Cobra Norato* (1931)—in their evocations of space, and why the Latin American geographical sequences have had to invent their own stands.

In *Alturas de Macchu Picchu*, the serial element of the first poems elaborates the spatial investigations I have already described. The speaker has implicitly promised to follow the axes of his geometrical grid and to discover further spaces for habitation within and among the objects of his world. A natural corollary to this sequential principle is that these openings and extensions will start to reveal something integral, that a coherent poetic continent will be episodically disclosed. In the third, fourth, and fifth lyrics of the sequence, however, it is not fully clear how this implicit promise will be redeemed. These poems, the least independent of the series, are given to the articulation of a thematic distinction between two varieties of death, each associated with one of the dimensions carried in Neruda's moral geometry. The third and fourth lyrics, respectively, address the ignominious demise that grows on contemporary humankind out of the moral tone of its debased existence, and a graver, more sudden and certain death.

The human soul was threshed out like maize in the endless
granary of defeated actions, of mean things that happened,
to the very edge of endurance, and beyond,
and not only death, but many deaths, came to each one:
each day a tiny death, dust, worm, a light
flicked off in the mud at the city's edge, a tiny death with coarse wings
pierced into each man like a short lance
and the man was besieged by the bread or by the knife,
the cattle-dealer: the child of sea-harbors, or the dark captain of the plough,
or the rag-picker of snarled streets:

everybody lost heart, anxiously waiting for death, the short death of every day:
and the grinding bad luck of every day was
like a black cup that they drank, with their hands shaking.

(Wright, 3)

Irresistible death invited me many times:
it was like salt occulted in the waves
and what its invisible fragrance suggested
was fragments of wrecks and heights
or vast structures of wind and snowdrift.

I had come to the cut of the blade, the narrowest
channel in air, the shroud of field and stone,
the interstellar void of ultimate steps
and the awesome spiral way:
though not through wave on wave do you attain us, vast sea of death,
but rather like a gallop of twilight,
the comprehensive mathematics of the dark.

(Tarn, 4.1–12)

The third lyric shows the quotidian landscape of its forerunners to be death's secret battleground, the scene of its unheralded victory: this *muerte pequeña* or "little death" advances under the cover of the "mean

things" Neruda likes to represent by horizontal movement.[26] The entire
contemporary setting, in fact, is disclosed as the site of a continual siege
against the upright tower of humanity ("the man was besieged by the
bread or by the knife") by smaller, supine objects. As the picture of belea-
guered humankind is refined, the kinds of men seen as particularly susceptible to the *muerte pequeña* are those who trace geodesic paths across
the globe: the drover, the plowman, the *roedor de las calles espesas* ("ro-
dent of the narrow streets"). The terrestrial itineracy of these people
leaves them vulnerable to daily assaults by petty death, as though death
suffuses the lowest plane of the atmosphere and creeps osmotically
into their lives. There is nothing for humankind to do but await the inevitable, daily assaults. In a closing scene that strikingly anticipates the
spread of toxins in the environment—a good present-day analogy for the
moral infirmity Neruda laments—they drink the little death in their cof-
fee.

The fourth lyric introduces a second sort of death—*la poderosa
muerte*, or "powerful death"—and forces its association with the speaker's retreat from geodesic movement into vertical exploration. At the first,
one sees again Neruda's relative lack of concern and discrimination for
the temporal element of his sequence. In the hands of a poet to whom
time was the most immediate dimension of human experience, the adverbial phrase *muchas veces* ("many times") in line 1 would not go uncon-
nected to other, particular utterances that might give the indefinite adjective emotional connotations. To this speaker and this poet, as I have said,
geography matters much more than history—or perhaps geography allows us to understand how history matters. The intuition of the *poderosa
muerte*, abrupt and unlooked for in the workings of process and character, recalls to the speaker not events but places and physical compositions.
It suggests, mysteriously but significantly, *mitades de hundimientos y altura / o vastas construcciones de viento y ventisquero* ("half-wrecks and
heights / or vast constructions of wind and snow-drift"): first a sort of
inspired imagining that seems to threaten the purity of the speaker's materialism with hints of transcendence and the supernatural, then a recovery in the second line to fix its image in empirical nature. These lines work
a quiet but unmistakable mandate of closing the landscape's vertical
reaches to the speaker's inquisitive eyes: the barrage of deformations
("halves of cave-ins") that precedes the tentative mention of "heights,"
and the next line's anticipation of an undisturbed silence, collaborate to
surround the idea of altitudes and depths, and especially that luminous
word *alturas*, with intimations of barrenness and inaccessibility. And af-
filiated with *la poderosa muerte*, the imagined reaches gain the sense of
an ending, as though to imply that earthly journeys finish there above or
below. Again, the supernatural tinge here in death's suggestion of *alturas*

and *hundimientos* is enough only to call the speaker's materialist outlook into momentary question, enough to provoke one's curiosity about the implied equation of these ultimate matters, this topos with that telos.[27]

What is this "powerful death"? Concha has written persuasively that *la poderosa muerte* achieves its power from its place in the organic cycle of terrestrial life, that it is literally the death of a flower or a man destined to live again in matter.[28] To this way of reading, the *hundimientos y altura* might imply the stations of such a cycle—the clouds or the deep processes in the earth—even as their vagueness admits they exceed the speaker's imagination here. Another critic fathoms "powerful death" not as a process but as "a completed and definitive fact like the total spread of the night when it covers the world":[29] in this interpretation, *la poderosa muerte* is a single end looming over the speaker's desiccated life. Both views are well rooted in Neruda's lines, which are as efflorescent with contingent meanings as any modern poet's. If it is thinkable (and to many of Neruda's Spanish American critics it is probably not), I propose that the exact nature of the various deaths is unimportant here. Many nominative sequences in the post-Petrarchan line, by definition occupied with the speaker's *vida*, give out their concern with death in an early installment, as in the first verses of *Canzoniere* 36. It matters most to Neruda's practice that the two sorts of death have strong and conflicting emotional colorings, and especially that each has its geographical expression. The setting of "petty death" is the more starkly developed to this point in the series; that of *la poderosa muerte* is less defined, but clings impressively to a locale of geographical, vertical extremes.

The speaker's itinerary and location are introduced evidentially in the second stanza of Canto 4 as though to satisfy the unspoken but always pertinent question: where were you when this intuition occurred? Each of his ways of addressing the geographical issue in lines 6 through 9 amounts to the same emotional conviction, for in each case he describes the terrestrial roam of the early lyrics as having arrived at a new condition of finality, and each locution in the anaphoric series of these lines is a means of saying that the margin has been reached, that a new pattern of movement (and by implication, of existence) must ensue. It scarcely counts how or why such a condition has been realized here and now. We and the speaker are simply confronted with a spatial imperative—"I came to the edge of the blade"—and must adjust accordingly, he to a freshly circumscribed world, we to a new and presumably less simple scheme of moral observation, as our touchstone of degradation and iniquity is withdrawn. The pause at the top of *la vertiginosa carretera espiral* ("the vertiginous spiral highway") appears to promise that the speaker is about to descend into the earth, corkscrewlike, to recover the meaning of his foreclosed existence.

Neruda then forces us across the roughest intellectual transition in the sequence:

> but broad sea, oh death! you come not wave by wave
> but like a gallop of nocturnal clarity
> or like the sums of the night.
>
> You never came to plunder a pocket, you could not
> come at all without red vestments:
> without an auroral carpet wrapped in silence,
> without raised or buried legacies of tears.
>
> (4.10–16)

The evident drift of the passage is to reinforce the diversion of the speaker's proper, mortal telos toward "powerful death," and to remind himself that his exhaustion of possibilities among geodesic paths has left him no closer to that mysterious, towering attainment. The repetitive motions of worldly life ("wave by wave") may wear us out or kill us, but they do not open onto this final and majestic condition (or "broad sea"). The speaker looks toward a kind of death that arrives richly but silently, suddenly but in a way that confers immortality ("raised or buried legacies of tears"). In the remainder of the lyric, which I have already quoted, the speaker tells of his disavowal of the urban, commercial struggle and his coincident, perhaps consequent exclusion from the "wounded inexistence" of humankind. The poem concludes with a frenzy of tracing paths and opening spaces, all to a frustrating and ominous end:

> I wanted to swim in the broadest lives,
> in the openest river mouths,
> and as men kept denying me little by little,
> blocking path and door so I would not touch
> with my streaming hands their wound of emptiness,
> then I went street after street and river after river,
> city after city and bed after bed,
> and my brackish mask crossed through waste places,
> and in the last low hovels, no light, no fire,
> no bread, no stone, no silence, alone,
> I roamed round dying of my own death.
>
> (Felstiner, 4.21–31)

The short, difficult fifth canto stalls over an apostrophe to *muerte grave*, and hears the speaker stipulate that his accumulating demise was not of this kind—it was baser, vaguer, and poorer.

It is appropriate that the most compelling climax of the work, when it comes, relies on movement and location rather than the personal and chronological events of most lyric and narrative climaxes. How, why, and when do not pertain here. The speaker—here as everywhere, "the primordial *here* and *zero-point* for every *objective* determination of space and spatial motion"[30]—has moved suddenly upward to find his object, and if we accept the fiction that offers perpendicular lines as signs of conflicting imperatives, then we will feel an exhilarating sense of arrival and fulfillment here.

> Then on the ladder of the earth I climbed
> through the lost jungle's tortured thicket
> up to you, Macchu Picchu.
> High city of laddered stones,
> at last the dwelling of what earth
> never covered in vestments of sleep.
> In you like two lines parallel,
> the cradles of lightning and man
> rocked in a wind of thorns.
>
> Mother of stone, spume of condors.
>
> High reef of the human dawn.
>
> Spade lost in the primal sand.
>
> This was the dwelling, this is the place:
> here the broad grains of maize rose up
> and fell again like red hail.
>
> Here gold thread came off the vicuña
> to clothe lovers, tombs, and mothers,
> king and prayers and warriors.
>
> Here men's feet rested at night
> next to the eagles' feet, in the ravenous
> high nests, and at dawn
> they stepped with the thunder's feet onto thinning mists
> and touched the soil and the stones
> till they knew them come night or death.
>
> I look at clothes and hands,
> the trace of water in an echoing tub,
> the wall brushed smooth by the touch of a face
> that looked with my eyes at the lights of earth,
> that oiled with my hands the vanished
> beams: because everything, clothing, skin, jars,
> words, wine, bread,
> is gone, fallen to earth.

And the air came in with the touch
of lemon blossom over everyone sleeping:
a thousand years of air, months, weeks of air,
of blue wind and iron cordillera,
that were like gentle hurricane footsteps
polishing the lonely boundary of stone.

(Felstiner, 6)

The first lines of the sixth canto offhandedly imitate the respiratory experience of arrival through Intipunku, the Gate of the Sun: one climbs a steep rock staircase and attains a promontory from which the city is visible suddenly and entirely. For Neruda's geometer, Machu Picchu is a literalizing presence. In this vivid and abruptly defined space, jutting toward the sky and bounded on every side by thousands of feet of empty air, nature frames a sanctuary from worldly concerns. Unroofed, without facades, and vacant, it expresses its geometry as nakedly as any place on earth. The throngs of right angles and hundreds of stairways, some with as many as 150 steps, starkly dramatize the speaker's moral landscape while harmonizing its drastic shifts of value. Here the contrasting values of ascendant and downward motion are purged in the process of exploration, since practically every site in the ruins lies at the ends of several paths running up and down the mountain, nearly everywhere both higher and lower than somewhere else. As George Kubler describes it, the "dimensions and directions of the town are 'around' and 'up' and 'down'; the units of urban space are contoured terraces, rising by pyramidal stages and spreading across the saddle like a blanket of ribbed and stony weave."[31]

Further, the speaker's quotidian moral geometry is reconciled not only in the dynamism of his exploring body but in the architectural statement of the *andenes*, the narrow terraces of cultivated land cut into the grades of the mountains. These functional compositions reconcile verticality and horizontality in a soothing steadiness of form: again, to trace them is to experience both axes as part of an integral pattern. The second paragraph of the sixth canto evokes the fresh geometry of the attained summit, dominated not by the tension of right angles but by the orderliness of parallel lines.

Two other lyric elements—kept separate in the previous poems to give a rougher piquancy to the speaker's unconverted experience—are united in the sixth poem: the time recovered by the speaker's narration and the occasion of the utterance itself. In this central episode of *Alturas de Macchu Picchu* the past shades into the present, and the sequence begins almost imperceptibly to move forward in time. This event is framed in properly geographical terms, however, as *here* is iterated before *now*, the spatial deictic of immediacy before its temporal counterpart. It is as though the speaker's sense of location rushes ahead of his capacity to devise his own actions in this setting, and he can only make a few mental impressions, musing on what once happened here, before going on to think and move for himself in the consecrated place. As he wanders and gazes, he gains his first intuition that the dead "hands" and "eyes" are living again through his presence, that with his arrival at Machu Picchu the history of that place, like his personal renewal, begins once more. He shares the present tense, the one in which the sequence is uttered, with the men and women who built the high city. This consolidation of tenses is not the sign of a new temporal reach on the order of the *Canzoniere*, but follows from the spatial order of Neruda's series: the speaker can sound and collect times only because he has achieved physical presence in the appropriate place, because he can get at them through matter. His contemporaneity with the Incas becomes important to the emotional logic of the sequence in the next poems, and ought to be taken not for a slackening of the work's priorities but for a rigorous keeping of them under the need to widen the import of *Alturas de Macchu Picchu*.

The seventh lyric is a go-between, and has only slight interest as part of Neruda's fictional program. The speaker continues to fuse past and present because, seen from the vantage of a spatial order, time loses its strata. As everywhere, his experience of physical reality conditions his view of its temporal dimension: throughout the canto, time is shown in corporeal terms,

> You dead of a common abyss, shades of one ravine—
>
> . . . .
>
> you plummeted like an autumn
> into a single death,
>
> (Tarn, 7.1, 8–9)

and the Incas' shared death is told by locating them somewhere together. The canto narrows the matter of the graver death, concentrating on Machu Picchu as its site:

> . . . as if to match
> the compass of your magnitude,
> this is how it came, the true, the most consuming death:
> from perforated rocks,
> from crimson cornices,
> and cataracting aqueducts,
> you plummeted. . . .
>
> (Tarn, 7.2–8)

We realize implicitly that the speaker's exploration of the hottest death will proceed past old borders of understanding because here he has a place to start; in the middle verses, we watch him finger the ruins for traces of a deposited essence. The last lines introduce Machu Picchu as the place where his precisely spatial view of the world originated, and where it will find its fulfillment as the series moves into the future.

> And yet a permanence of stone and language
> upheld the city raised like a chalice
> in all those hands: live, dead and stilled,
> aloft with so much death, a wall, with so much life,
> struck with flint petals: the everlasting rose, our home,
> this reef on Andes, its glacial territories.
>
> On the day the clay-colored hand
> was utterly changed into clay, and when dwarf eyelids closed
> upon bruised walls and hosts of battlements,
> when all of man in us cringed back into its burrow—
> there remained a precision unfurled
> on the high places of the human dawn,
> the tallest crucible that ever held our silence,
> a life of stone after so many lives.
>
> (Tarn, 7.22–35)

The strange epithet "glacial territories" works in a small but vital way to tighten the limits around the speaker's materialism, for it reminds us of the *altura* and the *vastas contrucciones de viento y ventisquero* that mysteriously occurred to him in Canto 4, that seemed to speak of a transcendence after *la poderosa muerte*. There was no fissure in his materialist outlook after all: high, lush Machu Picchu is the site he envisioned while stuck at the bottom, and the frosty air of the epithet here allows only a gently ironic glance at the partial inaccuracy of his expectations. Machu Picchu is also the site from which "a cluster of faces or masks," the vision of a distant perfection, was hurled down at the speaker in Canto 2. The city gives body to the hints of metaphysical destinations scattered through the early parts of the work. It is a site seemingly created to justify and exercise his materialist, geometrical cast of mind.

An invocation begins the eighth canto, the first imperative mood of the series and the first point at which the speaker shares his saving itinerary with humankind:

> Come up with me, American love.
>
> Kiss these secret stones with me.
> The torrential silver of the Urubamba

makes the pollen fly to its golden cup.
The hollow of the bindweed's maze,
the petrified plant, the inflexible garland,
soar above the silence of these mountain coffers.
Come, diminutive life, between the wings
of the earth, while you, cold, crystal in the hammered air,
thrusting embattled emeralds apart,
O savage waters, fall from the hems of snow.

Love, love, until the night collapses
from the singing Andes flint
down to the dawn's red knees,
come out and contemplate the snow's blind son.

(Tarn, 8.1–15)

His apostrophized "American love" is simply the fused and revivified *muertos* who were seen to plummet in the other canto, now tracing their former vertical line backwards to return to their earthly dwelling. He wants his forerunners to watch and reenact his tributes to Machu Picchu even as he implicitly supposes that he acts again their "secret" encounters with the site: the logic of time falls to the fullness and mystery of the place. The human actors of "American love" are designated by their continental residence, not their individual characters or their chronology. Drawn broadly, they include everyone who lives literally and figuratively below the "precision unfurled" at Machu Picchu, everyone who can make the journey upward. The geometer's ritualistic tribute to Machu Picchu, acted out to encourage his hypothetical imitator, is to touch it, kiss it, enter it. Contact and interposition matter here more than anywhere. The speaker notices "hollow" vegetable embraces of the ruins; we are inside these, and we show them up by our warmth and identity with what we hold.

John Felstiner has written that "with this canto, the poem's longest by far, I find myself awkwardly situated as a translator. It seems bloated, its metaphors merely jostling each other. . . . [My sense] is that in Canto VIII Neruda pulled out the stops on his verse without yet having a distinct dramatic purpose."[32] On the contrary, this lyric is among the most fictionally charged of the series if we understand where the geographical orientation of the work is tending. Which lines could we do without? The speaker celebrates the centered, domestic quality he feels at Machu Picchu and urges his addressee to enjoy the same sensation. Between the "steep night" and the "sonorous Andean flint" and the "red-kneed dawn," he says, "come out and contemplate the snow's blind son" (Tarn, 8.15). It seems clear that the *hijo* ("son") is the speaker himself: come out, he implores, and watch the capers and questions of your friend who was once caught in the *nieve aislada* ("lone snows") of civilization, who used to see as his prospect only vague and "vast constructions of wind and snow-drift." The self-reference here is elliptical because everything that touches person in the sequence is handled delicately, even reluctantly. For Neruda to say more about the speaker's altered outlook would be to elevate character to a principle of order at the expense of the spatial dimension.

Among the acts we and "American love" are to observe is the questioning of the canto's next, central portion, where the questions are in part an expressive formula for the speaker's turns of mind: one is meant to understand that this is the pattern of most responses of Machu Picchu, a place that constantly strains our capacities for intentness and puzzlement, and about which there can finally be only questions without answers. We have to remark, however, the trend of the questions toward largely irrelevant matters of time and person, the legacies of our quotidian and political lives in the world below. The energy of the comparisons in these lines, and the clogged sonorities, amount to Neruda's self-parody, as Felstiner observes; but one must listen for the aim of the parody, which is finally to discredit the nature of the questions before the stupefying reality of Machu Picchu:

> O Wilkamayu of the sounding looms,
> when you rend your skeins of thunder
> in white foam clouds of wounded snow,
> when your south wind falls like an avalanche
> roaring and belting to arouse the sky,
> what language do you wake in an ear
> freed but a moment from your Andean spume?
>
> Who caught the lightning of the cold,
> abandoned it, chained to the heights,
> dealt out among its frozen tears,
> brandished upon its nimble swords—
> its seasoned stamens pummeled hard—
> led to a warrior's bed,
> hounded to his rocky conclusions?
>
> What do your harried scintillations whisper?
> Did your sly, rebellious flash
> go traveling once, populous with words?
> Who wanders grinding frozen syllables,
> black languages, gold-threaded banners,
> fathomless mouths and trampled cries
> in your tenuous arterial waters?

Who goes dead-heading blossom eyelids
come to observe us from the far earth?
Who scatters dead seed clusters
dropping from your cascading hands
to bed their own disintegration here
in coal's geology?

Who has flung down the branches of these chains
and buried once again our leave-takings?

(Tarn, 8.16–44)

All compelling questions to a modern sensibility, but in each case the answer, the true answer, is close to the touch. The idiom of this chain of utterances answers the first query, and the geometrical harmony of the site answers all the rest. If some anthropomorphic force created and endowed this summit in a martial frenzy, that antique fact means nothing to the order and stillness of the place now; if there was once language to fill and honor Machu Picchu, there is no need to chase it into the past, for the presence of the speaker assures that it will speak again, and indeed that the words will be the same. History, its causes and results, do not matter here for the moment, and to suppose otherwise is to introduce the concerns of the urban world—modern, prosaic, academic—into a remote setting. The fit style of intercourse with the site is celebrated in the remaining verses of the canto.

Love, love, do not come near the border,
avoid adoring this sunken head:
let time exhaust all measure
in its abode of broken overtures—
here, between cliffs and rushing waters,
take to yourself the air among these passes,
the laminated image of the wind,
the blind canal threading high cordilleras,
dew with its bitter greetings,
and climb, flower by flower, through the thicknesses
trampling the coiling lucifer.

In this steep zone of flint and forest,
green stardust, jungle-clarified,
Mantur, the valley, cracks like a living lake
or a new level of silence.

Come to my very being, to my own dawn,
into crowned solitudes.
The fallen kingdom survives us all this while.

And on this dial the condor's shadow
cruises as ravenous as would a pirate ship.

                                                    (Tarn, 8.45–64)

Away with person and chronology, he says, and in their place strive to inhabit and commune with the native order of Machu Picchu. The warning away from "the border"—as I read it, a materialist's approximation of Milton's "be lowly wise"—contains both a pragmatic topography of the site, where the wandering visitor may suddenly plunge thousands of feet into the river, and a guide to its ontological assimilation. In the central verses of the longest stanza, "Between the ramparts and the quick water, gather to you the air of the gorge," the purpose of the pervasive tropes of interposition comes clear. By keeping the notion of interposition available through the sequence, almost literally by holding a space open in our understanding of the cantos, they have arranged for this final habitation at Machu Picchu, a place of utter betweenness. Much as a sequence unified by its fiction of person will set forth certain attributes to be gathered up and fulfilled later, Neruda has primed us to think in a particular, clefting fashion about the physical reality evoked in this work in order to settle us here. The speaker's former, persistent hunt for breaches was a rehearsal of escape from his debilitating worldly concerns, but Machu Picchu brings escape and interposition to life.

The way to understand Machu Picchu is to meet it with hand and foot, to enact its geometry on the stairs and cordilleras, to draw its unspoken history with touches into one's own voice. In the glow of this reading, it is natural to interpret the ninth canto—a chain of figurative epithets for Machu Picchu, much like the Germanic kennings—as a demonstration of the site under the speaker's active cognition. In these mostly hendecasyllabic lines are the qualities of apprehension and expression that will catch the nature of Machu Picchu: a set of rough but perceptible balances, an utter lack of hypotactic or temporal relation, an unconcern for historical exactitude and personal responsibilities. Certain poets treated in this study have situated revisions of their sequences within the poems themselves, and with this canto Neruda joins them. The ninth lyric is what *Alturas de Macchu Picchu* would be if he wrote freed from extant generic and cultural traditions, if he were not obliged to fashion a fictional context around his celebration of the place itself. The lyric clarifies the picture of the space with a string of largely metaphorical utterances, some of which build on the issues of the previous poems and some of which are startlingly fresh, even unassimilable:

Ultimate geometry, book of stone.
Iceberg carved among squalls.
Coral of sunken time.

> Finger-softened rampart.
> Feather-assaulted roof.
> Mirror splinters, thunderstorm foundations.
> Thrones ruined by the climbing vine.
> The blood-flecked talon's law.
> Gale at a standstill on a slope.
> Still turquoise cataract.
> Patriarchal chiming of the sleepers.
> Manacle of subjugated snows.
> Iron tilting toward statues.
> Storm inaccessible and closed.
>
> (Tarn, 9.11–24)

To read this canto closely is to be thrown onto the ad hoc affinities of words, the prevalent grammar, the regularity of some parts of speech and the near-absence of others. One notices the frequency of prepositions, for instance, and gradually arrives at their relevance. Prepositions often have a distinctly spatial designation: remember their clatter in Donne's notorious lines, "Licence my roaving hands, and let them go, / Before, behind, between, above, below" (Elegie 19, 25–26). They can be among the most pragmatic, least ambiguous parts of speech. Even so, the category houses some highly abstract, almost metaphysical referents, which often becomes evident when one tries to paraphrase prepositions in usage; unlike the class of nouns, which also carries a broad span of concrete and abstract meanings, the category of prepositions often holds its most abstract meanings in the same words—*to, for, in, by*—that house the simplest relations of place. Otto Jespersen has written that language continually betrays the degrees of abstraction and concreteness in life by fixing these at an arbitrary, convenient measure in its grammatical categories.[33] The prepositions in the ninth canto of *Alturas de Macchu Picchu* seem to invite an examination of this question: they suggest an elementary physical precision while concurrently carrying intuitive flashes about the universal resonances of the place. Once again, Neruda's metaphysics comes under the aspect of a geography, and we are made to contemplate the interpenetration of these levels of awareness. "The phrase *de piedra* ('of stone')," writes Robert Pring-Mill, recurs "like the 'Ora pro nobis' of a litany,"[34] and the conviction that ultimate things are being invoked—though they are called up by their material substance, a husk never to be discarded—is no less potent here than in a sacred ritual. The final epithet, *dirección del tiempo* ("direction of time," perhaps even "address" in the sense of a dwelling), staunchly holds to the spatializing of time that follows the speaker's recoil from his past. Time is local and available here at Machu

Picchu, he says, and you need not inquire for it further. Only look, and climb, and touch.

The first verses of Canto 10 answer and complicate the concerns of 9, initiating the close of the movement begun in that lyric.

> Stone within stone, and man, where was he?
> Air within air, and man, where was he?
> Time within time, and man, where was he?
>
> (Tarn, 10.1–3)

The geographical vision of the ninth canto is not, after all, a retreat from humanity, for that would give in unwittingly to the pressures of impersonality and indifference from which the speaker fled in the earliest poems. "American love" must have an object. The fruit of these unspoken imperatives appears in the first lines of the tenth canto, where the speaker at last integrates "man" into his understanding of Machu Picchu as more than an abstract presence that has built something of majesty. Having obtained the pure apprehension of the ninth canto, he is free here to consider matters of humanity without resorting to the historical, political, or arbitrarily personal focus of his earlier questions. At last he has come to think both spatially and compassionately, to understand humankind's place as the most important question he can frame on the way to plumbing men's and women's psychic lives and fates. The mode of inquiry that works through location here seems both especially objective and especially feeling, and is his first chance to give a practical repercussion to his old, dim belief of human identity with the material world.

Further, his new awareness of men and women as suffering organisms seems to lead abruptly to a stinging realization: that the indigenous dwellers may have been subjected to the exploitative, disintegrative working order from which he has escaped in coming to Machu Picchu. Did the people who built the city suffer the petty death of slaves? He thinks on the queer emptiness of the city: did famine quiet Machu Picchu?

> Were you also the shattered fragment
> of indecision, of hollow eagle
> which, through the streets of today, in the old tracks,
> through the leaves of accumulated autumns,
> goes pounding at the soul into the tomb?
> Poor hand, poor foot, and poor, dear life . . .
> The days of unraveled light
> in you, familiar rain
> falling on feast-day banderillas,

did they grant, petal by petal, their dark nourishment
to such an empty mouth?
> Famine, coral of mankind,
hunger, secret plant, root of the woodcutters,
famine, did your jagged reef dart up
to those high, side-slipping towers?

I question you, salt of the highways,
show me the trowel; allow me, architecture,
to fret stone stamens with a little stick,
climb all the steps of air into the emptiness,
scrape the intestine until I touch mankind.

Macchu Picchu, did you lift
stone above stone on a groundwork of rags?
coal upon coal and, at the bottom, tears?
fire-crested gold, and in that gold, the bloat
dispenser of this blood?

> (Tarn, 10.4–27)

Of all the work's intellectual and emotional turns, this one must be the hardest for the speaker to frame. It suggests that he finally understands the process related by these ten poems not as the path to a resting place, nor as a retreat from a site of evil to a dwelling of good, but as an experience of self-renewal and fresh seeing virtually dissociable from the places themselves. In his case Machu Picchu harmonized the conflicts and pressures of his past, and encouraged him to see his temporal and geographical life through a clean lens; but it may not have been so for everyone. The denizens of Machu Picchu itself might have lost sight of the things he has newly discovered, and might have needed the fresh perspective occasioned by his almost meditative attention to the harmonies of person and place. The movement away from his old fruitlessness and dull seeing—and not the spot or axis of his arrival—is the critical element in this renewal.

The possibility of an earthly fulfillment, then, is not in Machu Picchu but in himself and his continued investigation of his world. Perhaps the most confident thing Neruda can do with his quondam geometrical morality is to have his speaker, as here, grow into throwing it off and implicitly conceding its relativity. It was a mold that allowed him to reinterpret the past in light of the clear-sighted present, and it was a tool of self-discipline, but its uses are gone. Here and now the search can commence for his truest affinities with the population of Machu Picchu. He will attend closely to the Incas' complex relations with their earth and *arquitec-*

tura for omens of oppression as well as delight, admitting that Machu Picchu must be a site of psychic complication as much as any mundane place. And he tacitly allows that his contemporaneity with the people of Machu Picchu must be the warrant for his further exertion on their behalf, not for his rest and satisfaction:

> return unto me the slave you buried!
> Shake from the ground the hard bread
> of the wretched, show me the clothes
> of the serf and his window.
> Tell me how he slept when he was alive.
> Tell me if his sleep was
> raucous, half open, like a black hole
> bored by fatigue in the wall.
> The wall, the wall! Tell me if upon his sleep
> there weighed every floor of stone, and if he fell beneath it,
> as beneath a moon, with sleep!

(Flores, 10.28–38)

"The wall, the wall!": these squeals testify to his involvement in the new angle of vision that starts from matter and space. In full bloom, the speaker's geographical and material outlook gives the latter lyrics their delicate logic. It must be granted its importance where it appears.

As I have said, the serial conceit of *Alturas de Macchu Picchu* is that the speaker gradually extends two axes of movement in his first setting—the geodesic and subterranean lines of Cantos 1 through 5—and then in the sixth lyric suddenly attains a new place, which he consecutively explores only to run up against the need to reach beneath "the weave of bright matter" (10.47). These final cantos, then, are his admission of what matters most when the site has been mapped by his grateful and prescient eye, the destination of the Nerudean geography. In the first lines of the eleventh poem, the speaker openly avows that his sense of arrival at Machu Picchu will not suffice for others, and that much remains to be charted by him for others:

> Through a confusion of splendor,
> through a night made stone let me plunge my hand
> and move to beat in me a bird held for a thousand years,
> the old and unremembered human heart!
> Today let me forget this happiness, wider than all the sea,
> because man is wider than all the sea and her necklace of islands
> and we must fall into him as down a well to clamber back with
> branches of secret water, recondite truths.
> Allow me to forget, circumference of stone, the powerful proportions,

the transcendental span, the honeycomb's foundations,
and from the set-square allow my hand to slide
down a hypotenuse of hairshirt and salt blood.
When, like a horseshoe of rusting wing-cases, the furious condor
batters my temples in the order of flight
and his tornado of carnivorous feathers sweeps the dark dust
down slanting stairways, I do not see the rush of the bird,
nor the blind sickle of his talons—
I see the ancient being, the slave, the sleeping one,
blanket his fields—a body, a thousand bodies, a man, a thousand
women swept by the sable whirlwind, charred with rain and night,
stones with a leaden weight of statuary:
Juan Splitstones, son of Wiracocha,
Juan Coldbelly, heir of the green star,
Juan Barefoot, grandson to the turquoise,
[arise to birth with me, my brother].

                                                        (Tarn, 11)

The reintroduction of a downward, subterranean axis here annuls the pattern that led the speaker to Machu Picchu, and presses on him and us that the journey is only half done. Having achieved a clear sense of matter as psychic expression, he must "forget" geometry and remember history, must trace the human joy and suffering beneath the patterns of topography. The middle verses are the speaker's affirmation that in a line of movement, he will see neither the moving thing itself nor any abstract principle it may once have represented; he will see the harder thing, the patches of despair and inarticulateness caught in the shadows. He will forswear the clean discriminations that brought him here; he is drawn to mass sentience. The generic names celebrated in the last verses attest to the nature of his interest, and clarify its variance from the futile askings of the eighth canto. A sense of responsibility and compassion, which perhaps was suspended in the discipline of geometry, is fully restored here and made consequent to his materialism. Moreover, he conceives his task of recovery as mutual: it is not enough to "fall into" humankind; it must "rise to birth" with us as well. The juncture of these paragraphs, where a descending axis meets a line marked in the opposite direction, aptly stands for the fluid, contradictory patterns of spatial exploration that become necessary when the speaker gives up his own process of development for a communion with his "brothers." In meshing lines we meet the selves we were, fulfilling the vertical promise of the work's original, plunging hand but transcending the simplicity of its rectangular discrimination.

The last line of Canto 11, an imperative, is repeated as the first line of the final poem:

> Arise to birth with me, my brother.
>
> Give me your hand out of the depths
> sown by your sorrows.
> You will not return from these stone fastnesses.
> You will not emerge from subterranean time.
> Your rasping voice will not come back,
> nor your pierced eyes rise from their sockets.
>
> (Tarn, 12.1–7)

The aims of these verses are two: to place the speaker's preconquest brother under the *escala* ("ladder") of a dawning understanding that the speaker has already scaled for himself, showing by the return to the work's first climactic juncture how far the continued process of intuition and articulation will have to go when the series proper has ended; and to fix that Neruda imagines no supernatural event in these last poems, only the figurative revivification of the dead past through the contact of the speaker's alert senses with the material setting of the city. For all the excesses that become feasible when a living poet speaks openly for the past, the speaker's thorough materialism will be the check: the commerce between the dead Incas and the modern South American occurs only through the channels of the cityscape, and gets expressed only in the objective language of *here* and *there*:

> Show me your blood and your furrow;
> say to me: here I was scourged
> because a gem was dull or because the earth
> failed to give up in time its tithe of corn or stone.
> Point out to me the rock on which you stumbled,
> the wood they used to crucify your body.
> Strike the old flints
> to kindle ancient lamps, light up the whips
> glued to your wounds throughout the centuries
> and light the axes gleaming with your blood.
> I come to speak for your dead mouths.
>
> Throughout the earth
> let dead lips congregate,
> out of the depths spin this long night to me
> as if I rode at anchor here with you.
> And tell me everything, tell chain by chain,
> and link by link, and step by step;

sharpen the knives you kept hidden away,
thrust them into my breast, into my hands,
like a torrent of sunbursts,
an Amazon of buried jaguars,
and leave me cry: hours, days and years,
blind ages, stellar centuries.

And give me silence, give me water, hope.

Give me the struggle, the iron, the volcanoes.

Let bodies cling like magnets to my body.

Come quickly to my veins and to my mouth.

Speak through my speech, and through my blood.
(Tarn, 12.18–45)

The final verses not only introduce the remainder of Neruda's ambitious volume as a formal construction (*cadena a cadena* or "chain by chain"), they tell expeditiously the use that will govern the form: *Canto General* is one of the premier examples of something I have already defined as the artifactual sequence—better, it is a concatenation of such sequences under a "general" title. Its multiple speakers and changing perspectives, its historical play, and its widely varying poetic strategies all deepen the artifactual programs of the early modernists while affirming a broadly correspondent idea of political reality as overflowing the experience of any one subject. This is not to say that Neruda abandons the self-oriented vision of his earlier works in *Canto General*, for much of the collection is given to elaborating an intellectual and psychic anatomy of the principal speaker. It is probably obvious to most readers that Neruda learned the value of a capacious nominativity from Whitman, and put it to work in such divisions of *Canto General* as the bitter polemic "La arena traicionada" and the conclusion "Yo soy." Moreover, it is hardly fair to imply that Neruda's turns to artifactuality are all equally successful. The section "La tierra se llama Juan," in which poor South Americans of many sorts endorse the main speaker's historical redaction, never seems more than a puppet show by his literally supervising presence: "*Usted es Neruda?*" ("You are Neruda?") says one worker at an iodine factory in the eleventh lyric, "*Pase, camarada*" ("Come along, comrade"). But the dominant conception of *Canto General* is clearly artifactual, with a "double nature" of both personal and collective concerns, according to Emir Rodríguez Monegal.[35]

As Spanish American poetry has evoked a spatial dimension more consistently than that of Europe and the United States, Machu Picchu has been one of its most tenable topics. A number of New World poets have pondered the temporal reach of their lyric medium against the nature of their material, and decided with the Peruvian Alberto Hidalgo that

> la historia no comienza con h
> y no es tampoco historia
> pues la historia se llama Machu Picchu
> A ésta la escribieron con piedras unos hombres
> y la envidiaron unos dioses
> aquéllos nos fundaron a nosotros
> éstos fueron borrados como lápiz

(history does not begin with h, and is not history either, for history is called Machu Picchu. With stones men wrote to it, and gods envied it; the former founded us, the latter were erased like pencil-marks)[36]

Among several other works, Hidalgo's *Patria Completa* (1960), Mario Florián's "Oda heróica a Machu Piqchu" (1961), and César Toro Montalvo's *Torres y praderas de Machu Picchu* (1980) act out this conviction, appropriating the city in various ways as a place where cosmic, racial, and personal history can be read out of stones and into poetry.[37] For the most part, these works confine their spatial orientations to what they address rather than to what they make or are: except for some local deictic play in *Patria Completa* and an insistently circular movement around the city in Toro's lovely poem, these poets hardly exploit the properties of the lyric sequence to drive a sense of physical immediacy or make one feel motion as a lyric event. Like many of the Iberian poets of the Renaissance, they tend to dispose their collective works more as aggregations of individual lyrics than as fictions.

In one modern sequence about Machu Picchu, however, the possibilities of the spatial series are explored as radically and obsessively as can be imagined. I refer to *La Mano Desasida* by the Peruvian Martín Adán, a sequence that was published first in one version of three poems in 638 lines (1964), and later as ten lyrics in 180 pages (1980).[38] A stern challenge to the conceptual and compositional tenets of nearly every other text in this study, Adán's series (its English title is "The Hand Let Go") seems to risk everything, even its own interest and outcome, for an obsessively spatial orientation. Adán's speaker, like Neruda's in *Alturas de Macchu Picchu*, finds in the site a refuge from psychic stagnation and his sense of irrelevance to the quotidian world. For the Chilean poet's elegant process of discovery, however, Adán substitutes a rude, seemingly aimless thrashing. This much is clear from the start: *La Mano Desasida* is the cry of a speaker who adores Machu Picchu, and envies the lost city its isolation from human affairs, its physical integrity, its seeming atemporality. He wants, he says strangely and pathetically, to achieve these qualities in his own life. As though to leap across the ontological divide that keeps them apart, he calls Machu Picchu "I Myself." From the first verses, in fact, he muses abruptly about the conceivability of his identity with the site, as though to smash the rudiments of historicity and psychic process in the series before they can take hold. He disorients us with a militant strike:

> Si no eres nada sino en mí mi sima,
> Si no eres nada sino mi peligro,
> Si no eres nada allá sino mi paso,
> Que vengan todos, con su hedor y siglo.
> ¡Que venga el extranjero que me extraña!
> ¡Que venga el mal hallado!
> ¡Que baje el buey subido desde arriba
> El del belfo verde, desde humano vacío!
> Y que ronca y remira porque nace
> De vientre ajeno, que jamás es mío.
> ¡Aquí estoy muriéndome!
> ¡Así es toda mi vida!
> ¡De buey que rumia y que remira
> Y de yo que agoniza, que agonizo!
> Tú no eres bello porque no soy bello,
> Yo Mismo. Eres apenas profundo estar arriba
> De todo un vuelo interminable.
> Eres el ala que voló
> Y que bata todavía.

> (If you are nothing but in me my abyss,
> If you are nothing but my peril,
> If you are nothing there but my step,
> Then let them all come, with their histories and hot stink.
> Let him come, the stranger who finds me strange!
> Let him come, the fellow not well met!
> Let him come down from high, the ethereal ox,
> Green lips descending from human emptiness.
> He snorts and stares because he first saw light
> From out of a stranger's belly, none of mine.
> Here I am dying! So go all my days!
> Days of the ox that broods and looks about
> And of me, who is dying, am dying!
> You are not lovely because I am not lovely,
> Myself. You are hardly deep, being above
> Everything, a flight with no limits or corners.
> You are the wing that flew,
> And that still churns.)[39]

At one rate or another, it occurs to every reader that Adán's speaker seeks not to arrive at a new understanding through contemplation of Machu Picchu, but to become a place himself. That is, he wants to alter the dimensions of his existence, to enter the field of cool, objective relations that he imagines to exist between locales, to withdraw from the heat and pulse of humanity in favor of an imaginarily pure materialism. Such a stand is not unknown in other lyric settings, of course, especially where time is virtually a malevolent character:

> Aër felice, col bel vivo raggio
> rimanti; et tu corrente et chiaro gorgo,
> ché non poss'io cangiar teco vïaggio?

(Happy air, stay with that sweet living ray. And you, running, clear stream, why can I not exchange paths with you?)

(Canzoniere, 227.12–14)

But nowhere is it expressed with the primitive intensity of *La Mano Desasida*, nor with such drastic, deformative results for the lyric sequence. Much of his speech unfolds his struggle to converse with the genius loci of Machu Picchu far more directly and idiosyncratically than Neruda's speaker ever would, and to meditate on his own occupation of space, on his possibilities as a kind of landmark. He gets at his situation and his desires by alternating a relentlessly spatial view of the world with plaintive cries for relief and metamorphosis. An extended quotation will carry some of the qualities of the work:

> Mi deidad es como yo,
> Perecedera, miserable . . .
> Va preguntando y va errando
> Por entre el hueso y la sangre,
> Por entre el deslumbramiento y el desengaño
> Por entre el volumen y la imagen
> Por entre el llanto y el espejo,
> Por entre lo que agarra y lo que sabe;
> Por entre el tiempo y la memoria,
> Por entre la luz y el ave.
> Todo era entonces como es ahora:
> Todo era cielo,
> Todo era un no ver, todo de imagen
> Echada por exceso.
> Pero tú estabas, material,
> Sensible, imperfecto.

¿Qué eres tú, Machu Picchu,
Almohada de entresueño? . . .
¿Yo Mismo,
Si me acuerdo y no me acuerdo?
Era caudal de piedra,
Detenido.

Todo madre verdaderamente natural
Quiere contener el otro río.
La flor se puso verde de terror y de tierra
Y dejó pasar a cualquier gringo.
Y yo no soy y no seré nunca
Sino apenas un curso y mi sitio.

¡Sálvame, sálvame, Machu Picchu!
¡Sálvame, y no te huyas de mi peligro!
¡Ah, sí, Dios vive todavía!

(My deity is like me, mortal and miserable . . .
It goes asking, it goes wandering
Between the bone and the blood,
Between bewitchment and disillusion,
Between the volume and the likeness,
Between the tears and the looking glass,
Between what it clutches and what it knows,
Between time and memory,
Between the light and the bird.
Everything then was as now:
All was sky, all was a no see,
All was resemblance poured to excess.
But there you were: material, impressionable, unfinished.

What are you, Machu Picchu,
A pillow for the dreams between our nights,
Our daydreams? . . .
I Myself, if I remember and I do not?
I was a stream of stone,
Stopped.

All that is natural in the riverbed
Wants to gather the other river.
The flower went green, the color of earth and fear,
And let all the gringos pass.
And I am not, and never will be
Except, scarcely, a stream and my dwelling place.

Save me, save me, Machu Picchu!
Save me, and do not run from my peril!
O yes, my God, he lives, he lives!)

                              ("La sorpresa," 96–126)

This is hardly Neruda's geometrical grid and trope of interposition, but then *La Mano Desasida* is not a sequence of well-managed artifices. Instead it challenges most of the elements one learns to anticipate in the Western lyric sequence, bringing into question and not answering much that poets since Petrarch have tacitly assumed about the form's fictional uses of time and space, and about the satisfaction it confers out of these. Adán's is a trying, aggressive, dissonant piece of work.[40]

For one thing, the sense of temporality in *La Mano Desasida* contravenes most of the principles handed down from the *Canzoniere* and refined by later poets of both conservative and experimental bents. In another chapter I have written that many poets make little of the temporal interval between a lyric utterance and the event it relates, and perhaps at a glance Adán belongs in this class. The units of *La Mano Desasida* largely do not discriminate events through the striations of tense; instead the sole recoverable process of the work is the here and now of the utterances themselves, the present continuum in which the voice speaks to Machu Picchu and us. And though narrative and dramatic fragments are strewn across the verse, one can seldom or never pull these together into hypothetical episodes, as readers often do even with *The Waste Land* and *The Cantos*. Like everything in the sequence, temporality is shown being pressed into its flattest, ostensibly least ambiguous configuration in these poems.

Is Adán's then a ritual series? Because the poems are so intransitive, their resorts to an immediate materiality so readily cancelled by the voice's quarrels with itself, I tend to think not. But the negligible temporal interval answers the same urge as the speaker's insistence that he "is" Machu Picchu, the near-absence of coherent situations, and the continual spatializing of his history and concerns. That is, he actually wants to close down his present identity and get as near to Machu Picchu as the lyric medium allows; though he is simply one more poet of fictions about Machu Picchu, he wants to be its Whitman, its ritual celebrant and lover. *La Mano Desasida* is finally not so much a spatial or geographical sequence as the serio-temporal record of a mind literally trying to will itself into a new state of being. Of course we will have trouble reading the cry of someone who wishes to slip out of every element of his being, who fictionalizes the urge toward ritual; of course his temporal, spatial, and personal relations with Machu Picchu will waver unpredictably. He explicitly deforms the Petrarchan retrospective topos ("Everything then was as now"), the temporal *variatio* that enforces a fiction of process in innumerable settings through the twentieth century:

> You are the real and the true,
> The object of living and dying.
> Yes, but sadness lived in you, were you utterly!
> The sadness of human birth,
> Of being born human, the same old mutter.
> And every time I'm born I am the same.
> I am the same man to these narrow alleys
> Of existence I go there alone
> And to sex alley, and the way of loving women,
> And the alley that goes by the real, improbable road
> That runs to Death.
> Already I have told you so, Machu Picchu,
> Stone without a horizon for seeing itself.
>
>   ("La presencia," 189–202)

Stalled in a single instant, immune even to the intense consciousness of time's passing that afflicts many other lyric speakers, Adán's voice treats temporality as something that happens on an "improbable road" where he does not go, something to be remarked and deplored from a distance but seldom felt: "I take my stand in a space where there's no room for time," he says in the 1964 version ("La presencia," 223–24), and in 1980 adds, "You, Time, invade my space!" (252). The speaker looks over time as an unmappable labyrinth laid out beneath him, and defies the Petrarchan attitude much as, for example, Hinduism challenges Western historical thinking in certain cosmological anecdotes: "In one of the Purānic accounts of the deeds of Vishnu in his Boar Incarnation or Avatar, occurs a casual reference to the cyclic recurrence of the great moments of myth. The Boar, carrying on his arm the goddess Earth whom he is in the act of rescuing from the depths of the sea, passingly remarks to her: '*Every time I carry you this way.*' "[41] Substituting mean or unremarkable happenings for great moments, and debasing Vishnu into a shabby madman addressing his own goddess Earth, one can approximate the sense of time in these poems, and measure their unsettling effect on the received temporality of Adán's chosen form.

Fashioning his willful orientation to space and geography, Adán incites an oblique, polemical dialogue with the poet of *Alturas de Macchu Picchu* and, beyond, with the remains of a post-Petrarchan poetics. His poem articulates hard questions in full knowledge of the achieved uses of the form, the politics of the post-Petrarchan dramatis personae, and the subversive quality of these original, spatial claims. The title is the first clue to this revision. It introduces Adán's speaker as a tactile artist constantly grappling to dispose Machu Picchu and break its dominance over his imagination. Figuring the artist as "a wandering hand among the pairs," it anticipates the speaker's intuition that space and matter compose the primary dimension of human experience, and shows his commitment to take aesthetic and intellectual refuge there.

> Yes, first was Touch: all Knowledges came next.
> But what are these things, touching and understanding?
> Where, Machu Picchu, do I know myself?
> When . . . and why? . . .
> How do I die, my friend, that I may live you?
> Where does my wanting seize hold?
>
> ("La sorpresa," 74–81)

The implication for the work's spatial conceit—and therefore for its structure and appeal—is evident. Unlike that of *Alturas de Macchu Picchu*, the program of *La Mano Desasida* is one of a hand groping against an object: it plays over intriguing textures, collides with what it does not understand, returns to terrain already felt, and gathers a sense of its object by a patchwork of inferences rather than a tidy sum of advances and discoveries. The close, tactile relations between the speaker and Machu Picchu, indeed the speaker's sworn identity with the high city, is repeatedly played for contrast with the overtures of other admirers who cannot come so close: the discoverer Hiram Bingham, the archaeologists and philosophers, Pablo Neruda, and the ubiquitous gringo *turista* with his or her Kodak:

> Do not fear, Machu Picchu,
> Those tourists will not touch you.
> Neruda will cause you no harm,
> The gringa will cause you no harm!
> For I am alive and I defend myself,
> Your life is my own!
>
> (1980.214)

But the title's principal declaration, from a reading both informed by the preceding chapters and conditioned by the freestanding concerns of the work, is the disconnection of the speaker's hand. The verb *asir*, "to seize," often describes the actions of hands: a *mano desasida* is a hand let go or a hand released, perhaps a hand that lets go, or even a generous, open hand. But as the fiction of the series indicates, this is a hand unclasped not only by other hands but by the arm and body it might be connected to, a truly disjunct and independent instrument of the speaker's restless consciousness. Chilling and alienating him, the title motif sets his vision of human purpose against that embodied in Neruda's hand always groping for genitals: Adán prizes pure detachment over universal bonds, and distrusts nature too much to comprehend the exuberance of Neruda's materialism.[42] (Compare Hidalgo's less ideologically specific parody of the materialism of *Alturas de Macchu Picchu*: "Did they here learn to live connected to the land / By some sort of cable? / Who knows" [19.1–3].) The chief tone of Adán's sequence, though not the only one, is an irritability at humankind's "histories and hot stink." A *mano desasida*, seemingly cut free from the heart's clock and the body's temperate zones, the speaker can live out his feverish habituation to the place he admires. He can devote himself to exploring his shaping powers, a fount of renewed life, and plunge into the hard questions of mortality from the double position of both a creator and a terminal patient. Perhaps more to the point of our reading experience than anything else, the title involves a want of rest: his disconnected hand will continually hurry to new attitudes, using the evasive potential of sequentiality and its own dexterousness as barriers to a final admission of defeat. Each of these elements of the title figures in the following passage, a more or less random extract from the middle of "La presencia":

> If I retreat from my work,
> I lose my being from not creating.
> Yes, my body is this hand,
> The one I hold you with,
> The one that put your eons in an instant,
> Hideous stone, evil stone, stone of my thought!
> Keep still, I am doubting!
> Keep silent, my silence is veiling me in shadow
> Like the night of the dead!
> Keep still, for I want the valley
> With its green and its linnet!
> Keep quiet, I am human, you stone of augury!
> I take my stand in a space where there's no room for time,
> Where my hand keeps making and making,
> Makes the ruins and the walls and the feeling!
> O damned Machu Picchu!
> For what am I always born?
> Where am I killing him who never lives me—
> And I not living—to be he who never dies?
>
> ("La presencia," 207–32)

Still finer and more revealing, the title motif indicates a commonness between Adán's speaker and the inarticulate, disintegrated love objects of the post-Petrarchan sequences. In the *Canzoniere* and other works of that strain, the hand is typically an emblem of power. The suffering speaker's hands are impotent and insensate, with nothing available to them except an unmentioned masturbation.

> Piú volte incominciai di scriver versi:
> ma la penna et la mano et l'intellecto
> rimaser vinti nel primier assalto.

(Many times have I begun to write verses, but my pen and my hand and my intellect have been vanquished in the first assault.)

(20.12–14)

> Lasso, non di diamante, ma d'un vetro
> veggio di man cadermi ogni speranza,
> et tutti miei pensier' romper nel mezzo.

(Alas, I see all hope fall from my hands, made not of diamond but even of glass, and I see all my thoughts break in half.)

(124.12–14)

Meanwhile, the several agents that galvanize the Petrarchan lover's emotions (including not only Laura but Love and, especially in the later parts of the series, God) continually use their hands on him—or her, as in the third lyric of Vittoria Colonna's *Rime*. The Petrarchan confessional idiom tends to see these hands as willful, disembodied organs, partly to maintain an impression of the speaker's weakness before a supernatural power, partly to imply that he or she answers Love's continual threat of psychic disintegration by dissolving others in imagination.[43]

> Questa che col mirar gli animi fura,
> m'aperse il petto, e 'l cor prese con mano,
> dicendo a me: Di ciò non far parola.

(She, who with her glance steals souls, opened my breast and took my heart with her hand, saying to me: "Make no word of this.")

(23.72–74)

Even when Laura's hands are at rest, as in the seemingly adoring passages that provoked Marot and others to develop the blason, they are suffused with a latent menace. Therefore the speaker's arrangement and emotional coloring of them are, we know, merely a stay against her renewed assault, and these lyrics gain an ironic, suspenseful charge:

> O bella man, che mi destringi 'l core,
> e 'n poco spatio la mia vita chiudi;
> man ov'ogni arte et tutti loro studi
> poser Natura e 'l Ciel per farsi honore;

di cinque perle orïental' colore,
et sol ne le mie piaghe acerbi et crudi,
diti schietti soavi, a tempo ignudi
consente or voi, per arricchirme, Amore.

Candido leggiadretto et caro guanto,
che copria netto avorio et fresche rose,
chi vide al mondo mai sí dolci spoglie?

(O beautiful hand that grasps my heart and encloses in a little space all my life, hand where Nature and Heaven have put all their art and all their care to do themselves honor,

neat soft fingers, the color of five oriental pearls, and only bitter and cruel to wound me: to make me rich, Love now opportunely consents that you be naked.

White, light, and dear glove, that covered clear ivory and fresh roses: who ever saw in the world such sweet spoils?)

(199.1–11)

By contrast with these and later poems in the post-Petrarchan connection—from Maurice Scève's *Délie* 367 ("Asses plus long, qu'un Siecle Platonique") to Hart Crane's "Episode of Hands" (1948)—Adán's title suggests that the speaker suffers an alternating current of power and powerlessness, that he enacts the role not only of Petrarch's plangent lover but of his Laura as well. His degree of control over the site—his capacity, that is, to figure it in poetry—is pushed sharply to the foreground here as against the Petrarchan speaker's more tacit supervision of the *Canzoniere*. Adán's voice continually swears he will disfigure Machu Picchu, distort it, even erase it:

> Machu Picchu, if I choose to imagine it,
> You do not exist!
> There is only my soul and a stone,
> A river that runs between my feet
> And the heavens over my head
> And the house I made in my world,
> Not even inhabited by absence!
>
> ("La sorpresa," 44–49)

But as Adán's work makes the issue of the lover-poet's control cruder and more explicit, Machu Picchu itself is shown to be a subtler, more redoubtable object and foe than Laura could ever be. It is as anxiously solicited, and as silent, as Edward Taylor's God. The speaker finds that while in settings other than Machu Picchu his hand is an instrument of aesthetic

disposition, here at the site it only picks up the signals of an "Essence"
too large and daunting to be assimilated into art. A vestigial, ostensibly
manual creation, Machu Picchu nonetheless challenges—with its majesty,
its formal perfection, its otherworldliness—the idea of its human completion, and undoes the speaker's humanity. What, finally, can the speaker
have to do with it?

> When and how are you human,
> I the only human, and you human and mine?
> And what will I say if the word
> That weighs and travels so little like your balance?
> What will I say about your years?
> What will I say about the Urubamba?
> What will I say about the Indian girl
> Who washes herself unawares in the stream,
> An untaught flower of bluster, nude of love and hatred,
> Exact and superfluous and stinking and cloudy river?
>
> But you are here and now, all-enclosing stone,
> Huge and insufficient boundary, true word,
> You are what I flee from and hunt down,
> Concrete heavens and hard despondency,
> Symbol . . .
> Foul-smelling flesh that calls itself life,
> And life you are, filthy and odorless stone,
> With your brutish, lyrical way of looking at me;
> Human stone, terrifically human stone,
> All made of terrors and delights.
>
> ("La presencia," 15–35)

What can he say about it in a language of comparable exactitude? The
larger spectacle of its clean geometry, and the closer look at its precisely
matched stones, drive his language into an incoherence that yet carries his
frustration: "And what will I say if the word / That weighs and travels so
little like your balance?" Where it undermines his capacity as a poet, Machu Picchu also remakes his conception of the cosmos, and rewrites the
book of human and divine possibilities with one gesture. The speaker realizes that his anthropomorphic notions of God do not answer for the
makers of a place like Machu Picchu, and that he cannot understand the
mano divina that would shape this aerie of stones. The inadaptability of
his well-worn theology is suddenly vivid and frightening:

> But when you die, Machu Picchu,
> Where will I go, with what will I go, with my smile
> And my flesh and my bone and my house

And my heresy,
And my translation of the Catullan sparrow,
And my Mass,
And I don't know what, since being came late to me.
(It wasn't yet time, and life went tumbling down.)
And this being nothing but a speaking before the verses! . . .
And this shivering before God that they call life!
And this looking at you and dying, Stone there above! . . .
This feeling oneself a God before one's conscience,
Before one's own heresy! . . .
This having made you a human like myself,
Who was never the Prophet of the Bible,
Nor the Abominable Snowman, nor the Gorilla!

("La presencia," 48–66)

The mental experience told in *La Mano Desasida*, then, is the speaker's forced abandonment of his categories of understanding with only something all but incomprehensible taking their place. He learns to think of this *nada* ("nothing") as natural to the geographical existence he wishes to achieve, but the new habit of mind will defer moving into place through the entire sequence. The work's fictional program is to chart his groping around these questions, here his clutching them immediately, here his skittering away into doubts and evasions. Quarrying his sureties and casting him into an existential travail, Machu Picchu makes fresh poetry of the speaker's thoughts. Therefore the two layers of the title: before the series is well along Machu Picchu has made him both arranger and arranged, poet and poetry, so his hand must appear as both the artist's implement and the amputated, blasoned object. Both layers are sounded in every mention of the hand, for wherever it is made to stand for the share of power he holds over the high city, its disconnection invariably says something else. From a certain distance, moreover, the identification of a hand as lyric protagonist comes off as a parody of the entire nominative enterprise, as in what Charles Olson eagerly called "this most important shot against humanism" by the historian of paleolithic art, Max Raphael: "The hand is not a structure centered on an axis, it is unsymmetrical in shape, it has a one-sided direction just like an animal in motion, and its motions are free and independent of one another, because, unlike the human body as a whole, they do not constitute a single system of balance." (Olson comments to Robert Creeley, "that last sends me—is a thing i have been waiting for, the pertinence—what do you say!")[44] Such is the hand of *La Mano Desasida*, and its foregrounding here is probably one of postmodern poetry's most direct scores against the aesthetic and ideological complex that produced the fictional blason.

Further, the post-Petrarchan irony of *La Mano Desasida* extends well past the title to involve corruptions of several motifs from the *Canzoniere* and its successors. How are we to read these questions from "La sorpresa"?

> ¿Dónde me sé, Machu Picchu?
> ¿Cuándo? . . . ¿Por qué? . . .
> ¿Cómo me muero, Tú, para vivirte?
> ¿Dónde agarro para mi querer?
> ¿Cuándo yo dé con mi deseo
> Me huí el cuerno y espina en la sien?
> ¿Por qué lloro, a tu piedra pegado,
> Como si acabara de nacer?

> (Where, Machu Picchu, do I know myself?
> When . . . and why? . . .
> How do I die, my friend, that I may live you?
> Where does my wanting seize hold?
> When I meet my desire
> Did I flee
> The horn, the splinter in my temple?
> Why do I cry, stuck on your stone
> As though just born?)

(78–85)

The former questions are the organs of the sequence, the inquiries into his own ontology and spatiality that follow hard on the psychic dislocations wrought by Machu Picchu. At the penultimate question, the speaker attempts to clarify his predicament with what seems a Petrarchan allusion, an echo of the last lines of *Canzoniere* 23. Adán carries us back to a part of Petrarch's sequence where the speaker is most often and literally made Laura's object, as he suffers six Ovidian transformations at her *manos desasidas*. The Petrarchan speaker first looks back to the last days of his youth and wonders

> Lasso, che son! che fui!
> La vita el fin, e 'l dí loda la sera.
> Ché sentendo il crudel di ch'io ragiono
> infin allor percossa di suo strale
> non essermi passato oltra la gonna,
> prese in sua scorta una possente donna,
> ver' cui poco già mai mi valse o vale
> ingegno, o forza, o dimandar perdono.

(Alas, what am I? what was I? The end crowns the life, the evening the day. For that cruel one of whom I speak, seeing that as yet no blow of his arrows had gone beyond my garment, took as his patroness a powerful Lady, against whom wit or force or asking pardon has helped or helps me little.)

(23.30–37)

As he learns, he is only what Love makes him at any particular time. In one of the work's first extended records of accumulating process, the speaker finds that his physical and cerebral changes—from a man to a laurel, a swan, a stone, a fountain, an echo, and a stag—simply literalize the psychic alternations chronicled in the rest of the series. His anticipations of death, which begin early in the *Canzoniere*, gather force not simply as expressions of a mood but as the only feasible imaginings of closure in this lover's life and this series. His amatory existence is a chain of vicissitudes and metamorphoses, easily charted in time and space, without a destination. He knows he is literally going nowhere in love.

The canzone seems to retell a sustained episode of helplessness on the speaker's part. Showing his literal transformations after some of the patterns he often uses to alter and manage Laura—and nominating her in several episodes as the agent of his changes—the lover here gives full play to his occasional bent for reversing subject and object. It is only when we wonder why these metamorphoses seem so singularly neutralizing, so clamorous of authority acting on its dupe, that we disentangle the state of relations in the *Canzoniere* as a total fiction, and see who is changing whom in these poems.

At the end of Canzone 23, Petrarch's speaker recounts the transformation that allows for a contingent narrative conclusion but no halt to his sufferings. One notices the last detail in these lines, where Laura takes the part of Ovid's Diana and the speaker becomes Actaeon:

> I' seguí' tanto avanti il mio desire
> ch'un dí cacciando sí com'io solea
> mi mossi; e quella fera bella et cruda
> in una fonte ignuda
> si stava, quando 'l sol piú forte ardea.
> Io, perché d'altra vista non m'appago,
> stetti a mirarla: ond'ella ebbe vergogna;
> et per farne vendetta, o per celarse,
> l'acqua nel viso co le man mi sparse.
> Vero dirò (forse e' parrà menzogna)
> ch'i' sentí' trarmi de la propria imago,
> et in un cervo solitario et vago
> di selva in selva ratto mi trasformo:
> et anchor de' miei can' fuggo lo stormo.

(I followed so far my desire that one day, hunting as I was wont, I went forth, and that lovely cruel wild creature was in a spring naked when the sun burned most strongly. I, who am not appeased by any other sight, stood to gaze on her, whence she felt shame and, to take revenge or to hide herself, sprinkled water in my face with her hand. I shall speak the truth, perhaps it will appear a lie, for I felt myself drawn from my own image and into a solitary wandering stag from wood to wood quickly I am transformed and still I flee the belling of my hounds.)

(23.147–60)

Running away from the vision, the speaker comes forward into the present tense to break the narrative mise-en-scène: he runs off, of course, to write about the events of the strophe—as he implied he would (lines 10–12), and as he admits he is doing now (line 156)—and to reassert his control over them and their origin, Laura. The entire canzone, a chain of incidents involving what seems a more than usual exercise of power on Laura's part, appears here in retrospect as a carefully arranged history reflecting perhaps a more than usual disposition by the speaker. The lyric is vital to the early unfolding of the *Canzoniere* because, among other reasons, it shifts the ground under the work's relations of power so indeterminately and often. To mention it as Adán does is perhaps to imply that a configuration of power, even in the modern geographical series, is other than what it seems.[45]

Time in *La Mano Desasida* resists differentiation and mapping, of course, so Adán's speaker will undergo no literal changes, no Petrarchan *variatio* of the body, to mark the rush of process. The passage in "La sorpresa" that looks back to the canzone begins with spatial questions corresponding to Petrarch's "what am I? what was I?", and narrows his rendition of the metamorphoses into a few succinct verses. One hears a diminishing priority in the first three questions ("Where ... When ... and why?"), and then ("that I may live you?") the speaker's urge to become Machu Picchu as the end of his own search for order. By contrast, the Petrarchan canzone shows its speaker participating unwillingly in some simulations of Laura; he wishes implicitly to attain the godliness she is said to mirror. But it is a primary fact of that work's nominative orientation, and of its way of recovering amatory experience, that the personae are kept distinct as dramatized intelligences. They vary tacitly and delicately from that order as in Canzone 23, where Petrarch bares certain sensations in the lover's memory for local and climactic effect: the fluidity and indefinition of his control over the situation of loving, for example, or his helpless sense of having adapted always inappropriately to her stand of the moment. For everything in the sequence apart from these episodes of his intensified desolation, the speaker remains someone decidedly other than Laura, and leaves us always aware of the fact.

Adán, whose epithet for Machu Picchu is "I Myself," obviously gives away a program of distinct identities in favor of other interests. Continuing to grapple in "La sorpresa" with his and Machu Picchu's physical reality, he dispenses with the second-person pronoun in line 81 as though he and the city have coalesced and he explores his own body: "Where does my desire take hold?" he asks in the fashion of someone touching his interlocutor, someone to whom the pronoun *te* ("you") is made superfluous by an act of the body. The next lines, which introduce the unequivocally Ovidian-Petrarchan allusion, push the implication even harder. The key to the query appears, I suppose, in the first two words of line 83, which I have given in their own verse:

> ¿Cuándo yo dé con mi deseo
> Me huí el cuerno y espina en la sien?
>
> (When I meet my desire
> Did I flee
> The horn, the splinter in my temple?)

(82–83)

This rhetorical question must be emphatically answered with a no; unlike Petrarch's voyeur, who stops the chain of transformations and implies the origin of his utterance with his flight out of the grove, Adán's speaker wants to make it plain that he does not turn away from the source of his desire but rushes directly into its arms, into the heart of Machu Picchu. In view of his imagined identity with it, the unthinkable transgression would be not his approach but his guilty flight. He does not need to run off and recompose Machu Picchu in his imagination, but will meet it and dispose himself in its likeness. The discontinuity of the verbs—from an expectant present subjunctive to a preterite—suggests that the instant of fusion happens and then slips into pastness between these lines, falling through the serial cracks and demonstrating again the work's infidelity to matters of time. For that matter, the adverb *when* in the Spanish shifts rudely from an interrogative to a relative function between 82 and 83, as though the temporal specifications of grammar itself are literally breaking down. Like several other cruxes, these lines also argue that the verbal flow of *La Mano Desasida* is complemented by a repertory of implied gestures. Here, one guesses, he suddenly caresses Machu Picchu's stones again and instantly, perhaps involuntarily, reflects on his non-Ovidian thrust forward. The final question of the chain, "Why do I cry, stuck on your stone / As though just born?" (84–85), contains its own reply. He cries babylike because with the implicit fusion and (perhaps) touch, he has undergone this work's version of rebirth and metamorphosis, a provisional resolution into Machu Picchu that will be reenacted, examined, and disputed for the rest of the sequence. Such a buried climax is the only kind we can expect to find in a lyric sequence that throws out the differing exactitudes of Petrarch and Neruda in favor of a groping, imprecise coming to its materials. Rewritten into the shape of Adán's concerns, Petrarch's canzone provides the model for one attitude among many that the poet shuffles and reshuffles in his deliberately fumbling fashion.

Adán's colloquy with his forerunners resumes soon after the passage I have dissected, near the first of the poem called "La presencia," and continues sporadically through that lyric. Here three passages, with increasing distances between them, play out a Petrarchan motif:

> When and how are you human,
> I the only human, and you human and mine?
> And what will I say if the word
> That weighs and travels so little like your balance?
> What will I say about your years?
> What will I say about the Urubamba?
> What will I say about the Indian girl
> Who washes herself unawares in the stream,
> An untaught flower of bluster, nude of love and hatred,
> Exact and superfluous and stinking and cloudy river?
>
> ("La presencia," 15–24)

> Mother Desolation, give me your hardness!
> Let my foot tread on the nerve that brokenly flutters!
> Let my hand finger the hide it plucks!
> Let me go down from the rapture of terror and God
> To my flesh, my bone, my enervated idea!
> Let me wash myself with the naked Indian girl
> Where only some eddies will see me!
>
> (85–92)

> You are like the word:
> A certain hardness before Destiny and the infinite
> Philosophy will not show its face before your stones.
> Instead, a little below,
> What I see river
> Where she I feel Indian
> Gives drink to him I think her son.
> Yet do I believe? Yet do I exist?
> O do not turn on me, Machu Picchu, my own!

> Go, Machu Picchu, go! You are no gardener!
> With you or not, I remember or do not forget!
> Everything happened before the beginning,
> Everything of more or less!
> O soul that I am: it makes a body of me.
>
> (277–92)

Probably no chain of speeches can better show such definitive aspects of the speaker's love of Machu Picchu. Again, the Petrarchan dramatic element he evokes is part of the Ovidian narrative laid into Canzone 23, the myth of Actaeon and Diana. In the first of these Adanic passages, which occurs at the onset of the final and longest poem, the speaker relapses into looking on Machu Picchu as an artist contemplates his or her object. He implicitly understands that his geographical topic is too devastating to be caught in verse; as I have said, Machu Picchu destroys even the logic of the sentences that aim to recover something of its static calm and order. But he speaks vaguely as though he commands the temporal strata of a Petrarch, a Garcilaso de la Vega, a Yeats, as though the dramatic experience of "La presencia" and the recording of the poem are distinct events in time—as though Machu Picchu is not forcing the poetry out of him here and now. A terrific irony hovers in this list of questions—"what will I say," three times—because every reader of *La Mano Desasida* knows there is no immaculate post-Petrarchan breviary in the speaker's future. There is only the misshapen bulk of the work's extant versions, an admission of lost control, where, for example, in 1964 the second lyric is five times as long as the first and the third more than three times longer than that, and where all three constituent poems circle obsessively over the same issues again and again. "What will I say?": he is saying it now.

With the second passage in the chain, however, the speaker has come around to the conviction that truth is in presence more than absence, in immediate experience more than recollection, in space more than time:

> All is true if it is not history.
> All is life if it is life,
> And so goes my truth, my life.
>
> ("La presencia," 71–73)

It is useless to wonder how this sentiment was born, for like every mood of the speaker's it has always been alive in the sequence, though sometimes waiting just beneath the surface of his present outlook; in a temporally unmarked work such as Adán's (and to a certain degree, Neruda's), the transitional moments tend to slip out of prominence, here and there into downright invisibility. The work's program no more demands preparation for such a change than a hand needs to explain its altered grasp. This turn of thought compels the speaker to ask for the hardness of desolation, for tactile knowledge of the "hide" he will pluck by art, and finally for the experience of bathing with *la india desnuda* in a brook of this Andean Sorgue. Defining himself against the post-Petrarchan conception and identifying himself with the donna, he pleads to close his world even more tightly on itself, to eliminate every vestige of an interval between subject and object. He concedes that he is both the creative hand and the blasoned *mano desasida*. In this stream, where "only some eddies will see me," the plot of the Actaeon myth is closed down and emptied of tension: no possibility of voyeurism, nor of Diana's angry retribution, nor of flight and metamorphosis. As though continuing the enterprise of Pound's Canto 4, which retells the Ovidian-Petrarchan episode of Actaeon and Diana through an array of fragmentary voices (including one of Petrarch's likely Provençal sources, the troubadour Peire Vidal) until the subject of the utterance is posited as a transhistorical, transcultural first-person, Adán's "La sorpresa" and the rest of *La Mano Desasida* strenuously reimagine the status of the post-Petrarchan, New World object.[46]

The third revision of Petrarch's Ovidian episode occurs where the conclusion of "La presencia" and the series is underway and the speaker grows into his last thoughts. He has come to accept his intuition of a divinity without the human qualities that bring it down to the understanding of people; he knows that poetry, like life, happens in the here and now; and he knows that to exist among these facts is to suffer unspeakable fears and uncertainties. He takes Machu Picchu as the symbol of these tenets, of course, and has learned to live disconnected from his old cosmology. He savors the idea of his new identity as a place. If this is nothingness, he will grope around it feelingly and energetically.

> No, Machu Picchu is nothing!
> Every object is a secret!
> And an object and a form,
> Because I was hardly far!
> Everything is truth, and Death is getting born,
> Borning and making. If Machu Picchu dies,
> O then we shall never live.
> Everything will be some cloud
> And maybe not! Here in you, Machu Picchu,
> Where Nothing is a lump for touching, green and gray;
> Where my errant hand strikes, as my tongue speaks
> When it does not move!
> And the portraiture of my eyes
> Just now cannot!

Because I am your Spirit
That seizes you because it wants you, loves you
Because my soul, my You, are in travail
Now and always
Fear! Without limits or lights or snow,
Without burden of friends or lovers,
Without any words,
Without measure of measures, or meters, brief! . . .

You are like the word:
A certain hardness before Destiny and the infinite
Philosophy will not show its face before your stones.

("La presencia," 249–79)

When he goes on to observe

> Instead, a little below,
> What I see river
> Where she I feel Indian
> Gives drink to him I think her son,

(280–82)

one has to discern, through the odd syntax and languid tone, the speaker's commitment to a fresh way of living in and portraying the world: a way based on the primacy of geography and physical relations, and elaborated only to the resonances of elemental feelings and sensations. His crucial revision of the *india desnuda* here starts from her setting and proceeds not to an exercise of figuration or "philosophy," but to an inchoate awareness. The passage manifests his urge to think practically outside the categories of Indo-European grammar and Western poetics, to test an intellection and expression that will not compromise his hard-won understanding. The passage seems to allude precisely to *Canzoniere* 126, where Petrarch's speaker sings to the

> Chiare, fresche et dolci acque,
> ove le belle membra
> pose colei che sola a me par donna;
> gentil ramo ove piacque
> (con sospir' mi rimembra)
> a lei di fare al bel fiancho colonna;
> herba et fior' che la gonna
> leggiadra ricoverse
> co l'angelico seno;
> aere sacro, sereno,
> ove Amor co' begli occhi il cor m'aperse:

date udïenzia insieme
a le dolenti mie parole extreme.

(Clear, fresh, sweet waters, where she who alone seems lady to me rested her lovely body, gentle branch where it pleased her [with sighing I remember] to make a column for her lovely side, grass and flowers that her rich garment covered along with her angelic breast, sacred bright air where Love opened my heart with her lovely eyes: listen all together to my sorrowful dying words.)

(1–13)

For Petrarch, these verses introduce the second canzone in a subsequence given to searching out problems of expression and taking lyric stock. Canzoni 125 to 129 enact a pause after the early march of the sequence, and the lover's sense of place is a crucial element in this regeneration. Robert Durling interprets the subsequence convincingly:

The initial situation in 125 is one of impasse, split, alienation, resulting from the fact that Laura, the source of integration and inspiration, is absent. The block can only be broken by an upsurge of energy that will free the sources of feeling and resynthesize the existential situation, reunite inner and outer. . . .

In the fourth stanza the focus of attention is the setting of the meditation (we are meant to identify it as Vaucluse), and the gesture of addressing the landscape is represented as a defeated renunciation of direct address of Laura. Actually this is a first step toward evocation of her presence, but it begins as a demonstration of her absence. The lover's eye interrogates the scene, running discursively over it for the signs of her former presence. The poem ends on a note of provisional satisfaction afforded by imagining her "scattered footprints," which evoke the memory of disconnected moments— not synthesized—of the experience of the first day. . . .

Poem 126 begins where 125 leaves off, with a discursive interrogation of the place: it looks back to the unsynthesized past, then to the blocked, defeated present, then to the transcendent—and useless—future (in which Laura will interrogate the place); finally comes the ecstatic image, and the synthesis reintegrates both the lover's sense of Laura and the poet's evocative power. . . .

Poems 125 and 126, then, provide a model of the Petrarchan-Augustinian dialectic of dispersal and reintegration that governs the entire *Rime sparse*.[47]

It should be clear where Adán stands against Petrarch. Replacing time with space in the values of his sequence and in his local appropriation of *Canzoniere* 126, Adán shows his speaker casting his metaphysical discoveries in spatial terms and disentangling the synthesis of aesthetic redaction and immediate observation, "inner and outer," that matters to the

Petrarchan lover. This speaker is challenged by the presence of his beloved; it will continue to overpower him until he properly becomes a place himself. The glimpse he attains here, where "she I feel Indian" wades in the river below, tells of the feasibility of that geographical state, a condition in which he will be neither subject nor object, neither philosopher nor poet. In that event he will get disengaged from the cords of worldly life, shirk its relations of power and powerlessness, and remark the world as cleanly and faithfully as he tries to do here—as one place "sees" another. The triumph of these verses is meteoric, however, fixing nothing for the future: the next two lines, "Yet do I believe? Yet do I exist? / O do not turn on me, Machu Picchu, my own!" (283–84), mark the sudden, exasperating return of his bent for "philosophy," the obstacle to his aspirations. But these verses open the way for some of the most exquisite passages in *La Mano Desasida*, in which the usual entanglements fall away and he sees with the detached eyes of stone:

> And at our feet the quena sings,
> A cry with no suicides
> Nobody, nothing that I am.
> The callous nightingale
> Sings on in my boundless night
> Sings on, now harsh, now sibilant,
> Now breathless, now without a branch to hold him,
> Now with no wing to save him.
>
> ("La presencia," 293–301)

And it introduces the final struggle of the work, where the speaker makes his most potent effort to overturn received patterns of thought and assert what he has insensibly discovered. The series does not really conclude—does a hand have a terminal attitude?—but stops over a meditation on the meaning of solitude.

> Believe me, Machu Picchu,
> And horrible flora, make me to believe.
> Nothing is real but what you put
> Under what you touch.
> Nothing is real but your frown
> And a single rock
> And some man's hand that wanders making
> The vista, the object, the form . . .
> And the divinity of the immediate,
> And the instant of sense, and the abyss in darkness.
>
> Listen to me, Stone:
> I want to teach you and beguile you.

Solitude is a thing
Like those things you hold, and nothing more.
Solitude is like your heaven,
That is not your being . . . though yes, perhaps your being
Sometime or somewhere.
Or an evanescent being without a where,
Now without a way
To its ever over there.

Solitude is absolute:
It is desire's end.
The precious blue of heaven itself,
The icy water of the moraine . . .
The mountain is a delirium,
Your every word a surprise.

                                              ("La presencia," 445–68)

The most compact formulation of the speaker's stand might be in these last verses. He wants to leave off living in the manner of *ser* ("to be" or "to exist") and to take up his existence in *estar* ("to be" in a place, a condition, a moment); but he aspires to an *estar* unanchored to an actual place because he will be the place himself, a stationary and inert way of being, an utter recoil from the pulse and travels of humanity. His quarrel with Neruda over their respective appropriations of lyric space could not be clearer or more vehement, and the values of obsessive fidelity and immediacy, while not those of poetry itself, are all on his side.

"I take SPACE to be the central fact to man born in America, from Folsom cave to now."[48] So writes Charles Olson in *Call Me Ishmael* (1947), his interpretation of *Moby-Dick* as a prophetic text of the New World. Probably no other lyric products of the Americas show the phases of this idea more vividly than the sequences of Neruda and Adán. Like Olson's program called Objectism, they promise to unravel the postulates of a European humanism—in specifically lyric terms, a nominativity—that subdues space to time as it fashions its "history" with man at the center. They share some of Olson's postmodern project, "to restate man [in order] to repossess him of his dynamic," giving full play to spatial imperatives; Adán especially would recognize Olson's insistence that "man is himself an object, whatever he may take to be his advantages, the more likely to recognize himself as such the greater his advantages, particularly at that moment that he achieves an humilitas sufficient to make him of use."[49] Even in the climate that produced such geographically oriented sequences of the United States as Williams's *Paterson* (1946–58) and Olson's *Maximus Poems* (1960–75), however, *Alturas de Macchu Picchu* and *La Mano Desasida* stand uniquely situated for a strategic revision of poetic and cultural values. European and North American modernisms take apart their humanist legacies on almost predictable grounds, and produce lyric fictions that differ from each other mostly in the degrees of their revisions of post-Petrarchan values. Their extremities are often held in by a half-visible consensus, as Olson remarked of Williams's poetry.[50] But *Alturas de Macchu Picchu*, the texts that envelop it in *Canto General*, and other modern and postmodern sequences of Latin America dissent from the received program in ways appropriate to their Third World cultures. They can be political in ways that might not strike a North American reader, still less a European, as such: in some cases, as in Neruda's sequence, this means being highly attentive to matter until the boundary between its social and aesthetic dimensions dissolves, and the speaker's voice can invoke a freshly decompartmentalized humanism. They can be radical in ways that stick: these poets do not have the luxury of rejecting something—a temporality, an ideology of selfhood—and knowing that it will be read through their innovations anyway, giving shape to their newness. What they reject, they must do without, as Vallejo largely does in *Trilce*. Even so, the choice of geography as conceit might be fairly seen as the gesture that sums up their fictional innovations. It does not entail an outright abandonment of the humanist inheritance, but an informed revision of it. They simply and emphatically replace one axis with another, making manifest what was latent and vice versa; accordingly, the concerns of post-Petrarchan sequences and their modernist offshoots are hardly ruled out, but merely consigned to an alternate dimension, where they speak loudly enough to remind us they have been subordinated. For a poet of postcolonial Spanish America, after all, this is a way of defeating history with his or her indivisible possession, geography.

Adán raises the stakes. When he reads Neruda's tribute to Machu Picchu he sees not a text organized by space, but a covertly temporal fiction; not a true exploration of the site, but an allegorization of it. As de Man writes of Romantic sequences such as Wordsworth's *Duddon* sonnets, allegory of whatever origin honors time, not space, and we already know that all fictional sequences are (in one fashion or another) allegorical.[51] Or one might go back to W.V.O. Quine's observation that ordinary language is irremediably biased in favor of temporality, that "relations of date are exalted grammatically as relations of position, weight, and color are not,"[52] for a sense of Adán's conviction that Neruda's poems are poisoned at the cultural source. In reply, then, *La Mano Desasida* fictionalizes the urge to break free of fiction, to escape out of allegories and temporal specifications altogether and into an especially authentic realization of lyric's ritual dimension, one that privileges the nontemporal elements of that mode. Adán's speaker wants his poem, and himself, to be as ma-

terially available as the site itself—not a diary, certainly not a lyric character, but a place. Of course the series cannot attain ritual, for its substance is antithetical to the view of poems as songs or scripts: ritual poems
are not about escaping from fiction to become what they already are. But
La Mano Desasida cannot, will not elaborate a workable fiction either,
since everything that could constitute temporality is deliberately de-
formed into a spatial register, and in Adán's most disabling strike at the
nominative mode, the conceit of insensate object-as-subject thwarts the
emergence of even a substitute for a plot. Post-Petrarchism's most recent
and far-flung episode produces this babbling speaker, in some sense, the
heir to an entire generic and cultural tradition thrashing fitfully around in
his determination to escape from where aesthetic, intellectual, and political history has put him. Whatever one thinks of his complaint, we ought
to understand how that history becomes distilled into the event called the
lyric sequence; how that event circumscribes him, harasses him, and finally neutralizes his efforts to get free; and what the stakes still are, here
and elsewhere, where one of our contemporaries takes on a convention
so fully invested with deep-rooted literary and cultural values. Unending
by definition, and all but inescapable in practice, post-Petrarchism survives both mindless tributes and ruthless suicide missions until we realize,
if we ever do, that it is our own.

NOTES

INTRODUCTION
POST-PETRARCHISM

1. Frank Kermode, *The Sense of an Ending* (London: Oxford University Press, 1967), 39.

2. For a discussion of Petrarch's sensation of belatedness and the aesthetic and ideological issues that follow from it, see Thomas M. Greene, *The Light in Troy* (New Haven: Yale University Press, 1983), esp. 4–53, 81–103. Theodor E. Mommsen, "Petrarch's Conception of the Dark Ages," *Speculum* 17 (1942): 226–42, is a classic treatment of the poet's sense of removal from the culture of antiquity, while Charles Trinkaus, *In Our Image and Likeness*, 2 vols. (Chicago: University of Chicago Press, 1970), 1:3–50, situates him in a Christian context.

3. For one such philological essay, see K. P. Schulze, "Über das Princip der Variatio bei römischen Dichtern," *Neue Jahrbücher für das Klassische Altertum* 131 (1885): 837–78.

4. Octavio Paz, "Notes on *La realidad y el deseo*," in *Alternating Current*, trans. Helen R. Lane (1967; New York: Seaver Books, 1983), 10.

5. Stanley Jeyaraja Tambiah, *Culture, Thought, and Social Action* (Cambridge: Harvard University Press, 1985), 123–24. In the matter of ritual I have learned much from Tambiah's book, particularly the essays "The Magical Power of Words" (17–59) and "A Performative Approach to Ritual" (123–66), and from the following books by others: Clifford Geertz, *The Interpretation of Cultures* (New York: Basic Books, 1973), esp. 87–169; Sally F. Moore and Barbara G. Myerhoff, eds., *Secular Ritual* (Assen: Van Gorcum, 1977); Victor W. Turner, *The Forest of Symbols* (Ithaca: Cornell University Press, 1967); and Roy Wagner, *The Invention of Culture*, rev. ed. (Chicago: University of Chicago Press, 1981), esp. 71–132. In thinking about lyric's ritual mode I have used, along with the critical and theoretical texts cited below, Georges Poulet, "Phenomenology of Reading," *New Literary History* 1 (1969): 53–68, and Andrew Welsh, *Roots of Lyric* (Princeton: Princeton University Press, 1978).

6. Roman Jakobson, "Linguistics and Poetics," in *Style in Language*, ed. Thomas A. Sebeok (Cambridge: MIT Press, 1960), 359; Barbara Johnson, "Disfiguring Poetic Language" and "Apostrophe, Animation, and Abortion," in *A World of Difference* (Baltimore: Johns Hopkins University Press, 1987), 100–115, 184–99.

7. Denise Levertov, "Origins of a Poem," in *The Poet in the World* (New York: New Directions, 1973), 47; C. S. Lewis, *English Literature in the Sixteenth Century, Excluding Drama* (London: Oxford University Press, 1954), 491.

8. Victor Zuckerkandl, *Man the Musician*, trans. Norbert Guterman, vol. 2 of *Sound and Symbol*, Bollingen Series, no. 44, pt. 2 (Princeton: Princeton University Press, 1973), 19.

9. Gilbert Rouget, *Music and Trance*, trans. Brunhilde Biebuyck and Gilbert Rouget (Chicago: University of Chicago Press, 1985), 14.

10. Zuckerkandl, *Man the Musician*, 49. Justus George Lawler, *Celestial Pantomime: Poetic Structures of Transcendence* (New Haven: Yale University Press, 1979), 84, has argued more recently that figural, nondiscursive patterns in poetry may evoke fragments of universal human myths and empower the reader-participant to attain transcendence, or the "outpouring or overflowing ('influence' in the radical sense) of one person or reality into another."

11. Tambiah, *Culture, Thought, and Social Action*, 53.

12. Levertov, *Poet in the World*, 87. Arthur C. Danto, *The Transfiguration of the Commonplace* (Cambridge: Harvard University Press, 1981), is a broad-based philosophical study of what I observe here in lyric's ritual dimension.

13. Michael Riffaterre, *Semiotics of Poetry* (Bloomington: Indiana University Press, 1978), 12.

14. The first two essays in Octavio Paz, *Convergences*, trans. Helen Lane (San Diego: Harcourt Brace Jovanovich, 1987), 1–14, make a brief but important statement on the seldom-discussed topic of poetic glossolalia. Julia Kristeva's remarks on "le sémiotique" in "D'une identité l'autre" (trans. as "From One Identity to An Other"), in *Desire in Language*, ed. Leon S. Roudiez, trans. Thomas Gora et al. (New York: Columbia University Press, 1980), 131–40, concern such speech's heterogeneity to meaning as well as poetry's exertions on selfhood.

15. As a survey of numerological and calendrical structures in medieval and Renaissance English poems, see Alastair Fowler, ed., *Silent Poetry* (New York: Barnes and Noble, 1970), and Fowler, *Triumphal Forms* (Cambridge: Cambridge University Press, 1970); on the phenomenon in general, see Jerome Rothenberg, "The Poetry of Number," in *Pre-Faces and Other Writings* (New York: New Directions, 1981), 156–57.

16. Hans Robert Jauss, "*La douceur du foyer*: The Lyric of the Year 1857 as a Pattern for the Communication of Social Norms," *Romanic Review* 65 (1974): 201.

17. Veronica Forrest-Thomson, *Poetic Artifice* (Manchester: Manchester University Press, 1978), ix. The book explores the means of lyric's ritual element, proposing "its alternate linguistic orders as a new way of viewing the world" (xi).

18. Käte Hamburger, *The Logic of Literature*, trans. Marilynn J. Rose (Bloomington: Indiana University Press, 1973), 232–34.

19. Ibid., 271.

20. Ibid., 271–72.

21. Ibid., 286.

22. Ralph W. Rader, "The Dramatic Monologue and Related Lyric Forms," *Critical Inquiry* 3 (1976): 143.

23. Thomas G. Pavel, *Fictional Worlds* (Cambridge: Harvard University Press, 1986), 16.

24. Barbara Herrnstein Smith, *On the Margins of Discourse* (Chicago: University of Chicago Press, 1978), 28.

25. Ibid., 27, 30, 27. Cp. Félix Martínez-Bonati's critical extension of Smith's

ideas in *Fictive Discourse and the Structures of Literature*, trans. Philip W. Silver (Ithaca: Cornell University Press, 1981), 153–57.

26. Smith, *Margins of Discourse*, 27.

27. On person-representations and other notions of fiction I adapt here, see Nelson Goodman, *Languages of Art*, 2d ed. (Indianapolis: Hackett Publishing Co., 1976), 3–43, and *Ways of Worldmaking* (Indianapolis: Hackett Publishing Co., 1978). Jonathan Culler, "Poetics of the Lyric," in *Structuralist Poetics* (Ithaca: Cornell University Press, 1975), 164–70, describes the job of deictics in the construction of poetic subjectivity; Joel Fineman, *Shakespeare's Perjured Eye* (Berkeley: University of California Press, 1986), 5–9, situates deixis in Renaissance theories of language and poetics, and discusses how deictics shade into the epideictics of praise and the "self-inflation" of the fictional sonnet.

28. Hamburger, *Logic of Literature*, 13.

29. Pavel, *Fictional Worlds*, 38. His account of the "fictional ego" (85–93) bears on the present discussion; cp. Helen Vendler, "Contemporary American Poetry," in *The Harvard Book of Contemporary American Poetry* (Cambridge: Belknap Press of Harvard University Press, 1985), 8–9.

30. Barbara W. Lex, "The Neurobiology of Ritual Trance," in *The Spectrum of Ritual*, ed. Eugene G. d'Aquili et al. (New York: Columbia University Press, 1979), 139. Lex's entire essay, though it is pitched toward the physiology of ritual acts, potentially has something to say about the ritual dimension of lyric—especially such fundamental phenomena as rhythms, glossolalias, and the experience of sublimity.

31. Among concrete poems, see Pedro Xisto, "Epithalamium II" and "Epithalamium III," in *Concrete Poetry: A World View*, ed. Mary Ellen Solt (Bloomington: Indiana University Press, 1970), 114–15, and Haroldo de Campos's interpretive remarks on Décio Pignatari's poems "terra" and "hombre," in *An Anthology of Concrete Poetry*, ed. Emmett Williams (New York: Something Else Press, 1967), 248–49. For a recent account of some prose poems as utopias in a generic context—prophecying a fusion of genres and achieving an unprecedented contact between lyric discourse and material life—see Jonathan Monroe, *A Poverty of Objects: The Prose Poem and the Politics of Genre* (Ithaca: Cornell University Press, 1987), esp. 15–42.

32. I refer respectively, and at random, to the sonnet boom in England during the 1590s; the rise of an English Romantic poetry, represented by Wordsworth's dictum in the preface to the second edition (1800) of *Lyrical Ballads* (*Poetical Works*, ed. E. de Selincourt, 2d ed., 6 vols. [Oxford: Clarendon Press, 1952], 2:384); and the recent minor trend toward longer lyric and narrative poems.

33. Paul de Man, "The Rhetoric of Temporality," in *Blindness and Insight*, 2d ed. (Minneapolis: University of Minnesota Press, 1983), 194.

34. Ibid., 226.

35. Riffaterre, *Semiotics of Poetry*, 1–22; Octavio Paz and Julián Rios, *Solo a dos voces* (Barcelona: Lumen, 1973), n.p.; Jacques Derrida, *Of Grammatology*, trans. Gayatri Chakravorty Spivak (Baltimore: Johns Hopkins University Press, 1976), 27–73.

36. On the generic situation of lyric in the Middle Ages, see Hans Robert Jauss,

"Theory of Genres and Medieval Literature," in *Toward an Aesthetic of Reception*, trans. Timothy Bahti (Minneapolis: University of Minnesota Press, 1982), 98–109.

37. Paul de Man, "Autobiography as De-facement," in *The Rhetoric of Romanticism* (New York: Columbia University Press, 1984), 70.

38. Octavio Paz, introduction to *Renga: A Chain of Poems*, trans. Charles Tomlinson (New York: George Braziller, 1971), 22.

39. Cp. Hugh Kenner, "Art in a Closed World," *Virginia Quarterly Review* 38 (1966): 597–613; Kenner, *The Pound Era* (Berkeley: University of California Press, 1971), 355–81, 414–36; Michael André Bernstein, *The Tale of the Tribe* (Princeton: Princeton University Press, 1980), 127–61; and Vendler, "Contemporary American Poetry," 4.

40. Greene, *Light in Troy*, 124. On Petrarchan self-making, see esp. 104–26; on the artifactual dimension of humanist texts, 28–53.

41. Kenner, *Pound Era*, 369.

42. Francisco Rico, " 'Rime sparse,' 'Rerum vulgarium fragmenta,' para el título y el primer soneto del 'Canzoniere,' " *Medioevo Romanzo* 3 (1976): 133; Nancy J. Vickers, "Diana Described: Scattered Woman and Scattered Rhyme," in *Writing and Sexual Difference*, ed. Elizabeth Abel (Chicago: University of Chicago Press, 1982), 102; and Giuseppe Mazzotta, "The *Canzoniere* and the Language of the Self," *Studies in Philology* 75 (1978): 271–96.

43. Among the recent studies of narrative with which my assumptions largely agree are Roland Barthes, "Writing and the Novel," in *Writing Degree Zero*, trans. Annette Lavers and Colin Smith (Boston: Beacon Press, 1970), 29–40; Peter Brooks, *Reading for the Plot* (New York: Random House, 1984), 3–61; Northrop Frye, "Myth, Fiction, and Displacement," in *Fables of Identity* (San Diego: Harcourt Brace Jovanovich, 1963), 21–30; W. B. Gallie, *Philosophy and the Historical Understanding* (London: Chatto and Windus, 1964), 11–104; Gérard Genette, *Narrative Discourse*, trans. Jane E. Lewin (Ithaca: Cornell University Press, 1980); and James Phelan, *Reading People, Reading Plots* (Chicago: University of Chicago Press, 1989).

44. Walt Whitman, preface to *Leaves of Grass: The First (1855) Edition*, ed. Malcolm Cowley (New York: Penguin, 1976), 12, 11.

CHAPTER 1
FOUNDING FICTION

1. John Lyons, *Introduction to Theoretical Linguistics* (Cambridge: Cambridge University Press, 1969), 275. For other definitions of deixis, see Émile Benveniste, *Problems in General Linguistics*, trans. Mary Elizabeth Meek (Coral Gables: University of Miami Press, 1971), 218–19, 226–27; Charles J. Fillmore, "Deictic Categories in the Semantics of 'Come,' " *Foundations of Language* 2 (1966): 220–22; Fillmore, *Santa Cruz Lectures on Deixis* (Bloomington: Indiana University Linguistics Club, 1975), esp. 28–49; and Geoffrey N. Leech, *Linguistic Guide to English Poetry* (London: Longmans, 1969), where the author defines the notion (183–84), provides a chart of deictic words and expressions in English (191), and briefly discusses their uses in poetry (191–94).

2. But W. R. Johnson, *The Idea of Lyric* (Berkeley: University of California Press, 1982), 1–23, describes the fortunes of the deictic pronouns *I* and *you* in ancient and modern lyrics, and isolates particular deictic patterns much as I will do in this essay.

3. Uriel Weinreich remarks that "time deixis seems to be most typically associated with verb forms, although it is a perfectly conceivable component of noun designata as well (*the former, quondam, present, future king, the then king, the ex-king, the king-to-be*)." "On the Semantic Structure of Language," in *Universals of Language*, ed. Joseph H. Greenberg (Cambridge: MIT Press, 1963), 125.

4. Thomas Wyatt, "Heaven and Earth," 17–20, in *Complete Poems*, ed. R. A. Rebholz (New Haven: Yale University Press, 1981); William Shakespeare, 120.1–4, in *Sonnets*, ed. Stephen Booth (New Haven: Yale University Press, 1977); Walt Whitman, "When Lilacs Last in the Dooryard Bloom'd," 1–3, in *Leaves of Grass*, Variorum Edition of the Printed Poems, ed. Sculley Bradley et al., 3 vols. (New York: New York University Press, 1980), 2:529; Hart Crane, "Quaker Hill," 20–24, *The Bridge*, in *Complete Poems and Selected Letters and Prose*, ed. Brom Weber (New York: Liveright Publishing Corp., 1966); T. S. Eliot, "Burnt Norton," 44–46, *Four Quartets*, in *Complete Poems and Plays, 1909–1950* (New York: Harcourt, Brace, and World, 1971). The italics are mine. Except where I indicate otherwise, subsequent quotations of Shakespeare's *Sonnets* and Whitman's *Leaves of Grass* refer to these editions.

5. Benveniste, *Problems*, 226.

6. Fillmore, "Deictic Categories," 221.

7. Rodney Huddleston, "Some Observations on Tense and Deixis in English," *Language* 45 (1969): 799. Cp. Fillmore, *Santa Cruz Lectures*, 40–41.

8. Oswald Ducrot and Tzvetan Todorov, *Encyclopedic Dictionary of the Sciences of Language*, trans. Catherine Porter (Baltimore: Johns Hopkins University Press, 1979), 307.

9. M.A.K. Halliday, "Types of Process," in *System and Function in Language*, ed. G. R. Kress (London: Oxford University Press, 1976), 159.

10. Mircea Eliade, *The Sacred and the Profane*, trans. Willard R. Trask (New York: Harcourt, Brace, 1959), 68–70. Cp. Basil de Selincourt, "Music and Duration," in *Reflections on Art*, ed. Susanne Langer (Baltimore: Johns Hopkins University Press, 1958), 153, on the experience of musical process.

11. Gérard Genette, "Time and Narrative in *À la recherche du temps perdu*," trans. Paul de Man, in *Aspects of Narrative*, ed. J. Hillis Miller (New York: Columbia University Press, 1971), 93–94. The bracketed words were evidently inserted by de Man. Genette greatly develops his theory of narrative in *Narrative Discourse*.

12. On narrative's generic preference for the preterite, see Susanne Langer, *Feeling and Form* (New York: Charles Scribner's Sons, 1953), 160–66, and Hamburger, *Logic of Literature*, 70–110.

13. The narratives represented here by their first lines are Philip Sidney, *The Countess of Pembroke's Arcadia*, ed. Maurice Evans (Harmondsworth: Penguin, 1977), and Alfred Tennyson, "Enoch Arden," in *Poems*, ed. Christopher Ricks (London: Longmans, 1969).

14. Homer, *Odyssey*, trans. W.H.D. Rouse (New York: New American Library, 1937), 86.

15. Ovid, *Metamorphoses*, 1.1–4, trans. Rolfe Humphries (Bloomington: Indiana University Press, 1955).

16. *Odyssey*, trans. Rouse, 147, the end of book 12.

17. Miguel de Cervantes, *Don Quixote*, trans. Walter Starkie (New York: New American Library, 1964), 430.

18. *Don Quixote*, 2.44, ed. Martín de Riquer (Barcelona: Juventud, 1971), 848–49. The translation is mine.

19. Brooks Otis, *Virgil: A Study in Civilized Poetry* (Oxford: Clarendon Press, 1964), 41–46. The text and translation precede Otis's discussion. On the operation of tenses in the *Georgics*, see 205–8. Cp. Genette, "Time and Narrative," 117.

20. Martin Joos, *The English Verb* (Madison: University of Wisconsin Press, 1964), 131.

21. W. S. Merwin, introduction to his translation of the *Cid* (New York: New American Library, 1975), xxx. In his conservative edition of the *Cid* (Oxford: Clarendon Press, 1972), Colin Smith provides a bibliography of "the efforts which some have made to analyse the tense-structures of the poem" (182–84). Suzanne Fleischmann, "Evaluation in Narrative: The Present Tense in Medieval 'Performed Stories,' " *Yale French Studies* 70 (1986): 199–251, correlates the fact of tense-switching with oral performance.

22. Ramón Menéndez Pidal, *Romancero hispánico (hispano-portugués, americano, y sefardí): Teoría e historia*, 2 vols. (Madrid: Espasa-Calpe, 1953), 1:68.

23. Cp. George T. Wright, "The Lyric Present: Simple Present Verbs in English Poems," *PMLA* 89 (1974): 563–79.

24. Wordsworth, *Poetical Works*, 2:213–14.

25. Robert Herrick, "How Lillies Came White," in *Complete Poetry*, ed. J. Max Patrick (New York: New York University Press, 1963).

26. Seamus Heaney, *Preoccupations* (New York: Farrar, Straus and Giroux, 1980), 131.

27. Thomas Hardy, "In a Eweleaze Near Weatherbury," in *Complete Poetical Works*, ed. Samuel Hynes, 3 vols. (Oxford: Clarendon Press, 1982–85), 1:92.

28. John Milton, "Lycidas," in *Poems*, ed. John Carey and Alastair Fowler (London: Longmans, 1968).

29. Sharon Cameron, *Lyric Time* (Baltimore: Johns Hopkins University Press, 1979), 165.

30. The sixteenth-century critic Bernardino Daniello treats Catullus, Tibullus, Propertius, Ovid, Horace, and Virgil among Petrarch's Latin models: *Sonetti, canzoni, e triomphi di M. Francesco Petrarca con la spositione di Bernardino Daniello da Lucca* (Venice, 1549), esp. iii. Remigio Sabbadini, *Le scopete dei codici Latini e Greci ne' secoli XIV e XV*, ed. Eugenio Garin, 2 vols. (1905–14; Florence: Sansoni, 1967), circumstantiates the access that Renaissance bibliophiles such as Petrarch had to manuscripts of Callimachus (1:43–47), Catullus (2:207), Ovid (2:238), Propertius (2:246), and Tibullus (2:256). On the Latin elegists' importance to Petrarch, see Pierre de Nolhac, "Pétrarque et les poètes latins," in

Pétrarque et l'humanisme, rev. ed., 2 vols. (1907; Paris: Champion, 1965), 1:163–85; and B. L. Ullman, "Petrarch's Favorite Books," in *Studies in the Italian Renaissance* (Rome: Edizioni di Storia e Letteratura, 1955), 126–27. ·

31. Propertius, Loeb Classical Library (London: Heineman, 1939). The translation is mine. B. L. Ullman, "The Manuscripts of Propertius," *Classical Philology* 6 (1911): 282–301, and *Studies*, 181–200, discuss Petrarch's knowledge of Propertius.

32. The same deictic pattern organizes the first poem in Tibullus's collection, as well as the two proems discussed here. Otis, *Virgil*, 102–5, sees the construction in an epigram of Callimachus and in Catullus 72, and R.O.A.M. Lyne, *The Latin Love Poets* (Oxford: Clarendon Press, 1980), 22–23, 39, finds it in an epigram of Philodemus and in the same Catullan poem.

33. Ovid, *Amores*, Loeb Classical Library, 2d ed. (Cambridge: Harvard University Press, 1977), 1.1.1–12, 17–26. The translation is by Rolfe Humphries (Bloomington: Indiana University Press, 1957).

34. E. A. Havelock, *The Lyric Genius of Catullus* (1939; New York: Russell and Russell, 1967), 75.

35. Archibald W. Allen, "*Sunt qui Propertium malint*," in *Critical Essays on Roman Literature: Elegy and Lyric*, ed. J. P. Sullivan (London: Routledge and Kegan Paul, 1962), 117.

36. Gordon Williams, *Tradition and Originality in Roman Poetry* (Oxford: Clarendon Press, 1968), 480, and *Figures of Thought in Roman Poetry* (New Haven: Yale University Press, 1980), 129. Brooks Otis dissents: he observes a rough "temporal continuity" in the lyric collections of Catullus, Gallus, Tibullus, Propertius, and Ovid. His principal evidence is that here and there a poem seems to "recall" another, preceding one. It is certainly hyperbolical to leap from the admission that "one can, with perhaps somewhat less certainty, find more [than two] direct 'recalls' of one poem by another in Catullus" to the confident assertion that "here . . . we can descry a continuous narrative of personal experience" (*Virgil*, 104–5). Recent treatments of the Augustan books' nontemporal unities include Otis's review of Williams's *Tradition and Originality in Roman Poetry*, in *American Journal of Philology* 92 (1971): 325–26, and the essays by John Van Sickle and others in *Arethusa* 13, no. 1 (1980). The bibliography in that issue, 115–27, is especially valuable.

37. J.E.G. Zetzel, "Horace's *Liber sermonvm*: The Structure of Ambiguity," *Arethusa* 13, no. 1 (1980): 59.

38. Roland Barthes, *A Lover's Discourse*, trans. Richard Howard (New York: Hill and Wang, 1978), 7. Margaret Hubbard, *Propertius* (London: Duckworth, 1974), 47–53, discusses the temporal progress of that poet's lyric 2.28, which apparently borrows from the convention of the disconnected plot in contemporary mime; and Lyne, *Latin Love Poets*, 124–33, extends her observations to other lyrics of the same poet.

39. On the *vidas* included in the chansonniers, see Elizabeth Wilson Poe, *From Poetry to Prose in Old Provençal* (Birmingham, Ala.: Summa Publications, 1984), 83–95. On the parataxis of Provençal poetry at every formal remove, see Stephen G. Nichols, Jr., "Toward an Aesthetic of the Provençal *Canso*," in *The Disciplines*

of Criticism, ed. Peter Demetz et al. (New Haven: Yale University Press, 1968), 349–74, and Aldo Scaglione, "La struttura del *Canzoniere* e il metodo di composizione del Petrarca," *Lettere Italiane* 27 (1975): 132–33. On the Provençal materials in the *Canzoniere*, see Nicola Scarano, "Fonti provenzali e italiane della lirica petrarchesca," *Studi di Filologia Romanza* 8 (1901): 250–360. Pio Rajna, *Lo schema della* Vita Nuova (Verona, 1890), proposes that the alternating verse and prose of certain chansonniers (with their *vidas* of the poet and summaries of each lyric's provenance) make a better model for the form of the *Vita Nuova* than Boethius's *Consolation* does. Germaine T. Warkentin, "*Astrophil and Stella* in the Setting of Its Tradition," Ph.D. diss., University of Toronto, 1972, 386–94, extends Rajna's hypothesis to include nearly all the Provençal manuscripts that include prose segments as likely resources for Dante.

40. On the formal properties of classical Menippean satire, see J. P. Sullivan, *The* Satyricon *of Petronius: A Literary Study* (London: Faber and Faber, 1968), 81–114. P. G. Walsh, *The Roman Novel* (Cambridge: Cambridge University Press, 1970), 19–24, speculates on the aims of Varro of Reate and Petronius in their prosimetric innovation. In *English Literature in the Sixteenth Century*, 327, C. S. Lewis dispenses with the question of Menippean influence on Petrarch summarily: "The difference between the *Vita Nuova* and Petrarch's *Rime* is that Petrarch has abandoned the prose links." Marco Santagata describes a wider historical sight of the descent of the *Canzoniere* from narrative and didactic Romance forebears: see "La preistoria del genere canzoniere," in *Dal sonetto al canzoniere* (Padua: Liviana, 1979), 115–42.

41. Boethius, *Theological Tractates and the Consolation of Philosophy*, Loeb Classical Library (London: Heineman, 1918), 128. The translation is by Richard Green (Indianapolis: Bobbs-Merrill, 1962).

42. Dante, *Vita Nuova*, ed. Michele Barbi, national ed. (Florence: Bemporad, 1932), 4–8, the first lines of part 2. The translation is by Mark Musa (Bloomington: Indiana University Press, 1973). In his recent edition (Milan: Ricciardi, 1980), Domenico de Robertis annotates this passage with particular alertness to the temporal issues it engages. Charles S. Singleton, *An Essay on the* Vita Nuova (1949; Baltimore: Johns Hopkins University Press, 1977), 8, remarks the deictic structure established here for the "whole action" of the work.

43. Throughout this book, quotations of the *Canzoniere* are from Gianfranco Contini's edition (Turin: Einaudi, 1964). The translations are by Robert M. Durling, ed. and trans., *Petrarch's Lyric Poems* (Cambridge: Harvard University Press, 1976).

44. Ruth Shepard Phelps, *The Earlier and Later Forms of the* Canzoniere (Chicago: University of Chicago Press, 1925), 13, and Ernest Hatch Wilkins, *The Making of the* Canzoniere *and Other Petrarchan Studies* (Rome: Edizioni di Storia e Letteratura, 1951), 151–53, speculate on the compositional provenance of the proem. Bernard Weinberg, "The *Sposizione* of Petrarch in the Early Cinquecento," *Romance Philology* 13 (1960): 374–86, alludes to the opinions of some Renaissance commentators concerning the relations of the proem and its successors. See also Rico, " 'Rime sparse,' " 101–38.

45. Among the first hundred pieces in the series, for example, this construction

can be plainly recognized in at least twenty-five: 1, 2, 3, 4, 21, 23, 25, 34, 37, 43, 44, 47, 50, 52, 55, 61, 62, 65, 67, 84, 85, 87, 88, 89, 90, 91, 96, 97, and 99. Cp. Mazzotta, "Language of the Self," 275.

46. For a more general catalogue (with a running commentary) of the allusions to passing time in Petrarch's sequence, see Giuseppe Caione, *Il sentimento del tempo nel* Canzoniere *del Petrarca* (Lecce, Italy: ITES, 1969).

47. See Aldo S. Bernardo, "The Importance of the Non-Love Poems of Petrarch's 'Canzoniere,' " *Italica* 27 (1950): 302–11.

48. Cp. Ricardo J. Quinones, *The Renaissance Discovery of Time* (Cambridge: Harvard University Press, 1972), 106–71.

49. Greene, *Light in Troy*, 29–30.

50. Ibid., 31.

51. Wilkins, *Making of the* Canzoniere, 155–56; see 75–194 for a history of the sequence's versions.

52. Langer, *Feeling and Form*, 264.

53. The dated poems (and their cumulative years from Petrarch's first sight of Laura) are as follows: 30 (seven years) 50 (ten years), 62 (eleven years), 79 (thirteen years), 101 (thirteen years), 107 (fourteen years), 118 (sixteen years), 122 (seventeen years), 145 (fifteen years), 212 (twenty years), 221 (twenty years), 226 (eighteen years), 271 (twenty-one years), 278 (twenty-four years), and 364 (thirty-one years).

54. Warkentin, "Tradition," 168, observes the imitation of Petrarch's self-dating poems by his followers, but overlooks the evident aim of these gestures: to pay a formal tribute to the achievement of process, even by reproducing what may be accidental, illogical features of the *Canzoniere*. On the wide use of anniversary lyrics, see 429, n. 39.

55. Thomas P. Roche, Jr., "The Calendrical Structure of Petrarch's *Canzoniere*," *Studies in Philology* 71 (1974): 152, 165. Roche elaborates his argument in *Petrarch and the English Sonnet Sequences* (New York: AMS Press, 1989), 1–69. On the ritual function of the sestine, see Marianne Shapiro, *Hieroglyph of Time* (Minneapolis: University of Minnesota Press, 1980).

56. Eliade, *Sacred and Profane*, 104.

57. As a random sample of numerological and calendrical explications in fictional sequences of the Renaissance and later, see Fowler, *Triumphal Forms*; A. C. Bradley, *A Commentary on Tennyson's* In Memoriam, 3d ed. (1910; Hamden, Conn.: Archon Books, 1966), 20–23; Forrest Read, *'76: One World and the Cantos of Ezra Pound* (Chapel Hill: University of North Carolina Press, 1981); Norman Holmes Pearson, foreword to *Trilogy*, by H.D. (New York: New Directions, 1973), ix–x; and Barry Ahearn, *Zukofsky's* "A": *An Introduction* (Berkeley: University of California Press, 1983), esp. 231–41.

58. Luigi Tansillo, *Canzoniere edito ed inedito*, ed. Erasmo Pèrcopo, 2 vols. (Naples: Società Editrice della Biblioteca di Scrittori Meridionali, 1927), 1:48, 111–12. The translations are mine.

59. Juan Boscán Almogáver, 65.1–6, in *Obras*, ed. Martín de Riquer et al. (Barcelona: Universidad de Barcelona, 1957). The translation is mine. Boscán introduced the Petrarchan sonnet and canzone to Spain.

60. Bernardino Rota, *Rime* (Naples, 1572), 65ᵛ. The translation is mine.

61. Mary Wroth, *Pamphilia to Amphilanthus*, P67.1–8 and P99.5–8, in *Poems*, ed. Josephine A. Roberts (Baton Rouge: Louisiana State University Press, 1983).

62. Pablo Neruda, *Veinte poemas de amor y una canción desesperada*, 6.1–9, *Obras completas*, 4th ed., 3 vols. (Buenos Aires: Losada, 1973). All quotations of Neruda's poetry and prose are from this edition. The translation here is by W. S. Merwin (New York: Penguin, 1976).

63. Francesco Petrarca, *Lettere senili*, trans. Giuseppe Fracassetti, 2 vols. (Florence, 1870), 2:301.

64. David Rapport Lachterman, *The Ethics of Geometry: A Genealogy of Modernity* (New York: Routledge, 1989), 1–24, gives an account of "construction as the mark of the modern" that seems highly Petrarchan in view of the present chapter.

CHAPTER 2
CONSTRUCTING CHARACTER

1. The pre-Petrarchan history of the lyric mode I call nominativity is properly too diverse to cite here, but one recent study stands out as especially relevant: Sylvia Huot, *From Song to Book* (Ithaca: Cornell University Press, 1987), 211–41, treats the assembling of single-author codices in Old French lyric during the fourteenth century in a way that suggests the formation of what I call an ideology of generic purpose. From Petrarch forward, a composite account of the nominative mode might be extracted from the following studies, most of which treat major lyric sequences: Mazzotta, "Language of the Self," 271–96; Greene, *Light in Troy*, esp. 81–146; Anne Ferry, *The "Inward" Language: Sonnets of Wyatt, Sidney, Shakespeare, Donne* (Chicago: University of Chicago Press, 1983); Richard C. McCoy, *Sir Philip Sidney: Rebellion in Arcadia* (New Brunswick: Rutgers University Press, 1979), 1–35, 69–109; Fineman, *Shakespeare's Perjured Eye*, esp. 187–241; Helen Vendler, *The Poetry of George Herbert* (Cambridge: Harvard University Press, 1975); and Timothy Peltason, *Reading In Memoriam* (Princeton: Princeton University Press, 1985). For a discussion of some of the political issues involved in nominativity, see Gayatri Chakravorty Spivak, "Finding Feminist Readings: Dante—Yeats," in *In Other Worlds* (New York: Methuen, 1987), 15–29.

2. For recent studies of the fiction of *Astrophil and Stella*, see Carol Thomas Neely, "The Structure of English Renaissance Sonnet Sequences," *ELH* 45 (1978): 359–89; Alan Sinfield, "Astrophil's Self-Deception," *Essays in Criticism* 28 (1978): 1–18; McCoy, *Sir Philip Sidney*, 69–109; Sinfield, "Sidney and Astrophil," *Studies in English Literature, 1500–1900* 20 (1980): 25–41; Murray Roston, *Sixteenth-Century English Literature* (New York: Schocken Books, 1982), 147–53, 181–82; Ann Rosalind Jones and Peter Stallybrass, "The Politics of *Astrophil and Stella*," *Studies in English Literature, 1500–1900* 24 (1984): 53–68; and Nona Fienberg, "The Emergence of Stella in *Astrophil and Stella*," *Studies in English Literature, 1500–1900* 25 (1985): 5–19. Fineman, *Shakespeare's Perjured Eye*, esp. 189–98, and Heather Dubrow, *Captive Victors* (Ithaca: Cornell

University Press, 1987), 169–271, have a great deal that is useful to say about Sidney's sequence in relation to Shakespeare's, especially in the matter of person.

3. The principle of function in characterization has a rich past in structuralist criticism, from which I borrow it. Étienne Souriau, in *Les deux cent mille situations dramatiques* (Paris: Flammarion, 1950), resolves drama into a play of functions or abstract roles, and uses colorful terms to propose a largely grammatical picture of literary action: his actor called the "Lion" catalyzes the action of the play, the "Sun" (or "Desired Good") is the direct object of his will, the "Earth" (or "Desired Recipient of the Good") the indirect object, "Mars" the opponent, and so forth. Robert Scholes summarizes Souriau's scheme in *Structuralism in Literature* (New Haven: Yale University Press, 1974), 50–58. Seven years after Souriau, Northrop Frye argues in *Anatomy of Criticism* (Princeton: Princeton University Press) that "in drama, characterization depends on function; what a character is follows from what he has to do in the play" (171). He goes on to present a typology of characters for each of his four mythoi or pregeneric plots, but his treatment of comic types, following the *Tractatus Coislinianus* of the fourth century B.C.E., is best-known: Frye allows for something like my crossroads of function and attributes in the various intersections of actor-types (the hero, the object of the hero's desire, the blocking character, and so on) and attitude-types (the *eiron* or self-deprecator, the *alazon* or impostor, the buffoon, and the churl). A. J. Greimas, in *Sémantique structurale* (Paris: Larousse, 1966), 172–91, has proposed a bank of functions or *actants* distributed much like Souriau's; the account of his work in Ducrot and Todorov, *Encyclopedic Dictionary*, 225, is brief but useful. Fredric Jameson, "Magical Narratives: On the Dialectical Use of Genre Criticism" in *The Political Unconscious* (Ithaca: Cornell University Press, 1981), 112–19, argues for a still more flexible understanding of these "traditional categories" and their historical determinations than Frye, for instance, allows. Phelan, *Reading People*, ingeniously tests a structuralist-influenced criticism of character against several modern novels.

4. Cp. Arthur Colby Sprague's analysis of the first scene of *Othello*, in *Shakespeare and the Audience* (Cambridge: Harvard University Press, 1935), 108–9.

5. Robert Scholes and Robert Kellogg, *The Nature of Narrative* (New York: Oxford University Press, 1966), 165–70, account for the Christian origins of development as a characterological factor. For much ancient literature as well as classical and modern Eastern cultures, characterization—insofar as it exists as a relevant phenomenon, for it does not appear everywhere—is a matter of function and attributes alone.

6. Alain Robbe-Grillet and Alain Resnais, *Last Year at Marienbad*, trans. Richard Howard (New York: Grove Press, 1962), 14. The emphasis is mine.

7. Ibid., 30. The emphasis is mine.

8. V. Propp, *Morphology of the Folktale*, trans. Laurence Scott, 2d ed. (1928; Austin: University of Texas Press, 1968). The actions are numbered and remarked in the third chapter (25–65), from which I excerpt freely.

9. Ibid., 22.

10. Ibid., 22.

11. Ibid., 21.

12. Ibid., 91.

13. M. M. Bakhtin published his *Marxism and the Philosophy of Language* under the name of V. N. Volosinov in 1929; I use the translation by Ladislav Matejka and I. R. Titunik (New York: Seminar Press, 1973). The chapters "Language, Speech, and Utterance" (65–82), "Verbal Interaction" (83–98), and "Theory of Utterance and Problems of Syntax" (109–14) pertain most strongly to my argument. On Bakhtin's identity as the author of this book, see Michael Holquist's introduction to Bakhtin's *Dialogic Imagination*, trans. Caryl Emerson and Michael Holquist (Austin: University of Texas Press, 1981), xxvi.

14. Smith, *Margins of Discourse*, 60–64, remarks on the boundaries of the utterance and its uses in fiction (though not specifically in characterization).

15. Aristotle, *Poetics* 1450a9–b17, trans. S. H. Butcher, 4th ed. (London: Macmillan, 1911).

16. By "modal" characters I mean those person-representations, sometimes called "humours" or "flat" characters, that are built on a single value. The most important documents concerning modal characters in Western literature include the *Nicomachean Ethics* 1115a–1128b, where Aristotle defines several moral virtues and vices, and the *Rhetoric* 1388b–1391b and 1408a, where the notion gets its first critical airing as an affective strategy of rhetoric; the *Characters* of Theophrastus, surely the transitional work that turns a principle of persuasion into a principle of representation; Christopher Marlowe's tragic and Ben Jonson's comic "humours," each the supreme English application of modal conceptions in its genre; and Strindberg's preface to *Miss Julie* (1888), a forceful rejection of modal characters as bourgeois, non-naturalistic, and antimodern.

17. Bakhtin, *Marxism*, 96.

18. Fernando Ferrara, "Theory and Model for the Structural Analysis of Fiction," *New Literary History* 5 (1974): 250.

19. William Shakespeare, *Macbeth*, 4.3.39–48, 50–54, 57–65, 77–84, 91–99, 101–2, in G. Blakemore Evans's Riverside edition (Boston: Houghton Mifflin, 1974). Subsequent quotations of the plays are from this edition.

20. Cp. W. J. Harvey, *Character and the Novel* (London: Chatto and Windus, 1965), 53. Lennard J. Davis, *Resisting Novels* (New York: Methuen, 1987), 102–61, is a bracing reintroduction to the matter of characterological speech.

21. Leo Spitzer, "Soy quien soy," *Nueva Revista de Filología Hispánica* 1 (1947): 113–27, discusses the biblical context of the utterance, which comes to have not only theological but characterological importance in a number of Renaissance genres and settings.

22. Cp. other characterological interpretations of Sonnet 129 by Helen Vendler, "Jakobson, Richards, and Shakespeare's Sonnet cxxix," in *I. A. Richards: Essays in His Honor*, ed. Reuben Brower et al. (New York: Oxford University Press, 1973), 179–98, and Dubrow, *Captive Victors*, 209–10.

23. Joachim Du Bellay, *Les Regrets*, 39, in *Poésies françaises et latines*, ed. E. Courbet, 2 vols. (Paris: Garnier Frères, 1918), 2:188. The translation is by C. H. Sisson (Manchester: Carcanet, 1984).

24. Robert Lowell, "Home After Three Months Away," in *Life Studies* (New York: Noonday Press, 1956), 83–84.

25. Frances Ferguson, "Appointments with Time: Robert Lowell's Poetry through the *Notebooks*," in *American Poetry Since 1960*, ed. Robert B. Shaw (Cheadle: Carcanet, 1973), 18–20, offers a noncharacterological reading of the poem that takes its claims to divided selfhood at face value and (somewhat strenuously) sees its unity in "the complicated allusion to Richard II" (19).

26. Kenneth Burke, "Four Master Tropes," appendix to *A Grammar of Motives* (1945; Berkeley: University of California Press, 1969), 511–13. Much of the material in Burke's *Grammar* is invaluable to an extensive theory of characterization, though in my brief sketch I have used it only here.

27. Leslie Fiedler, *Love and Death in the American Novel*, rev. ed. (New York: Stein and Day, 1966), 270; see the complete treatment of the "Good Bad Boy" at 259–90.

28. *Don Quixote*, 2.43, trans. J. M. Cohen (Harmondsworth: Penguin, 1950), 742.

29. Charles Dickens, *David Copperfield*, ed. Nina Burgis (Oxford: Clarendon Press, 1981), 1. For a recent, mimetically oriented treatment of characterological contradiction, see Baruch Hochman, *Character in Literature* (Ithaca: Cornell University Press, 1985), 50.

30. All quotations of *Astrophil and Stella* are from William A. Ringler's edition of Sidney's *Poems* (Oxford: Clarendon Press, 1962).

31. I have considerable sympathy for Hallett Smith's old-fashioned essay on *Astrophil and Stella* in *Elizabethan Poetry* (Cambridge: Harvard University Press, 1952), 142–57. He sees character as a ruling principle in the sequence, though he does not treat the peculiar capacity of the form for projects of this sort: see esp. 147–48. Richard B. Young, "English Petrarke: A Study of Sidney's *Astrophel and Stella*," in *Three Studies in the Renaissance: Sidney, Jonson, Milton*, Yale Studies in English 138 (New Haven: Yale University Press, 1958), calls Astrophil "a character in a love story" (7), and often sees "the substantial character, the material fact of the personality, emerging from the impersonal, verbal manners of the convention" in the sequence (23).

32. Cp. Young, "English Petrarke," 8, and Smith, *Elizabethan Poetry*, 148–49. Other treatments of Sidney's personifications are those by J. W. Lever, *The Elizabethan Love Sonnet* (London: Methuen, 1956), 83–88, and Robert L. Montgomery, Jr., *Symmetry and Sense* (Austin: University of Texas Press, 1961), 90–96, both of which compare the personified objects to a cast of subordinate characters.

33. Bakhtin, *Marxism*, 72, 95.

34. Thomas P. Roche, Jr., "*Astrophil and Stella*: A Radical Reading," *Spenser Studies* 3 (1982): 141, correctly perceives (as many readers do not) Astrophil's dislocation from conventional assessments of protagonism, but insists that no reconstituted "hero" remains when these are swept away. Roche goes too quickly, I believe, past two facts: in most readers' experience Astrophil's example is not entirely negative, and works of all sorts may offer native realizations of function

that inflect our prior attitudes without destroying them. Roche extends his reading in *Petrarch*, 193–242.

35. Cp. Roche, "*Astrophil and Stella*," 171.

36. Smith, *Elizabethan Poetry*, 154. Cp. Montgomery, *Symmetry and Sense*, 103, and Lever, *Elizabethan Love Sonnet*, 74–75.

37. Cp. David Kalstone, *Sidney's Poetry* (Cambridge: Harvard University Press, 1965), 143–44.

38. Ibid., 119.

39. This is perhaps to depart slightly from the important work on counter-Petrarchan poetries by sixteenth-century women recently done by feminist critics (where the poet's gender alone is sometimes claimed to be a radical disruption of convention), and to say that we ought to read factors such as nominativity more rigorously into those texts. Among the best such work is that of Ann Rosalind Jones, especially in four influential essays: "Assimilation with a Difference: Renaissance Women Poets and Literary Influence," *Yale French Studies* 62 (1981): 135–53; "Surprising Fame: Renaissance Gender Ideologies and Women's Lyric," in *The Poetics of Gender*, ed. Nancy K. Miller (New York: Columbia University Press, 1986), 74–95; "City Women and Their Audiences: Louise Labé and Veronica Franco," in *Rewriting the Renaissance*, ed. Margaret W. Ferguson et al. (Chicago: University of Chicago Press, 1986), 299–316; and the aforecited collaboration with Peter Stallybrass, "Politics of *Astrophil and Stella*."

40. Young's entire essay, "English Petrarke," discusses Astrophil's various "transformations" over the course of the sequence. And Neil L. Rudenstine, *Sidney's Poetic Development* (Cambridge: Harvard University Press, 1967), 222–69, marks Astrophil's development from Sonnet 21 and its immediately following poem, where Rudenstine sees "the first important signs of change in Astrophel's manner" (222).

41. Cp. Montgomery, *Symmetry and Sense*, 118.

42. On the various endings of sixteenth-century sequences, see Thomas P. Roche, Jr., "Shakespeare and the Sonnet Sequence," in *English Poetry and Prose, 1540–1674*, ed. Christopher Ricks (London: Barrie and Jenkins, 1970), 105–9; Neely, "Structure," 375–82; and Dubrow, *Captive Victors*, 209.

43. Thomas Watson, headnote to 79, *The Hekatompathia or Passionate Centurie of Love*, ed. S. K. Heninger (Gainesville: Scholars' Facsimiles, 1964).

44. Barnabe Barnes, Madrigall 17, in *Parthenophil and Parthenophe*, ed. Victor A. Doyno (Carbondale: Southern Illinois University Press, 1971).

45. Fineman, *Shakespeare's Perjured Eye*, 197.

45. Phelan, *Reading People*, esp. 133–62, examines the "foregrounding of the synthetic" in several modern prose fictions. Making the necessary allowances for genre and period, one might adapt Phelan's argument to make a good case for Sidney's radicalism where the poetics of fiction is concerned, though of course it is the prose *Arcadias* that are most often discussed in this connection, and even then are seldom given their due as experiments. The possibility has not been seriously entertained that (of all things) *Astrophil and Stella* might be even more experimental.

CHAPTER 3
TWO RITUAL SEQUENCES

1. At least since the 1950s, it has been common to treat *Leaves of Grass*, and often "Song of Myself," as the head of a new line in American poetry. Most often this conviction is explained by a metaphor—that Whitman's sequence is the first successful American realization of the epic impulse. Since *Leaves* can be an epic only grossly or figuratively, by virtue of its extent and importance, it is fair to ask what the literal facts behind the metaphor might be; here, I think, we come into contact with its phenomenal innovation. Among the critics who see Whitman as an originary poet in one way or another, cp. Roy Harvey Pearce, *The Continuity of American Poetry* (Princeton: Princeton University Press, 1961), 69–83; Fernando Alegría, *Walt Whitman en Hispanoamérica* (Mexico City: n.p., 1954); James E. Miller, Jr., Karl Shapiro, and Bernice Slote, *Start with the Sun* (Lincoln: University of Nebraska Press, 1960); Albert Gelpi, "Walt Whitman: The Self as Circumference," in *The Tenth Muse* (Cambridge: Harvard University Press, 1975), 155–216; James E. Miller, Jr., *The American Quest for a Supreme Fiction* (Chicago: University of Chicago Press, 1979); and M. L. Rosenthal and Sally M. Gall, *The Modern Poetic Sequence* (New York: Oxford University Press, 1983), 25–44.

2. For a recent account of *variatio* in post-Petrarchan lyric, see Germaine Warkentin, " 'Love's Sweetest Part, Variety': Petrarch and the Curious Frame of the Renaissance Sonnet Sequence," *Renaissance and Reformation* 11 (1975): 11–23.

3. Georg Luck, *The Latin Love Elegy* (London: Methuen, 1959), 66.

4. Matthew Santirocco, "Horace's *Odes* and the Ancient Poetry Book," *Arethusa* 13, no. 1 (1980): 46.

5. Octavio Paz, "Primitives and Barbarians," in *Alternating Current*, 25–26.

6. Vickers, "Diana Described," 96.

7. Two influential definitions of the blason are those of Albert-Marie Schmidt in his edition of *Poètes du XVIe siècle* (Paris: Gallimard, 1953), 293–94, and Roland Barthes in *S/Z*, trans. Richard Miller (New York: Hill and Wang, 1974), 113–14. Besides Vickers's essay, prominent treatments of the blason include Julia Kristeva's brief remarks in *Desire in Language*, 51–54; Robert E. Pike's survey of "The 'Blasons' in French Literature of the Sixteenth Century," *Romanic Review* 27 (1936): 223–42; V.-L. Saulnier, *Maurice Scève*, 2 vols. (Paris: Klincksieck, 1948), 1:72–87; D. B. Wilson, *Descriptive Poetry in France from Blason to Baroque* (Manchester: Manchester University Press, 1967), particularly the first two chapters (1–99); and Alison Saunders's exhaustive historical study, *The Sixteenth-Century Blason Poétique* (Bern: Peter Lang, 1981). Smith, *Elizabethan Poetry*, 26–27 and 53–54, briefly discusses English blasons.

8. George Puttenham, *The Arte of English Poesie*, in *Elizabethan Critical Essays*, ed. G. Gregory Smith, 2 vols. (Oxford: Clarendon Press, 1904), 2:46–47.

9. Douglas Peterson, *The English Lyric from Wyatt to Donne* (Princeton: Princeton University Press, 1967), 170–76, describes the objections to profane poetry by writers such as Robert Southwell and Nicholas Breton, and shows how the devotional lyrics they incited remained in heavy rhetorical debt to the Pe-

trarchans. Louis L. Martz, *The Poetry of Meditation*, rev. ed. (New Haven: Yale University Press, 1962), 183–93, remarks on Southwell's "sacred parody" of love poetry as the fount of a stylistic movement that extends down to Herbert and Vaughan. And William L. Stull, "Sacred Sonnets in Three Styles," *Studies in Philology* 79 (1982): 78–99, observes that the religious sonneteers seem to exercise a much wider range of styles than the Petrarchan love poets.

10. Thomas Carew, "Elegie upon the Death of the Deane of Pauls, Dr. John Donne," in *Poems*, ed. Rhodes Dunlap (1949; Oxford: Clarendon Press, 1964), 74.

11. Both quotations appear in Izaak Walton's *Life of George Herbert* (1670; London: Oxford University Press, 1973), 268. Other English voices for the same view, such as Miles Coverdale, Thomas Becon, and Thomas Brice, are quoted in the first pages of Lily B. Campbell, "The Christian Muse," *Huntington Library Bulletin* 8 (1935): 29–70.

12. George Herbert, "Providence," in *Works*, ed. F. E. Hutchinson (Oxford: Clarendon Press, 1941).

13. All quotations of Donne's poetry are from Herbert J. C. Grierson's edition, *The Poems of John Donne*, 2 vols. (Oxford: Clarendon Press, 1912). The quoted poems here are *La Corona* 2 ("Annunciation") and *Holy Sonnets* 4.

14. Henry Vaughan, "Jesus Weeping (2)," "Repentance," and "The World," in *Works*, ed. L. C. Martin, 2d ed. (Oxford: Clarendon Press, 1957).

15. All quotations of Taylor's *Preparatory Meditations* are from Donald E. Stanford's edition of the *Poems* (New Haven: Yale University Press, 1960).

16. Barbara K. Lewalski, *Protestant Poetics and the Seventeenth-Century Religious Lyric* (Princeton: Princeton University Press, 1979), gives the most comprehensive scrutiny to the devotional verse of this period. Her discussion of biblical compendiums and psalters as forerunners of religious lyric collections (32–53) pertains especially to the present chapter, although she emphasizes the collective rather than the sequential element in seventeenth-century works.

17. Perry Miller, *The New England Mind: The Seventeenth Century* (New York: Macmillan, 1939), 11–13. There is an exposition of the doctrine of attributes in Adolph Harnack, *History of Dogma*, trans. James Millar, 3d ed., 7 vols. (London, 1897), 3:241–47; Herschel Baker, *The Wars of Truth* (Cambridge: Harvard University Press, 1952), 9–12, discusses the vitality of the doctrine in seventeenth-century English thought. Walter Farquhar Hook, *Church Dictionary*, 7th ed. (London, 1854), 355, gives a useful list of the biblical passages that define some of the attributes.

18. John Preston, *Life Eternall, or, A treatise of the Knowledge of the Divine Essence and Attributes*, 2d ed. (London, 1631), 98–99, 157–58, first pagination.

19. Ibid., 45–46, second pagination.

20. Isaac Newton, *The Mathematical Principles of Natural Philosophy* (1687), trans. Andrew Motte, 2 vols. (London, 1729), 2:391; see esp. 389–93, the conclusion of book 3.

21. Thomas Ken, *Hymnarium*, in *Works*, 4 vols. (London, 1721), 2:14, where the *Hymnarium* has its own pagination. Ken, Izaak Walton's brother-in-law, died in 1711.

22. Ibid., 102.

23. Ibid., 11.

24. Samuel Willard, *A Compleat Body of Divinity* (Boston, 1726), 42–43. Willard's exposition of God's attributes occurs at 49–94. Willard had died in 1707.

25. Herbert, *A Priest to the Temple*, in *Works*, 234.

26. Henry Constable, *Poems*, ed. Joan Grundy (Liverpool: Liverpool University Press, 1960).

27. Taylor gathered fourteen of his sermons into a book called *Christographia*, ed. Norman S. Grabo (New Haven: Yale University Press, 1962).

28. Martz, foreword to Taylor, *Poems*, xxi. Lewalski, *Protestant Poetics*, 396–97, sketches the thematic outlines of the First and Second Series, and observes some subsequences unmentioned by Martz.

29. Karl Keller, *The Example of Edward Taylor* (Amherst: University of Massachusetts Press, 1975), 92–93.

30. Richard Baxter, *The Saints Everlasting Rest*, 5th ed. (London, 1654), 133–34, third pagination. Baxter's book was, according to Martz, "the first Puritan treatise on the art of methodical meditation to appear in England, and one of the most popular Puritan books of the seventeenth century" (*Meditation*, 154). It went through thirteen editions in Taylor's lifetime.

31. Martz, *Meditation*, xxii–xxiii.

32. Ibid., 4.

33. Ibid., 16.

34. Ibid., 30.

35. Gelpi, *Tenth Muse*, 43. Norman S. Grabo, *Edward Taylor* (New York: Twayne Publishers, 1961), 138–42, remarks usefully on the identity of the lyrics and the absence of *variatio*; he argues that the subsequences observed by Martz are illusory, that the appearance of "sequence is quite accidental" (139).

36. Riffaterre, *Semiotics of Poetry*, 20.

37. Other Puritan lyric sequences include A[nn] L[ok], *A Meditation of a Penitent Sinner: Written in Maner of a Paraphrase upon the 51. Psalme of David*, appended to *Sermons of John Calvin, vpon the songe that Ezechias made after he had bene sicke . . .* (London, 1560), STC 4450; the works of her son Henry Lok, *Sundry Christian Passions* (1593), *Sundry Affectionate Sonets* and *Peculiar Prayers* (1597), in *Poems*, ed. Alexander B. Grosart, Fuller Worthies' Library (Blackburn, 1871); and perhaps Arthur Golding's translation of *The Psalmes of David and others*, which was published with Calvin's commentaries (London, 1571), STC 4395. For very brief appraisals of Henry Lok's poetry, see Lewalski, *Protestant Poetics*, 239–40; William L. Stull, " 'Why Are Not *Sonnets* Made of Thee?': A New Context for the 'Holy Sonnets' of Donne, Herbert, and Milton," *Modern Philology* 80 (1982): 133, and "Elizabethan Precursors of Donne's 'Divine Meditations,' " *Comitatus* 6 (1975): 38–40; and more extensively on both Loks, Roche, *Petrarch*, 154–66.

38. Cp. Sacvan Bercovitch, *The Puritan Origins of the American Self* (New Haven: Yale University Press, 1975), 35–71, and John F. Lynen, *The Design of the Present* (New Haven: Yale University Press, 1969), 29–86.

39. Mircea Eliade, *The Myth of the Eternal Return*, trans. Willard R. Trask (New York: Pantheon Books, 1954), 35, 89.

40. Eliade, *Return*, 34.

41. Bercovitch, *Puritan Origins*, 13–14. On the humanist attitudes mentioned here, cp. Trinkaus, *In Our Image and Likeness*.

42. Bercovitch, *Puritan Origins*, 30.

43. Golding, introduction to *Psalmes*, vʳ.

44. Miller, *New England Mind*, 12.

45. Ibid., 12–13.

46. Leo Bersani, *The Culture of Redemption* (Cambridge: Harvard University Press, 1990), 153–54.

47. Karen E. Rowe, *Saint and Singer* (Cambridge: Cambridge University Press, 1986), 1–23.

48. Paul Zweig, *Walt Whitman: The Making of the Poet* (New York: Basic Books, 1984), 232. Cp. Malcolm Cowley, introduction to *Leaves of Grass: The First (1855) Edition*, vii–viii.

49. See, for instance, the many papers and tributes directed to Whitman's work in Jim Perlman et al., ed., *Walt Whitman: The Measure of His Song* (Minneapolis: Holy Cow! Press, 1981).

50. Walt Whitman, *An American Primer*, ed. Horace Traubel (Boston: Small, Maynard, and Co., 1904), vii.

51. Charles Feidelson, Jr., *Symbolism and American Literature* (Chicago: University of Chicago Press, 1953), 18–19. Cp. Pearce, *Continuity*, 69–83.

52. Floyd Stovall, *The Foreground of* Leaves of Grass (Charlottesville: University Press of Virginia, 1974), 131. The most explicit treatment of *Leaves* as a nominative text of its own peculiar kind is Quentin Anderson, *The Imperial Self* (New York: Alfred A. Knopf, 1971), 88–118.

53. Following each quotation from *Leaves of Grass*, I give the date of the relevant version and the poem's (eventual) title.

54. "Note at End of *Complete Poems and Prose*," in *Prose Works 1892*, ed. Floyd Stovall, 2 vols. (New York: New York University Press, 1964), 2:734.

55. Pearce, *Continuity*, 73–74.

56. Robert Bernard Martin, review of *The Victorian Imagination*, by William E. Buckler, *Times Literary Supplement*, 10 April 1981, 415.

57. *The Complete Writings of Walt Whitman*, ed. Richard Maurice Bucke et al., 10 vols. (New York: G. P. Putnam's Sons, 1902), 10:14.

58. Cowley, introduction to *Leaves of Grass*, xxviii. Cp. Carl F. Strauch, "The Structure of Walt Whitman's 'Song of Myself,' " *English Journal* 27 (1938): 597–607; James E. Miller, Jr., " 'Song of Myself' as Inverted Mystical Experience," in *A Critical Guide to* Leaves of Grass (Chicago: University of Chicago Press, 1957), 6–35; Ferguson, "Appointments with Time," 15.

59. Cp. Leo Spitzer, *La enumeración caótica en la poesía moderna*, trans. Raimundo Lida (Buenos Aires; Universidad de Buenos Aires, 1945). Suzanne Beth Schneider, "Porches of the Sun: The Problem of Form in Whitman's 'Song of Myself,' " Ph.D. diss., Yale University, 1977, 35–122, is especially enlightening on the topic of Whitman's catalogues; her discussion (104–10) of the anticatalogue

"Poem of the Propositions of Nakedness" (1856, later retitled "Respondez!") suggests striking parallels with the antiblasons by Marot and others.

60. Cp. Steven Kagle, "Time as a Dimension in Whitman," *American Transcendental Quarterly* 12 (1971): 55–60; "Temporal Structure in *Leaves of Grass*," *Illinois Quarterly* 33 (1971): 42–49; and Lynen, *Design of the Present*, 273–339.

61. Fulke Greville, *Caelica*, 103.10–14, in *Poems and Dramas*, ed. Geoffrey Bullough, 2 vols. (New York: Oxford University Press, 1941–45), 1:149.

62. Eliade, *Sacred and the Profane*, 69.

63. Cp. Cowley, introduction to *Leaves of Grass*, x, xxvii–xxxvii.

64. Zweig, *Walt Whitman*, 232–33.

65. Tambiah, "A Performative Approach to Ritual," in *Culture, Thought, and Social Action*, 139–46, following Roman Jakobson's work on poetry, treats parallelism or "stacking" as a feature of ritual.

66. *Leaves of Grass*, Comprehensive Reader's Edition, ed. Harold W. Blodgett and Sculley Bradley (New York: New York University Press, 1965), 206.

67. Kermode, *Sense of an Ending*, 45.

68. See, for instance, David Perkins, *A History of Modern Poetry: From the 1890s to the High Modernist Mode* (Cambridge: Belknap Press of Harvard University Press, 1976), and Marjorie Perloff, *The Poetics of Indeterminacy* (Princeton: Princeton University Press, 1980).

69. Ezra Pound, Canto 99, *The Cantos* (New York: New Directions, 1970), 708. The lines of *The Cantos* go unnumbered by scholarly convention, which instead respects pages as the (appropriately material) units of Pound's sequence. Pound treats the canzoni of the Provençals and Dante as "ritual" in the important essay "Psychology and Troubadours" (1916), in *The Spirit of Romance* (1910; New York: New Directions, 1952), 87–100.

70. Christine Froula, *To Write Paradise: Style and Error in Pound's* Cantos (New Haven: Yale University Press, 1984), 153. In the book's central chapter, 139–70, Froula makes inferentially clear how much of Whitman returns in Pound; her conceits of "wandering" and "error" are in fact restatements of the openness of the ritual text, though she develops them with a wealth of historical and textual material and demonstrates how a ritual or performative dimension may be constituted diachronically and editorially. Ronald Bush, *The Genesis of Ezra Pound's* Cantos (Princeton: Princeton University Press, 1976), is also deeply concerned with exposing the ritual element of the sequence, which he sees in Pound's vatic plan as "a structure that could include the whole of life and that was based on upon the perception of limited patterns of recurrence and divine intervention" (110). Both critics, of course, build on the fundamentally ritual notion of Pound's poetics presented in Kenner, *Pound Era*, esp. 349–81 and (on Canto 82's propitiation of Whitman) 486–88.

71. Ibid., 154.

72. Unpublished letter to Norman Holmes Pearson, quoted ibid., 175.

73. Ezra Pound, "What I Feel About Walt Whitman," in *Selected Prose, 1909–1935*, ed. William Cookson (London: Faber and Faber, 1973), 115–16. Pound's relations with Whitman are discussed by Hugh Witemeyer in *The Poetry of Ezra*

Pound: Forms and Renewal, 1908–1920 (Berkeley: University of California Press, 1969), 135–38, and more recently in George Bornstein, ed., *Ezra Pound Among the Poets* (Chicago: University of Chicago Press, 1985), 81–105. On the attitudes of the other American modernist poets to Whitman, see William Carlos Williams, "An Essay on *Leaves of Grsass*," in Leaves of Grass *One Hundred Years After*, ed. Milton Hindus (Stanford: Stanford University Press, 1955), 22–31, reprinted in *Whitman: A Collection of Critical Essays*, ed. Roy Harvey Pearce (Englewood Cliffs: Prentice-Hall, 1962), 146–54; John Berryman, " 'Song of Myself': Intention and Substance," in *The Freedom of the Poet* (New York: Farrar, Straus and Giroux, 1976), 227–41; and Stephen Tapscott, *American Beauty: William Carlos Williams and the Modernist Whitman* (New York: Columbia University Press, 1984).

74. Ezra Pound, "Histrion," 6–7, in *Collected Early Poems*, ed. Michael John King (New York: New Directions, 1976), 71.

75. I know of no extended treatment of Pound in relation to Petrarch, but there are many books and articles on Pound's uses of Petrarch's sources, for to a large extent, their poets are the same (Ovid and the other Roman elegists, Daniel, Cavalcanti, and of course Dante). On Pound's adaptations of his classical and Romance models, see the various essays in Eva Hesse, ed., *New Approaches to Ezra Pound* (London: Faber and Faber, 1969), and in Bornstein, *Pound Among the Poets*; Stuart Y. McDougal, *Ezra Pound and the Troubadour Tradition* (Princeton: Princeton University Press, 1972), esp. 43–44; Peter Makin, *Provence and Pound* (Berkeley: University of California Press, 1978); and James J. Wilhelm, *Dante and Pound* (Orono, Maine: University of Maine Press, 1974). Humphrey Carpenter, *A Serious Character: The Life of Ezra Pound* (Boston: Houghton Mifflin, 1988), contains a great deal of suggestive information about Pound's aspirations toward a "Renaissance."

76. Stuart Y. McDougal, "Dreaming a Renaissance: Pound's Dantean Influence," in Bornstein, *Pound Among the Poets*, 75.

77. In "What I Feel About Walt Whitman," Pound perhaps echoes—in a complex transposition—Petrarch's notorious letter to Boccaccio, *Familiares* 21.15, in which the former's ambivalence toward (the unnamed) Dante shows through his protests of admiration; in a sense, Pound consistently uses Dante as Petrarch here uses Virgil, to keep another (potentially) major influence (for Petrarch, Dante; for Pound, Petrarch) unacknowledged. See Petrarch, *Letters on Familiar Matters: Rerum familiarium libri*, trans. Aldo S. Bernardo, 3 vols. (Baltimore: Johns Hopkins University Press, 1975–85), 3:202–7.

78. Ezra Pound, "A Retrospect" (1918), in *Literary Essays*, ed. T. S. Eliot (New York: New Directions, 1954), 9; Hugh Kenner, *The Poetry of Ezra Pound* (1951; Lincoln: University of Nebraska Press, 1985), 234.

79. Ezra Pound and Dorothy Shakespear, *Letters, 1909–1914*, ed. Omar Pound and A. Walton Litz (New York: New Directions, 1984), 38; the second quotation is from the title page of *A Draft of XVI. Cantos* (Paris: Three Mountains Press, 1925).

80. Pound, *Guide to Kulchur* (New York: New Directions, 1970), 263; "Hell"

(1934), in *Literary Essays*, 208. Cp. *Literary Essays*, 154, and *Spirit of Romance*, 166.

81. Noel Stock, *The Life of Ezra Pound* (New York: Pantheon Books, 1970), 184, quoted in Carpenter, *Serious Character*, 287.

CHAPTER 4
NOMINATIVE TO ARTIFACTUAL

1. For a survey of artifactuality in modern European poetry, see Hugo Friedrich, *The Structure of Modern Poetry*, trans. Joachim Neugroschel (1956; Evanston: Northwestern University Press, 1974), and the following recent and representative studies of particular American sequences: on Eliot's *Waste Land*, Calvin Bedient, *He Do the Police in Different Voices*: The Waste Land *and Its Protagonist* (Chicago: University of Chicago Press, 1986); on Vallejo's *Trilce*, Jean Franco, *César Vallejo* (Cambridge: Cambridge University Press, 1976), 79– 137; on Mário de Andrade's *Paulicéa Desvairada*, Luiz Costa Lima, *Lira e antilira* (Rio: Civilização Brasileira, 1968), 33–56; on Williams's *Spring and All*, James E. B. Breslin, "*Spring and All*: A New Lyric Form," in *William Carlos Williams: An American Artist* (1970; Chicago: University of Chicago Press, 1985), 50–86; on Williams's *Paterson*, Joseph N. Riddel, *The Inverted Bell* (Baton Rouge: Louisiana State University Press, 1974); and on Pound's *Cantos*, Kenner, *Pound Era*, esp. 94–144, 349–81, and 414–36; Bernstein, *Tale of the Tribe*, esp. 29–182; and Herbert Schneidau, "Pound's Book of Cross-Cuts," *Genre* 11 (1978): 505–21. See also the other essays on Eliot, Crane, Williams, Stevens, and Ashbery in that special issue of *Genre*, ed. Joseph N. Riddel, on "the long poem in the twentieth century"; and David Perkins's discussions of those poets in *A History of Modern Poetry: Modernism and After* (Cambridge: Belknap Press of Harvard University Press, 1987). On the transition from one phase to the other, see Michael Hamburger, *The Truth of Poetry* (London: Weidenfeld and Nicolson, 1969), which is broadly concerned with subjectivity in European poetry; Georges Poulet, *Exploding Poetry: Baudelaire/Rimbaud*, trans. Françoise Meltzer (Chicago: University of Chicago Press, 1984), where a meticulous phenomenological reading of the two poets seems to disclose the former's affiliations with a Petrarchan first-person poetics and the latter's decomposition of Baudelairean time and identity; and the following books, all instances of a certain elegiac genre of 1960s critical writing on the changing fortunes of selfhood in modern literature: Robert Langbaum, *The Poetry of Experience* (New York: W. W. Norton, 1963); Langbaum, *The Mysteries of Identity* (New York: Oxford University Press, 1977), esp. 83–119 and 147–247; Wylie Sypher, *Loss of the Self in Modern Literature and Art* (New York: Random House, 1962); and Erich Kahler, *The Disintegration of Form in the Arts* (New York: George Braziller, 1968).

2. Guillaume Apollinaire, *The Cubist Painters*, trans. Lionel Abel, Documents of Modern Art 1 (New York: Wittenborn, 1962), 25. Yeats's sequences and collections have often been read as such, though never with any careful or sustained resort to the achievement of Petrarch and his successors, nor for the purposes I have here. The inaugural essay on sequentiality in the poems is Hugh Kenner, "The Sacred Book of the Arts," *Sewanee Review* 64 (1956): 574–90, reprinted in

Gnomon (New York: McDowell, Obolensky, 1958), 9–29. The most notable treatments of the sequences are John Unterecker, *A Reader's Guide to William Butler Yeats* (New York: Noonday Press, 1959); Sarah Youngblood, "The Structure of Yeats's Long Poems," *Criticism* 5 (1963): 323–35; M. L. Rosenthal, *Sailing into the Unknown* (New York: Oxford University Press, 1978), 26–44; and Rosenthal and Gall, *Modern Poetic Sequence*, 96–145. The only significant discussions I know of the two sequences I treat in this chapter are Unterecker, *Reader's Guide*, 194–96 and 235–40, and Rosenthal and Gall, *Modern Poetic Sequence*, 109–21.

3. All quotations of Yeats's verse are from Richard J. Finneran's edition of the *Poems* (New York: Macmillan, 1983), except where I specify otherwise. In that edition the poems of *A Man Young and Old* are numbered 227–36, *A Woman Young and Old* 293–303.

4. Samuel Daniel, *Delia*, 31.9–14 and 32.1–4, in *Poems and a Defence of Ryme*, ed. Arthur Colby Sprague (Cambridge: Harvard University Press, 1930); Edmund Spenser, *Amoretti*, 22.1–4, in *Minor Poems*, ed. Charles Grosvenor Osgood and Henry Gibbons Lotspeich, 2 vols., in the variorum edition of the *Works*, ed. Edwin Greenlaw et al. (Baltimore: Johns Hopkins Press, 1943–57); Tennyson, *In Memoriam A.H.H.*, 15.1–4, in *Poems*.

5. On narrative distance, see J. Hillis Miller, *The Form of Victorian Fiction* (Notre Dame: University of Notre Dame Press, 1968), 53–90; and Genette, *Narrative Discourse*, esp. 29–32 and 185–211. Wayne C. Booth, *The Rhetoric of Fiction* (Chicago: University of Chicago Press, 1961), is largely given to considering varieties of narrative distance, though it has most to do with the intervals among narrators, authors, and readers (but see 156). Pavel, *Fictional Worlds*, 85–93 and 145–46, treats the topic more generally than the narrative theorists, while Cameron's *Lyric Time* is a specialized treatment of lyric interval that stresses the temporal relations between lyric speakers and their histories. Loy D. Martin, *Browning's Dramatic Monologues and the Post-Romantic Subject* (Baltimore: Johns Hopkins University Press, 1985), esp. 82–105, is also usefully engaged with lyric interval.

6. Miller, *Form*, xi, 88.

7. Ibid., 66.

8. W. H. Auden, introduction to the *Sonnets*, in the *Complete Signet Classic Shakespeare*, ed. Sylvan Barnet (New York: Harcourt Brace Jovanovich, 1972), 1724.

9. Miller, *Form*, 76–77.

10. Historically speaking, "reticence" is almost a polite code word for the disruptions of first-person conventions occasioned by the rise of artifactuality: see Eliot's early remarks (1918) about *The Cantos* ("it is an objective and reticent autobiography"), quoted in Bush, *Genesis of Pound's Cantos*, 5.

11. On the reticence of "Human Dignity," cp. Richard Ellmann, *Yeats: The Man and the Masks* (1948; New York: W. W. Norton, 1978), 263–64.

12. The excursive nature of metaphor (in poetry) and analogy (in rhetoric) is a constant principle in Western literary theory: the identity of the Greek *analogy* with the Latin *proportio*—or "symmetry," "proportion"—and I. A. Richards's

widely adopted, two-episode definition of metaphor in his *Philosophy of Rhetoric* (New York: Oxford University Press, 1936) should suffice by themselves to demonstrate that an original, inhabitant argument or subject is invariably thought to abide under the excursive element in a trope, and to remain in clear relation to it. Yeats's stroke in "The Mermaid" and other lyrics is to disrupt this formalist balance by throwing away the inhabitant term and making the excursive term serve temporarily in its place. The indeterminacy of this lyric's entrance to the series is apparent in Marjorie Perloff's reading, which perhaps prompts more questions than it answers: " 'Heart Mysteries': The Later Love Lyrics of W. B. Yeats," *Contemporary Literature* 10 (1969): 270. Perloff says nothing about whether the "swimming lad" is the speaker of the sequence or not, because that is exactly the identification Yeats has left out.

13. Geoffrey N. Leech, *Meaning and the English Verb* (London: Longmans, 1971), 32.

14. Otto Jespersen, *The Philosophy of Grammar* (London: Allen and Unwin, 1924), 269–71, discusses the distinction between the perfect and the preterite in some ancient and modern tongues.

15. Cp. Rosenthal and Gall, *Modern Poetic Sequence*, 144.

16. W. B. Yeats, *Letters*, ed. Allan Wade (London: Rupert Hart-Davis, 1954), 721–22.

17. For a very different version of the ode in English, see Sophocles, *Oedipus at Colonus* 1211–48, trans. Robert Fitzgerald (New York: Harcourt, Brace, and World, 1969), 145–46. R.W.B. Burton, *The Chorus in Sophocles' Tragedies* (Oxford: Clarendon Press, 1980), 284–92, places this choral ode in the continuum of the play and of Greek thought. Yeats's interest in the *Colonus* can be traced through his *Letters*: 537, 720–24, 728–29.

18. Yeats designed the *Woman* series "to balance that of 'The Young and Old Countryman,' " as he wrote in 1927 (*Letters*, 725). In the notes to *The Winding Stair*, he remarks that the sequence "was written before the publication of *The Tower*, but was left out for some reason I cannot recall." See the variorum edition of the *Poems*, ed. Peter Allt and Russell K. Alspach (New York: Macmillan, 1957), 831. Unterecker, *Reader's Guide*, 203, 236, believes that the *Woman* series and its accompanying volume *The Winding Stair* are Yeats's calculated "answer" or "refutation" to the *Man* series and *The Tower*, though no one has tried to interpret the two sequences with strict reference to one another.

19. Jones, "Assimilation with a Difference," treats the rhetorical overlappings and answerings in the sequences of Maurice Scève (1544) and Pernette du Guillet (1545) and those of Louise Labé (1555) and Olivier de Magny (1556); in "City Women and Their Audiences," she discusses Franco in relation to Labé.

20. On the nominative dimension in confessional poetry of the 1950s and 1960s, cp. Geoffrey Thurley, *The American Moment* (London: Edward Arnold, 1977), 30; Steven K. Hoffman, "Impersonal Personalism: The Making of a Confessional Poetic," *ELH* 45 (1978): 687–709; Charles Altieri, *Self and Sensibility in Contemporary American Poetry* (Cambridge: Cambridge University Press, 1984), 40; James E. B. Breslin, *From Modern to Contemporary* (Chicago: University of Chicago Press, 1984), esp. 52–76; Alan Williamson, *Introspection and*

Contemporary Poetry (Cambridge: Harvard University Press, 1984), esp. 7–25; and Paul Breslin, *The Psycho-Political Muse* (Chicago: University of Chicago Press, 1987), esp. 42–58.

21. Aristotle, *Poetics* 1449a10–b9, trans. Butcher.

22. Siegfried Kracauer, *Theory of Film* (New York: Oxford University Press, 1960), 32–33. Gerald Mast, "Kracauer's Two Tendencies and the Early History of the Film Narrative," *Critical Inquiry* 6 (1980): 455–76, criticizes the earlier theorist's binary distinction as he seeks a fresh conceptual lexicon for film's narrative means.

23. Ezra Pound, *Selected Letters, 1907–1941*, ed. D. D. Paige (New York: New Directions, 1971), 294; and Haroldo de Campos, "The Informational Temperature of the Text," trans. Jon M. Tolman, *Poetics Today* 3, no. 3 (1982): 184. Where *The Cantos* are concerned, assertions such as Campos's hold up an interpretive (or willfully noninterpretive) tradition that goes back to Yeats's introduction to the *Oxford Book of Modern Verse, 1892–1935* (New York: Oxford University Press, 1937), xxiv–xxvi. Cp. R. P. Blackmur, "The Masks of Ezra Pound," in *The Double Agent* (New York: Arrow Editions, 1935), 31, and Allen Tate, "Ezra Pound," in *The Man of Letters in the Modern World: Selected Essays, 1928–1955* (New York: Meridian Books, 1955), 258.

24. Delmore Schwartz, "An Unwritten Book," *Southern Review* 7 (1941): 485; reprinted in *The Permanence of Yeats*. ed. James Hall and Martin Steinmann (New York: Macmillan, 1950), 323.

25. Among the recent expository treatments of gender relations in artifactual discourse like those Yeats anticipates, see the following three essays in film criticism: Linda Williams, "When the Woman Looks," in *Re-visions: Essays in Feminist Film Criticism*, ed. Mary Ann Doane et al. (Frederick, Maryland: University Publications of America, 1984), 83–99; and Kaja Silverman, "Lost Objects and Mistaken Subjects; A Prologue," and "Disembodying the Female Voice: Irigaray, Experimental Feminist Cinema, and Femininity," in *The Acoustic Mirror: The Female Voice in Psychoanalysis and Cinema* (Bloomington: Indiana University Press, 1988), 1–41, 141–86.

26. My treatment of the woman's character in this chapter is not concerned to engage the complicated psychology of *A Vision* (1925), though that system is presumably her pattern. The best exposition of *A Vision* is Helen Hennessy Vendler, *Yeats's* Vision *and the Later Plays* (Cambridge: Harvard University Press, 1963), esp. 1–123. Langbaum, *Mysteries of Identity*, 147–74, and J. Hillis Miller, *Poets of Reality* (New York: Atheneum, 1974), 88–100, have useful things to say about the influence of *A Vision* on Yeats's lyrics.

27. Rudolf Arnheim, *Visual Thinking* (Berkeley: University of California Press, 1969), 262.

28. A note on the dating of "Her Triumph" and the sequence at large: Richard Ellmann, *The Identity of Yeats* (New York: Oxford University Press, 1954), 293, assigns the poem to November 1929; A. Norman Jeffares, *Commentary on the Collected Poems* (Stanford: Stanford University Press, 1968), 393, names "29 November 1929" as the date of composition. Obviously both scholars have used the same manuscript as their source for the date: this sheet is an intermediate draft

of "Her Triumph" with the poet's notation "Nov. 29." Ellmann interprets this inscription as designating month and year; Jeffares, assuming Ellmann's year to be correct, takes the same notation to mean month and day. In view of the fact that "Her Triumph" was published in October 1929, and Yeats's statement that the entire sequence was finished before the publication of *The Tower*, it seems evident that "Nov 29" means November 29, 1927 or perhaps 1926. This matter has some importance for the dating of the series, for now all the poems can be seen as strictly contemporary. I have studied the drafts of "Her Triumph" and several other lyrics at the W. B. Yeats Archive, a deposit collection at the State University of New York at Stony Brook (SUSB). I cite the manuscripts by reel, volume, and page, as for instance the draft that contains the disputed date: SUSB 30.4.16.

29. SUSB 30.2.247, a draft of "A First Confession."

30. Yeats wrote to Olivia Shakespear in June of 1927: "Here is an innocent little song ["A First Confession"]—one of the first [of] my woman series to balance that of 'The Young and Old Countryman,' and after that one ["Consolation"] not so innocent." *Letters*, 725.

31. The two most notable treatments of "Chosen" and "Parting" are F.A.C. Wilson's Platonic exegesis of the first poem in *W. B. Yeats and Tradition* (London: Victor Gollancz, 1958), 205–11, and Jon Stallworthy's manuscript study of both in *Between the Lines* (Oxford: Clarendon Press, 1963), 137–63. "Chosen" is the formal child of Donne's brilliant lyric "A Nocturnall upon St. Lucies Day": writing to Herbert Grierson about Donne's poem in 1926, Yeats says "I have used the arrangement of the lines in the stanzas for a poem of my own, just finished" (*Letters*, 710).

32. Stallworthy, *Between the Lines*, 161.

33. F. E. Sparshott, "Basic Film Aesthetics," in *Film Theory and Criticism*, ed. Gerald Mast and Marshall Cohen (New York: Oxford University Press, 1974), 219.

34. Yeats's modal conception of his old age may be traced through his letters to Dorothy Wellesley in the last month of 1936—see *Letters on Poetry from W. B. Yeats to Dorothy Wellesley* (1940; London: Oxford University Press, 1964), 107, 109, 110—and in a letter of the same time to Ethel Mannin (*Letters*, 872).

35. The translation is based on *Antigone* 781–805, and spans the short fourth stasimon on love and *commos* or lament for Antigone's death. As with the other Sophoclean version, Yeats used a French translation as his model. H.D.F. Kitto, *Form and Meaning in Drama* (London: Methuen, 1960), 166–67; H. C. Kamerbeek, *The Plays of Sophocles: Commentaries*, 7 vols. (Leiden: Brill, 1978), 3:20–21; and Burton, *Chorus*, 112–18, consider the ode in the play's context. The ode's vestigial rhyme scheme is ABCACD BDEFEFG HGH. Yeats had worked out a more conventional ABABCDCDEFEFGHGH in a single stanza, but he yielded to Ezra Pound's strong suggestion—represented by a boldly drawn arrow in the surviving typescript, SUSB 30.4.76—that he move the "inhabitant" line to its present position near the top of the poem.

36. Yeats, *Letters*, 758. The choral idea is offered by Walter E. Houghton,

"Yeats and Crazy Jane: The Hero in Old Age," *Modern Philology* 40 (1943): 323, reprinted in Hall and Steinmann, *Permanence of Yeats*, 376.

37. Houghton struggles to make *Words for Music Perhaps* seem more nominative than it is by working the twentieth lyric, "I Am of Ireland," into the lives of Jane and Jaçk: "let us say that a woman very like Crazy Jane is in a pub somewhere outside of Ireland. As she looks at the rowdy scene (even the orchestra is drunk—the fiddlers are all thumbs), suddenly she thinks of Ireland, of everything romantic the name can suggest, its heroic past, its holy miracles, its national aspiration, its beauty—everything which Yeats has captured in her song. No one pays any attention, except perhaps one man, another Jack the Journeyman" (Hall and Steinmann, *Permanence of Yeats*, 379). There is, of course, no reason to insist on these stringent naturalizations unless the critic is uncomfortable watching the nominative sequence turning artifactual as he or she reads.

38. For a nostalgic treatment of the turn from a strict nominativity in Yeats's later collections, see Peter Ure, "Yeats's Supernatural Songs," *Review of English Studies*, n.s., 7 (1956): 50–51.

39. Cp. Thomas Parkinson, *W. B. Yeats: The Later Poetry* (Berkeley: University of California Press, 1971), 54–55, concerning one of the functions of the poet according to Yeats's aesthetic program.

40. Victor Knoll, *Paciente arlequinada: Uma leitura da obra poética de Mário de Andrade* (São Paulo: Editora HUCITEC-Secretaria de Estado da Cultura, 1983); and Marjorie Perloff, *The Dance of the Intellect: Studies in the Poetry of the Pound Tradition* (Cambridge: Cambridge University Press, 1985), esp. her context-setting first chapter (1–32).

CHAPTER 5
MEASURING SPACE, BECOMING SPACE

1. On the phenomenology of fictional space, see Pavel, *Fictional Worlds*, 94–105.

2. *Il Petrarcha con l'espositione d'Alessandro Vellutello* (Venice, 1547), v^{v-r}. The translation is mine.

3. *Il Petrarcha* (1547), 5^v. Weinberg, "*Sposizione* of Petrarch," 378–79, and Roche, *Petrarch*, 73–77, discuss Vellutello as commentator; Jan Lawson Hinely, "The Sonnet Sequence in Elizabethan Poetry," Ph.D. diss., Ohio State University, 1966, 81–82, treats him as mapmaker.

4. *Il Petrarcha con nuoue spositioni, nelle quali, oltre l'altre cose, si dimostra qual fusse il vero giorno & l'hora del suo innamoramento* (Lyons, 1564).

5. Throughout this essay and in the rest of the study I use the common spelling *Machu Picchu* for the site and *Macchu Picchu* in mentioning Neruda's title.

6. The nominative dimension of Neruda's poetic collections, which I can only glance at here, is treated briefly by Emir Rodríguez Monegal, *Neruda: El viajero inmóvil*, rev. ed. (Caracas: Monte Avila, 1977), 17–25, and more extensively by Enrico Mario Santí, *Pablo Neruda: The Poetics of Prophecy* (Ithaca: Cornell University Press, 1982). Santí also offers one of the best treatments of the temporality of Neruda's sequences (56–58, 104–75), and produces a statement by Neruda

that reveals something of the priorities among the "autobiographical" and "local" or geographical conceits in *Alturas de Macchu Picchu* (117–18).

7. A few obvious errors in the fourth edition of Neruda's *Obras completas* have been silently replaced with readings from the second edition (1957). Besides my own translations, as here, I use several English versions of *Alturas de Macchu Picchu*: Angel Flores's "Summits of Macchu Picchu," in *The World's Best*, ed. Whit Burnett (New York: Dial Press, 1950), 355–67; Nathaniel Tarn's *Heights of Macchu Picchu* (New York: Farrar, Straus and Giroux, 1966); James Wright's translation of the third canto in *Neruda and Vallejo: Selected Poems*, ed. Robert Bly (Boston: Beacon Press, 1971); and John Felstiner's usually literal version in his *Translating Neruda* (Stanford: Stanford University Press, 1980). The source of each translation appears immediately afterward; unattributed translations are mine.

8. The first lyric's proemial nature is confirmed by Mario Rodríguez Fernández, "El tema de la muerte en 'Alturas de Macchu Picchu' de Pablo Neruda," *Anales de la Universidad de Chile* 131 (July–September 1964): 27, who discusses it in terms that evoke the proem to the *Canzoniere*: "The lyric speaker expresses himself from a new mastery—which, although we cannot yet describe its exact character, is superior to what has been revealed to this point—and a temporal posteriority" (my translation).

9. On this geometrical tension, cp. Jaime Concha, "Interpretación de *Residencia en la tierra* de Pablo Neruda," *Mapocho* 1, no. 3 (July 1963): 5–39, reprinted in *Hispanic Studies* 1 (1974): 31–84 (but all citations refer to the former printing); and Cedomil Goic, "*Alturas de Macchu Picchu*: La torre y el abismo," *Anales de la Universidad de Chile* 157–60 (January–December 1971): 153–65, reprinted in *Pablo Neruda*, ed. Emir Rodríguez Monegal and Enrico Mario Santí (Madrid: Taurus, 1980), 219–44.

10. Plato, *Republic* 527b, trans. Paul Shorey, in *Collected Dialogues*, ed. Edith Hamilton and Huntington Cairns (Princeton: Princeton University Press, 1963), 759.

11. John Stuart Mill, *On Liberty: Essays on Politics and Society*, ed. J. M. Robson, *Collected Works* (Toronto: University of Toronto Press, 1977), 18:244.

12. Wesley C. Salmon, "The Twin Sisters: Philosophy and Geometry," in *Space, Time, and Motion*, 2d ed. (Minneapolis: University of Minnesota Press, 1982), 1–29, offers a lucid discussion of the forces that overturned the primacy of Euclidean geometry in the nineteenth and twentieth centuries. Roberto Bonola, *Non-Euclidean Geometry*, trans. H. S. Carslaw (1912; New York: Dover Publication, 1955), is more technical but still has great historical reach. My understanding has also been helped by Charles Fefferman's unpublished lecture on "Twentieth-Century Geometry," delivered at Bard College on 14 April 1984. For a discussion of space as a factor in twentieth-century ideologies and aesthetics, see Stephen Kern, *The Culture of Time and Space, 1880–1918* (Cambridge: Harvard University Press, 1983), 131–80; and for a more specific engagement with geometrical constructivism as a factor in modernity, see Lachterman, *Ethics of Geometry*.

13. Willard Van Orman Quine, *Word and Object* (Cambridge: MIT Press, 1960), 252.

14. Wilhelm Worringer, *Abstraction and Empathy*, trans. Michael Bullock (1908; London: Routledge and Kegan Paul, 1953), 20. On Worringer's impact

on the Anglo-American modernists, see William C. Wees, *Vorticism and the English Avant-Garde* (Toronto: University of Toronto Press, 1972), 78–85.

15. Jacques Derrida, *Edmund Husserl's Origin of Geometry: An Introduction*, trans. John P. Leavey, Jr., ed. David B. Allison (Stony Brook, N.Y.: Nicolas Hays, 1978), 83.

16. Concha, "Interpretación," and Alain Sicard, *El pensamiento poético de Pablo Neruda*, trans. Pilar Ruiz Va (Madrid: Gredos, 1981), 99–167.

17. Pablo Neruda, "Sobre una poesía sin pureza" (1935), *Obras completas* 3:636–37, trans. Margaret Sayers Peden, in Neruda, *Passions and Impressions* (New York: Farrar, Straus and Giroux, 1983), 128. The Spanish title of *Passions and Impressions* is *Para nacer he nacido*.

18. Amado Alonso, "From Melancholy to Anguish," trans. Enrique Sacerio Garí, *Review*, Center for Inter-American Relations (Spring 1974): 17. The original passage appears in Alonso, *Poesía y estilo de Pablo Neruda*, 3d ed. (Buenos Aires: Sudamericana, 1966), 19–21. Rodríguez Monegal, *Neruda*, 272, emphasizes Neruda's affinities with Joyce, Proust, and especially *The Waste Land* in this matter of disintegration. Alonso's view is qualified in Alfredo Lozada's chapter on the materialism of the *Residencia* volumes: *El monismo agónico de Pablo Neruda* (Mexico City: Costa-Amic, 1971), 215–82.

19. Concha, "Interpretación," 13.

20. Ibid., 18, my translation.

21. Sicard, *Pensamiento poético*, 137, my translation.

22. Neruda, "Ritual of My Legs," 37–41 and 52–67, in *Residence on Earth*, trans. Clayton Eshleman ([San Francisco]: Amber House Press, 1962). I have added lines 54 and 55, which Eshleman leaves out.

23. William Wordsworth, "Essay, Supplementary to the Preface" (1815), *Poetical Works* 2:433.

24. Wordsworth, *Poetical Works* 3:508.

25. Cameron, *Lyric Time*, 240–41. On Wordsworth's temporal geography in the *Duddon* sequence and elsewhere, see de Man, "Temporality," 205–7.

26. Rodríguez Fernández, "Tema de la muerte," 36, observes the influence of Rainer Maria Rilke's epithet and idea of a *kleine Tod* or "little death." To me the marks of influence here are less intriguing as evidence of an immediate intellectual debt than as a clear transhistorical link between Neruda and the post-Petrarchan writers I have already considered. Rilke, a translator of Louise Labé and Michaelangelo whose lyric sequences show the latter's influence, embodies that link.

27. Goic, "*Alturas de Macchu Picchu*," 157–58, gives a properly complicated account of the ideas of death I can only sketch here.

28. Jaime Concha, "El descubrimiento del pueblo en la poesía de Neruda," *Hispanic Studies* 1 (1974): 88–90. The essay was originally published in *Aurora* (Santiago) 3–4 (July–December 1964): 128–38.

29. Rodríguez Fernández, "Tema de la muerte," 38, my translation.

30. Derrida, *Husserl's Origin of Geometry*, 85.

31. George Kubler, "Machu Picchu," *Perspecta* 6 (1960): 49. Machu Picchu is described thoroughly and sometimes fancifully by its American discoverer Hiram Bingham, *Lost City of the Incas* (1948; Westport: Greenwood Press, 1981), and

more authoritatively by Hermann Buse, *Machu Picchu*, 3d ed. (Lima: Librería Studium, 1978).

32. Felstiner, *Translating Neruda*, 177.

33. Jespersen, *Philosophy of Grammar*, 63–64.

34. Robert Pring-Mill, preface to Tarn's translation of *Heights of Macchu Picchu*, xvii.

35. Rodríguez Monegal, *Neruda*, 323. Rodríguez Monegal's discussion of *Canto General* (310–34) is excellent. René de Costa, *The Poetry of Pablo Neruda* (Cambridge: Harvard University Press, 1979), 105–43, and Manuel Durán and Margery Safir, *Earth Tones* (Bloomington: Indiana University Press, 1981), 81–105, assign *Canto General* to the ever-widening category of the modern "epic"; de Costa, however, also concentrates on the artifactual element of the collection, the "oracular pose [that] permitted the author to speak out through a host of other distinct narrative voices in the remaining cantos [after *Alturas de Macchu Picchu*], turning his *Canto general* into a truly general song, a choral epic" (124). Alternately, Gordon Brotherston, *Latin American Poetry* (Cambridge: Cambridge University Press, 1975), 42–55, examines an aspect of what might be called the work's nominative dimension: the rest of his third chapter, which begins at p. 27 and runs through the Neruda section, examines other "songs of America" by the Chilean Andrés Bello, the Nicaraguan Ruben Darío, and the Peruvian José Santos Chocano for Whitman's influence in the relation between self and continent. Brotherston's sixth chapter (94–137) is generally about self-representation in the collections of the Peruvian César Vallejo and Neruda's other volumes.

36. Alberto Hidalgo, 25.13–19, in *Patria Completa* (Lima: Juan Mejía Baca, 1960). All quotations of *Patria Completa* refer to this edition, and all translations are mine.

37. Mario Florián, "Oda heróica a Machu Piqchu," in *Obra poética escogida, 1940–1976* (Lima: Studium, 1977); César Toro Montalvo, *Torres y praderas de Machu Picchu* (Lima: Ediciones Arybalo, 1980); Faustina Espinosa Navarro, *Machu Pikchu, poemas del Inka en quechua i castellano* (Cusco, Peru: Wiraqocha Biblioteca, [1978]). Jesús Cabel, *Opera de piedra* (Arequipa, Peru: Ediciones Dirección Universitaria de Investigación, 1981), anthologizes segments of lyric sequences and discrete lyrics on the same topic. Hugo Montes, *Machu Picchu en la poesía* (Madrid: Ediciones Cultura Hispánica, 1976), summarizes and discusses pertinent works by Neruda and others.

38. Adán's work on this sequence was published in several fragments before its gathering in a limited edition in 1964: *La Mano Desasida* (Lima: Juan Mejía Baca), a single series of three lyrics and 638 lines. This version was reprinted twice, in Adán's *Obra poética (1928–1971)* (Lima: Instituto Nacional de Cultura, 1971), and in the revised edition of the same (1976). The appearance of Adán's *Obra poética*, ed. Ricardo Silva-Santisteban (Lima: Edubanco, 1980), brought a much longer version of *La Mano Desasida*, ten poems in more than 180 pages. Hubert P. Weller, "The Poetry of Martín Adán," in *Romance Literary Studies: Homage to Harvey L. Johnson*, ed. Marie A. Wellington and Martha O'Nan (Potomac: Studia Humanitatis-Turanzas, 1979), 151–60, offers a bare summary of Adán's career.

39. All quotations of *La Mano Desasida* are from the 1964 edition, unless I

indicate otherwise; extracts from the *Obra poética* of 1980, for instance, are followed by that year and the page number in Silva-Santisteban's edition. All translations of 1964 are from my English version in *Extramares* 1 (1989): 91–108.

40. In general the quality of criticism of Adán's verse is not high, and his critics have sometimes dimly seen the radical spatialism of *La Mano Desasida*, sometimes not. The longest studies so far are Edmundo Bendezú Aibar, *La poética de Martín Adán* (Lima: P. L. Villanueva, 1969); two dissertations, Miroslav [Mirko] Lauer, "Un ensayo sobre la obra poética de Martín Adán," Universidad de San Marcos, 1972, and John Kinsella, "The Tragic and Its Consolation: A Study of the Work of Martín Adán," University of Liverpool, 1977; and the better of the books, Mirko Lauer, *Los exilios interiores: Una introducción a Martín Adán* (Lima: Hueso Húmero, 1983). The more notable shorter treatments of Adán's poetry in general are José Carlos Mariátegui, "El Anti-Soneto," *Amauta* 17 (September 1928): 76, reprinted in Adán, *Obra poética (1928–1971)*, 237–39; Emilio Adolfo Westphalen, "Homenaje a Martín Adán," *Amaru* 9 (March 1969): 42–43, reprinted in Adán, *Obra poética (1928–1971)*, 287–93; Mirko Lauer, "Martín Adán: Mano asida al absoluto," *Amaru* 9 (March 1969): 44–45; Julio Ortega, "Nota sobre la poesía de Martín Adán," *Razón y Fábula* 22 (November–December 1970): 54–60, reprinted in his *Figuración de la persona* (Barcelona: Edhasa, 1971), 157–64, and in Adán, *Obra poética (1928–1971)*, 304–12; and James Higgins, *The Poet in Peru* (Liverpool: Francis Cairns, 1982), 145–66. The few studies of *La Mano Desasida* include Ortega's review in the *Revista Peruana de Cultura* 6 (October 1965): 133–34; Juan Larrea's brief remarks in "Machupicchu, piedra de toque," *Del surrealismo a Machupicchu* (Mexico City: Joaquín Mortiz, 1967), 192–93; Montes, *Machu Picchu*, 31–34; Kinsella, "Tragic and Its Consolation," 239–44; and Lauer, *Exilios*,46–52.

41. Heinrich Zimmer, *Myths and Symbols in Indian Art and Civilization*, ed. Joseph Campbell (New York: Bollingen-Pantheon, 1946), 18.

42. Félix Schwartzmann, *El sentimiento de lo humano en América*, 2 vols. (Santiago: Universidad de Chile, 1953), 2:63–80, treats the Nerudean urge to overreach individual identities and forge universal links. Alonso, *Poesía y estilo*, esp. 24–26, relates the frequent *membra disjecta* in Neruda's other works to his early, insistent theme of the disintegration of reality. Saúl Yurkiévich, "La imaginación mitológica de Pablo Neruda," in *Fundadores de la nueva poesía latinoamericana* (Barcelona: Seix Barral, 1971), 196–98, and Eliana S. Rivero, "Simbolismo temático y titular en *Las manos del día*," *Mester* 4 (1974): 75–81, account for the hand in Neruda's stock of images.

43. James V. Mirollo, "In Praise of *La bella mano*: Aspects of Late Renaissance Lyricism," *Comparative Literature Studies* 9 (1972): 31–43, treats the post-Petrarchan uses of the often disembodied hand.

44. Charles Olson and Robert Creeley, *The Complete Correspondence*, ed. George F. Butterick, 8 vols. (Santa Rosa: Black Sparrow Press, 1987), 8:47–48.

45. The fullest discussion of Canzone 23 is Dennis Dutschke, *Francesco Petrarca Canzone XXIII from First to Final Version* (Ravenna: Longo, 1977). Dutschke is especially good with the speaker's startling oscillations into Laura's

usual terms (85) and the implied lyric interval of the final lines (195–99). Classical and Renaissance versions of the myth of Actaeon and Diana are examined for alternate significances by Leonard Barkan, "Diana and Actaeon: The Myth as Synthesis," *English Literary Renaissance* 10 (1980): 317–59.

46. On Petrarch's extensive use of Peire Vidal, see Scarano, "Fonti provenzali." Froula, *To Write Paradise*, 11–136, traces the evolving design of Pound's Canto 4 and provides a genetic text for the years 1915–25. Cp. the account of the Actaeon motif in Canto 91 in Christine Brooke-Rose, *A ZBC of Ezra Pound* (Berkeley: University of California Press, 1971), 189.

47. Durling, introduction to *Petrarch's Lyric Poems*, 22–24.

48. Charles Olson, *Call Me Ishmael* (New York: Reynal and Hitchcock, 1947), 11. Perhaps the best discussion of Olson's ideas of geography is Bernstein, *Tale of the Tribe*, 239–50.

49. Charles Olson, *Selected Writings*, ed. Robert Creeley (New York: New Directions, 1966), 59, 24–25.

50. See the long discussion of the "wcw crisis" (8:192) in Olson and Creeley, *Complete Correspondence*, 7:63–123, an exchange that begins with Olson's fan letter (based on a mistake) to Louis Martz; and see Robert von Hallberg, *Charles Olson: The Scholar's Art* (Cambridge: Harvard University Press, 1978), 52–59.

51. De Man, "Temporality," 204–8.

52. Quine, *Word and Object*, 170.

INDEX

acrostics, 8, 106
Actaeon, 138, 243, 247–48, 285nn. 45 and 46
Adán, Martín: *La Mano Desasida*, 17, 18, 196, 230–54, 283n.38, 284n.40
Alighieri, Dante, 150, 151, 264n.1, 273n.69, 274nn. 75 and 77; *Vita Nuova*, 22, 38–41, 262nn. 39, 40 and 42
allegory, 12, 13, 116, 121, 253
Allen, Archibald W., 37
Alonso, Amado, 206
Andrade, Mário de, 194; *Paulicéa Desvairada*, 15, 275n.1
Apollinaire, Guillaume, 154
Aristotle: *Nicomachean Ethics*, 266n.16; *Poetics*, 68, 172; *Rhetoric*, 189, 266n.16
Arnheim, Rudolf, 176–77
artifactuality. *See* lyric sequence: artifactual
attributes, doctrine of, 115–19, 130, 131, 270n.17, 271n.24
Auden, W. H., 158–59
Augustan poetic collections, 41, 52, 111, 261n.36. *See also* Callimachus; Catullus; Ovid; Propertius; Tibullus; Virgil
Augustine, Augustinianism, 115, 117, 250

Baïf, Jean-Antoine de, 114
Bakhtin, M. M., 68–69, 84–85, 266n.13
Barnes, Barnabe: *Divine Centurie of Spiritual Sonnets*, 113–14; *Parthenophil and Parthenophe*, 92, 106–7, 113
Barthes, Roland, 38, 258n.43, 269n.7
Baudelaire, Charles, 275n.1
Baxter, Richard, 121, 130, 271n.30
Beatrice, 39–40
Becon, Thomas, 270n.11
Bembo, Pietro: *Rime*, 114
Benveniste, Émile, 24
Bercovitch, Sacvan, 130
Berryman, John, 108, 172, 274n.73
Bersani, Leo, 132
Bible: Canticles, 120; 1 Corinthians, 120; 2 Corinthians, 118; Exodus, 74, 266n.21; Genesis, 25; John, 140; Song of Songs, 17; Zechariah, 125
Bingham, Hiram, 236, 282n.31
Bishop, Elizabeth, 32
blason, 112, 118–19, 139, 207–8, 237–39, 241, 248, 269n.7, 284nn. 42 and 43
Boethius, 38
Booth, Wayne C., 276n.5
Bopp, Raul: *Cobra Norato*, 210
Boscán, Juan: *Obras ("Cancoines y sonetos")*, 59, 263n.59
Braque, Georges, 154
Breton, Nicholas, 269n.9
Brice, Thomas, 270n.11
Bucke, Richard Maurice, 135
Bunting, Basil: *Briggflatts*, 17
Buonarroti, Michelangelo: *Rime*, 282n.26
Burke, Kenneth, 78–82, 267n.26
Bush, Ronald, 273n.70

calendars, 8, 13, 56–57, 62, 138, 140–41, 153, 178, 182, 256n.15, 263n.57
Callimachus, 260n.30, 261n.32
Cameron, Sharon, 34, 209, 276n.5
Campos, Haroldo de, 257n.31, 278n.23
canzone, 18
Carew, Thomas, 114
Carpenter, Humphrey, 274n.75
catachresis, 7, 128
Catullus, 37, 38, 241, 260n.30, 261nn. 32 and 36
Cavalcanti, Guido, 150, 274n.75
Cervantes Saavedra, Miguel de: *Don Quixote*, 28, 49, 79
chansonniers. *See* Provençal chansonniers
character. *See* lyric: character in
Cid, Poema de mío, 30, 260n.21
Coleridge, Samuel Taylor, 12
Colonna, Stefano: *Sonnetti . . . di M. Laura*, 171
Colonna, Vittoria: *Rime*, 171, 238
Concha, Jaime, 205–6, 213, 281n.9
concrete poetry, 11, 19, 196, 257n.31. *See also* lyric: materiality of
Constable, Henry, 114; *Diana*, 118–19